NABOKOV'S

Pale Fire

BRIAN BOYD

NABOKOV'S
Pale Fire

The Magic of Artistic Discovery

PRINCETON UNIVERSITY PRESS · PRINCETON, NEW JERSEY

Library of Congress Cataloging-in-Publication Data

Boyd, Brian, 1952–
Nabokov's pale fire : the magic of artistic
discovery / Brian Boyd.
p.   cm.
Includes bibliographical references and index.
ISBN 0-691-00959-7 (cloth : alk. paper)
1. Nabokov, Vladimir Vladimirovich, 1899–1977.   Pale fire.
I. Title.   II. Title: Pale fire.
PS3527.A15P3334   1999
813'.54—dc21   99-30682

This book has been composed in Palatino

The paper used in this publication meets the minimum
requirements of ANSI/NISO Z39.48-1992 (R1997)
(*Permanence of Paper*)

http://pup.princeton.edu

Printed in the United States of America

10 9 8 7 6 5 4 3 2 1

To BRONWEN

We are discoverers: and discovery
is a creative art.

(KARL POPPER, *Conjectures and Refutations*)

Contents

Acknowledgments

I WOULD LIKE to thank those who accepted and supported parts of my earlier case—readers like Chris Ackerley, Paul Tudor, Gennady Barabtarlo, John Morris, Andrew Hoyem, and Sergey Il'yn; those who resisted it, especially those who did so with specific arguments, like David Lodge, Ellen Pifer, and Charles Nicol; and those who have written well on *Pale Fire* while focusing on other aspects of the novel altogether, like Robert Alter, Richard Rorty, and Michael Wood.

In this story of what can be gradually discovered in reading, I would like to acknowledge all who have contributed in print to our growing understanding of *Pale Fire*, from early readers like Mary McCarthy and Carol T. Williams to the Kinboteans, Shadeans, the Kinbote-or-Shadeans, and the anti-Shadeans who emerged from the mid-1960s on: Page Stegner, Andrew Field, Julia Bader, Peter Rabinowitz, Alvin B. Kernan, D. Barton Johnson, Pekka Tammi, Gerard de Vries, and many others. Some, including Lisa Zunshine, Omry Ronen, and Robert Dirig, have supplied details or prompted ideas at conferences, while other keen readers who have never published on *Pale Fire* or on Nabokov at all have privately offered me information that had escaped professional scholars and critics. An observation by Tony Fazio precipitated half a chapter.

Chris Ackerley, Matthew Brillinger, D. Barton Johnson, Gennady Barabtarlo, Galya Diment, Michael Wood, and Andrew Langridge all read the whole manuscript with care. I am indebted to Professor Barabtarlo for a particularly meticulous reading and one very fruitful suggestion and to Professor Wood for such firm and articulate resistance. Beth Gianfagna has once again proved an ideally sensitive copy editor.

I would especially like to thank Dmitri Nabokov for his contribution to the Internet discussion of *Pale Fire* that pointed out his father's amusement at both Kinbotean and Shadean stances; Zoran Kuzmanovich, editor of *Nabokov Studies* (where an earlier version of chapters 8 and 13 appeared), for prodding me with further questions, even after I had passed beyond a Shadean reading; Dieter E. Zimmer, for following up a particular line of inquiry for me, as so often before, and for the service he has provided to all of those working on the Lepidoptera in Nabokov in his *Guide to Nabokov's Butterflies and Moths*; MacDonald P. Jackson, for urging me to write the book without delay; and above all, Bronwen Nicholson, for her criticism, suggestions, forbearance, support, and much more; and Vladimir Nabokov, for eventually making it possible to find a much more exciting explanation of what really happens and what is really at stake in *Pale Fire*. I wish he could read this centenary offering.

NABOKOV'S
Pale Fire

To Véra

Vanessa incognita

from V
Mont Reux
April 23   1962

Nabokov drew this invented *Vanessa incognita* for Véra on a copy of *Pale Fire* the week it was published. Its blue color is impossible for a real *Vanessa*. (Courtesy of Glenn Horowitz Bookseller)

Introduction

VLADIMIR NABOKOV'S *Pale Fire* invites readers to discovery in a way no other novel does, and for that very reason it can excite readers like no other book. Witness the breathlessness of Mary McCarthy's renowned, much-reprinted review: "*Pale Fire* is a Jack-in-the-box, a Fabergé gem, a clockwork toy, a chess problem, an infernal machine, a trap to catch reviewers, a cat-and-mouse game, a do-it-yourself kit. . . . This centaur-work of Nabokov's, half-poem, half-prose, this merman of the deep, is a creature of perfect beauty, symmetry, strangeness, originality, and moral truth."[1] Because it invites us to discovery, *Pale Fire* also prompts us to disagree radically about what we think we have found. Nabokov's finest novel has become a paradigm of literary elusiveness, a test case of apparent undecidability.[2]

That seems to suit our muddled times, when "advanced" thinkers claim we must all accept as a universal truth that there is no such thing as truth, only local versions. The very notion of the difficult pursuit of the complex truth of things seems outdated to many a postmodernist—until he or she needs, say, the latest medical treatment arrived at through just such a struggle for truth.[3] In an age that has become particularly skeptical of the possibility of *artistic* discovery, both *in* art and *about* works of art, I want to affirm that writers and readers can discover new ways of writing and reading and that these discoveries have much in common with the process of scientific discovery.[4]

DISCOVERY

Nabokov himself was passionately committed to discovery all his life, as a scientist, a scholar, an artist, and a man. His scientific work on butterflies was small in scope—he had only a few years in the 1940s when he could snatch time from teaching and writing for laboratory work—and has only in the 1990s come to be fully appreciated by researchers in his field,[5] but he knew nothing like the spell of the microscope, the challenge of unravelling nature's riddles—or so he would say in the throes of discovery.[6] But in the heat of other pursuits, he could think equally irresistible the excitement of the literary research he undertook in the 1950s for his edition of Pushkin's *Eugene Onegin*, or the sustained sixty-year thrill of literary invention, or his lifelong quest to locate our position in "the universe embraced by consciousness."[7]

As he matured as a novelist, he found new ways to offer readers the same challenge of discovery, on the same range of levels, that he encountered in life. Nowhere does he succeed better than in *Pale Fire*, which detonates in the creative reader's mind a chain reaction of explosive discoveries that become still more explosive the more we reread.

Reveling in the find after find that she had made—or thought she had made—in *Pale Fire*, Mary McCarthy ended her review by hailing it "one of the very great works of art of this century." Most keen readers of Nabokov concur, happily singling out *Pale Fire* as his highest achievement. But it proves a good deal harder for them to interpret than to evaluate the novel. Whereas *Lolita* sparks moral debate especially among those who have never read it, *Pale Fire* has ignited a critical controversy among those who have read and *re*read it that burns more fiercely every year.

Rereaders of the novel incline to one of four major positions, three of which have been around almost since *Pale Fire* was published in 1962, and the fourth, arguing that we must move beyond the first, but only to find the second and third readings locked in intentionally irresolvable competition, has circulated for at least two decades.[8] Indeed it is primarily because of the continuing debate among these positions that, in John Burt Foster, Jr.'s words, *Pale Fire* is "often viewed as a masterpiece of emerging postmodernism in fiction. Thus Matei Calinescu contends that it furthered the process by which the term 'postmodern' shifted from its original narrowly American application to the broad international meaning it holds today."[9]

The debate among these four positions recently re-erupted onto the Internet,[10] and as the staunchest proponent of one of them, I ejected a little lava of my own. I restated my case, citing old evidence that had already persuaded many and adducing new evidence that was inclining still others to waver, and was asked to present a complete statement of the case in print. But as I reread *Pale Fire*, a few niggles in the novel itself and in the critical debate around it forced me to reconsider my position and drove me to a radical new reading that no one had yet glimpsed. This new interpretation contradicts all the others—and confutes the claim that the novel is quintessentially "postmodern"—yet explains their appeal and their partial truth.

Nabokov's "Pale Fire" leads toward this interpretation through the series of discoveries Nabokov invites the first-time reader to make, then the more elusive discoveries he offers the rereader,[11] and the even more resistant and astonishing discoveries he prepares for those ready to make a still further imaginative effort.

As a researcher into one particularly complex family of butterflies, the Blues, Nabokov had found dizzying degrees of difficulty in understanding their relationships and their evolution. In an interview two months after the publication of *Pale Fire*, he reflected that experience when he declared: "You can get nearer and nearer, so to speak, to reality; but you can never get near enough because reality is an infinite succession of steps, levels of perception, false bottoms, and hence unquenchable, unattainable."[12] One of his greatest achievements as a writer was to invent a way to entice his readers to discover little by little the increasing complexity of the world of one of his novels, to lure them, as he felt lured by the mystery of the world around him, into trying to advance along that infinite succession of steps. By focusing intently on the psychology of discovery, he learned to write fiction that was immediately accessible but that almost immediately encouraged us to begin exploring deeper—fiction that would be found to be endlessly complex yet would neither overburden the reader from the first, like Joyce's *Finnegans Wake* or even parts of *Ulysses*, nor introduce intricacy for its own sake or at the expense of character and life, like Perec's *Life: A User's Manual*.

Frank Kermode called *Pale Fire* "one of the most complex novels ever written."[13] True, but John Barth's comment seems closer to the experience of the novel: "*Pale Fire* is a joy." It is a joy that intensifies with time and effort, as we inch toward its recessed surprises and the possibility that the surprises it intimates may lie in wait in the world around us. The reading of *Pale Fire* I propose suggests a way of reading all of Nabokov that runs counter to the still widespread notion that he was an ironist who skewers with the elegant épée of his prose all he dislikes in life, an artist who flaunts his artifice, a supreme stylist with nothing to say. Nabokov is an ironist, but his ultimate irony is that people fail to see the bewildering bounty of life. He is an artist who does indeed flaunt some of his artifice, but only to leave much more concealed, as he thinks life itself hides most of its unending surprises. He works with unusual care at the surface of his style, but he does so to open up unusual depths of feeling and thought. Unlike a Mann or a Musil, he quickly becomes impatient with ideas, but he may one day be seen as one of the most philosophical of all novelists.

The subtitle of this book, *The Magic of Artistic Discovery*, reflects several of its directions: the excitement of discovery awaiting us in *Pale Fire*; the artistic discoveries Nabokov had to make in order to allow *us* to discover so much; the process of critical discovery surrounding the novel; and the explanation of the nature of discovery advanced by Karl Popper from the time of his *Logic of Scientific Discovery* (1934) and until his death.[14]

As Bryan Magee has recently observed, Popper's argument, "despite appearances, . . . is radical—revolutionary in a historic sense, and epic in its implications."[15] Magee sums up Popper's claims:

> . . . that . . . all philosophy and all science involving the pursuit of certainty must be abandoned, a pursuit which had dominated Western thinking from Descartes to Russell; that because we do not, and never can in the traditional sense of the word "know," know the truth of any of our science, all our scientific knowledge is, and always will remain, fallible and corrigible; that it does not grow, as for hundreds of years people believed that it did, by the perpetual addition of new certainties to the body of existing ones, but by the repeated overthrow of existing theories by better theories, which is to say chiefly theories that explain more or yield more accurate predictions; that we must expect these better theories in their turn to be replaced one day by better theories still, and that process will have no end; so that what we call our knowledge can only ever be theories; that our theories are the products of our minds; that we are free to invent any theories whatsoever, but before any such theory can be accepted as knowledge it has to be shown to be preferable to whatever theory or theories it would replace if we accepted it; that such a preference can be established only by stringent testing; that although tests cannot establish the truth of a theory they can establish its falsity—or show up flaws in it—and therefore, although we can never have grounds for believing in the truth of a theory, we can have decisive grounds for preferring one theory to another; that therefore the rational way to behave is to base our choices and decisions on "the best of our knowledge" while at the same time seeking its replacement by something better; so if we want to make progress we should not fight to the

death for existing theories but welcome criticism of them and let our theories die in our stead.[16]

Much recent thinking aims to reject foundationalism, the assumption that we can have a secure foundation or authority for what we think we know. In advancing what he calls his "non-authoritarian theory of knowledge,"[17] Popper shows that we must reject all claims to be able to reach truth through some sure method—tradition, intuition, reason, observation, experiment, or whatever—and that we can nevertheless still explain the explosive growth of provisional human knowledge.[18] Unlike a Derrida or a Rorty, he removes foundations without removing the search for truth.[19]

Like Nabokov, Popper stresses that there is always more to discover, and no right road to discovery. We sense a problem, to which we freely invent solutions that we then need to test against alternatives, by comparing their consistency, their consequences, their explanatory power. In *Pale Fire* Nabokov poses a whole series of problems, problems within problems and problems overlapping problems, and the history of *Pale Fire* criticism shows exactly the fitful advance toward attempts to engage with deeper problems that Popper or Nabokov would expect in tackling a complex world or work.

On the strength of his philosophy of science and the political philosophy that he develops from it,[20] claims Magee, Popper is "the outstanding philosopher of the twentieth century." Yet he also points out that Popper overlooks major areas that matter: "the things that are most important of all to us, which Kant (and for that matter the Wittgenstein of the *Tractatus*) saw as rooted in the world of the unknowable—the meaning of life as a whole, the meaning of death; morality; values; the significance of art—are things that Popper has not written about, or at any rate not much."[21] But these things are exactly what interests Nabokov most of all. A scientist himself, impatient with the old answers, the old approximate descriptions and explanations, Nabokov knows that modern science has discovered worlds within unexpected worlds, what his John Shade calls

> A system of cells interlinked within
> Cells interlinked within cells interlinked
> Within one stem.

But he thinks that behind the endless complexity of things we can discover in science lurks "something else, something else, something else"—"and I must not be overexplicit."[22] In his poem "Pale Fire,"

Shade arrives at the conclusion "not text, but texture": that he cannot express the truth he sees behind things directly, but only through the interrelationships between things. In the same way, Nabokov allows his readers to find through the interrelationships between the parts of *Pale Fire* what he must not make overexplicit, to approach closer and closer to the "something else" hidden behind the world of his work, a reflection of the "something else," the great surprise that he thinks hidden behind life and death by the mysterious generosity somehow hidden still further behind.

READING

Introducing his course "Masterpieces of European Fiction" at Cornell, Nabokov would tell his students: "Curiously enough, one cannot *read* a book: one can only reread it. A good reader, a major reader, an active and creative reader is a rereader."[23] Presumably he wanted his own readers to be active and creative rereaders. What exactly *did* he think and expect of us? In a chapter of *Speak, Memory* written just months before he first gave that Cornell lecture, he discusses the chess problems he often composed in his years of European exile. That he wants chess to cast light on his writing he lets us see in one famous sentence:

> It should be understood that competition in chess problems is not really between White and Black but between the composer and the hypothetical solver (just as in a first-rate work of fiction the real clash is not between the characters but between the author and the world), so that a great part of a problem's value is due to the number of "tries"—delusive opening moves, false scents, specious lines of play, astutely and lovingly prepared to lead the would-be solver astray.[24]

To an interviewer who quoted part of the parenthesis back at him, Nabokov replied "I believe I said 'between the author and the reader,' not 'the world,'"[25] which is plainly what he had originally intended.

To some, the comparison of the relationship between author and reader to that between problem-composer and problem-solver epitomizes just what disturbs them in reading Nabokov: that he seems to see the reader as an antagonist whom he wants to outwit and convince of his own superiority. But although a chess *game* involves an attempt by one player to outdo another, a chess *problem* is quite different—and

Nabokov was always much more interested in the composition and art of chess problems than in the competition of chess games. Despite the resistance a good problem must have to easy solution, others must be able to solve it, or it is a failure. *Because* of the resistance, successful solvers can enjoy knowing they have exercised the imagination and intelligence to discard false solutions and persevere to find the true one. The relationship between composer and solver is fundamentally a generous one: the composer invites the solver as close to creative equality as the difference in their roles allows.

Nabokov thinks it a key to his world that the world itself invites us to share in the creativity we find in it, and he makes that in turn a key to his work. In an article on fictional audiences that begins and ends with *Pale Fire*, Peter Rabinowitz writes: "Nabokov appears to derive an almost sadistic satisfaction from knowing that his authorial audience [the hypothetical audience an author writes for] is intellectually well above his actual readers—although it is possible that Nabokov in fact writes for an authorial audience quite close to his actual readers but writes in order to make that audience feel intellectually inadequate."[26] This seems to me exactly the reverse of the truth. Nabokov thinks that the world itself is "intellectually well above" us all. As a scientist exhilarated by the discoveries he makes in the natural world, he is also aware that each new discovery reveals more that now suddenly needs explanation. Science, he insists, does nothing to dispel the mystery of the world and in fact has turned each of us into "a trillion of mysteries."[27] Yet he thinks that there is something fantastically generous, curiously playful, even, in the fact that the world is far more complex, dense, and deceptive than it seems, in its providing such inexhaustible scope for inquiry.

Once, shortly after his years in the laboratory at Harvard's Museum of Comparative Zoology, Nabokov was ready to write an ambitious book on the subject of animal mimicry,[28] which he thought often manifested an artistic perfection and wit in excess of any possible advantage it could have in the struggle for survival, and "seemed to have been invented by some waggish artist precisely for the intelligent eyes of man" to discover.[29] He suspects that in general nature buries so much precisely so that we will always have more to unearth. Echoing the first modern philosopher of science, Sir Francis Bacon, who echoes Proverbs, he writes in *Bend Sinister* that "the glory of God is to hide a thing, and the glory of man is to find it."[30] Nabokov feels that the inexhaustibility of the world is nowhere more munificent than in offering endless opportunities for the delights of discovery. He tries to provide equivalents in his fiction as he invites us to discover more and more about our world, or the world of literature, or the world of the particular work, to become, as nearly as possible, the co-creators of one of his miniature worlds, as we solve the artistic problems it poses.

Always passionately concerned with freedom, Nabokov sought it in a metaphysical even more than in a political sense, in the possibility that somehow human freedom might escape what he saw as the amazingly spacious but still unbreachable prison of time, personality, mortality. At the beginning of the chapter of his autobiography that ends with the chess problem, he writes:

> The spiral is a spiritualized circle. In the spiral form, the circle, uncoiled, unwound, has ceased to be vicious; it has been set free. I thought this up when I was a schoolboy, and I also discovered that Hegel's triadic series (so popular in old Russia) expressed merely the essential spirality of all things in their relation to time. Twirl follows twirl, and every synthesis is the thesis of the next series. If we consider the simplest spiral, three stages may be distinguished in it, corresponding to those of the triad: We can call "thetic" the small curve or arc that initiates the convolution centrally; "antithetic" the larger arc that faces the first in the process of continuing it; and "synthetic" the still ampler arc that continues the second while following the first along the outer side. And so on.[31]

This spiral runs through all of Nabokov's metaphysics and his art. He sketches its metaphysical implications in the next and final chapter of *Speak, Memory*: "Every dimension presupposes a medium within which it can act, and if, in the spiral unwinding of things, space warps into something akin to time, and time, in its turn, warps into something akin to thought, then, surely, another dimension follows—a special Space maybe, not the old one, we trust, unless spirals become vicious circles again."[32] He dwells on the esthetic implications of the spiral at more length, in the chess problem ending the previous chapter:

> I remember one particular problem I had been trying to compose for months. There came a night when I managed at last to express that particular theme. It was meant for the delectation of the very expert solver. The unsophisticated might miss the point of the problem entirely, and

discover its fairly simple, "thetic" solution without having passed through the pleasurable torments prepared for the sophisticated one. The latter would start by falling for an illusory pattern of play based on a fashionable avant-garde theme (exposing White's King to checks), which the composer had taken the greatest pains to "plant" (with only one obscure little move by an inconspicuous pawn to upset it). Having passed through this "antithetic" inferno the by now ultrasophisticated solver would reach the simple key move (bishop to c2) as somebody on a wild goose chase might go from Albany to New York by way of Vancouver, Eurasia and the Azores. The pleasant experience of the roundabout route (strange landscapes, gongs, tigers, exotic customs, the thrice-repeated circuit of a newly married couple around the sacred fire of an earthen brazier) would amply reward him for the misery of the deceit, and after that, his arrival at the simple key move would provide him with a synthesis of poignant artistic delight.

The problem is not just an elaborate metaphor but a genuine chess problem: on the next page, Nabokov provides both the position of the pieces on the board and the key, and the problem has more than once been analyzed purely in chess terms.[33] But in view of the comparison he makes on the previous page between chess and fiction, Nabokov plainly intends us to take this particularly successful problem as an analogy to the aims of his most successful fiction.[34] In his fiction he offers all readers a straightforward, accessible reading, which nevertheless itself requires *some* imaginative problem-solving to arrive at the "fairly simple, 'thetic' solution," just as life itself offers its own kind of problems and rewards to the unintellectual. He then places greater demands on his more sophisticated readers, subjects them even to the "pleasurable torments" of the "antithetic inferno," an unexpected tour of the world of the work or the problem that is its own "ampl[e] reward," before they can reach the ultimate solution in "a synthesis of poignant artistic delight," just as life itself sets before the inquiring mind the additional challenge of attempting to wrest out its secrets and sense and the additional reward of the thrill of discovery.

As Martin Amis observes, Nabokov, whatever else he may do, "spins a jolly good yarn, with believable characters, a strong story-line, and vivid, humorous prose. . . . He does all the usual things better than anybody else."[35] Unlike many modernists, Nabokov treats us to the pleasures of striking characters and storylines involving love and death, those staples of life and literature, in unusually dramatic and colorful forms. Even at this level, of course, he invites us to be active and imaginative: to guess at the reality and the identity of Humbert's pursuer and his intended victim; to intuit the link between Kinbote and Charles II; to notice the true family relationship between Van and Ada. By incorporating even into his plots problems that we can all solve in the course of a single reading, he invites us to sample the delights of discovery, while by leaving still more that remains elusive, he encourages us to return for more. Just as he slowly turns the "would-be solver" of his chess problem into "the by now ultrasophisticated solver," so he develops us into the ultrasophisticated readers he knows we can become.

In this, his procedure could not be more different from Joyce's. For Joyce the subject and the style appropriate to the subject were everything, and the reader be damned. Joyce's radical pursuit of appropriate form opened up extraordinary new possibilities in fiction, in his unrivalled and varied handling of interior monologue, in the amplitude and precision of his realism, in the exuberance of his artifice, in styles ranging from the headlines and rhetoric of the "Aeolus" chapter of *Ulysses* to the lyrical pseudoscientism of "Ithaca" to the dream-palimpsests of *Finnegans Wake*, but for most readers it also meant a sense of overload, even in *Ulysses* ("Ineluctable modality of the visible: at least that if no more, thought through my eyes . . ."), let alone in the nightslur and oneirobabble of *Finnegans Wake*. Writing for the professors he wanted to keep busy for a thousand years, or for the ideal reader with the ideal insomnia, Joyce does not compromise the density of his Dublin references, the crowdedness of Stephen's mind, the virtual stasis of his plots, the details left unexplained until hundreds of pages later.

Nabokov, by contrast, writes with an acute awareness of the range and capacity of his readers, whom he thinks—*pace* Rabinowitz—"the most varied and gifted in the world."[36] He handles story and style at a swift pace, and though he often issues brief local challenges, he allows us easily to pass them by and to enjoy the imaginative leaps that we *can* make. Even his vocabulary operates this way. He cannot attain a Joycean luxuriance in his English, but he studs his text with curios— "versipel," "kinbote," "lemniscate," "lansquenet," "stillicide," "luciola" are a few that might stump us in *Pale Fire*—that send us to our fattest dictionary to locate the explosive surprise waiting in each word. He spaces and grades his challenges, so that we can handle enough of them to continue at speed, so that we can solve enough to want to look out for more, but so that we do not even suspect the deeper problems until we are well on the way to becoming expert solvers.

None of Nabokov's other novels seems closer to the chess problem model than *Pale Fire*.[37] A first reading of the book introduces us as it were to its thetic phase, where Nabokov as part of the "good yarn" he spins sets us all problems to solve as we read, though each of us may solve them in different ways and at different rates.[38] By the time we reread the novel and have a knowledge of the whole at our disposal, we have entered the antithetic phase, where new problems appear as we try to trace an echo, or account for the role a particular part plays in the whole. While some problems solve themselves almost as soon as we glimpse them, others resist us. Some seem isolated, but many appear to relate to each other in elusive patterns we want to identify and explain, and even to add up to the promise of some major new meaning. We make discoveries rapidly, but with each new find we sense there is still more to discover, or our apparent discoveries start to unravel or to suggest something still more important beyond. Suddenly, we hit on one key move, we enter the synthetic phase, we find the solution that transforms the whole novel and its world, and discovery cascades down upon discovery. And even there the magic and the mystery have not reached their end.

A word about method. I quote at length from *Pale Fire*, often returning to the same quotations a number of times. This should not be taken as an insult to the reader's intelligence but as a tribute to Nabokov's. Any passage in the novel works on a first reading, and in its local context; but many also conceal unanticipated discoveries for the rereader or re-rereader. Partly to establish such passages' immediate self-sufficiency, partly to show that they are not being distorted by selective quotation, partly to point up ironic reversals of implication from reading to rereading or re-rereading, and above all to have all necessary clues at hand, and to stress the surprises lurking behind natural-seeming surfaces, I return to particular quotations, as readers keep returning to them in successive readings of *Pale Fire*, with a new sense of the novel's problems and possibilities each time.

Part One

THESIS: READING

Story as Discovery

its fairly simple, "thetic" solution

I.

Foreword

IF YOU HAVE NOT read *Pale Fire*, read it before reading on. You will not be able to unlock all its surprises, but you should not risk having sprung for you here what you could have had the pleasure of finding for yourself.

Pale Fire consists of four parts—a Foreword, signed Charles Kinbote; the long poem "Pale Fire," by John Shade; Kinbote's line-by-line Commentary to the poem; and his Index.[1] One of the many jokes of this very funny novel is that when we reach the end of the Foreword, we do not know which way to continue. But let us begin at the beginning, at the start of a first reading, to see how Nabokov primes us for discovery. Kinbote starts off with a sober description of the poem he is presenting to the public for the first time in this annotated edition: "*Pale Fire*, a poem in heroic couplets, of nine hundred ninety-nine lines, divided into four cantos, was composed by John Francis Shade (born July 5, 1898, died July 21, 1959) during the last twenty days of his life, at his residence in New Wye, Appalachia, U.S.A." Nothing could be less like "Lolita, light of my life, fire of my loins. My sin, my soul . . . " than this dry academic self-effacement.

All the same, the jokes have already begun, even before the playful transformation of a town in upstate New York into "New Wye, Appalachia." Once when teaching *Pale Fire* I had in my graduate class, as well as bright young students, the recently retired former head of our English Department. I began to describe the book as consisting first of "a poem in heroic couplets, of nine hundred ninety-nine lines" when his white head jerked back, perplexed. Unlike the students, he had not missed the absurdity of the opening line—as if I had said that a family has nine children, all twins.

The second paragraph continues in the same apparently bloodless critical vein but its pulse soon starts to twitch erratically: "The short (166 lines) Canto One, with all those amusing birds and parhelia, occupies thirteen cards.* Canto Two, your favorite, and that shocking tour de force, Canto Three, are identical in length (334 lines). . . ." "Your favorite"? When we have only just opened the book? When it is always absurd to prejudge another's taste? When this familiarity instantly violates the impersonal decorum? What sort of a person *is* this commentator?

The third paragraph resumes the orderly exposition: "A methodical man, John Shade usually copied out his daily quota of completed lines at midnight but even if he recopied them again later, as I suspect he sometimes did, he marked his card or cards not with the date of his final adjustments, but with that of his Corrected Draft or first Fair Copy. I mean, he preserved the date of actual creation rather than that of second or third thoughts. There is a very loud amusement park right in front of my present lodgings." By now academic calm has been shattered completely, as Kinbote's "I mean" discloses a first sign of distractedness before he erupts in the impatient petulance of his complaint about the noise, doubly comic for the way it chimes so oddly with the previous sentence: here, if anywhere, is the moment of actual creation preserved, with no sign of second or third thoughts exerting any control.

The sentence that follows returns to discreet scholarly distance ("We possess in result a complete calendar of his work"), but we are on guard for the next sign of instability, the next quirk of chaos. Before we reach it, Kinbote raises the stakes of our curiosity in another way:

> It contains not one gappy line, not one doubtful reading. This fact would be sufficient to show that the imputations made (on July 24, 1959) in a newspaper interview with one of our professed Shadeans—who affirmed *without having seen the manuscript of the poem* that it "consists of disjointed drafts none of which yields a definite text"—is a malicious invention on the part of those who would wish not so much to deplore the state in which a great poet's work was interrupted by death as to

---

* Parhelia? A parhelion, Nabokov's favorite dictionary, Webster's Second, explains as "a mock sun, any one of several bright spots, often tinged with color, on the parhelic circle. Several parhelia, symmetrically distributed, are often seen at once. They are due to the same cause as halos, of which they may be regarded as intensified parts." Our first invitation to discover, and our first "pale fire."

asperse the competence, and perhaps honesty, of its present editor and
commentator. (14)

We have heard him already explode into expostulation. *Can* he prove
a competent commentator?

The intrigue swirling around the manuscript intensifies as Kinbote
names "Prof. Hurley and his clique" as his antagonists, and insists on
the poem's completeness. For Shade

> the third canto was the penultimate one, and thus I myself have heard
> him speak of it, in the course of a sunset ramble, when, as if thinking
> aloud, he reviewed the day's work and gesticulated in pardonable self-
> approbation while his discreet companion kept trying in vain to adapt
> the swing of a long-limbed gait to the disheveled old poet's jerky shuffle.
> Nay, I shall even assert (as our shadows still walk without us) that there
> remained to be written only *one* line of the poem (namely verse 1000)
> which would have been identical to line 1 and would have completed
> the symmetry of the structure, with its two identical central parts, solid
> and ample, forming together with the shorter flanks twin wings of five
> hundred verses each, and damn that music. (14–15)

So Kinbote is not just an academic editor, but a close personal associate
of the poet. What exactly is the relationship between this poet, given,
it seems, to "pardonable self-approbation," and the commentator who
calls himself a "discreet companion" but can again burst out with "and
damn that music"? And *is* the poem complete, in the way Kinbote
suggests?

Concluding his case, Kinbote adds: "And if all this were not
enough—and it is, it is enough—I have had the dramatic occasion of
hearing my poor friend's own voice proclaim on the evening of July 21
the end, or almost the end, of his labors. (See my note to line 991.)"
Why that urgency, that desperation, in his "it is, it is enough"? And
why does he urge us to see his note to line 991? He presumably has his
reasons, but we can already suspect he is a man easily engulfed in his
own immediate predicament. Yet behind his outbursts, his "amusement park," his "and damn that music," we can sense Nabokov's irony
and control. Does Nabokov too want us to skip forward to the note to
line 991?

If we imagine he does, and we flip forward to the note, we find ourselves indeed on the evening of July 21, and we find something very
odd in the relationship of poet and commentator. They are neighbors,

and Kinbote tells us he had just met Shade's wife Sybil "speeding townward and therefore nursed some hopes for the evening. I grant you I very much resembled a lean wary lover taking advantage of a young husband's being alone in the house!" In a flash the Foreword's first glimpses of Kinbote's relationship to Shade takes on a startling new tinge. It seems Nabokov *will* make it worth our while to follow these cross-references. The note continues: "Through the trees I distinguished John's white shirt and gray hair: he sat in his Nest (as he called it), the arborlike porch or veranda I have mentioned in my note to lines 47–48." Should we check that out too; should we finish note 991; or should we just scuttle safely back to the Foreword at once?

If we succumb to our curiosity, and our hope that Nabokov might still make it worthwhile to do so, we find a description of Shade's home in the note to lines 47–48 cede place in the second paragraph to the house Kinbote rents next door and "the charming, charmingly vague lady (see note to line 691) who secured it for me. . . ." Now wait a minute! Does Nabokov really want us to to follow even *this* trail? If we do, will we ever get back? Has he prepared us a labyrinth just so that he can laugh at our getting lost? Let's try trusting him just one more time.

The note to line 691 begins: "John Shade's heart attack (Oct. 17, 1958) practically coincided with the disguised king's arrival in America where he descended by parachute. . . ." Disguised king! What is this? Three sentences later: "While Kingsley, the British chauffeur, an old and absolutely faithful retainer, was doing his best to cram the bulky and ill-folded parachute into the boot, I relaxed on a shooting-stick he supplied me with." "*I* relaxed"? What? Is the disguised king who has just parachuted into America none other than our commentator? It seems so, as the note proceeds, for the Sylvia O'Donnell who meets him and whom he characterizes by her "vagueness of manner" (248) has indeed rented him a house in New Wye near the Shades. She may be "charmingly vague," but she knows just who she's speaking to. Shade is already much better after his heart attack, she reports, "but the boy is strictly hetero, and, generally speaking, Your Majesty will have to be quite careful from now on." (248) The force of Kinbote's comparing himself to "a lean wary lover" abruptly becomes clear.

If we have followed this far, we now know to trust Nabokov. Or so we think. We finish note 691, return to note 47–48, with its hilarious description of Kinbote as tenant in the Goldsworth house, and yet another cross-reference—uh-oh!—to the note to line 62. Can we keep track of where we are? OK: one more try. Note 62 begins: "Often, almost nightly, throughout the spring of 1959, I had feared for my life. Solitude is the playfield of Satan. I cannot describe the depths of my loneliness and distress. . . . Everybody knows how given to regicide Zemblans are: two Queens, three Kings, and fourteen Pretenders died violent deaths, strangled, stabbed, poisoned and drowned, in the course of only one century (1700–1800)." So our commentator is the king of *Zembla*!

As his description of his harrowing night sweats darkens, Kinbote refers us to his note to lines 47–48 (we smile: we know that note, we'll get back and finish it as soon as we're out of this one) and then to the note to line 691 (smile: we've read that, and know its secret). We finish the note, return to where we left off note 47–48, finish that (no more cross-references, but we do read: "it also dawns upon me *now* that . . . [Sybil] made him tone down or remove from his Fair Copy everything connected with the magnificent Zemblan theme with which I kept furnishing him and which, without knowing much about the growing work, I fondly believed would become the main rich thread in its weave!" [91]), and return to near the start of the trail, note 991. There we carry on from where we left off, and, passing Shade saying that apart from a "few trifles to settle . . . I've swung it, by God"—and this was what prompted Kinbote's initial cross-reference—we reach this:

> "A suggestion," I said, quivering. "I have at my place half a gallon of Tokay. I'm ready to share my favorite wine with my favorite poet. We shall have for dinner a knackle of walnuts, a couple of large tomatoes, and a bunch of bananas. And if you agree to show me your 'finished product,' there will be another treat: I promise to divulge to you *why* I gave you, or rather *who* gave you, your theme."
>
> "What theme?" said Shade absently, as he leaned on my arm and gradually recovered the use of his numb limb.
>
> "Our blue inenubilable Zembla, and the red-capped Steinmann, and the motorboat in the sea cave, and—"
>
> "Ah," said Shade, "I think I guessed your secret quite some time ago. But all the same I shall sample your wine with pleasure. Okay, I can manage by myself now."

Kinbote has a secret he has not divulged even to his friend and neighbor Shade, yet after reading only two and a half pages into the Foreword we already know that secret: Kinbote is the disguised king of Zembla. We can see already that Kinbote has been feeding Shade the story of the king, passed off as someone else's, as the theme for the poem "Pale Fire," and that Shade has probably not had the least inclination to make this the subject for his poem. Two pages into the Foreword, and twenty pages of surprises through the Commentary, and we seem to know a secret that Kinbote has been desperately keeping to himself, and a conclusion that has not yet dawned on the Kinbote of this late note.

If we have followed this trail to the end, we know to trust Nabokov; we know to follow our curiosity, even when it can lead at times to uncertainty and frustration, as well as to the surprise of discovery. I first followed this particular path when I was sixteen years old and ever since have let Nabokov lead me to discoveries more rewarding than we have any right to expect. Nabokov knows that not every reader will trust him enough to follow this trail. Those who think he aims only to tease, to taunt, to prove his own superiority, will of course resist starting up the track at all. But Nabokov knows that life also offers too many simultaneous prompts to our curiosity for us to be able to follow them: what's the name of that flower? what's this really made of? how does this work? why does that happen? Life can frustrate us, bombard us with what we do not know, so that we can give up on curiosity, unable to choose where to turn next, but Nabokov suggests that not to trust in our curiosity at all, not to follow any trail, is the surest way of missing out on life's limitless surprises.

He plants only one cross-reference within the Foreword, in the hope that we will have the energy to follow this one trail. If we do not follow it at all—and most readers seem not to—he still primes our curiosity in many ways essential to the unfolding story:

(1) About Kinbote's competence as editor and commentator: The "amusement park," "and damn that music," the explicit criticism others make of Kinbote's plans to publish the poem, even the question whether "Mrs. Shade's tremulous signature [on the contract giving Kinbote the right to publish] might not have been penned 'in some peculiar kind of red ink'" (16–17).

(2) About the finishedness of the poem he sets before us: The 999 lines of heroic couplets, Kinbote's admission of the "devastating erasures and cataclysmic insertions" (14) on the last index cards of the manuscript, Hurley's claim, Kinbote's counter-claim.

(3) About Kinbote's relationship to Shade: "The thick venom of envy began squirting at me as soon as academic suburbia realized that John Shade valued my society above that of all other people. Your snicker,

my dear Mrs. C., did not escape our notice" (24); "I had my full reward in John's friendship. This friendship was the more precious for its tenderness being intentionally concealed, especially when we were not alone" (25).

(4) About Kinbote's personality: He may call himself Shade's "discreet companion" (14), yet he prides himself on his "powerful red car" (19); he responds to a taunt—not the sole taunt or snicker or denunciation he earns even in the short space of the Foreword—by contenting himself "with pulling Gerald Emerald's bow-tie loose" (24).

(5) About Kinbote's very sanity: "'You are a remarkably disagreeable person. I fail to see how John and Sybil can stand you,' and, exasperated by my polite smile, she added: 'What's more, you are insane.' But let me not pursue the tabulation of nonsense" (25).

(6) About Kinbote's sexuality: His mention of "a moody, delicate, rather wonderful boy" (21); his two ping-pong tables, and "a kind of little seminar at home followed by some table tennis, with two charming identical twins and another boy, another boy" (23); "a treatise on certain Zemblan calisthenics"—what?—"in which I proposed to interest that young roomer of mine" (26).

(7) And about some other secret we can sense but not define:

> Imagine a soft, clumsy giant; imagine a historical personage whose knowledge of money is limited to the abstract billions of a national debt; imagine an exiled prince who is unaware of the Golconda in his cuff links! This is to say—oh, hyperbolically—that I am the most impractical fellow in the world. Between such a person and an old fox in the book publishing business, relations are at first touchingly carefree and chummy, with expansive banterings and all sorts of amiable tokens. I have no reason to suppose that anything will ever happen to prevent this initial relationship with good old Frank, my present publisher, from remaining a permanent fixture. (17–18)

That could pass some readers by, but this cannot:

> There was also the morning when Dr. Nattochdag, head of the department to which I was attached, begged me in a formal voice to be seated, then closed the door, and having regained, with a downcast frown, his swivel chair, urged me "to be more careful." In what sense, careful? A boy had complained to his adviser. Complained of what, good Lord? That I had criticized a literature course he attended ("a ridiculous survey of ridiculous works, conducted by a ridiculous mediocrity"). Laughing

> in sheer relief, I embraced my good Netochka, telling him I would never
> be naughty again. I take this opportunity to salute him. He always be-
> haved with such exquisite courtesy toward me that I sometimes won-
> dered if he did not suspect what Shade suspected, and what only three
> people (two trustees and the president of the college) definitely knew.
> (24–25)

What is there to suspect about him? Is it his homosexuality? Is it
something more mysterious? Does it link in some way with that
"imagine a historical personage"? Just who and what *is* this strange
commentator?

   After having our curiosity and our doubts about Kinbote raised in
so many ways, we reach the last paragraph of the Foreword, about to
begin the poem, only to have Kinbote explain the notes that follow,
and add:

> Although those notes, in conformity with custom, come after the poem,
> the reader is advised to consult them first and then study the poem with
> their help, rereading them of course as he goes through its text, and per-
> haps, after having done with the poem, consulting them a third time so
> as to complete the picture. I find it wise in such cases as this to eliminate
> the bother of back-and-forth leafings by either cutting out and clipping
> together the pages with the text of the thing, or, even more simply, pur-
> chasing two copies of the same work which can then be placed in adja-
> cent positions on a comfortable table—not like the shaky little affair on
> which my typewriter is precariously enthroned now, in this wretched
> motor lodge, with that carrousel inside and outside my head, miles
> away from New Wye. (28)

What sort of an imbalanced egoist is this commentator anyway, to expect us to read the notes three times for the one time we read the
poem? What sort of crazy carrousel is his mind? Perhaps we could
follow his advice and read the notes first—some readers do—but there
seems something highly doubtful about him. Let us just turn the page,
and read the poem.

2.

Poem

JOHN SHADE'S "Pale Fire" opens with an extraordinary series of images whose initial impact lingers in the mind as it expands in implication throughout the poem:

> I was the shadow of the waxwing slain
> By the false azure in the windowpane;
> I was the smudge of ashen fluff—and I
> Lived on, flew on, in the reflected sky.

As we learn more about Shade's lifelong attempt to understand a world where life is surrounded by death, we realize the full resonance of these opening lines: that he is projecting himself in imagination into the waxwing, as if it were somehow still flying beyond death, and into the reflected azure of the window, as if that were the cloudlessness of some hereafter, even as he stands looking at "the smudge of ashen fluff" of the dead bird's little body. Alvin Kernan comments that the bird "has died flying into the hard barrier of the image which promises freedom but only reflects the world it is already in,"[1] and that irony persists:

> And from the inside, too, I'd duplicate
> Myself, my lamp, an apple on a plate:
> Uncurtaining the night, I'd let dark glass
> Hang all the furniture above the grass,
> And how delightful when a fall of snow
> Covered my glimpse of lawn and reached up so
> As to make chair and bed exactly stand
> Upon that snow, out in that crystal land!

10

The contrast between the mundaneness of Shade's room—"Myself, my lamp, an apple on a plate"—and the magic of the reflection reflects in turn off those other contrasts already intimated between real and imagined, between life and the hint of something beyond life in the "reflected sky," to create a sustained tension throughout the poem between the taken-for-granted, the freshly seen, the vividly projected, and the unseen beyond. This is major poetry, by any standard, fully justifying Kinbote's awe at the end of the Foreword as he watches "John Shade perceiving and transforming the world, taking it in and taking it apart, re-combining its elements in the very process of storing them up so as to produce at some unspecified date an organic miracle, a fusion of image and music, a line of verse" (27).

The next verse paragraph seems to gaze in the same direction but blinks to a different beat:

> Retake the falling snow: each drifting flake
> Shapeless and slow, unsteady and opaque,
> A dull dark white against the day's pale white
> And abstract larches in the neutral light.
> And then the gradual and dual blue
> As night unites the viewer and the view.

Shade still stresses sight, but sharpness fades to shapelessness, opacity, dullness, paleness, abstractness, neutrality, so that like Keats compensating for the darkness of stanza 5 of "Ode to a Nightingale" by steeping it in smell, he now turns up the sound. Internal rhyme and off-rhyme (initial and end: *Retake, flake*; medial: *snow, slow; dark, larches*) and assonance (*flake / Shapeless, opaque*) accumulate toward the explosion of

> And then the gradual and dual blue
> As night unites the viewer and the view.

For all his peculiarities, Kinbote will prove to have a deep passion for poetry and a fine ear for verbal music, and will often single out for special delectation Shade's ability to counterpoint sound and sense. But as he reads these particular lines he has too much else on his mind to comment on the way Shade compounds the end-rhyme with the triple internal rhyme, the burst of *u* sounds, the strange fusion and fission and reflection of syllables (*gradual . . . dual, night unites, viewer . . . view*) that matches the slow fusion of the light blue of the west with the dark blue of the east as night consolidates itself, and the viewer standing inside, lights on, finds himself now reflected in the window looking onto the darkened view.

The soft, snowy evening yields to a crisp dawn:

> And in the morning, diamonds of frost
> 20   Express amazement: Whose spurred feet have crossed
> From left to right the blank page of the road?
> Reading from left to right in winter's code:
> A dot, an arrow pointing back; repeat:
> Dot, arrow pointing back . . . A pheasant's feet!

As Robert Alter comments,[2] we do a double take as we read Shade's words, sense our eyes gliding left to right over a once-blank page and see through Shade's metaphor to the pheasant's tracks. These lines show in new ways Shade's closeness of observation, his easy knowledge of natural kinds built up from a lifetime of active curiosity, his precision and play of image (• ← • ←), his wry self-consciousness, his ingenious incorporation of other structures, visual and verbal, into the exigencies of that last rhyming couplet. Shade at his most playful, as here, is also, we will discover later in the poem, Shade not far from his most philosophical, disclosing his delight in the combinations of the world around him, sensing what almost seems the inherent playfulness of things, apprehending and reshaping his world with an answering spirit of play.

Although many have no doubt that Shade's "Pale Fire" is major poetry, many have no doubt that it is not. Why? When we come from the tantalizing promise of Kinbote's character in the Foreword, the hints of mysteries not quite stated but perhaps soon to be solved, Shade's world can seem drab and flat. "All colors made me happy: even gray," he writes as he retrieves his autobiographical record, and to a superficial eye there may indeed seem too much gray in his story. Everything in the Foreword suggests that there are surprises to come in Kinbote, that he is wildly eccentric, to say the least, perhaps completely unbalanced, and that we will have a high time reading around him. But Shade contains no secrets, no surprises. No one will ever tell him *he* is insane. As "Pale Fire" shows us, he is stability itself, living all his life in his parents' home, in the same comfortable small academic town, marrying his childhood sweetheart and in forty years never wavering in his love. He records his undramatic surroundings, recounts his quiet life, and that is all. No wonder, especially after what we see (and before what we *will* see) of Kinbote, that Shade's world can seem insipid, especially when encased in a verse form that fell out of fashion in English almost two centuries ago.

Yet as those opening lines suggest, he can make the ordinary extraordinary. If there are no surprises or secrets *in* him, he finds surprises in his world, in a waxwing's death, in a pheasant's tracks, in a newspaper clipping (*Red Sox Beat Yanks 5–4 / On Chapman's Homer*), in what he dubs an iridule, a rainbow reflected in a cloud from a thunderstorm in a distant valley: he wants us to see that "we are most artistically caged." Caged, all the same. Even more crucial to his life and his poem than the surprises of life are the far greater surprises he suspects around us. (As he will say to Kinbote in the Commentary: "Life is a great surprise. I do not see why death should not be an even greater one." [C.549, 225]) Canto Two begins:

> There was a time in my demented youth
> When somehow I suspected that the truth
> About survival after death was known
> To every human being: I alone
> Knew nothing, and a great conspiracy
> Of books and people hid the truth from me.
>
> There was the day when I began to doubt
> Man's sanity: How could he live without
> Knowing for sure what dawn, what death, what doom
> Awaited consciousness beyond the tomb?
>
> And finally there was the sleepless night
> When I decided to explore and fight
> The foul, the inadmissible abyss,
> Devoting all my twisted life to this
> One task. Today I'm sixty-one. Waxwings
> Are berry-pecking. A cicada sings.

170 (line marker for "To every human being: I alone")

180 (line marker for "Devoting all my twisted life to this")

In "Pale Fire" Shade presents the story of his life as one lifelong quest to explore the "inadmissible abyss" of death, a quest pursued with passion and play, stinging skepticism and quiet trust.

Whereas in the Foreword we expect to make discoveries about Kinbote, in the poem we feel the constant pressure of the discoveries that Shade would dearly like to make about death. We begin Canto One with the waxwing, Shade's mature attempt as poet to imagine for a moment projecting himself into that "reflected sky," and we end the canto with the series of childhood fits or trances, in which he felt "tugged at by playful death," that leads to his dedicating himself to his quest at the start of Canto Two.

Canto Two culminates in the dreadful discovery that the Shades must make about their only child's suicide, one March night in 1957, two years before the poet undertakes "Pale Fire." The counterpoint between Hazel's last hours and her parents' uneasy vigil at home while waiting for their unattractive daughter to return from her first blind date creates an unbearable tension and poignancy as time swings back and forth, ticking away to the irretrievable moment of her death at the very midpoint of the poem.

For all his sense of the mystery behind death, Shade knows he cannot force the door to the beyond. Canto Three shows him arriving, through two major encounters with the ironies of death, at a new sense of the unknown that looms beyond life. First, a term of lectures some twenty years ago at what Shade wryly redubs "I.P.H., a lay / Institute (I) of Preparation (P) / For the Hereafter (H), or If, as we / Called it"—"To speak on death ('to lecture on the Worm,' / Wrote President McAber)."

> That tasteless venture helped me in a way.
> I learnt what to ignore in my survey
> Of death's abyss. And when we lost our child
> I knew there would be nothing: no self-styled
> Spirit would touch a keyboard of dry wood
650 > To rap out her pet name; no phantom would
> Rise gracefully to welcome you and me
> In the dark garden, near the shagbark tree.

Then in October 1958, a year and a half after Hazel's death, he has his own near-death experience during a sudden collapse after giving a public lecture. Returning from this blackout, he feels sure he has slipped into death and back, and has seen there, "dreadfully distinct / Against the dark, a tall white fountain."

Galvanized by the thought that this vision offers him a promise of something beyond death, he then reads in a magazine about a woman "whose heart had been / Rubbed back to life by a prompt surgeon's hand" and who reports that she "glimpsed a tall white fountain— and awoke." Convinced he is on the brink of discovering what has eluded him all his life, Shade tracks the woman down, only to find her impossibly gushy. Rather than have her swamp him with claims to a mystical bond between them, he backs off, and calls on the journalist who had written the story:

> He took his article from a steel file:
> 800 "It's accurate. I have not changed her style.
> There's one misprint—not that it matters much:
> *Mountain*, not *fountain*. The majestic touch."
>
> Life Everlasting—based on a misprint!
> I mused as I drove homeward: take the hint,
> And stop investigating my abyss?
> But all at once it dawned on me that *this*
> Was the real point, the contrapuntal theme;
> Just this: not text, but texture; not the dream
> But topsy-turvical coincidence,
> 810 Not flimsy nonsense, but a web of sense.
> Yes! It sufficed that I in life could find
> Some kind of link-and-bobolink, some kind
> Of correlated pattern in the game,
> Plexed artistry, and something of the same
> Pleasure in it as they who played it found.
>
> It did not matter who they were. No sound,
> No furtive light came from their involute
> Abode, but there they were, aloof and mute,
> Playing a game of worlds, promoting pawns
> 820 To ivory unicorns and ebon fauns. . . .

After the exhilarating discoveries he thought he had made comes the rude shock of the misprint that wryly confirms for him how impossible it must always remain, on this side of death, to see beyond it. It is not that deflating recognition, however, but the resolve that follows it, that forms the core and key to the poem. It is a resolve he shares with his maker. In a kind of postscript to *Speak, Memory* that he withheld from publication during his lifetime, and that has just been published for the centenary of his birth, Nabokov dons the mask of a reviewer of his autobiography, and writes, among amusingly disparaging comments, of the "retrospective acumen and creative concentration that the author had to summon in order to plan his book according to the way his life had been planned by unknown players of games."[3] Shade writes his autobiographical poem in exactly the same spirit. Conscious, after the *fountain-mountain* confusion, that his very quest to explore the beyond makes him seem a mere toy of the gods, he derives a sense of the playfulness hidden deep in things, and feels that he can perhaps understand and participate a little in this playfulness, if only obliquely, through the pleasure of shaping his own world in verse, through playing his own game of worlds, through sensing and adding to the design in and behind his world.

In Canto Four Shade focuses precisely on the way he shapes his verse, on the way he composes, in the midst of what seems anything but a life permeated by design. The Canto starts with the word "Now" and remains in the present moment of composition throughout, exploring the nature of poetic inspiration as it arrives amid the clutter of the everyday. Repeatedly Canto Four seems to promise some mighty theme ("Now I shall cry out as / None has cried out. Now I shall try what none / Has tried. . ."), only to lapse back into the mundanity of the moment, as Shade soaps his leg or shaves.

Shade ends the canto and the poem by looking around him as he writes, in the late afternoon of July 21, 1959, at the chance harmonies of the present. He answers the highly wrought image of waxwing and window at the start of the poem by finishing with a fade-out into the world around him, a slow dissolve into the here and now, which nevertheless builds on the discovery he has reached at the end of Canto Three, that there is some mysterious match between the artifice of his art and his attempt to see behind life:

> Gently the day has passed in a sustained
> Low hum of harmony. The brain is drained
> And a brown ament, and the noun I meant
> To use but did not, dry on the cement.
> Maybe my sensual love for the *consonne*
> *D'appui*, Echo's fey child, is based upon
> A feeling of fantastically planned,
> 970   Richly rhymed life.
>   I feel I understand
> Existence, or at least a minute part
> Of my existence, only through my art,
> In terms of combinational delight;
> And if my private universe scans right,

So does the verse of galaxies divine
Which I suspect is an iambic line.
I'm reasonably sure that we survive
And that my darling somewhere is alive,
As I am reasonably sure that I
980   Shall wake at six tomorrow, on July
The twenty-second, nineteen fifty-nine,
And that the day will probably be fine;
So this alarm clock let me set myself,
Yawn, and put back Shade's "Poems" on their shelf.

But it's not bedtime yet. The sun attains
Old Dr. Sutton's last two windowpanes.
The man must be—what? Eighty? Eighty-two?
Was twice my age the year I married you.
Where are you? In the garden. I can see
990   Part of your shadow near the shagbark tree.
Somewhere horseshoes are being tossed. Click. Clunk.
(Leaning against its lamppost like a drunk.)
A dark Vanessa with a crimson band
Wheels in the low sun, settles on the sand
And shows its ink-blue wingtips flecked with white.
And through the flowing shade and ebbing light
A man, unheedful of the butterfly—
Some neighbor's gardener, I guess—goes by
Trundling an empty barrow up the lane.

Even as he affirms the relationship between his art and his confidence in the ultimate design of life, Shade here seems ready to renounce the high artifice of the poem's opening images, to accept serenely the quiet continuities of life. The poem breaks off in the midst of things, amid the casual circumstances of the hour—a chance extra ("Some neighbor's gardener"), an offhand phrase ("I guess"), a low-key rhyme ("goes by"), a last line without its expected matching rhyme—amid the quotidian, the undesigned, the artlessness of life.

The poem breaks off, yet everything indicates that it probably needs just one more line to be finished. The story of Shade's past has caught up with his present, with the day and the very hour of writing; he is ready to set his poems back on their shelf as he awaits the sunset. The design of the poem, too, seems to confirm the subdued closure. It consists of four cantos; Cantos Two and Three match each other exactly in

length; with one more line, Canto Four would be exactly the length of
Canto One, and these two outer flanks together would add up to a
third of the whole, or the equivalent of each of the inner two cantos. Or
to tally things another way: Hazel's death, at line 500, the end of Canto
Two, seems to have been placed exactly halfway to the end of a thousand-line poem.

Shade ends quietly, after the shock of the start, and yet he satisfies
his own urge for hidden design, for what he calls in his Canto Three
epiphany "some kind of link-and-bobolink." Just before "Gently the
day has passed," but already on the last day of composing the poem,
he writes:

> *Dim Gulf* was my first book (free verse); *Night Rote*
> Came next; then *Hebe's Cup*, my final float
> In that damp carnival, for now I term
> 960   Everything "Poems," and no longer squirm.
> (But *this* transparent thingum does require
> Some moondrop title. Help me, Will! *Pale Fire*.)

He appears to grasp for a stopgap title, and to sound not quite convinced. The line suggests he may have borrowed from Shakespeare,
and if we reach for a concordance, we find our hunch is right:

> I'll example you with thievery:
> The sun's a thief, and with his great attraction
> Robs the vast sea; the moon's an arrant thief,
> And her pale fire she snatches from the sun;
> The sea's a thief, whose liquid surge resolves
> The moon into salt tears. (*Timon of Athens*, 4.3.435–40)

In the past Shade has followed the common academic habit (which
Kinbote will roundly denounce) of stealing his titles from other authors' phrases, but he has reformed, reverting to the plain "Poems"
before, as he pretends, succumbing today to the need for some name
for the long poem now drawing to an end. With his usual modesty he
reaches for a title that implies his poem can shed only a pallid glow
compared to the heat and light Shakespeare radiates over the landscape of English literature.[4]

In fact the title Shade lifts from Shakespeare also puts a highly ironic
twist on the whole practice of purloining another's phrase, since it wittily steals from Timon's denunciation against universal thievery. Even
that self-deprecatory "some moondrop title" (a moondrop, Webster's

Second notes, is "a liquid of magical potency, supposed to be shed by the moon") subtly echoes Timon's image, and like the whole passage from which the title comes, harks back to the images of reflection that open the poem.[5]

Now at the close of the day and the close of his poem, describing in his last verse paragraph the sun sinking even as he writes, its "flowing shade and ebbing light," Shade once again echoes the tide and light imagery from *Timon*, once again links back to his poem's beginning, and does exactly what he said in Canto Three he had wanted to do, to imitate those "Playing a game of worlds . . . / . . . Making ornaments / Of accidents and possibilities." In that same passage in Canto Three, Shade had also said that it sufficed that he could find in life "Some kind of link-and-bobolink." This oddly misleading phrase links the very idea of linkage with the name of an American bird, and here at the end of the poem Shade can link the ending of the poem deceptively with the beginning it seems so little to resemble, through the butterfly, the "Vanessa with a crimson band" on its wing, that allows a hide-and-seek visual echo of the bright red streak on the wing of that other American bird, the waxwing, in the poem's first line.

The waxwing slain by the false azure in the windowpane, as we can see from a later vantage point in the poem, has strongly personal associations with people Shade has lost: his parents were ornithologists, and as we learn in the Commentary, his father even had a Mexican waxwing, *Bombycilla shadei*, named after him; and Shade will evoke Hazel in her last hour of life standing "Before the azure entrance" of the Hawaiian bar where she has just been rudely spurned. Like the waxwing at the start that reflects those he has lost, the Vanessa at the end of the poem pays a private tribute, this time to the one person still by his side, his wife, Sybil. Much earlier in the poem, after recounting how they first became sweethearts, he turns to her:

> Come and be worshiped, come and be caressed,
> 270   My dark Vanessa, crimson-barred, my blest
> My Admirable butterfly! .   .   .
>
>   .   .   .   .
>
> We have been married forty years.   .   .   .
>
>   .   .   .   .
>
> I love you when you're standing on the lawn
> Peering at something in a tree: "It's gone.
> It was so small. It might come back" (all this

Voiced in a whisper softer than a kiss).
I love you when you call me to admire
A jet's pink trail above the sunset fire.
I love you when you're humming as you pack
A suitcase or the farcical car sack
With round-trip zipper. And I love you most
290   When with a pensive nod you greet her ghost
And hold her first toy on your palm, or look
At a postcard from her, found in a book.

At the very beginning of his last day's composition, Shade again turns to his wife:

And all the time, and all the time, my love,
950   You too are there, beneath the word, above
The syllable, to underscore and stress
The vital rhythm. One heard a woman's dress
Rustle in days of yore. I've often caught
The sound and sense of your approaching thought.
And all in you is youth, and you make new,
By quoting them, old things I made for you.

In the last paragraph of the poem, not only does the Vanessa that he has identified with her flit back, but he looks out to see Sybil herself, and all the attitudes he has said he particularly loves in her: her standing in the garden, poised near a tree; her admiring something in "the sunset fire," as the setting sun now "attains / Old Dr. Sutton's last two windowpanes"; and especially the times when he loves her with the sharpest pang of all, "When with a pensive nod you greet her ghost," some little memento of Hazel's past, for here he sees her "shadow near the shagbark tree" that he has himself so indelibly associated with Hazel's childhood:

I had a favorite young shagbark there
50   With ample dark jade leaves and a black, spare,
Vermiculated trunk. The setting sun
Bronzed the black bark, around which, like undone
Garlands, the shadows of the foliage fell.
It is now stout and rough; it has done well.
White butterflies turn lavender as they
Pass through its shade where gently seems to sway
The phantom of my little daughter's swing.

After Hazel's death Shade had said that I.P.H. had taught him that "no phantom would / Rise gracefully to welcome you and me / In the dark garden, near the shagbark tree." Nevertheless at the end of his poem, as he looks at the world unwinding around him, he fuses together, through the force of his art, the shagbark, the setting sun, another butterfly, the "phantom" recollection of Hazel's swing, Sybil's "shadow" near the tree, and implicitly their tenderly stored image of Hazel. What seems an ordinary evening turns out to be part of an intricate texture Shade has bravely woven to celebrate all he shares with his wife and to commemorate what they have lost in their daughter. Here, more delicately and deceptively than in the starker scoring of the counterpoint of Hazel's last night, he plays his "game of worlds," answering the turmoil of that night with his own design and his own sense of confidence in the ultimate design of things, even amid the accidents of the passing day.

3.

Commentary

MARTIN AMIS's observation that Nabokov "does all the usual things better than anybody else" applies with special force to one of the most *un*usual things ever twisted into a tale, the Commentary that occupies most of *Pale Fire*. More than two hundred pages of line-by-line annotations might seem a disastrous recipe for narrative, yet Nabokov here tells three colorfully contrasting stories, one homely, one exotic, one splenetic—Kinbote's intimate friendship with Shade in New Wye, Charles II's escape from Zembla, and Gradus's pursuit of the disguised king—that converge to a climax right in the final note. He simultaneously invents settings that offer both the recognitions of realism (small-town American academia) and the dislocations of romance (the fairyland of Zembla); places in them one of the most original and unforgettable of characters, the preposterously comic, inescapably tragic Charles Kinbote; and, amid all the mayhem Kinbote causes, allows us the pleasures of form, the satisfaction of sensing the author's order everywhere behind the commentator's chaos.

One sustained irony shapes the whole Commentary. Instead of presenting readers of his vast *apparatus criticus* with the result of prodigious labors in labyrinthine libraries, instead of assembling for them identifications they will have no time to make themselves, Kinbote acknowledges that he has "no library in the desolate log cabin where I live like Timon in his cave" (C.39–40) and except for one interview has undertaken no research whatever. Unlike *Kinbote's* readers, though, *Nabokov's* are invited to make their own easy and surprising discoveries about what the commentator cannot see. Most of these discoveries demand no infinite Borgesian library—just a good dictionary, a complete Shakespeare, and curiosity, memory, imagination. What we can find in the Commentary depends less on the esoterica of the erudite than simply on an alert assessment of human behavior and character.

NOTE TO LINES 1–4

On a first reading we may not consciously appreciate, but we certainly *feel*, the control Nabokov exerts through the Commentary despite Kinbote's mental disarray. The first note begins with a welcome and elegant paraphrase of the waxwing image that requires us to turn back to the poem itself, so establishing a pattern essential to our enjoyment of the whole Commentary. At the end of the Foreword, Kinbote had claimed: "Let me state that without my notes Shade's text simply has no human reality at all since the human reality of such a poem as his (being too skittish and reticent for an autobiographical work), with the omission of many pithy lines carelessly rejected by him, has to depend entirely on the reality of its author and his surroundings, attachments and so forth, a reality that only my notes can provide. To this statement my dear poet would probably not have subscribed." Kinbote's first note does indeed provide some of the human reality Shade omits: some of it imagined with the indulgent fancifulness of *biographie romancée* ("We can visualize John Shade in his early boyhood, a physically unattractive but otherwise beautifully developed lad, experiencing his first eschatological shock, as with incredulous fingers he picks up from the turf that compact ovoid body and gazes at the wax-red streaks ornamenting those gray-brown wings"), and some of it mildly helpful, but largely prompted by Kinbote's inability to focus for long on anything but himself:

> When in the last year of Shade's life I had the fortune of being his neighbor in the idyllic hills of New Wye (see Foreword), I often saw those particular birds most convivially feeding on the chalk-blue berries of junipers growing at the corner of his house. (See also lines 181–182.)
>
> My knowledge of garden Aves had been limited to those of northern Europe but a young New Wye gardener, in whom I was interested (see note to line 998), helped me to identify the profiles of quite a number of tropical-looking little strangers and their comical calls. . . .

Already impossibly egocentric as critical commentary, the note scales new heights of absurdity as he draws our attention to a waxwing-like bird in the heraldic crest "of the Zemblan King, Charles the Beloved (born 1915), whose glorious misfortunes I discussed so often with my friend." The Zemblan theme had been introduced obliquely four times in the Foreword, but only in passing. Now Kinbote seems to feel it cannot be too early to introduce on center stage the real hero of the Commentary, the man whose misfortunes he discussed so often with Shade and who *should* have been the subject of Shade's poem.

The final paragraph of the first note provides one helpful biographical detail ("The poem was begun at the dead center of the year, a few minutes after midnight July 1") only to lapse instantly into Kinbotean self-concern and a hint, already, of another sexual appraisal ("while I played chess with a young Iranian enrolled in our summer school"), and then into a mysterious but clearly outrageous admission: "I do not doubt that our poet would have understood his annotator's temptation to synchronize a certain fateful fact, the departure from Zembla of the would-be regicide Gradus, with that date. Actually, Gradus left Onhava on the Copenhagen plane on July 5." This is the first mention of Gradus, and we are interested to find out how he will have such a "fateful" impact on the story, but the very facts that Kinbote thinks Gradus deserves mention in this first note, that he has been tempted to alter what he believed to be the historical truth of the matter for the sake of symmetry, and that he thinks Shade would have understood this temptation, confirm all the suspicions he engendered in the Foreword. This man who thinks himself in a unique position to present Shade's poem seems to understand neither his own role as commentator nor the man he claims as his friend.

While it offers some helpful paraphrase of the poem and some welcome biographical context, the first note offers us far more of Kinbote's egotism, his incomprehension of Shade, his sexual pursuits, his preoccupation with Zembla, and his fixation on Gradus. Through Kinbote's disordered note Nabokov sounds each of the main themes of the Commentary and invites us to read *through* Kinbote rather than with him, to enjoy the outrageousness of his character and his scholarship.

All it takes to detect most of the ironies is a sense of what one person owes to another. If we remain alert to that, we can read through the heroic story Kinbote projects—his "glorious friendship" with Shade and his singular suitability as the poet's companion, inspiration, and editor, as well as the "glorious misfortunes" in his own past—to see the comedy and pathos of an insane and insufferable self-regard that drives others from him until he is left alone in terror and despair.

There are four major areas of discovery in a first reading of the Commentary. The central discovery, the central joke of the novel, is that Kinbote's notes bear so little relation to Shade's poem. Within that larger surprise are a series of slightly more deferred discoveries, about the true relationships between Kinbote and Shade, between Kinbote and Charles II of Zembla, and between Kinbote and Gradus. Let us examine each of these in turn, in order of increasing distance from Shade's poem.

ONE. KINBOTE AS COMMENTATOR

The gaps between poem and commentary offer us a series of miniature comic discoveries, the simplest of which require no more than flicking back to the poem to see the effrontery, usually the vainglory, sometimes the desperation, of Kinbote's shameless self-concern. "*Line 62*: often," reads one headnote, and Kinbote's gloss opens: "Often, almost nightly, throughout the spring of 1959, I had feared for my life. Solitude is the playfield of Satan . . . ," when the poem in fact reads: "TV's huge paperclip now shines instead / Of the stiff vane so often visited / By the naïve, the gauzy mockingbird." We notice the comedy of Kinbote's failure to explain words (lemniscate); numbers (see note to lines 120–121); natural objects (the Toothwort White); social customs ("*Line 130*: I never bounced a ball or swung a bat": "Frankly I too never excelled in soccer and cricket; I am a passable horseman, a vigorous though unorthodox skier, a good skater, a tricky wrestler, and an enthusiastic rock-climber": European Kinbote fails to see, of course, that American Shade means basketball and baseball—*and* that he should keep himself out of this note); and especially literary allusions (the Sherlock Holmes stories, Hardy, Eliot, Frost, Browning, Poe, Shakespeare). While he fails to identify the source of Shade's title, despite the poet's clear hint, the high-churchy Kinbote glosses the Pope in

> I listened to the buzz downstairs and prayed
> For everybody to be always well,
> Uncles and aunts, the maid, her niece Adèle
> Who'd seen the Pope, people in books, and God

with the proud precision of "Pius X, Giuseppe Melchiorre Sarto, 1835–1914; Pope 1903–1914." Unprepared to track down Shade's references, he reroutes the Commentary to his own obsessions and fantasies:

> My own boyhood was too happy and healthy to contain anything remotely like the fainting fits experienced by Shade. It must have been

with him a mild form of epilepsy, a derailment of the nerves at the same spot, on the same curve of the tracks, every day, for several weeks, until nature repaired the damage. Who can forget the good-natured faces, glossy with sweat, of copper-chested railway workers leaning upon their spades and following with their eyes the windows of the great express cautiously gliding by? (C.162)

Here his own incidental metaphor can cause his mind to jump before he guides it into the groove of his own past, his sexual predilections, his craving for admiration. And as so often, Nabokov allows Kinbote a nostalgia and a lyricism inseparable from the absurdity of his irrelevance.

"pale fire"

At each level of the Commentary there seems to be one particular discovery that Nabokov stresses as an opportunity or a problem inviting our special attention. As in the Foreword, Nabokov especially rewards the especially curious, but still leaves a solution open to others.

In Kinbote's second note he records that "The last king of Zembla—partly under the influence of his uncle Conmal, the great translator of Shakespeare (see notes to lines 39–40 and 962), had become, despite frequent migraines, passionately addicted to the study of literature." If we follow both cross-references, we arrive first at Kinbote's comment on a draft couplet that Shade decided against. Citing the discarded lines, Kinbote adds:

> One cannot help recalling a passage in *Timon of Athens* (Act 4, Scene 3) where the misanthrope talks to the three marauders. Having no library in the desolate log cabin where I live like Timon in his cave, I am compelled for the purpose of quick citation to retranslate this passage into English prose from a Zemblan poetical version of *Timon* which, I hope, sufficiently approximates the text, or is at least faithful to its spirit:
>
> > The sun is a thief: she lures the sea
> > and robs it. The moon is a thief:
> > he steals his silvery light from the sun.
> > The sea is a thief: it dissolves the moon.
>
> For a prudent appraisal of Conmal's translations of Shakespeare's works, see note to line 962.

The translation back from the Zemblan should invite the curious or suspicious reader to look up the Shakespearean original, which offers us not only the expected comedy of the absurd garbling in the second-generation translation, but also, unexpectedly, the title of Shade's poem.[1] If we follow the second cross-reference in the note to line 12, now backed up by this new cross-reference, we head for the note to line 962, which turns out to be Kinbote's gloss on Shade's "But this transparent thingum does require / Some moondrop title. Help me, Will! *Pale Fire*." Kinbote correctly deduces that the poet has lifted a phrase from Shakespeare, but adds: "But in which of the Bard's works did our poet cull it? My readers must make their own research. All I have with me is a tiny vest pocket edition of *Timon of Athens*—in Zemblan! It certainly contains nothing that could be regarded as an equivalent of 'pale fire' (if it had, my luck would have been a statistical monster)" (285).

We can solve the riddle of the title, then, as early as our reading of the note to line 12, and as a bonus for consulting the cross-references, we return to Kinbote saying that the last king of Zembla "had become . . . passionately addicted to the study of literature." If we have been consistently curious enough to follow the cross-references we will know from the Foreword that Kinbote is that "last king"and will see at once the irony that despite his professed passion for literature he has too little interest in Shade's poem—as opposed to the poem he wanted Shade to write and is now forcing on him in the Commentary—even to search out a Shakespeare concordance.

If however we do not follow those first cross-references from the note to line 12, we come in the course of a page-after-page reading to the note to line 39–40, with *its* cross-reference to the note to line 962. If we *still* remain incurious, still do not chase down the references, the next note contains strange echoes of the Zemblan lines from *Timon* still resounding in Kinbote's mind from the previous note. He complains that despite all his pressure on Shade to "recreate in a poem the dazzling Zembla burning in my brain," he now sees how sadly misplaced were his hopes:

> Although I realize only too clearly, alas, that the result, in its pale and diaphanous final phase, cannot be regarded as a direct echo of my narrative (of which, incidentally, only a few fragments are given in my notes—mainly to Canto One), one can hardly doubt that the sunset glow of the story acted as a catalytic agent upon the very process of the

sustained creative effervescence that enabled Shade to produce a 1000-line poem in three weeks. There is, moreover, a symptomatic family resemblance in the coloration of both poem and story. I have reread, not without pleasure, my comments to his lines, and in many cases have caught myself borrowing a kind of opalescent light from my poet's fiery orb, and unconsciously aping the prose style of his own critical essays. (C.42, 81)

The echo of "pale fire" in "pale and diaphanous final phase," and of the Zemblan *Timon* (unbeknownst to him, Kinbote's phrase echoes the English *Timon* even more closely) should trigger our suspicion, if we have still have not reached for Act IV Scene 3 of *Timon* in our one-volume Shakespeare.

If even that resonant echo does not make us curious, there are more references to a copy of the Zemblan *Timon* that the future Charles II discovers in a cupboard leading to a secret tunnel and that thirty years later, after the Zemblan revolution, he takes with him as a good-luck talisman as he escapes through the tunnel to emerge near Timon Alley and Coriolanus Lane. And if even that insistence does not seem like a problem or a clue, perhaps all the references to *Timon* and to one particular passage might be recalled when we come to the start of Kinbote's note declaring that his tiny vest pocket edition of the Zemblan *Timon* "certainly contains nothing that could be regarded as an equivalent of 'pale fire.'" At any rate, the problem of the title has at last clearly been posed, and the alert reader already given half-a-dozen chances to solve the problem that Kinbote remains too fixated on his vision of Zembla to attend to.

I find it staggering that readers can think someone as playfully generous as Nabokov is out to frustrate them. He does find incuriosity funny—and sad—but he always rewards the curious.

Two. New Wye: Kinbote and Shade

Kinbote does not bother to stoop to such "humdrum potterings" (C.747–748) as a serious commentary entails because he thinks he enhances the poem by revealing "the underside of the weave" (F, 17), the much more thrilling story that he pressed Shade so often to tell, that Shade *should* have told and *would* have told had he been free. Kinbote assumes without question that Shade and Shade's readers will naturally be far more interested in the "glorious misfortunes" of Charles II of Zembla than in the quiet life of the "gray poet" (C.12) of New Wye. This leads us naturally to the second and third levels of the Commentary, to Kinbote and Shade as neighbors, and to the Zembla Kinbote thinks they should share.

Kinbote claims that Shade "valued my society above that of all other people." The claim sounded suspect enough in the Foreword, especially when he argued that although they had not known each other long "there exist friendships which develop their own inner duration, their own eons of transparent time, independent of rotating, malicious music" (F, 18–19), or when he admitted that Shade "intentionally concealed" his tenderness toward him when they were not alone, but it looks quite preposterous after Shade's intentionally *revealed* devotion to his wife in "Pale Fire." When Kinbote now complains that Professor Hurley's memoir of Shade "contains *not one reference* to the glorious friendship that brightened the last months of John's life" (C.71, 101), he intends it as proof of Hurley's rancorous envy and bias, but even on a first reading, even this short a distance into the Commentary, we have reason to believe that Hurley omits Kinbote because his relationship with Shade was neither glorious nor even friendship. After all, only two notes earlier, lamenting the terrors of his solitude, Kinbote reports that

> it was then, on those dreadful nights, that I got used to consulting the windows of my neighbor's house in the hope for a gleam of comfort (see note to lines 47–48). What would I not have given for the poet's suffering another heart attack (see line 691 and note) leading to my being called over to their house, all windows ablaze, in the middle of the night, in a great warm burst of sympathy, coffee, telephone calls, Zemblan herbal receipts (they work wonders!), and a resurrected Shade weeping in my arms ("There, there, John"). (C.62, 96)

Kinbote also claims to be the "only begetter" (F, 17) of "Pale Fire," but his judgment rests on nothing more than his sense of his own importance: "How persistently our poet evokes images of winter in the beginning of a poem which he started composing on a balmy summer night! The mechanism of the associations is easy to make out (glass leading to crystal and crystal to ice) but the prompter behind it retains his incognito. One is too modest to suppose that the fact that the poet and his future commentator first met on a winter day somehow impinges here on the actual season" (C.34–35). "One is too modest to suppose," he says, with all the pompous impersonality of false modesty, yet he not only supposes, he mentions, he insists: he *is* "the prompter behind."

Although this particular claim merits only ridicule, Nabokov injects into Kinbote's desperate urgency toward Shade a passionate exuberance and enthusiasm that almost convince, even as they amuse: Kinbote's need to thrust Zembla on Shade with a "drunkard's wild generosity," his sexual excitement at filling him with his story ("I knew he was ripe with my Zembla, . . . ready to spurt at the brush of an eyelash"),[2] his uncontrollable urge to spy on Shade at work on a "really big poem" (C.47–48, 86) that he will not talk about, his sense of stunned betrayal when he realizes that, evening after evening, Shade reads his latest lines out to Sybil, his agony of disappointment when he learns that his visions of Zembla have not after all been fixed forever in the amber of Shade's verse.

Nabokov lets Kinbote express his needs as fervently as Humbert expresses his. Just as Humbert almost persuades some who read *Lolita* without a critical eye to what the urgency of his feelings means for those around him, Kinbote can persuade some into thinking Shade *should* have put the colorful Zembla story in verse. But here lies the main task of readerly discovery in this second, New Wye, level of the Commentary. We are invited to see, behind Kinbote's enthusiasm for his own viewpoint, how insufferable his obsessive behavior is—his thrusting his story at Shade, his shamelessly intrusive and potentially terrifying snooping on his neighbors, his vicious disregard for the man he thinks of as his friend, or indeed for anyone but himself, and his complete failure to understand the unique trust of married love—and how generous and gentle Shade is to his interesting and desperate but deeply disagreeable neighbor.

One scene must suffice. Walking home from church one morning Kinbote has the impression he hears Shade's voice say "Come tonight, Charlie," but there is no one there:

> I at once telephoned. The Shades were out, said the cheeky ancillula, an obnoxious little fan who came to cook for them on Sundays and no doubt dreamt of getting the old poet to cuddle her some wifeless day. I retelephoned two hours later; got, as usual, Sybil; insisted on talking to my friend (my "messages" were never transmitted), obtained him, and asked him as calmly as possible what he had been doing around noon when I had heard him like a big bird in my garden. He could not quite

remember, said wait a minute, he had been playing golf with Paul (whoever that was), or at least watching Paul play with another colleague. I cried that I must see him in the evening and all at once, with no reason at all, burst into tears, flooding the telephone and gasping for breath, a paroxysm which had not happened to me since Bob left me on March 30. There was a flurry of confabulation between the Shades, and then John said: "Charles, listen. Let's go for a good ramble tonight, I'll meet you at eight." It was my second good ramble since July 6 (that unsatisfactory nature talk); the third one, on July 21, was to be exceedingly brief.

Where was I? Yes, trudging along again as in the old days with John, in the woods of Arcady, under a salmon sky.

"Well," I said gaily, "what were you writing about last night, John? Your study window was simply blazing."

"Mountains," he answered.

The Bera Range, an erection of veined stone and shaggy firs, rose before me in all its power and pride. The splendid news made my heart pound, and I felt that I could now, in my turn, afford to be generous. I begged my friend not to impart to me anything more if he did not wish it. He said yes, he did not, and began bewailing the difficulties of his self-imposed task. He calculated that during the last twenty-four hours his brain had put in, roughly, a thousand minutes of work, and had produced fifty lines (say, 797–847) or one syllable every two minutes. He had finished his Third, penultimate, Canto, and had started on Canto Four, his last (see Foreword, see Foreword, at once), and would I mind very much if we started to go home—though it was only around nine— so that he could plunge back into his chaos and drag out of it, with all its wet stars, his cosmos?

How could I say no? That mountain air had gone to my head: he was reassembling my Zembla! (C.802)

There are obvious comic ironies to detect here: the discrepancy between Shade's curt "mountains"—the mountain Mrs. Z. sees in her near-death experience, and her "Mont Blanc" in Canto Three of the poem—and Kinbote's assumption that Shade is writing about Charles II's escape over the mountains; the echo of the "fountain"/ "mountain" mistake in the poem in the "mountains"/"mountains" mistake here; the narcissistic sexual pride Kinbote takes in his story, in the double entendres of "The Bera Range,[3] an erection of veined stone and shaggy firs." But they are almost a distraction from the more revealing discoveries the attentive reader needs to make about Kinbote the man.

His contempt for the "ancillula, an obnoxious little fan who . . . no doubt dreamt of getting the old poet to cuddle her some wifeless day" reveals how little his self-obsession has in common with self-aware-ness. He too is a Shade fan, derives a sexual charge from his relation-ship to Shade, and relishes visiting when Sybil is away. His scorn for the ancillula reflects his snobbery, his natural lack of generosity, and his misogyny, his failure to comprehend any kind of claim or attach-ment between a woman and a man.

Shade, shielded by Sybil at the telephone, rises from his work at Kin-bote's insistence, and, unable not to respond to Kinbote's tears, agrees to break the flow of inspiration—he has just been working on the cen-tral passage of the poem—to meet Kinbote for a walk. Kinbote cannot imagine that Shade does not look forward to their strolls as passion-ately as *he* does, or that the poet withstands his incessantly turning any conversation back to Zembla only out of a sense of curiosity, kindness, and pity for someone most people in New Wye reject as insufferable. Once their stroll begins, Kinbote basks in the tranquillity of triumph ("Where was I? Yes, trudging along again as in the old days with John, in the woods of Arcady, under a salmon sky") while Shade diplomati-cally parries his intrusiveness, and after an hour gently asks Kinbote's leave to return to the concentrated fever of his composition. Kinbote agrees without a qualm only because he supposes Shade is today as happily glorying in Charles II as he always does himself.

"pale light"

Despite his ridiculous pride in Zembla and in everything from his powerful car and his erect bodily carriage to his imagined social poise, his intimacy with Shade, and his all-round fascination, Kinbote, pre-cisely because of his relentless self-satisfaction, drives away everybody in New Wye apart from Shade and a few passing sexual partners, leav-ing himself alone, conscious of the dislike he generates, and subject to despair and a dread of persecution. He thinks constantly about the ter-rors of solitude and darkness, and about suicide as an end to his fears.

For that reason he feels a special affinity for Hazel Shade—although he has never actually asked Shade about either his daughter or his par-ents (meanwhile telling him all about Charles II's parents, Alfin the Vague and Blenda), and although he complains that there is rather too much of Hazel in Shade's poem and too little of Zembla ("his picture of Hazel is quite clear and complete; maybe a little too complete, architectonically, since the reader cannot help feeling that it has been expanded and elaborated to the detriment of certain other richer and rarer matters ousted by it" [C.230, 164]). The one piece of research Kinbote does undertake is to see Jane Provost, Shade's former secretary, who had arranged Hazel's first and last blind date, and who tells him more about Hazel's poltergeist experiences, not even hinted at in the poem, and her night in "The Haunted Barn," which Shade refers to only in the coyest of terms. From a transcript Jane Provost has made of Hazel's notes in the barn comes the most urgent invitation to discovery in the New Wye element of the Commentary. Like the identification of the *Timon of Athens* passage in the first level, but in a much more mysterious way, it reflects the words "pale fire."

On the one night Hazel visits the Haunted Barn alone, she sees a "roundlet of pale light" darting about the walls. She puts questions to the "luminous circlet," spelling out the alphabet until it seems to give "a small jump of approval" at the right letter, and Kinbote transcribes what she records: "pada ata lane pad not ogo old wart alan ther tale feur far rant lant tal told." (C.347, 188) Because his own thoughts return inexorably to suicide—and he wonders at the end of a note on the subject whether "We who burrow in filth every day may be forgiven perhaps the one sin that ends all sins" (C.493)—Kinbote tries with particular urgency to detect in the message any kind of reference to Hazel's suicide, which took place less than six months after her night in the barn. *His* urgency provokes ours. After trying to construe the line every way he can, he feels he would like to abandon the quest

> had not a diabolical force urged us to seek a secret design in the abracadabra,
>
> 812   Some kind of link-and-bobolink, some kind
> 813   Of correlated pattern in the game
>
> I abhor such games; they make my temples throb with abominable pain—but I have braved it and pored endlessly, with a commentator's infinite patience and disgust, over the crippled syllables in Hazel's report to find the least allusion to the poor girl's fate. Not one hint did I find. Neither old Hentzner's specter, nor an ambushed scamp's toy flashlight, nor her own imaginative hysteria, express anything here that might be construed, however remotely, as containing a warning, or having some bearing on the circumstances of her soon-coming death. (C.347, 189)

Kinbote's lingering over the message Hazel records, his throbbing conviction that it *must* have some hidden meaning, and his linking it with
the central epiphany of Shade's "Pale Fire," prompt us to try to decipher those "crippled syllables." But if some discoveries come easily,
others resist us. If the curious reader can find the source of "pale fire"
even before the origin of the title has been posed as a problem, a first-
time reader of *Pale Fire* simply cannot at this point detect the source
and significance of *this* "pale light." The *re*reader, however, will have
the key.

THREE. ZEMBLA: KINBOTE AND CHARLES II

        Within the frame of the Commentary and the story of Kin-
bote and Shade comes the story of Zembla that Kinbote foists on Shade
in the hope that he will compose a long poem, "a kind of *romaunt*,
about the King of Zembla" (C.1000, 296). For most readers, Zembla is
pure enchantment, and its uncertain status adds a shimmer to its radiant crispness. No country at all to us, it seems blandly enough accepted by people in New Wye. What exactly is its shifting relation to
Novaya Zemlya or Nova Zembla, to Russia or Scandinavia, to reality
and romance?

Kinbote has a boundless enthusiasm for Zembla's cloudless skies
and crystal clarities and the reign of its last king. In the first note introducing the subject directly, a note to Shade's "that crystal land," which
he suggests is "Perhaps an allusion to Zembla, my dear country," he
describes the harmony that was the password of Charles the Beloved's
reign: "A small skyscraper of ultramarine glass was steadily rising in
Onhava. The climate seemed to be improving. Taxation had become a
thing of beauty. The poor were getting a little richer, and the rich a
little poorer" (C.12, 75).

Strangest of all the dislocations in Zembla is the sexual inversion
that makes male homosexuality if not quite the norm, at least the
"manly" Zemblan form of love. Shade's "my bedroom" (his childhood
bedroom in the house he still inhabits) triggers this glorious note from
Kinbote that foregrounds the sexual theme:

> Our Prince was fond of Fleur as of a sister but with no soft shadow of
> incest or secondary homosexual complications. She had a small pale face
> with prominent cheekbones, luminous eyes, and curly dark hair. It was

rumored that after going about with a porcelain cup and Cinderella's slipper for months, the society sculptor and poet Arnor had found in her what he sought and had used her breasts and feet for his *Lilith Calling Back Adam*; but I am certainly no expert in these tender matters. Otar, her lover, said that when you walked behind her, and she knew you were walking behind her, the swing and play of those slim haunches was something intensely artistic, something Arab girls were taught in special schools by special Parisian panders who were afterwards strangled. Her fragile ankles, he said, which she placed very close together in her dainty and wavy walk, were the "careful jewels" in Arnor's poem about a *miragarl* ("mirage girl"), for which "a dream king in the sandy wastes of time would give three hundred camels and three fountains."

On ságaren werém tremkín tri stána
Verbálala wod gév ut trí phantána

(I have marked the stress accents). (C.80)

Right from the start, from the slipperiness of "no soft shadow of incest or secondary homosexual complications," the note defocalizes our response to Zemblan sexuality. The hints of myth and fairy tale in Lilith and Cinderella, the delicious unlikelihood of a "society sculptor" testing the feet and breast size of all Zembla's women, the exoticism of Arab girls and "special Parisian panders who were afterwards strangled," where the gruesome remains harmless behind its veil of remoteness, the suggestion that female beauty is a mere mirage—all this only prepares for the even stranger scene that dominates the note. Pushed by her ambitious mother the Countess, Fleur de Fyler lays siege to the King in his bedroom in the days between his mother's death and his coronation, but she proves "a poor seducer." Fleur's nymphlike, all-but-naked body floating through the scene in a kind of half-hearted and hopeless assault ("The sight of her four bare limbs and three mousepits (Zemblan anatomy) irritated him") makes heterosexual sex seem so bizarre that it thoroughly naturalizes Charles II's "manlier pleasures." Only gradually will Kinbote's guard drop to reveal that the King's homosexuality has a more sordid side in his predilection for young boys.

The major discovery in the Commentary's Zemblan story, *the* first major discovery on a first reading of the novel, is that Charles II of Zembla *is* Kinbote. Kinbote keeps it a secret from all those around him in New Wye and from us until well into the Commentary, and enjoys the secret *as* secret, as something both to be kept and to be bestowed as a priceless reward. He says to Shade on one of their evening rambles: "as soon as your poem is ready, as soon as the glory of Zembla merges with the glory of your verse, I intend to divulge to you an ultimate truth, an extraordinary secret" (C.433–34, 215). Commenting just a little earlier on Shade's dropping from his draft a quotation from Pope ("The sot a hero, lunatic a king"), Kinbote asks: "Or was he afraid of offending an authentic king? In pondering the near past I have never been able to ascertain retrospectively if he really had 'guessed my secret,' as he once observed (see note to line 991)" (C.417–421). There can be few readers who will *not* have guessed the secret by this point, and apart from those who have already followed the cross-reference from the Foreword to the note to line 991, there will be few who will not flick forward now to that note for the pleasure of confirming the hunch. Again the secret is not openly disclosed, yet is all but divulged: Kinbote says to Shade that if he shows him the manuscript of the poem that he has just declared practically finished, "I promise to divulge to you *why* I gave you, or rather *who* gave you, your theme."

If we do not discover that Kinbote is Charles II via the first trail of cross-references from the Foreword, we can still reach his secret through many possible alternative routes. Through Kinbote's strong desire to disclose who he really is, even while preserving his incognito, as in the Foreword's "Imagine a soft, clumsy giant; imagine a historical personage . . . ; imagine an exiled prince . . ." (F, 17). Through the slip in his initial eulogy of Charles II's reign: "The poor were getting a little richer, and the rich a little poorer (in accordance with what may be known some day as Kinbote's Law)" (C.12, 75). Through our hunch that someone as narcissistic as Kinbote could be so entranced with Charles II only if he *is* Charles II, a guess we may well make by early in the first long note on Zembla, describing Charles II's parents (C.71). Through the possibility of checking such a hunch at any time by glancing ahead to the Index we saw listed on the Contents page, for there the headnote announces: "The capital letters G, K, and S (which see) stand for the three main characters in this work." (There is no C for Charles II, which already offers a clue; if we follow the "which see" we find "K, see Charles II and Kinbote"; if we overlook the headnote and search directly for Charles II, we see at the end of the entry: "See also Kinbote.") Through the vivid detail and charged emotion of certain scenes, like the night the Prince is informed his mother has died (C.71, 105–6), that seem to place the narrator as participant and principal. Through Charles's telling Disa he will go to America to teach literature (C.433–434, 213), where we know Kinbote has recently arrived to do just that. Through Shade's question, after he hears of Charles II's last meeting with his Queen, Disa: "How can you know that all this intimate stuff about your rather appalling king is true?" (C.433–434, 214). Through the shift of pronoun from third person to first in the note describing the King's arrival by parachute in America (C.691, 247), as if Kinbote feels he can relax his guard now that his story has landed him safely here. Through the letter to Disa that gives his American address as "Dr. C. Kinbote, Kinbote (*not* 'Charles X. Kingbot, Esq.,' as you, or Sylvia, wrote; *please*, be more careful—and more intelligent)" (C.768, 257). The series of clues becomes gradually more unequivocal, so that by this last one surely *every* reader must know what Kinbote still does not say explicitly, so that we *all* have the pleasure of discovering for ourselves Kinbote's "ultimate truth," his "extraordinary secret."

"dim light"

Within the Zemblan level of the Commentary, as within the others, there is one special focus of discovery, and like the other special foci, it involves the title of the poem and the image of "pale fire." To Kinbote the high point of his "glorious misfortunes" is his escape through the tunnel and over the mountains. He recounts the tunnel episode in the longest note of all, a note tense with the excitement of discovery and the exultation of escape. Kinbote tells us that the King, imprisoned in a tower of his own palace after the Zemblan revolution, feels himself "the only black piece in what a composer of chess problems might term a king-in-the-corner waiter of the *solus rex* type" (C.130, 118–19). So crucial is this episode to the Zembla saga that Kinbote suggests to Shade he should call his whole poem about Charles II "Solus Rex" (C.1000, 296). The entire tunnel note in fact seems to be constructed as a kind of chess problem for us as well as for the King: can we solve the problem of his escape?

As the King sits in the dismal lumber room to which he has just been transferred, light glints off a key in a closet door and triggers in his mind a thirty-year-old recollection. As a thirteen-year-old looking for a set of toys that he and his special playmate Oleg can play with, he is directed to the lumber room in which he now sits as deposed king. Dislodging a piece of black velvet at the back of the closet with the toys, the boy discovers a secret tunnel. Armed with flashlights, he and Oleg explore the tunnel together, ticking off 1,888 yards on a pedometer, when they reach a door behind which they hear "Two terrible voices, a man's and a woman's, now rising to a passionate pitch, now sinking to raucous undertones, . . . exchanging insults in Gutnish as spoken by the fisherfolk of Western Zembla. An abominable threat made the woman shriek out in fright. Sudden silence ensued, presently broken by the man's murmuring some brief phrase of casual approval ('Perfect, my dear,' or 'Couldn't be better') that was more eerie than anything that had come before" (C.130, 127). They flee in terror back through the tunnel, but once in the palace, they have other discoveries to make: two weeks earlier they had for the first time shared the same bed, and now the "recent thrill of adventure had been superseded already by another sort of excitement. They locked themselves up. The tap ran unheeded. Both were in a manly state and moaning like doves" (127).

The discovery of the tunnel, and the discovery of sex, flash through Charles II's mind as he sits in his prison and realizes he has also discovered his means of escape. He asks to be allowed to play the piano, and is led to the music room, where Odon, an actor and staunch Royalist, poses as an Extremist guard: "'Never heard of any passage,' muttered Odon with the annoyance of a chess player who is shown how he might have saved the game he has lost" (129). Odon asks him to stay put for another day, until he can make arrangements for the escape—he will be busy that night performing an old melodrama at the Royal Theater—but the anxious King, returning to his room, opens the closet door in the dark, pulls on over his pajamas some sportsclothes he finds in a heap on the floor, removes the shelves, takes with him as a talisman a little book he dislodges, a tiny vestpocket version of *Timon Afinsken* he had noticed there thirty years before, enters the tunnel, replaces the shelves, and switches on his flashlight to find that he is now "hideously garbed in bright red" (133). He walks along the remembered tunnel, still not sure where it will come out.

Where *will* he emerge? A plethora of insistent patterns adds an odd urgency to the comparison of the King's imprisonment to a *solus rex* chess problem and of the tunnel to its solution. When the Prince first discovers the tunnel, his tutors Monsieur Beauchamp and Mr. Campbell sit down to a game of chess just as the boys set off to explore and finish just as they emerge; when the King descends into the tunnel, soldiers outside play a game of lansquenet. The lumber room had had a full-length mirror and a green silk sofa when it was the dressing room of the King's grandfather, Thurgus the Third. Above the closet leading to the tunnel hangs a portrait, framed in black velvet, of the actress Iris Acht, whose surname means "eight" in German and who "for several years, ending with her sudden death in 1888," had been Thurgus's mistress. The boys head down green-carpeted steps into the tunnel. Oleg walks in front, and "his shapely buttocks encased in tight indigo cotton moved alertly, and his own erect radiance, rather than his flambeau, seemed to illume with leaps of light the low ceiling and crowding walls. Behind him the young Prince's electric torch played on the ground and gave a coating of flour to the back of Oleg's bare thighs" (126–27). They have tocked off 1,888 yards on their pedometer when they reach a green door to which the key of the closet door fits, but they are startled by that strange argument and by the strange approval it elicits into running back before they find what lies behind that door.

Soon after discovering the secret passage, the Prince almost dies of pneumonia and "in his delirium he would strive one moment to follow a luminous disk probing an endless tunnel and try the next to clasp the melting haunches of his fair ingle" (128). He is sent to the south of Europe to recuperate, and Oleg's death at fifteen helps "to obliterate the reality of their adventure" (128). Now when the King switches on his flashlight inside the tunnel, the

> dim light he discharged at last was now his dearest companion, Oleg's ghost, the phantom of freedom. He experienced a blend of anguish and exultation, a kind of amorous joy, the like of which he had last known on the day of his coronation, when, as he walked to his throne, a few bars of incredibly rich, deep, plenteous music (whose authorship and physical source he was never able to ascertain) struck his ear, and he inhaled the hair oil of the pretty page who had bent to brush a rose petal off the footstool, and by the light of his torch the King now saw that he was hideously garbed in bright red. (132)

The images of the "luminous disk" and the "dim light" that recalls Oleg so vividly for the King as to seem like his ghost will resonate oddly with the "luminous circlet" and the "roundlet of pale light" we encounter in the Haunted Barn episode, but already have an eeriness of their own. The red garb the King finds himself wearing stands in vivid contrast with the pattern of greens at both ends of the tunnel. What on earth is the point of these patterns, and where will the tunnel lead?

When the King reached the end of the tunnel,

> he unlocked the door and upon pulling it open was stopped by a heavy black drapery. As he began fumbling among its vertical folds for some sort of ingress, the weak light of his torch rolled its hopeless eye and went out. He dropped it: it fell into muffled nothingness. The King thrust both arms into the deep folds of the chocolate-smelling cloth and, despite the uncertainty and the danger of the moment, was, as it were, physically reminded by his own movement of the comical, at first controlled, then frantic undulations of a theatrical curtain through which a nervous actor tries vainly to pass. This grotesque sensation, at this diabolical instant, solved the mystery of the passage even before he wriggled at last through the drapery into the dimly lit, dimly cluttered *lumbarkamer* which had once been Iris Acht's dressing room in the Royal Theater. (133–34)

At last the problem is solved, at least for the moment. The tunnel had connected Thurgus and his lover; the greens had linked her greenroom* and his dressing room; the sounds the boys had heard had been from the rehearsal of an old melodrama, the very melodrama that has just been revived and that Odon now stars in—fortunately, for between scenes Odon encounters the King in his bright red and whisks him away from apprehension.

Now it is possible but extremely unlikely that a first-time reader could guess, before the King does, just where his escape will bring him out, or could recognize all of these patterns. Yet the chess-problem frame, the game of chess and the later game of lansquenet, the doubled names of Beauchamp and Campbell, the doubling of Acht and 1888 and of 1888 as a marker in space and in time, the green and red pattern, the performance then and now of a Gutnish melodrama, the overtones of a descent into the underworld in the description of the tunnel, the references to the flashlight as Oleg's ghost—all accumulate to charge the atmosphere in a way that even a first-time reader can register. But charge with what? A sense of the fates deciding between someone's death or his imminent escape into freedom? A sense that all depends on Charles II making some right move?

---

* Greenroom: a room once provided in theaters where actors and actresses could meet or mingle with others between scenes.

A first release comes for us, as for the King, at the moment he finds where that green door leads. The initial mystery stands suddenly solved, but what else lies behind these pervasive patterns? Do they somehow cohere into a single design or a problem we can eventually resolve?

Four. Kinbote and Gradus

The fourth level of the Commentary, and the third of its three plot strands, sets out Gradus's approach to his assassination attempt on Charles II. Kinbote, who finds such triumph in the story of the King, exults in a different way in the narrative vengeance he wreaks on his would-be assassin. Always vindictive, whether spontaneously undoing Gerald Emerald's tie as he passes or deliberately wounding Sybil Shade for not inviting him to John's birthday party, Kinbote dedicates a large portion of his Commentary to Gradus in a spirit of unsparing revenge. He vents his animosity through the control he exerts and asserts over Gradus's appearance in the narrative, through recording details that he indicates the unobservant gunman fails to register,[4] through the insatiable insults embedded in his direct descriptions, through his gloating over the misfortunes that befall Gradus—his failed plans, his family woes, his physical ailments.

We glimpse Gradus only in distant summary when he is first introduced, although Kinbote, working from an interview with the killer, conscientiously and contemptuously fills in his background, his birth in Riga, his childhood in Strasbourg, his arrival in Zembla in the 1940s, his first dabblings in Extremism, the botched crimes of his early days as a revolutionary, his selection as assassin, perhaps so that no "son of Zembla" need "incur the dishonor of actual regicide" (C.171, 150). As Gradus reaches Paris, Geneva, Nice, and New York, we see him in tighter and tighter focus, until when he flies from New York to New Wye we watch him in extreme—and extremely unpleasant—close-up, as Kinbote has us peer with superiority and scorn into "his magenta and mulberry insides" as he starts to succumb to food-poisoning, the details of which we are also not spared (C.949/2, 278).

In the last detailed note describing Gradus's approach, Kinbote records that after his explosive discharge in the toilet of a hotel near the New Wye campus, Gradus "was still groaning and grinding his dentures when he and his briefcase re-offended the sun" (C.949/2, 280).

He heads for the campus, is directed to the library, asks for Dr. Kinbote. A girl at the main desk suggests he try the Icelandic Collection, but he cannot find it, and when he eventually makes his way back to the main desk, the girl asks, "Didn't you— . . . Oh, there he is!" "Along the open gallery that ran above the hall, parallel to its short side, a tall bearded man was crossing over at a military quick march from east to west. He vanished behind a bookcase but not before Gradus had recognized the great rugged frame, the erect carriage, the high-bridged nose, the straight brow, and the energetic arm swing, of Charles Xavier the Beloved" (281–82). At last Kinbote as storyteller admits in triumph that he is no less a man than the ex-king of Zembla, his identity confirmed by the man who has traveled thousands of miles to put him to death.

But, incompetent as ever, Gradus again loses himself in the library, and on returning to the desk once more is told Dr. Kinbote has left for the day. He is offered a lift to Dulwich Hill by someone passing that way, and dropped off outside the Goldsworth home. "One finds it hard to decide what Gradus alias Grey wanted more at that minute: discharge his gun or rid himself of the inexhaustible lava in his bowels" (283). Gradus remains there, at the end of the second note to line 949, both ominous and odious, this clockwork man under Kinbote's taunting control, while Kinbote in the three notes on the last ten lines of the poem describes the evening atmosphere evoked in Shade's final verses, and his inviting the poet back to his own home to share half a gallon of Tokay.

Note to Line 1000

In the final note, to line 1000, the four parts of the Commentary (commentary, New Wye, Zembla, Gradus) confront one another as in any classic climax. No cross-references have directed us here in advance, and although the note's events have long been dimly foreshadowed, they come as a complex surprise.

Gradus steps right into the foreground, into the same scene as Kinbote and Shade, only for a moment, only in this last note, as he suddenly shoots at Shade—no, at Kinbote—as they cross from Shade's house to the Goldsworth house Kinbote rents: "His first bullet ripped a sleeve button off my black blazer, another sang past my ear. It is evil piffle to assert that he aimed not at me (whom he had just seen in the library—let us be consistent, gentlemen, ours is a rational world after all), but at the gray-locked gentleman behind me. Oh, he was aiming at me all right but missing me every time, the incorrigible bungler" (294).

Shot through the heart, Shade slumps to the ground as Kinbote's gardener brings a spade crashing down on the gunman. At last we find out how Kinbote comes to be in possession of the poem: leaving Shade lying bleeding on the ground, he spirits the manuscript away, hides it in his closet, and only then calls 11111. The man who had wished his friend might have a heart attack so that he could rush over with his wonder-working Zemblan herbal receipts returns to the garden with no more than a glass of water to find Shade already lying "with open dead eyes directed up at the sunny evening azure" (295).

In the turmoil of that night, Kinbote snatches time to read the poem, only to learn in a fury of disappointment that it contains nothing of the Zemblan lore he had lavished on Shade. When Sybil, hearing the gardener's version of the death scene, and thinking Kinbote has thrown himself between the gunman and Shade, says "There are things for which no recompense . . . is great enough" (298), Kinbote suggests with quick presence of mind that there *is* a recompense, if he be allowed to edit and publish the poem. In her distraction and gratitude she agrees, and Kinbote escapes to record in the Commentary not only his unique friendship with Shade, and the Zembla story he offered him, but also the Gradus story that proves his kingship matters even in New Wye.

grey shadow

Kinbote has wanted us to discover the great secret of the Commentary, that he is no less a personage than King Charles the Beloved of Zembla. What he does not expect is that we will also make another discovery, that the man he calls Jakob Gradus is in fact really an American, Jack Grey, an escapee from an institution for the criminally insane who has come to wreak vengeance on Goldsworth, the judge who sent him there and whom Shade happens to resemble.

Kinbote knows that the police identify the killer only as Grey, but in his sometimes anxious, sometimes cocky attempts to refute that story he only shows how coherent the Jack Grey version is, how consistent with the circumstances, how much more probable than his own account, no matter how painstakingly he has elaborated it. Hints of the version that he wants to suppress occur in one early note (C.47–48), but the first explicit statement that the account he has given of Gradus does not square with the police's Jack Grey version does not occur until the end of the last long note about Gradus, after he has been dropped off in front of the Shade and Goldsworth homes (C.949/2). Only in the final note, to line 1000, does Kinbote, in attempting to resist the New Wye version of events, inadvertently prompt us to recognize that it makes far more sense than his own. Even his attempt to explain how he knows the details of Gradus's past seems so uncertain as to be self-refuting:

> I did manage to obtain, soon after his detention, an interview, perhaps even two interviews, with the prisoner. He was now much more lucid than when he cowered bleeding on my porch step, and he told me all I wanted to know. By making him believe I could help him at his trial I forced him to confess his heinous crime—his deceiving the police and the nation by posing as Jack Grey, escapee from an asylum, who mistook Shade for the man who sent him there. A few days later, alas, he thwarted justice by slitting his throat with a safety razor blade salvaged from an unwatched garbage container. He died, not so much because having played his part in the story he saw no point in existing any longer, but because he could not live down this last crowning botch— killing the wrong person when the right one stood before him. In other words, his life ended not in a feeble splutter of the clockwork but in a gesture of humanoid despair. Enough of this. Exit Jack Grey. (299)

"An interview, perhaps even two interviews"—or, far more likely, no interviews at all.

But if Kinbote has invented the regicide Jakob Gradus from the bare name Jack Grey and the fact that he has deliberately shot someone on the property Kinbote rents, then the consequences are momentous. The gunman did not know that Kinbote was "really" Charles II and was not shooting at him at all, as Kinbote so strenuously insists he was. The elaborately orchestrated account of Gradus's approach, which fills almost as much space in the Commentary as the story of the King's escape, disintegrates into fabrication or fantasy. If that circumstantial story, following a trail that begins in Zembla, is entirely unreal, then so too in all probability is Kinbote's claim to be Charles II, and perhaps even the very existence of the country of Zembla.

Kinbote has admitted throughout the Commentary to relentless fears of persecution, and Jack Grey's mistakenly shooting Shade instead of Goldsworth has merely provided our commentator with the occasion to name a persecutor and invent a conspiracy that confirms his own importance. The concerted reactions of those around him in New Wye have given us reason to suspect Kinbote's insanity from as early as the Foreword. We have still more grounds for suspicion in the Commentary, in the extravagance of his claims and his behavior as neighbor and annotator, and in his readiness to see imputations against his sanity even where there are none.[5] Yet he is an intelligent and eloquent man and tells a thoroughly coherent if fabulous story. Only in this last note does the alternative account of Jack Grey clinch our doubts and confirm for us that Kinbote is indeed thoroughly mad.

With Gradus identified as Grey and Kinbote marked as mad, we can diagnose from his behavior and his Commentary that he suffers from classical paranoia in all its three main forms. Those with delusions of grandeur have the rarest and usually the severest kind of paranoia, and their delusions, unlike those of schizophrenia or mania sufferers, tend to be detailed, coherent, stable, and persistent, like Kinbote's conviction that he is the last king of Zembla. That fantasy may well reflect an unbearable nostalgia for a real homeland, perhaps Russia, since he certainly speaks Russian and admits to its being the fashionable language of Zembla when he was a child, and since his story involves deposition by a revolution *à la russe*. Those with erotic paranoia believe themselves loved sexually by someone else, usually famous, who reveals affection through countless small signs, as Kinbote is convinced the celebrated American poet John Shade values his company "above that of all other people" (F, 24). Kinbote has also shown all the traits of the third form of paranoia, persecution mania. At a level beneath his unshakeable self-satisfaction he is aware of the intense dislike he generates around him for his homosexuality and his megalomaniac narcissism.[6] His sense of beleaguered isolation produces terrors, sweats, a panicky dread of solitude at night, in which a fear of assassination and his own strong temptation to escape his despair by killing himself repeatedly fuse: "At times I thought that only by self-destruction could I hope to cheat the relentlessly advancing assassins who were in me, in my eardrums, in my pulse, in my skull, rather than on that constant highway looping up over me and around my heart" (C.62, 97).

Once Shade is shot, once Kinbote sees that Shade's long poem eschews Charles II of Zembla, he hangs on to the manuscript of the poem in order to attach to it a Commentary that will tell the Zembla story and reflect his triple centrality, as Charles the Beloved, as the neighbor and friend whose Zembla saga inspired the creative explosion in which Shade wrote "Pale Fire," and as the intended victim of a vast plot stretching from Zembla across Europe to America. But the very strand of his story that in his final note brings "proof" of his identity all the way to New Wye starts to unravel and to take the whole Commentary with it. Kinbote wants us to discover "an ultimate truth, an extraordinary secret" in the course of the Commentary. We do discover the secret of his true self, but not the one he means us to find (that he is Charles II), but the one that he tries to keep hidden even from himself: that he is a pathetic, lonely paranoid, utterly deluded about himself and his importance to Shade, to Zembla, to anything outside the desperate compensations in his own mind.

The Levels Tilt

But just when we make this unsettling discovery that reveals half of the Commentary to be sheer delusion, and yet allows everything in it to settle into a new kind of stability and sense, the last four paragraphs of the last note tilt and twist in a series of unstable surprises, as Kinbote seems either to lose control completely ("Well, folks, I guess many in this fine hall are as hungry and thirsty as me, and I'd better stop, folks, right there") or to see through the mirages of his madness glimpses of unexpected, inadmissible truths, not only that he is mad, but that he is invented:

> God will help me, I trust, to rid myself of any desire to follow the example of two other characters in this work. I shall continue to exist. I may assume other disguises, other forms, but I shall try to exist. I may turn up yet, on another campus, as an old, happy, healthy, heterosexual Russian, a writer in exile, sans fame, sans future, sans audience, sans anything but his art. I may join forces with Odon in a new motion picture: *Escape from Zembla* (ball in the palace, bomb in the palace square). I may pander to the simple tastes of theatrical critics and cook up a stage play, an old-fashioned melodrama with three principals:[7] a lunatic who intends to kill an imaginary king, another lunatic who imagines himself to be that king, and a distinguished old poet who stumbles by chance into the line of fire, and perishes in the clash between the two figments. Oh, I may do many things! History permitting, I may sail back to my

recovered kingdom, and with a great sob greet the gray coastline and the gleam of a roof in the rain. I may huddle and groan in a madhouse. But whatever happens, wherever the scene is laid, somebody, somewhere, will quietly set out—somebody has already set out, somebody still rather far away is buying a ticket, is boarding a bus, a ship, a plane, has landed, is walking toward a million photographers, and presently he will ring at my door—a bigger, more respectable, more competent Gradus.

After all our discoveries in the Commentary, none more startling than those of the last few pages, we leave it with a whole new slew of surprises as we head for the Index.

4.

Index

AFTER THE WILD wobbling of Kinbote's world at the end of the Commentary, he establishes a tighter control than ever in the Index. Here at last he has no competition: no other voice can be heard, no other reality can press for recognition, he can sum up his world just as he sees it. The orderliness of the alphabetic sequence highlights the rigorous coherence of his Zembla, almost seeming to verify its validity and refute our recent dismissal, until we remember that it confirms only the relentless method of his particular madness.

With the voice of others suppressed, the Index offers what Robert Martin Adams calls a "convulsively funny"[1] outlet for Kinbote's egotism. In the first publication of the major work of a major American poet, Kinbote indexes only his own Foreword and Commentary, not Shade's "Pale Fire" at all. He allows entries for only five people in New Wye: three Shades, Kinbote, and a "*Botkin*, V., American scholar of Russian descent." This Botkin is disturbing: why him, when if we check the references, we see that he appears never as a character but only as a name, in three separate notes,[2] yet has five lines of index, ending with "botkin or bodkin, a Danish stiletto" (which points unmistakably to Hamlet the Dane's "To be or not to be" soliloquy: "... who would bear the whips and scorns of time, ... When he himself might his quietus make / With a bare bodkin ... / But that the dread of something after death, / ... puzzles the will ..." [3.1.69–79])? As for the Shades, Sybil is dismissed in one word ("*passim*"), as if to allow her no grounds for complaint (and John Shade has written in his poem: "And all the time, and all the time, my love, / You too are there"), while simultaneously voicing *Kinbote's* complaint that she was always in the way of his attempts to see and inspire her husband. The indexer comments on Hazel, "deserves great respect, having preferred the beauty of death to the ugliness of life," a gruesome remark, considering that it is her own lack of beauty, her *own* ugliness, that drives her to suicide. Shade receives a page of subentries, which seems generous enough until we compare it with the two pages for Kinbote, and until we notice that every subentry under "Shade" always maximizes *K*'s role: "his first brush with death as visualized by *K*, and his beginning the poem while *K* plays chess at the Students' Club, *1*; . . . *K*'s drawing *S*'s attention to a pastel smear crossing the sunset sky, *286*; . . . ."

Apart from the three pages of the Index taken up by Shade as seen by Kinbote and by Kinbote as seen by Kinbote in all his charm and glory ("his good-natured request to have *S* use his stories, *12*; his modesty, *34*; his having no library in his Timonian cave, *39*"), the remaining seven pages focus entirely on the Matter of Zembla, often disclosing new details about characters, places, and events and provoking Kinbote's comical praise ("heterosexual man of fashion and Zemblan patriot") or contempt ("a puny traitor"). The coherence and sheer detail seem all the more absurd now that we are convinced he is crazy, now that we see the elaborate lengths to which he has gone in order to place himself more grandly than ever at the center of things.

Yet he also discloses his pettiness, as in his gleeful asides about Prof. H., Prof C., and Gerald Emerald—all indicated as "(not in Index)"; his homosexuality; his misogyny (s.v. *Odon*: "ought not to marry that blubber-lipped cinemactress, with untidy hair"); and his pedophilia ("his logcabin in Cedarn and the little angler, a honey-skinned lad, naked except for a pair of torn dungarees, one trouser leg rolled up, frequently fed with nougat and nuts, but then school started or the weather changed"). One comic way his homosexuality manifests itself in the Index is in the entries on Shade's game Word Golf, a game that requires changing one word into another in a given number of one-letter-at-a-time changes, where all the intermediary stages must also be valid words: "*Lass*, see Mass"; "*Male*, see Word Golf"; "*Mass, Mars, Mare*, see Male"; "*Word golf*, S's predilection for it, *819*; see Lass."

That is playful, wholesome fun, as it were, for Kinbote, whatever others might think of pedophilia. Another playful chain of cross-references is a deliberate taunt: "*Andronnikov and Niagarin*, two Soviet experts in quest of a buried treasure, *130, 681, 741*; see Crown Jewels"; "*Crown Jewels, 130, 681*; see Hiding Place"; "*Hiding place, potaynik* (q.v.)"; "*Niagarin and Andronnikov*, two Soviet 'experts' still in quest of a buried treasure, *130, 681, 741*; see Crown Jewels"; "*Potaynik, taynik (q.v.)*"; "*Taynik*, Russ., secret place; see Crown Jewels." Kinbote jeers here at Niagarin and Andronnikov, who were looking for the Zemblan crown jewels and inching dangerously nearer the King's tunnel just before he made his escape. But has Kinbote perhaps hidden the Crown Jewels among all the Zemblan place-names in the Index, or somewhere else left us a clue as to where they really are?

Whether or not he has (and a good reader should by now realize that indeed Kinbote probably *has* disclosed where the jewels are), the Index plays everywhere with the impulse to discovery that runs throughout *Pale Fire*, thwarted in the case of Niagarin and Andronnikov, so often richly rewarded for the reader. It prompts our curiosity (the Word Golf trail, the Crown Jewel trail); challenges our attention but repays us with surprising cadences or details ("his bald spot, his two teenage mistresses, Fleur and Fifalda (later Countess Otar), blue-veined daughters of Countess de Fyler, interesting light effects, *71*"); and tests our memories, inviting us to recall or return to a note to detect the comedy of Kinbote's even-more-skewed summary of a scene, or to find out more about his world.

In one of the last entries, *Variants*, Kinbote lists the discarded draft passages he has cited. Unable not to claim credit for something he is pleased with, he identifies 13 lines dropped from the poem as "K's contribution."[3] If we return to these, we discover that they reveal there is not a single line in the variants that Kinbote has praised so much, and that he advances as proof that Shade would have written about Zembla had he been allowed, that has actually been written by Shade. (The starkest fabrication of all the variants, supplied in the note to line 12, even Kinbote knows is so unsuccessful and unconvincing that he withdraws it within the text of his Commentary.) Kinbote's egotism, never more comically to the fore than in the Index, explodes itself, explodes his pretext for surrounding Shade's poem with Zembla, but what does it matter, he almost seems to think, here *is* Zembla, and nothing but Zembla, and he is its king.

Nabokov told his students that we cannot read novels but only reread them. Kinbote tells *us* at the end of the Foreword to read his notes, reread the poem with their help, rereading them of course as we go, and then perhaps read them again to complete the picture. We laugh at his eagerness, but with all the cross-references in the Commentary, and with all the invitations in the Index to relive—and spot the self-aggrandizement in—all that Kinbote has brought to life, Nabokov almost manages to make us rereaders, even as we enjoy the suprises and discoveries of a first reading, and to make us realize that there remain many more surprises and discoveries ahead if we return to reread from start to finish.

5.

Pale Fire

POEM AND COMMENTARY

Each part of *Pale Fire* has its own charm, issues its own challenges, and constitutes a natural phase in a consistent story, but why ever did Nabokov choose to write a novel in the form of a foreword, poem, commentary and index? One answer obvious from outside the novel is that its design owes much to Nabokov's translation of and commentary to the greatest of Russian poems, Alexander Pushkin's verse novel *Eugene Onegin* (1823–31), which he worked on between 1949 and 1957.[1] In published form, Nabokov's prefatory matter occupies 110 pages; his translation of Pushkin's poem, 240; the commentary, 1,087; and the index, 109—making four volumes in all, roughly four times the size of *Pale Fire* but in much the same proportions.

In planning *Pale Fire* Nabokov must have been attracted by the technical challenge of telling a story, in fact several intertwined stories, in such an unpromising format as the foreword-poem-commentary-index structure he had been working with for a decade. Yet unlike many modern novelists, from the Joyce who switches styles from chapter to chapter of *Ulysses* to the Woolf who alters focus and rhythm from section to section of *To the Lighthouse* or the Faulkner who jumps from narrator to narrator in *The Sound and the Fury* and spawns a fashion for telling fiction by unmotivated switches from voice to voice, Nabokov always devises stories that *require* the surprising new forms he invents. Here the whole situation of Kinbote and Shade—Kinbote's desperation that Shade tell his story in the verse he cannot write himself, his resolving to tell it via a commentary to the poem when he finds Shade has not obliged him—can *only* be fully told in the form Nabokov devises for *Pale Fire*.

Readers often suppose—especially if they know of Nabokov's strong literary opinions and his indignation in *Eugene Onegin* at the absurdities others have inflicted on Pushkin—that the form of *Pale Fire* and the conduct of Kinbote must make the novel an extended literary satire, a product of the creative artist's disdain for criticism, a sustained send-up of the follies of critics and readers. And *Pale Fire* does indeed present a comic nightmare of all that could go wrong in criticism. In Kinbote we encounter a critic who ignores the artist's work to focus solely on his own interests, yet who claims a unique, unchallengeable position of insight into his author (no one else was such a treasured friend) and a unique access to the text (no one else has even *seen* it), and who also claims not only that he has actually inspired the text but that he has revamped it to bring it closer to its original inspiration or to what it really *should* have said.

But although Kinbote's Commentary is a critical nightmare, Nabokov was far from thinking the process of trying to understand a literary masterpiece inherently absurd or insignificant. Some readers have idly assumed that there is something of Kinbote in Nabokov's commentaries to *Eugene Onegin*. The only thing they have in common is that neither is colorless, but the color of Nabokov's commentary is the result of prodigious, painstaking inquiry. He consecrated years of intense effort—often working day after day from 9 A.M. to 2 A.M.—to researching *Eugene Onegin* in the libraries of Harvard and Cornell, at a time when he was at his own creative peak, in the decade between starting *Lolita* and finishing *Pale Fire*. In the year he first noted down waxwings' fatal weakness for windows, for instance, he wrote to Katharine White: "I long to finish my huge Pushkin opus and go back to fiction. The monster has grown far beyond whatever I planned originally but I am glad now that I did not shrink from the task—eight years ago. It is not only going to make 'Eugene Onegin' accessible to the foreign reader but will also give the American reader, and the English-reading Russian, a unique and exhaustive work on the subject."[2]

Far from disdaining the task of critical annotation, Nabokov approached it with dedication and excitement, hoping to present an edition of *Eugene Onegin* "as true to the original as scholarship and art can make it,"[3] and finding that "the more difficult it was, the more exciting it seemed."[4] Eager to return to fiction, he kept hoping he was near the end of his work, but kept on finding more: "Pushkin should have been finished long ago," wrote Véra Nabokov late in 1956, "but he just goes on and on making new discoveries."[5] "But what things I'm finding, what discoveries I'm making!" Nabokov told a friend three months later.[6]

In *Pale Fire* he tried to create for his readers something of the same magic of discovery he had felt in exploring *Eugene Onegin*. He thought carefully about discovery, about both the excitement it produces and the effort it can involve. *Pale Fire*'s form requires that from the first we become active rather than passive readers, following at least some cross-references, comparing the divergences and the occasional concurrence between poem and commentary, perhaps returning from some items in the Index to revisit, even if only in memory, the relevant note in the Commentary. But in order to welcome the creative and curious reader, Nabokov arranges that on a first encounter we sense the excitement much more than the effort of discovery as we unpack the successive surprises in Kinbote. Although even at this stage we may be aware of some minor uncertainties (does that message in the Haunted Barn really tell us something? where *are* the Crown Jewels?), he all but leads us to the finds that matter, like the identification of Shade's source for "pale fire." *Our* efforts of inquiry and imagination make Kinbote's failure to search out anything that might elucidate Shade's poem all the funnier.

Nabokov knows that a genuine commentary to a literary masterpiece necessitates a good deal of hard, selfless work. His *Pale Fire* will itself become steadily more demanding as it becomes still more rewarding, but Kinbote does not even *begin* to face the demands of writing a commentary to *Shade's* "Pale Fire." He does not bother to trace sources in the original language, fails to identify natural objects, and misconstrues the mores and milieu of his poet because he is too preoccupied with his own Zembla. He does not try to understand Shade or his work or his world: he disapproves of the tenderness Shade shows toward Sybil in the poem, sees only that "the passage devoted to her (lines 246–292) has its structural use as a transition to the theme of his daughter" (C.246), and laments that the space Shade allots Hazel is "to the detriment of certain other richer and rarer matters ousted by" her (C.230, 164).

But the serious—and hilarious—shortcomings of Kinbote's Commentary function much less as literary satire than as brushstrokes in Nabokov's larger-than-life portrait of Kinbote's egotism, and as part of the contrast that portrait makes with the more subdued tones of the picture the novel paints of Shade. The real reason for the poem-and-commentary form is to be found here, in the human contrast between the fireside poet and the insane commentator.

Nabokov may have developed *Pale Fire* out of his critical labors on *Eugene Onegin*,[7] but it is vastly more than a satire on criticism. It is indeed a very literary work, but if it is a comment on other literature, it is a reflection on the whole history of literature, on the shift from romance to realism, from the old kind of hero with whose glory the reader is invited to identify, the kings of immortal old tales whom Kinbote craves to join, to the modern image of everyman as artist, the suburban Shade, in the modest circumstances of the real, coping with courage and self-control, with imagination, curiosity, tenderness, and kindness, with the fact of his mortality and his losses past and still to come.

CONFLICT AND CONTRAST

Although Nabokov declares that in a first-rate work of fiction the real clash is not between character and character but between author and reader, this does not seem obviously true of most first-rate fiction. In the *Odyssey* we focus on Odysseus battling monster after monster and then confronting the assembled multitude of Penelope's suitors; in *Anna Karenina*, more subtly, we watch, aghast, as Anna and Vronsky destroy their own passion through slight misalignments in their motives, and relieved, as Kitty and Lyovin manage to reconcile *their* inevitable cross-purposes.

But *Nabokov's* novels at least bear out his dictum. The special role discovery plays even on a first reading of *Pale Fire* shows his remark to be particularly pertinent here. Yet if Nabokov sees the clash between author and reader as primary, it does not mean he neglects the clash of character and character. Far from it. Character conflict plays a less overwhelmingly dominant role in Nabokov than in most fiction partly because, as he says himself, "His best works are those in which he condemns his people to the solitary confinement of their souls."[8] Yet in *Pale Fire* the "solitary confinement of the soul" provides the very basis of what conflict we find. For here we encounter a Kinbote who boasts, from the outset, of his singular rapport with Shade, and soon boasts more and more openly of his glorious escape from Zembla, but who as we gradually discover had no real closeness to or understanding of

Shade or anyone else, and who remains enclosed within his desperate self-delight. And from the start we have to discover the real Shade.

Though he hides surprises for us, we can hardly fail to recognize Kinbote's bold contours, since he is so extravagant and extreme, so comically un-self-aware, so shamelessly eager to thrust himself forward. We can also see Shade directly, though in a much more subdued light, in the poem, if we ignore Kinbote's advice to read the poem only in snatches between readings and rereadings of the Commentary. Despite its autobiographical form, "Pale Fire" avoids self-display, but Shade's very reticence and restraint tell us much. He invites our attention not because his poem records *his* experience but because he has wrought it to the right artistic pitch and brought it to the right philosophical focus: his lifelong quest to discover what lies beyond the self, especially in the ultimate, all-resisting secret of death, and to make what he can of life in the face of the uncertainty of death.

Because Kinbote dominates in the rest of the text not only as storyteller but as subject—as hero, in fact—and because he has almost no interest in others, even in Shade, except as the man who might authorize his passport to eternity, we find it difficult to see Shade plain in the Commentary. Our situation as readers resembles very much our predicament in reading *Lolita* or *Ada*: there too intelligent and eloquent narrators, imprisoned in their own self-regard, make it anything but easy for us to discern the real Lolita or Lucette and *their* claims on our consideration. But as in *Lolita* and *Ada* we can nevertheless apprehend and appreciate the key character whom the narrator presents as being so much less beguiling than himself.

In his verse, Shade exercises his imagination to step outside himself and encounter the world around him. In life, too, he remains always alert to his world. He is curious about natural phenomena—to the irritation of Kinbote, always eager to return to the subject of Charles II— and respectful and ready to learn from someone who knows "the names of things" (C.347, 185), like the uneducated but astute amateur naturalist Paul Hentzner. He tries to see things from viewpoints other than his own, as he shows in his poem from the moment he places himself in the position of a waxwing. Unlike everybody else in New Wye, including his wife, he even tries to see as if through Kinbote's eyes. At a party at the Hurleys', Kinbote does not hear Mrs. Hurley, who has evidently called him mad, but comes in only for Shade's reply: "'That is the wrong word,' he said. 'One should not apply it to

a person who deliberately peels off a drab and unhappy past and replaces it with a brilliant invention. That's merely turning a new leaf
with the left hand'" (C.629, 238). Sensing Kinbote's neediness, Shade
agrees to sunset rambles with his neighbor, knowing that Kinbote will
ignore the usual give-and-take of conversation and try to divert the
flight of the discussion toward Onhava. Shade will even break off from
his own urgent need, when his inspiration is at its strongest, to be
available for Kinbote at a moment of particular desperation. Where
Kinbote's self-obsession soon drives others away, even his numerous
sexual partners, Shade transcends his own solitude through his responsiveness to others and especially through all that he can share
with his wife. Although Shade tolerates his impossible neighbor better
than anybody else in New Wye, his conduct as poet and person is a
resounding critique of Kinbote's as character and commentator.[9]
Where Shade uses his imagination to reach beyond himself, Kinbote in
his life and in his commentary refuses any escape from his solitude
except in his doomed dream of foisting an idealized image of himself
on his world.

   Pale Fire, then, shows a clash between two kinds of minds. The real
story of the novel, we discover on a first reading, is not the uncanny
harmony between Kinbote and Shade that allows Kinbote to gloss
Shade's last and greatest work, and that even licenses him to tell the
story Shade *would* have told had he been free, but the tension between
a Kinbote condemned to the solitary confinement of his soul and a
Shade who makes every effort to overcome the natural confinement
of consciousness, between a Kinbote who attempts to impose his glory
on Shade and the world, and the Shade who must resist, must hang on
to his own life and work, while going as far as he can in kindness toward Kinbote. And in the tussle between poem and commentary this
quiet clash of wills persists even after Shade's death. The poem-and-
commentary structure allows Nabokov to dramatize two competing
attitudes toward the self—one, Shade's, that seeks a way beyond it,
versus another, Kinbote's, that pretends the whole world will soon
share his triumphant satisfaction with himself.

   Even in stories shaped much more than *Pale Fire* by the
clash of characters, the greatest storytellers seek more than to concen-
trate on conflict. Although they try to encompass as much as they can
of life, the supreme fictionists cannot possibly include everything, and

know that even were they to succeed, they could never impose shape on it all. Instead they opt for character and plot contrasts to suggest the range of life without losing the focus of art. Homer sets Odysseus's long and dangerous attempt to return to his home and his faithful Penelope against Telemachus's brief quest from his home in search of his father, against Menelaus's long wanderings before he reaches home and his once unfaithful Helen, against Agamemnon's swift return to his home and the faithless Clytemnestra lying in wait to kill him; nearly three millennia later Tolstoy intercuts the love-stories of Anna and Vronsky and Kitty and Lyovin, one starting in excitement and ending in despair, the other starting in painful embarassment and passing through rapture to a complex, never quite unclouded happiness.

So natural a solution do character and plot contrasts provide for the artistic problem of reconciling scope and shape that they can easily become mechanical, lifeless, stale. Lyly, Marlowe, Jonson, and Middleton all offer facile parallel plots of a kind that Shakespeare, alone of his contemporaries, always has the intuition and imagination to avoid. Almost four centuries later, Graham Greene in *The Comedians* fails to defuse the danger by bestowing on his carefully contrasted leads the ironically commonplace names of Smith, Jones, and Brown.

Through the poem-and-commentary form of *Pale Fire*, Nabokov reanimates character and plot contrast. Just as Shakespeare can interweave four plots and almost as many worlds, Nabokov juxtaposes, insets, and intercuts Shade quietly musing through his window with various versions of Kinbote, as Shade's friend or nosy neighbor, as Zembla's escaping king, or as the target drawing Gradus inexorably nearer. Just as Shakespeare can shift from the stilted verse romance of Silvius to the crass realism of Touchstone's prose to the romantic realism of Rosalind's, so Nabokov switches us from verse to prose, realism to romance, Appalachia to Zembla. And just as Shakespeare, in the words of A. D. Nuttall, "likes to take a stereotype and then work against it"[10]—when for instance he makes Prince Hal rebel against the gravity of his father's age and authority by spending his time not so much with other wild youths as with a man older than his father and grave only in girth—so Nabokov takes the expected opposition of poetry and scholarship and inverts it. Instead of offering us a turbulent poet and a dry, methodical scholar, he presents us with a poet who is controlled, serene, happily homely, rather realistic, somewhat prosaic, almost static, and a scholar who is a proud romantic exile, a natural storyteller full of vivid, extravagant invention, who careens chaotically from ecstasy to despair.

Only one term links these two stark opposites: loss. Shade composes his poem because he has lost his daughter, Kinbote compiles his Commentary because he has lost what he looks back at as a kingdom beyond the seas. Shade confronts his grief with courage, dignity, and artistry, facing up to the real but probing in imagination for a way beyond it. Kinbote responds with fantasy, evading the real in a dream of his own glorious centrality. Together they suggest the range of our human ways of coping with our condition.

Shade speaks for us all in his efforts to make sense of his world despite his losses in life and the impending loss of life itself. Kinbote, by contrast, seems to speak only for himself, yet for all the extravagance of his impulse he too represents something at the core of experience. Each of us is inevitably central in our world but peripheral to the world of others, and there are times when we crave that our experience might be not *just* ours, not confined to this mind and moment, not consumed in the course of ongoing life, not doomed to oblivion when we die, but might be somehow registered and recognized by others, in the way *we* want them to feel it, with all the color and the vibrancy it has for us. With all his gifts, and with the shared life of a happy marriage, Shade can find a partial way out of this predicament. Without either, Kinbote at first thinks he too can find an escape through Shade, but learns that Shade has his own life and work, and that only *he*, Kinbote, can render the magic of the world that will die with him. In *that* sense Kinbote too, in his hopes and his helplessness, speaks for us all, for the radiant dreamy escapism of our wishes and the rawness of our frustrations and fears.

Part Two

ANTITHESIS: REREADING

In Search of the Story Behind

this "antithetic" inferno . . . the pleasant experience of the roundabout route

6.

Intrusions of the Real: Shade

Loss, Loss, and Loss Again

If a first reading of *Pale Fire* begins with the joke of "a poem in heroic couplets, of nine hundred ninety-nine lines," the joke has a far bitterer new twist as we begin to reread. We now know why Shade never had the time to adjust the last draft verse paragraph, with its "devastating erasures and cataclysmic insertions," or to find a way to round the poem out to line 1000: he was killed before he had the chance to finish the day's revisions. He dies an utterly senseless death, victim of the would-be revenge of the madman Jack Grey, who has aimed, as if on the orders of some mocking fate, at a man who merely happens to resemble Judge Goldsworth and to step onto Goldsworth's garden at the worst possible moment. Even that absurd death is further drained of meaning when another madman appropriates it to form the basis for his Jakob Gradus fantasy, just as he hijacks Shade's greatest—if forever uncompleted—achievement to serve his own megalomaniac ends.

At the end of his poem, as he approaches line 1000, Shade expresses his confidence, despite his daughter's suicide, in the sense of harmony he feels around him in the slowly gathering summer evening, in the accidents of the real:

> ... And if my private universe scans right,
> So does the verse of galaxies divine
> Which I suspect is an iambic line.
> I'm reasonably sure that we survive
> And that my darling somewhere is alive,
> As I am reasonably sure that I
> Shall wake at six tomorrow, on July

980

> The twenty-second, nineteen fifty-nine,
> And that the day will probably be fine.

His confidence in waking at his usual time the next morning seems modest and eminently reasonable, yet it could not be more grotesquely misplaced. Line 976 may be an iambic line, but Shade's private universe loses its pattern when the poem breaks off before he can complete its final couplet and fit the right line 1000 into place. The verse of galaxies divine seems a mocking chaos, not a benignly ordered cosmos.

When we first read the final note in the Commentary we may be appalled at the sudden shot from a killer's gun, but Kinbote distracts us from the death by his concern to conceal his poem, by his mortification on discovering it is not the Zemblan *romaunt* he thought he had inspired, and by his adamant dismissal of the police's Jack Grey version of events. Because Grey suddenly calls into question not only the Gradus story but Zembla itself, we find it hard to pay Shade's death sufficient heed. The Index, hilariously self-contained within Kinbote's world of delusion, makes it still harder to focus on the murder. Kinbote calls his last note, the note in which Shade's death is reported, note to line 1000, on the basis that the poem should conclude with its first line: it is essential to his whole enterprise that he can present the poem as complete in order to have the right to publish. In the Index, line 1000 is reported under the names of four people: Charles II, whose last entry is merely "Solus Rex, *1000*"; Gradus, Jakob, whose story ends with "the crowning blunder, *1000*"; Kinbote, Charles, Dr., "his unsuccessful attempt to save *S*'s life, and his success in salvaging the MS, *1000*"; and Shade, John Francis, "his death from a bullet meant for another, *1000*." Shade's death deserves few words in a world so focused on Zembla.

But when we begin to reread, the knowledge of that death hangs heavily over Kinbote's initial explanations about the manuscript, and especially over the poem itself, where Shade had fought so bravely to wrest an affirmation from life in the face of death, even in the face of Hazel's suicide, only for death to have the last cruel laugh. No matter how much control we think we can impose in life, no matter how much sense and shape we think we can find in our world, we can do nothing to stave off the havoc of death.

That this has a special force for Nabokov we will realize if we know that his father's birthday was July 21, the day of Shade's death, and that Nabokov senior was shot through the heart by a gunman aiming to assassinate someone else.[1] Shade's death only repeats what Kinbote calls "the farce of fate" (C.1000, 294) in Nabokov's own life. Nabokov had more than enough provocation for the mordant irony that saturates his work. Yet if we feel the presence of death and disorder when we return to reread *Pale Fire*, we also see much more that we had not seen on a first reading: more life, and more design.

OUTER SOURCES

As we reread, we are likely to brood more on the sources of the strikingly fictional elements of the story: Wordsmith University, New Wye, Zembla and Charles II.

Wordsmith and New Wye are stylized versions of Cornell University and Ithaca, where Nabokov taught and lived from 1948 to 1959. Nabokov had an office in Goldwin Smith Hall, not far from the library, renowned for its Wordsworth collection, and the two exchange syllabic partners to form the "Goldsworth and Wordsmith" combination of Shade's poem and Kinbote's note to lines 47–48. New Wye engagingly reflects the recycling of English place names from New Jersey to New Hampshire, and of course particularly New York state, the locus of Ithaca.[2]

Since Kinbote insists on the distinction between his Zembla and "Nova Zembla" (C.894, 267), his own Zembla must be different from those slim polar islands once called Nova Zembla. Now known more often by their Russian name, Novaya Zemlya, or "new land," they were formerly, as the Popean quotation in Shade's manuscript note at line 937 indicates ("At Greenland, Zembla, or the Lord knows where"),[3] a byword for remoteness and coldness, connotations Pope's friend Swift exploited when in his *Battle of the Books* he announces that "a malignant deity, call'd *Criticism* ... dwelt on the Top of a snowy Mountain in *Nova Zembla*."[4] Judging by geographical and linguistic indications, Kinbote's Zembla is sometimes very close to Novaya Zemlya but shifts at times toward Scandinavia, perhaps toward Finland, where until November 1917 the Russian language had something like the presence it has in the Zembla of Kinbote's youth, or perhaps toward Norway or Sweden, whose languages combine with Slavic traces to produce Zemblan.

Writing in March 1957 to the young publisher Jason Epstein, then of Doubleday, to outline an early version of a novel already to be called

Pale Fire, Nabokov noted that "the story starts in Ultima Thule, an insular kingdom, where a palace intrigue and some assistance from Nova Zembla clear the way for a dull and savage revolution. My main creature the King of Thule, is dethroned. After some wonderful adventures he escapes to America. . . . He lives more or less incognito, with the lady he loves, somewhere on the border of Upstate New York and Montario: the border is a little blurry and unstable, but there is a bus to Goldenrod, another to Calendar Barn, and on Sundays the Hudson flows to Colorado. Despite these—on the whole quite innocent—little defocalizations, the locus and life-color are what a real-estate mind would call 'realistic.'"[5] The Utana from which Kinbote writes his Commentary cannot be far from Montario, and Zembla must be closer to the mythic Ultima Thule than to the actual Novaya Zemlya or the relative "realism" of New Wye.

As others have pointed out—perhaps it is a mere coincidence, more likely a seed that nearly sprouted another way—Zembla occurs in an article published on July 30, 1939, in the Paris-based Russian émigré daily *Poslednie novosti*, to which Nabokov contributed. The article recalls the first days of the League of Nations, when each nation was entitled to five seats for its delegates: "Those who were not members of the delegation could occupy the peripheral seats where one could see or hear nothing. Daniele Varè, a member of the Italian secretariat, decided to take the vacant seats behind the Venezuela delegation for his compatriots. He sneaked into the Assembly Hall at night and on a placard where the name of a country was to be displayed, wrote 'Zembla.' On the following day, pundits cast one quick glance at the placard and nodded significantly, 'Zembla, of course.'"[6] Since Nabokov began working later in 1939 on his last, abandoned Russian novel, *Solus Rex*, which revolves around Ultima Thule and eventually in *Pale Fire* would evolve into Zembla, it seems quite possible this strange intrusion of an almost legendary land into modern politics may have precipitated something in his imagination and lingered there quietly in suspended germination for twenty years.

Charles II, also known as Charles the Beloved, owes his title to several other kings of this name.[7] The foremost is England's Charles II, whom Kinbote happily evokes in his Commentary, because of his flair, looks, and popularity, and especially his romantic escape after the battle of Worcester in 1651: "Many times that night our King cast himself upon the ground with the desperate resolution of resting there till dawn that he might shift with less torment what hazard soever he ran. (I am thinking of yet another Charles, another long dark man above two yards high)" (C.597–608, 233). In the first sentence, Kinbote quotes almost verbatim from the *History of the Rebellion* (1702–4) by Edward Hyde, the Earl of Clarendon,[8] and he later gives the name of the farm where Charles II of England lay in hiding to a treasured locale in Zembla: "*Boscobel*, site of the Royal Summerhouse, a beautiful, piny and duny spot in W. Zembla, soft hollows imbued with the writer's most amorous recollections; now (1959) a 'nudist colony'—whatever that is, *149, 596*." Kinbote would be less happy to know that Charles VI of France (1368–1422), who was first known as Le Bien-Aimé (the Beloved), came to be called Le Fol (the Mad). He may have forgotten, but Nabokov clearly has not, the roots of his own fantasy in the fate of his contemporary, King Carol II of Romania (1893–1953), who was forced to renounce his rights to the throne in 1925 because of a romantic liaison, but returned from exile to be proclaimed king in 1930, and in 1938 established a personal dictatorship. After the outbreak of World War II he found himself unable to resist Russian, Hungarian, and Bulgarian claims on Romania, and was forced to abdicate in September 1940.

Pale Fire can be glossed in this way for the real world sources of even the most bizarre Zemblan details:

> Parachuting had become a popular sport. Everybody, in a word, was content—even the political mischiefmakers who were contentedly making mischief paid by a contented *Sosed* (Zembla's gigantic neighbor). But let us not pursue this tiresome subject.
>
> To return to the King: take for instance the question of personal culture. How often is it that kings engage in some special research? Conchologists among them can be counted on the fingers of one maimed hand. The last king of Zembla—partly under the influence of his uncle Conmal, the great translator of Shakespeare (see notes to lines 39–40 and 962), had become, despite frequent migraines, passionately addicted to the study of literature. (C.12, 75)

Sosed is Russian for "neighbor," and an echo of *Sovietskiy Soyuz*, the Soviet Union, and its support for "revolutionary" movements elsewhere. Charles II's father's being briefly a conchologist (see Kinbote's Index) recalls both Emperor Hirohito, who had a laboratory for marine biology, his special hobby, and Prince Albert I of Monaco, a passionate oceanographer who founded Monaco's Oceanographic Museum. Conmal, Charles II's uncle and a risibly inept translator of Shakespeare into Zemblan, stands in for Grand-Duke Konstantin Konstantinovich, the son of Tsar Alexander III's uncle, a mediocre poet and dramatist who completed a Russian translation of Shakespeare, whose work, Nabokov implies, he conned rather badly.

"But," to quote Kinbote, "let me not pursue the tabulation of non-sense": let me remark instead that the exotic details of this and other Zemblan passages, quite self-sufficient in their shimmer of strange-ness, often conceal close equivalents in the real world just where they seem strangest, yet identifications like these, while amusing to remem-ber or momentarily exciting to discover, tend to miss the point.[9] If Na-bokov wants us to understand something essential, he plants it firmly within the covers of his book, or indicates—if we exercise just a little curiosity, memory, and imagination—exactly where we should look for it elsewhere.

INNER SOURCES: REALITY INTRUDES

Almost all that Nabokov invites us to discover in *Pale Fire* requires only that we look closely at the novel itself. In time we may find there things quite unexpected, quite at variance with the apparent limits of its fictive world, but we will also find that the human relation-ships within this world are far more tenderly imagined, far more fully realized, than even the initial vividness of its details suggest.

One "hot, black, blustery night," convulsed by curiosity about the progress of Shade's poem, Kinbote steals around the Shade home, three sides of which are dark. He sees a faint square of light, sees

> Sybil and John, her on the edge of a divan, sidesaddle, with her back to me, and him on a hassock near the divan upon which he seemed to be slowly collecting and stacking scattered playing cards left after a game of patience. Sybil was alternatively huddle-shaking and blowing her nose; John's face was all blotchy and wet. Not being aware at the time of the exact type of writing paper my friend used, I could not help wonder-ing what on earth could be so tear-provoking about the outcome of a game of cards. As I strained to see better, standing up to my knees in a horribly elastic box hedge, I dislodged the sonorous lid of a garbage can. This of course might have been mistaken for the work of the wind, and Sybil hated the wind. She at once left her perch, closed the window with a great bang, and pulled down its strident blind. (C.47–48, 90)

"Later considerations and deductions have persuaded me," writes Kinbote, "that the night of great need on which I decided to check the matter"—whether they were in fact home on nights when the Shade house seemed dark from next door—"was July 11, the date of his completing his Second Canto" (C.47–48, 89–90). Nabokov regularly uses dates as a means of indicating relationships that may not at first be apparent, and that a narrator may even want to suppress. Here, however, Kinbote has virtually provided the explanation himself: the Shades have been crying because John has been reading Sybil the section of the poem he has just completed, the harrowing account of Hazel's last night. The comedy of Kinbote's subsiding into the box hedge and dislodging the garbage disguises the horror of the situation: the intense privacy of the couple, reliving the most painful moment of their life, shattered by Kinbote's intrusion, their chance to sit and share their grief denied by the sudden clatter. The "hot, black, blustery night" and Sybil's hatred of the wind take on still more poignancy when we remember that when Hazel died it was also "a night of thaw, a night of blow, / With great excitement in the air."

Kinbote returns to his solitude "with a heavy heart and a puzzled mind," but solves the puzzle a few days later, "very probably on St. Swithin's Day, for I find in my little diary under that date the anticipatory 'promnad vespert mid J.S.,' crossed out with a petulance that broke the lead in midstroke." He waits and waits for Shade to join him in the lane, and when he does not come, walks to the dark front door and then around the house, seeing Sybil through a window

> with so rapt a look on her face that one might have supposed she had just thought up a new recipe. The back door was ajar, and as I tapped it open and launched upon some gay airy phrase, I realized that Shade, sitting at the other end of the table, was in the act of reading to her something that I guessed to be a part of his poem. They both started. An unprintable oath escaped from him and he slapped down on the table the stack of index cards he had in his hand. Later he was to attribute this temperamental outburst to his having mistaken, with his reading glasses on, a welcome friend for an intruding salesman; but I must say it shocked me, it shocked me greatly, and disposed me at the time to read a hideous meaning into everything that followed. "Well, sit down," said Sybil, "and have some coffee" (victors are generous). I accepted, as I wanted to see if the recitation would be continued in my presence. It was not. "I thought," I said to my friend, "you were coming out with me for a stroll." He excused himself saying he felt out of sorts, and continued to clean the bowl of his pipe as fiercely as if it were my heart he was hollowing out. (C.47–48, 90–91)

Kinbote deduces immediately that Shade reads to Sybil each new
phase of the poem as he completes it, and now as he writes the Commentary arrives at the battier conclusion that she must have regularly
excised the "magnificent Zemblan theme." But look at the scene from
the Shades' point of view. *Shade* deduces from Kinbote's intrusion at
the rear of the darkened house that the cacophony outside several
nights before was caused not by the wind but by Kinbote. No wonder
he hollows that pipe out so fiercely.

St. Swithin's Day (Kinbote, recall, is a high-church protestant) is
July 15. That night (as we can calculate from his rate of composition,
and the dated lines 596 and 699),[10] Shade has been reading out the
following passage, reflecting on what the experience of I.P.H., the Institute of Preparation for the Hereafter, has taught him now that he has
to confront Hazel's death:

> That tasteless venture helped me in a way.
> I learnt what to ignore in my survey
> Of death's abyss. And when we lost our child
> I knew there would be nothing: no self-styled
> Spirit would touch a keyboard of dry wood
> 650   To rap out her pet name; no phantom would
> Rise gracefully to welcome you and me
> In the dark garden, near the shagbark tree.
>
> "What is that funny creaking—do you hear?"
> "It is the shutter on the stairs, my dear."
>
> "If you're not sleeping, let's turn on the light.
> I hate that wind! Let's play some chess." "All right."
>
> "I'm sure it's not the shutter. There—again."
> "It is a tendril fingering the pane."
>
> "What glided down the roof and made that thud?"
> 660   "It is old winter tumbling in the mud."
>
> "And now what shall I do? My knight is pinned."
>
> Who rides so late in the night and the wind?
> It is the writer's grief. It is the wild
> March wind. It is the father with his child.

Sybil's tension here in the poem, when she hears a funny creaking on
the stairs, or a tendril fingering the pane, or "old winter tumbling in

the mud"—noises she could almost suppose a sign from the daughter who died exactly a year ago, on a night like this, a daughter linked in life with poltergeist phenomena in this very house and ghostly lights in a haunted barn not far away—adds a new poignancy to the alarm the Sybil of the Commentary felt at the noise Kinbote caused outside several nights earlier. Here in the poem, Shade soothes her jumpiness in the only passage of extended dialogue between them: no wonder the Sybil of the Commentary sits listening with such rapt fascination. Then, in the last three lines above, he evokes, as Kinbote notes, the beginning of "Erlkönig," "the well-known poem by Goethe about the erlking, hoary enchanter of the elf-haunted alderwood, who falls in love with the delicate little boy of a belated traveler" (C.662).[11]

Presumably the scene of alarm at the noises outside that Shade writes into "Pale Fire" has been prompted in his imagination, or rekindled in his memory, by his and Sybil's alarm at the noise Kinbote caused outside three nights before. Ironically, Kinbote tries to insist that his "glorious friendship" and his tales of Zembla have inspired something in Shade's poem. What he does not realize is that his total incomprehension of what it might mean to be a friend, to think about others with the concern they might have for you, appears to have helped nudge into life one tiny portion of Shade's poem.

And what Shade does not realize, but we can see, is that it was indeed in a sense the sinister "Elf King" of Goethe's poem who was out there in that night of wind, another fantastic king, another pedophile. For Charles II, escaping in the night over the mountains, at an altitude of "elfinwood" and, with "a shiver of *alfear* (uncontrollable fear caused by elves)" (C.149, 142–43), keeps "repeating these haunting lines [of Goethe's poem] to himself both in Zemblan and German, as a chance accompaniment of drumming fatigue and anxiety" (C.662). But despite that haunted repetition, one of the many things Kinbote cannot understand is a parent's anxious love for a child that runs through Goethe's poem and Shade's agonizing echo. No wonder, indeed, that when Shade realizes four nights later that it was Kinbote who was out there prowling, he has to focus so fiercely on his pipe to avoid following up his "unprintable oath" with an outburst of raw anger.

Kinbote simply cannot see from a point of view other than his own. In a note a little later, he describes, via the appalling record of Zemblan regicide, his panics in his lonely nights at the Goldsworth castle:

> Stealthy rustles, the footsteps of yesteryear leaves, an idle breeze, a dog touring the garbage cans—everything sounded to me like a bloodthirsty

prowler. I kept moving from window to window, my silk nightcap
drenched with sweat, my bared breast a thawing pond, and sometimes,
armed with the judge's shotgun, I dared beard the terrors of the terrace.
I suppose it was then, on those masquerading spring nights with the
sounds of new life in the trees cruelly mimicking the cracklings of old
death in my brain, I suppose it was then, on those dreadful nights, that
I got used to consulting the windows of my neighbor's house in the hope
for a gleam of comfort . . . (C.62, 96).

Precisely because *he* feels panic in the night, he turns to the Shades'
windows for comfort, and then once he hears Shade is at work on the
long poem that he is sure commemorates Zembla, even stalks the
house to cause *them* an alarm and a distress that he never considers.
Yet three days later, on July 19, when Kinbote rings up desperate to see
Shade, and breaks down on the phone, Shade agrees to come for a
ramble with him that evening, despite the pressure of the inspiration
still coursing through him, despite now knowing Kinbote for the sick-
ening stalker he is. For Nabokov, the kind of sensitivity to particulars
and the attention to the interrelations of things that he invites us to see
and shows Kinbote to be blind to is no mere aesthetic fussing over
details: it carries a moral charge.

INNER SOURCES: ATTENTION TO THE REAL

On a first reading of *Pale Fire*, we enjoy the absurdity of
Kinbote's conviction not only that Shade should have written a poem
about Zembla but that, despite his failure to do so, he has somehow
been deeply influenced by his neighbor's inspiring story. As we reread
and reread, we find more and more ironies underlying the sources of
Shade's poem, or for that matter, of Kinbote's fantasy. Already we
have seen that the one concrete impetus Kinbote provides Shade
comes not through his Zembla story, but through his collapsing noisily
from a box hedge as he pries into the Shades' privacy in order to ascertain just how far Shade has reached in transmuting into verse Kinbote's own imagined flight from reality. But as we reread, we should
notice someone less pushy who stimulates Shade's imagination much
more—by his attention to the real.

Before Kinbote arrived in New Wye, Shade used to undertake evening rambles with one other man we learn of, Paul Hentzner, whom

he would walk with "every other evening" until he sold his farm in 1950. Kinbote of course cannot understand very well the attraction of any companion other than himself. He describes Hentzner as

> an eccentric farmer of German extraction, with old-fashioned hobbies such as taxidermy and herborizing. . . . Although by academic standards an uneducated man, with no real knowledge of far things in space or time, he had about him a colorful and earthy something that pleased John Shade much better than the suburban refinements of the English Department. He who displayed such fastidious care in his choice of fellow ramblers liked to trudge with the gaunt solemn German, every other evening, up the wood path to Dulwich, and all around his acquaintance's fields. Delighting as he did in the right word, he esteemed Hentzner for knowing "the names of things." . . . (C.347, 185)

If Kinbote cannot see the appeal of such a companion for a poet, we surely can. Kinbote wants to focus on his own story, and have Shade impart that to posterity. Hentzner simply allows Shade to see his world better and do what he wants with his verse. But Kinbote continues:

> Now he was walking with another companion. Limpidly do I remember one perfect evening when my friend sparkled with quips, and marrowskies, and anecdotes which I gallantly countered with tales of Zembla and harebreath escapes! As we were skirting Dulwich Forest, he interrupted me to indicate a natural grotto in the mossy rocks by the side of the path under the flowering dogwoods. This was the spot where the good farmer invariably stopped, and once, when they happened to be accompanied by his little boy, the latter, as he trotted beside them, pointed and remarked informatively: "Here Papa pisses." Another, less pointless, story awaited me at the top of the hill. . . . (C.347)

Whenever we hear something called "pointless" in Nabokov, we should look for the hidden point. Kinbote's very disdain for Hentzner, and the comic image of the little boy's declaration, may be point enough on a first reading, but if we catch the amusing twist on the title of Browning's verse drama *Pippa Passes* (1843), we might suspect by the time we return to the joke that *there* lies the point that passes Kinbote by. Mrs. Sutherland Orr, a close friend of Browning, explained the origins of the poem: "Browning was walking alone, in a wood near Dulwich, when the image flashed upon him of some one walking thus alone through life; one apparently too obscure to leave a trace of his or her passage, yet exercising a lasting though unconscious influence at every step of it; and the image shaped itself into the little silk-winder of Asolo, Felippa, or Pippa."[12] Just as the obscure Pippa passes by characters whose lives she affects without her ever meaning to— including a sculptor whose art she redirects—so the outwardly unprepossessing Hentzner proves an inspiration to John Shade when the self-important Kinbote, the incognito king, cannot stir his fancy. Shade will shape his art from seeing for himself, with Hentzner's help, the inner grain of the real, not from succumbing to Kinbote's fantasy of himself at the center of a world he barely notices.

7.

Excursions from the Real: Kinbote

KINBOTE SEES all too little of the world around him, and yet we have to see most of *Pale Fire* through his eyes. We can make out how much is false in his image of himself—his conviction that he is Charles the Beloved, say, or that he was the intended target of the bullet that killed Shade—but can we ascertain how much is true?

Explaining the chess problem in *Speak, Memory*, Nabokov compares the "antithetic" stage of approaching a solution to "a wild goose chase ... from Albany to New York by way of Vancouver, Eurasia and the Azores. The pleasant experience of the roundabout route (strange landscapes, gongs, tigers, exotic customs, the thrice-repeated circuit of a newly married couple around the sacred fire of an earthen brazier)"[1] amply rewards us for the delay. As we reread *Pale Fire*, we gradually sense a curiously concealed congruence between part and part, between Shade's poem and Kinbote's commentary, and as we shall see in the next chapter, that becomes a problem that more and more urgently demands some kind of solution. But as we reread we also learn more about local features of the novel's world and ours.

On our first reading, we may admire Shade and recognize that he gets short shrift from Kinbote, but we are happy to have the cracked commentator command more of our attention than the poet he claims to serve. We enjoy Kinbote's comic vitality and his romantic fancies, and the challenge of discovery he presents, the triumphant secret he cannot wait to disclose (that he is Charles II), the shameful secret he cannot manage to contain (that he is insane). On a rereading, conscious throughout of Shade's death, we pay Shade more heed,[2] and find him more admirable the more tragic we know him to be. And on a rereading, aware from the first of Kinbote's insanity, we find him more pathetic, more exasperating, more outrageous, more self-defeating, more doomed, as he presents us with a new challenge to discovery: just what is the reality he is trying to flee?

Let's begin *this* roundabout route.

KINBOTE'S ORIGINS

Kinbote's Zembla speaks a language that mixes Slavic and Germanic elements, and its court once spoke Russian as the "fashionable language *par excellence*" (C.894, 268): "When I was a child, Russia enjoyed quite a vogue at the court of Zembla" (C.681, 245). Situated somewhere near the border between Russia and Scandinavia, Zembla has suffered a revolution that with Soviet aid has toppled a monarchy. One particularly hysterical note, to Shade's melancholy evocation of the exile who "suffocates and conjures in two tongues / The nebulae dilating in his lungs," glosses "two tongues" as: "English and Zemblan, English and Russian, English and Lettish, English and Estonian, English and Lithuanian, English and Russian, English and Ukrainian, English and Polish, English and Czech, English and Russian, English and Hungarian, English and Rumanian, English and Albanian, English and Bulgarian, English and Serbo-Croatian, English and Russian, American and European" (C.615). The combination "English and Russian" recurs four times, and apart from Zemblan, every pairing with English involves a language of the Soviet bloc, whether Slavic or otherwise.[3] The loss of Russia and the rise of the Soviet Union stand somewhere behind Kinbote's sense of a lost kingdom. Kinbote's "Alfin the Vague (1873–1918; regnal dates 1900–1918, but 1900–1919 in most biographical dictionaries, a fumble due to the coincident calendar change from Old Style to New)" (C.71, 101–2) also indicates a Russian subtext, since it was only in Russia that the calendar change from Julian to Gregorian took place in 1918. "Charles the Beloved," Kinbote even tells us, "could boast of some Russian blood" (C.681, 245).

Early in the Index the listing of "*Botkin, V.*, American scholar of Russian descent" strikes us as surprising for several reasons: because so few people in New Wye rate Index entries (the only others are the Shades and Kinbote); because in the Commentary Botkin is never featured as an onstage character, but only as a name; because his initial, V., that letter no other language uses quite so frequently as Russian, chimes oddly with the double "v" of Charles Xavier Vseslav, the King's full name that we learn a few lines below; and because his entry alone in the Index places the notes referred to in back-to-front order,[4] starting with 894, then 247, then 71, then the kind of etymological glosses to explain a name that we would expect at the start of an entry (as in "*Emblem*, meaning 'blooming' in Zemblan; a beautiful bay . . . , 433").

Kinbote is an expert on surnames, and if we follow the Index references, we notice that he rushes to introduce "Botkin (one who makes bottekins, fancy footwear)" (C.71, 100) in a context where it does not fit, as if acting under some private compulsion.[5] Another Index reference takes us to this:

> Professor Pardon now spoke to me: "I was under the impression that you were born in Russia, and that your name was a kind of anagram of Botkin or Botkine?"
> Kinbote: "You are confusing me with some refugee from Nova Zembla" [sarcastically stressing the "Nova"]. (C.894, 267)

"Botkin" is indeed a Russian name, and, like "Nabokov," a distinguished one. Vasily Botkin (1812–69), a writer and translator, was a friend of Turgenev.[6] Dr. Evgeny Botkin, the family doctor of Tsar Nicholas II, was shot with the imperial family at Ekaterinburg on July 16, 1918. S. D. Botkin was the most prominent figure in monarchical civic associations in the thriving Russian émigré Berlin of the early 1920s, as Nabokov's father V. D. Nabokov was the most prominent in liberal émigré organizations until *he* was shot in another aftershock of the Russian Revolution.[7]

Particularly curious is the one reference to Professor Botkin in the Commentary that is *not* listed in the Index, as if it gave away far too much: "Speaking of the Head of the bloated Russian Department, Prof. Pnin, a regular martinet in regard to his underlings (happily, Prof. Botkin, who taught in another department, was not subordinated to that grotesque 'perfectionist') . . ." (C.172, 155). Since "Prof. Botkin" has not been mentioned before and never appears in person, his very introduction here implies that to anyone who knows the Wordsmith faculty, a Professor Botkin will immediately come to mind, someone so Russian it would be natural to suppose he *did* teach in the Russian Department, while the "happily" applied to a person who otherwise plays no part in the Commentary seems explicable only if this Botkin is in fact Kinbote himself.[8]

Kinbote teaches in a department headed by Dr. Nattochdag, a Swede, to judge by his name, and apparently often carries out research

in the Icelandic Collection of the Wordsmith University Library (see
C.949/2, 281). He is asked, but refuses, "to speak on the subject of 'The
Hally Vally' (as she put it, confusing Odin's Hall with the title of a
Finnish epic)" (F, 25), as if he were an expert on Valhalla or the *Kalevala*
or some such. He seems, in other words, to belong to a Department of
Scandinavian Studies, and indeed his Zemblan reflects strong Nordic
as well as Slavic elements, while the Zemblan place names Odevalla,
Falkberg, Gothland, and Kronberg echo places in southern Sweden,
the city of Uddevalla, the town of Falkenberg, the island of Gotland,
and the district of Kronoberg.

Professor Kinbote is certainly a new arrival in New Wye: he says he
has known Shade for only a few months, a time span nothing could
make him understate. He says he parachuted into America, under the
alias of Kinbote, in October the previous year, 1958, and though we
may doubt the manner, again the time seems right: the recent date
would explain why he still knows so little of such all-American activi-
ties as basketball or baseball.

Kinbote, or rather Botkin (but let us call him Kinbote, since he places
his new identity so squarely over the old), seems likely to be a Russian
émigré who has lived until recently in Scandinavia. Nevertheless, his
English is impeccable, if slightly stiffish: he is no Pnin. He translated
Shade twenty years ago, he says, into Zemblan. He can ape Shade's
prose style in his Commentary and attain wonders of eloquence. He
knows English poetry well, correctly referring a rare word ("stillicide") by memory to a poem of Thomas Hardy, or casually punning on
the name of a versifier as obscure as Thomas Flatman. Except for
Shade himself, he despises those members of the English department
whom he mentions—Prof. Hurley, Prof. C., and the teaching assistant,
Gerald Emerald.

If he has been brought up with governess English in a monarchist
émigré Russian household,[9] in the sort of émigré family "that had not
yet had time to grow poor, and still subsisted on the phantasmata of its
old St. Petersburg habits" that Nabokov pictures in *The Eye*,[10] if he has
lived most of his life in Scandinavia, probably in Sweden,[11] if he taught
there in a university English Department, then all the evidence makes
sense, or as much sense as we can expect: his languages (English, Russian, and Zemblan), his learning, his present position at Wordsmith
and his condescension to its English Department;[12] Zembla's geogra-
phy (its north-south spine of mountains, its being cut off at the south,
as he puts it in his colorful way, "by an impassable canal from the

mainland of madness" [C.149, 137–38]), its polity, and even the name of its king (Charles has been by far the most favored name for Swedish monarchs; Charles XVI Gustav—whose name is surely as close as we can come to Charles XaVIer Vseslav—was already Crown Prince at the time *Pale Fire* was written); and above all the intense nostalgia Kinbote feels for a country that is neither Scandinavian nor Russia.[13]

FLIGHT AND FRIGHT

If Kinbote has had a position in a Scandinavian university, why has he now come to America, and why does he live there in such fear of pursuit? He tells us that when he arrived in the United States, he was warned by Sylvia O'Donnell to be careful in his relationship with Shade: "the boy is strictly hetero, and, generally speaking, Your Majesty will have to be quite careful from now on" (C.691, 248). Nevertheless, Kinbote is incautious, and he pays for it, at least in his mind. Early in a first reading we will be struck by the glaring and absurd name of the "young instructor in a green velvet jacket, whom I shall mercifully call Gerald Emerald," who makes a mocking reference to Kinbote as "the Great Beaver" and whose bow-tie Kinbote pulls in retaliation (F, 24). Throughout the Commentary Kinbote's animosity toward Emerald persists, and the reason becomes clear by the Index if no earlier: Emerald has rebuffed his advances and now makes him feel vulnerable to exposure and ridicule. Every new sign that Emerald is decidedly "hetero" and indeed rather homophobic ("Quite the fancy pansy," he says of an old photograph of Charles II [C.894, 268]) adds to Kinbote's dread and detestation.

Kinbote reports that one night the Goldsworths' black cat suddenly reappears "sporting a neck bow of white silk which it could certainly never have put on all by itself" (C.62, 97). Perhaps Emerald is indeed paying him back for pulling his bow tie, but Kinbote senses something much more sustained and sinister:

> It is so easy for a cruel person to make the victim of his ingenuity believe that he has persecution mania, or is really being stalked by a killer, or is suffering from hallucinations. Hallucinations! Well did I know that among certain youthful instructors whose advances I had rejected there was at least one evil practical joker; I knew it ever since the time I came home from a very enjoyable and successful meeting of students and

teachers (at which I had exuberantly thrown off my coat and shown several willing pupils a few of the amusing holds employed by Zemblan wrestlers) and found in my coat pocket a brutal anonymous note saying: "You have hal . . . . . s real bad, chum," meaning evidently "hallucinations," although a malevolent critic might infer from the insufficient number of dashes that little Mr. Anon, despite teaching Freshman English, could hardly spell. (C.62, 97–98)

Only because he suffers already from persecution mania can Kinbote read a note warning him about his halitosis as an insinuation about hallucinations, as proof that Emerald wants to persecute him into thinking he has persecution mania. He imagines a pattern of persecution that supposedly culminates in Emerald's driving Gradus from the Wordsmith campus to the scene of what he construes as the assassination upon him. But of course, he predicts bitterly, Emerald will never admit to such a thing: "I am sure that Mr. Emerald will interrupt briefly his investigation of some mammate student's resilient charms to deny with the vigor of roused virility that he ever gave anybody a lift to my house that evening" (C.1000, 298).

If Kinbote's sense of persecution in New Wye springs mainly from his indiscreet homosexual advances, details of the King's flight from Zembla suggest that the real Kinbote or Botkin may have had to flee northern Europe because of his sexual relations with young boys. Zembla's "boy choirs are the sweetest in the world" (C.549, 224), and Charles II can also amuse himself there "with a band of Eton-collared, sweet-voiced minions imported from England" (C.433–434, 209). As the King escapes Zembla, as he reaches the tunnel from the lumber room, he feels himself suddenly as if in the presence of thirteen-year-old Oleg, his first sexual partner, and experiences a sudden "blend of anguish and exultation, a kind of amorous joy" that he has not felt since his coronation, when he "inhaled the hair oil of the pretty page who had bent to brush a rose petal off the footstool" (C.130, 132–33)— and at this very moment he looks down to find himself dressed in a dangerously conspicuous shade of red. Risking immediate capture if he lingers, he has to flee Onhava and scramble desperately over the mountains, reciting "Erlkönig" to himself through the darkness, as if this red-clad king racing through the night were Goethe's boy-catching Elf-King himself.

On his way to America, Kinbote lingers in Switzerland[14] and Nice, perhaps because he had to leave "Zembla" in haste and mark time in central and southern Europe before he could find an American teach-

ing post. With the pressure of pursuit relaxed once he arrives in Switzerland, he enjoys there the favors of Gordon—then a boy of thirteen
or fourteen—and will eventually gain the sweetest revenge of all
against his pursuers as he imagines Gradus following on his trail and
failing even to notice the skimpy covering that surrounds the young
loins the King remembers so well and that metamorphoses from "a
leopard-spotted loincloth" to "ivy," "black bathing trunks," "white
tennis shorts," and a "Tarzan brief . . . cast aside on the turf" (C.408).

Kinbote's sense of persecution is all but inextricable from his longing for suicide: "At times I thought that only by self-destruction could
I hope to cheat the relentlessly advancing assassins who were in me, in
my eardrums, in my pulse" (C.62, 97). But his temptation to suicide in
turn seems difficult to detach from his temptation to pedophilia. In his
note on suicide he first explains that the "more lucid and overwhelm-
ing one's belief in Providence, the greater the temptation to get it over
with, this business of life, but the greater too one's fear of the terrible
sin implicit in self-destruction" (C.493, 219) and then elaborates on the
temptation even a nebulous trust in an afterlife offers:

> A good Zemblan Christian is taught that true faith is not there to supply
> pictures or maps, but that it should quietly content itself with a warm
> haze of pleasurable anticipation. To take a homely example: little Chris-
> topher's family is about to migrate to a distant colony where his father
> has been assigned to a lifetime post. Little Christopher, a frail lad of nine
> or ten, relies completely (so completely, in fact, as to blot out the very
> awareness of this reliance) on his elders' arranging all the details of de-
> parture, passage and arrival. He cannot imagine, nor does he try to
> imagine, the particular aspects of the new place awaiting him but he is
> dimly and comfortably convinced that it will be even better than his
> homestead, with the big oak, and the mountain, and his pony, and the
> park, and the stable, and Grimm, the old groom, who has a way of fon-
> dling him whenever nobody is around.
>
> Something of this simple trust we too should have. With this divine
> mist of utter dependence permeating one's being, no wonder one is
> tempted, no wonder one weighs on one's palm with a dreamy smile the
> compact firearm in its case of suede leather hardly bigger than a castle-
> gate key or a boy's seamed purse, no wonder one peers over the parapet
> into an inviting abyss.
>
> I am choosing these images rather casually. There are purists who
> maintain that a gentleman should use a brace of pistols, one for each
> temple, or a bare botkin (note the correct spelling), and that ladies

should either swallow a lethal dose or drown with clumsy Ophelia.
(C.493, 220)

Kinbote may have chosen his images casually, but Nabokov certainly
has not.

Kinbote proposes what he thinks is an image of simple trust, a little
boy's trust in the absolute security of family and home, a parable of the
Christian's unspecific trust in an afterlife as still better than here, and
tries to present that world of childhood security as in no way threat-
ened, in fact as only spiced and enhanced, by "Grimm, the old groom,
who has a way of fondling him. . . ." We might wonder if acting on
that attitude has not led to *Kinbote's* having "to migrate to a distant
colony." Still dwelling on the temptation to suicide, he declares: "no
wonder one weighs on one's palm with a dreamy smile the compact
firearm in its case of suede leather hardly bigger than . . . a boy's
seamed purse." Those last few words refer to a prepubertal boy's tight
little scrotum.[15] Kinbote can think of nothing weighed in one's palm
more likely to produce a dreamy smile. Yet his visions of bliss easily
tip into despair, and the comparison of scrotum and suicide pistol
seems to reveal that despite his indulgent fancies, he feels a guilt that
hounds him close to suicide. "We who burrow in filth every day," he
says at the end of his "suicide note," "may be forgiven perhaps the one
sin that ends all sins."

If it was the recklessness of his pedophilia that forced him to flee his
"Zembla," Kinbote's recurrent fears of pursuit, however hysterically
exaggerated, have some slender basis in reality. But he cannot stay
there long. He pictures his flight from northern Europe in terms of a
red-clad king escaping through the night, and now in New Wye sees
himself still chased by his opposite, the vividly green and vigorously
heterosexual Emerald, the "young instructor in a green velvet jacket"
who drives an assassin to meet him before whizzing on "to some tryst
in the valley" (F, 24; C.949/2, 284).

ZEMBLA

If a scenario like this—Russian birth, English education,
Scandinavian situation, sexual indiscretion, panicky flight—explains
the past of the real Botkin or Kinbote, what of his unreal world, his
Zembla? When did that fantasy form?

Even a Kinbote would hardly invest his imagination in a lost "distant northern land" if he was still living in a northern land not distant at all from and in fact practically overlapping with Zembla. The Commentary, moreover, seems to indicate that Kinbote's delusions begin to develop only after he arrives in New Wye and sets himself up in what he repeatedly calls the Goldsworth "chateau" or "castle." When he moves into this rented home,

> Family photographs met me in the hallway and pursued me from room to room, and although I am sure that Alphina (9), Betty (10), Candida (12), and Dee (14) will soon change from horribly cute little schoolgirls to smart young ladies and superior mothers, I must confess that their pert pictures irritated me to such an extent that finally I gathered them one by one and dumped them all in a closet under the gallows row of their cellophane-shrouded winter clothes. . . . I did not bother, though, to do much about the family books which were also all over the house— four sets of different Children's Encyclopedias, and a stolid grown-up one that ascended all the way from shelf to shelf along a flight of stairs to burst an appendix in the attic. Judging by the novels in Mrs. Goldsworth's boudoir, her intellectual interests were fully developed, going as they did from Amber to Zen. The head of this alphabetic family had a library too. . . . (C.47–48, 83)

Alphabetic indeed: "Alphina" and "Betty" all but embody the first two letters of the Greek alphabet, and the reversed order of daughters and letters implies a deliberate countdown, a comically confident case of family planning. But the girls' names also oddly prefigure the names of the four principals of the Zemblan royal family, in descending order of age, King Alfin, Queen Blenda, their son Charles and his queen Disa.[16] The unique "Alphina" especially seems to have inspired the equally unprecedented "Alfin," to serve as a starting point, as her name implies, for the whole Zemblan saga, and the first character Kinbote introduces in his first long Zemblan note is indeed Alfin the Vague.

The children's closet in the Goldsworth home, where an irritated Kinbote stores the girls' photos (his reaction would have been different, no doubt, had they been boys of the same age), will be the place where he also hurriedly hides the manuscript of Shade's poem immediately after the poet is shot: "Leaving the gardener to watch over him I hurried into the house and concealed the invaluable envelope under a heap of girls' galoshes, furred snowboots and white wellingtons heaped at the bottom of a closet, from which I exited as if it had been the end of the secret passage that had taken me all the way out of my enchanted castle and right from Zembla to *this* Arcady" (C.1000, 295). Again note the alphabet reversed, Z to A. At this point Kinbote still expects the poem he hides in the closet to be called "Solus Rex," the name he suggested to Shade, after the chess-problem term he applies to his position of apparently exitless imprisonment in his Zemblan castle, before he found the solution, a tunnel concealed in a closet that he had come across as a child. Has the Goldsworth closet somehow expanded in Kinbote's mind to become the Zemblan closet leading to the secret passage that makes possible the King's escape?

Mrs. Goldsworth's novels show, Kinbote notes wryly, that "her intellectual interests were fully developed, going as they did from Amber to Zen." Another comic alphabetism, this reflects the four sets of Children's Encyclopedias in another key, but "Amber" specifically suggests Kathleen Winsor's *Forever Amber* (1944), a steamy-for-the-time historical blockbuster (two million copies already sold!) of romantic intrigues centering on the court of England's Charles II.[17] "Zen" at the other end of Mrs. Goldsworth's intellectual range suggests the preoccupation with Zen Buddhism in J. D. Salinger's then-recent stories about the Glass family,[18] which chime in curious harmony with Zembla, that "crystal land" (C.12, 74) whose revolution "flickered first" in its Glass Factory (C.130, 120).

If, as Alvin Kernan comments, there lies beneath the strangeness of Kinbote's Zembla a "conventional romance of faraway kingdoms, secret passages, hair-breadth escapes, exotic landscapes, and secret band of murderers. . . . A retelling of a standard romance,"[19] there may be good reason for that: Zembla appears to emerge, in a sense, from the books Kinbote finds around him. In the solitude of the Goldsworth castle, doubly dislocated from the Russia of his birth and the Scandinavia where he had felt sexually free, still harrowed by a sense of persecution but exhilarated to have a great American poet for neighbor and occasional companion, the dangerously egomaniacal Kinbote rapidly develops a fantasy that sublimates his past and will carry him forever into the future, if only he can persuade Shade to turn his vision into verse. As his Zembla develops into a more vivid and viable alternative to the "drab and unhappy past" (C.629) that he wants to flee, the alphabetic hints of the Goldsworth chateau consolidate in his mind until they form the almost entirely self-enclosed delusions that in the Index guide us methodically through Zembla from A to Z.

REVENGE

While Kinbote shapes most of Zembla to celebrate himself, he also constructs parts of it to avenge himself against others. He wreaks bitter narrative vengeance not only on Gradus but on all the Shadows. We can easily discern Jack Grey behind Gradus, but who are his supposed co-conspirators?

The next identification proves only slightly more difficult than Gradus himself. In Nice, Gradus meets "one of the greater Shadows":

> He was a merry, perhaps overmerry, fellow, in a green velvet jacket. Nobody liked him, but he certainly had a keen mind. His name, Izumrudov, sounded rather Russian but actually meant "of the Umruds," an Eskimo tribe sometimes seen paddling their umyaks (hide-lined boats) on the emerald waters of our northern shores. Grinning, he said friend Gradus must get together his travel documents, including a health certificate, and take the earliest available jet to New York. . . . Our man, who interrupted the herald of success to say he had never—was bidden not to display so much modesty. A slip of paper was now produced on which Izumrudov, shaking with laughter (death is hilarious), wrote out for Gradus their client's alias, the name of the university where he taught, and that of the town where it was situated. No, the slip was not for keeps. He could keep it only while memorizing it. This brand of paper (used by macaroon makers) was not only digestible but delicious. The gay green vision withdrew—to resume his whoring no doubt. How one hates such men! (C.741, 256)

The "green velvet jacket," the "emerald" and the "herald" perhaps stir only a sense of an uncaught echo in our first reading, unless we know Russian (*izumrudov*—as one word—means "of emeralds" and "herald" becomes *gerald* in Russian transliteration).[20] But when we reach the Index—where we might have noticed that there is no entry on Gerald Emerald—we read, under "Kinbote," "his loathing for a person who makes advances, and then betrays a noble and naïve heart, telling foul stories about his victim and pursuing him with brutal practical jokes, 741." Even without checking the note, we can recognize this as explaining Emerald, whom we encounter a few lines later, still under "Kinbote": "his final rupture with E. (not in the Index)." If the earlier reference did not prompt us to turn to note 741, perhaps this one will. Yet when we check that note, it contains no reference to Emerald or to anything in New Wye, but only to the meeting between Gradus and Izumrudov.

Nabokov makes it possible for a good first-time reader, and certainly for any alert rereader, to see that Kinbote has constructed Izumrudov as a vengeful version of the Gerald Emerald who has made fun of Kinbote's identity and sexuality and has even, last treachery of all—so he cannot help imagining—driven the killer to the scene of the assassination.[21] Izumrudov therefore becomes the agent who at last informs Gradus of the King's incognito and address and orders him to New York.

Among the Shadows pursuing Kinbote, Nabokov prepares for us a graded series of challenges to discovery, some we can meet quickly, others we may vaguely sense but not readily resolve, still others that take time even to catch our curiosity. If we soon spot Emerald in Izumrudov, we may also suspect that Kinbote's imagination has transformed those he calls "our professed Shadeans" (F, 14) of New Wye into the Shadows he sees radiating out from Zembla toward him.[22] These "professed Shadeans," Shade's fellow professors in the Wordsmith English Department, claim to represent his interests against what they see as the unbalanced, probably insane, editor who disappeared with and threatens to publish Shade's last manuscript; Kinbote sees the Shadeans as mediocrities envious of his special relationship with the poet, as he sees the Shadows as blunt-witted assassins who envy the King his distinction and pursue him out of mere malice. Yet the hunch that Shadeans and Shadows have much in common hardly suffices for us to say the Shadows are only a transmutation of the Shadeans, especially when each of the named Shadows—Gradus, Izumrudov, and Baron A.—has a character and role of his own. If Gradus is really Grey and Izumrudov merely Emerald, moreover, neither is an associate or a defender of Shade.

The two most vivid of those who hound the King and help Gradus to New Wye are Niagarin and Andronnikov, the two Soviet espionage experts brought to Onhava after the Zemblan revolution to locate the missing Crown Jewels. They cannot find them, but are still tapping and testing the walls of the palace, inching toward the room where the King is imprisoned, when he makes his escape. Even after he flees the country, the Extremists assume he still has not left Zembla, and the gloomy Russians continue their search, while Kinbote taunts: "they continued their elaborate excavations until the palace was all honeycombed and partly demolished, an entire wall of one room collapsing one night, to yield, in a niche whose presence nobody had suspected, an ancient salt cellar of bronze and King Wigbert's drinking horn; but you will never find our crown, necklace and scepter" (C.681, 244). He treats them with all the contempt that he lavishes on Gradus: "Their names (probably fictitious) were Andronnikov and Niagarin. One has seldom seen, at least among waxworks, a pair of more pleasant, presentable chaps. Everybody admired their clean-shaven jaws, elementary facial expressions, wavy hair, and perfect teeth" (244). Despite their "expertise" and some rudiments of humanoid functionality, this Rosencrantz and Guildenstern pair[23] bungle every assignation, and it is only by a massive compounding of mistakes that they are directed to burgle Queen Disa's Côte d'Azur villa, where they find a jewel box in a bureau with, of course, no crown jewels, but a letter from Charles II in which his Kinbotean incognito and address are fully spelled out. For all their incompetence, it is they who make it possible for Gradus to pursue his prey all the way to his "crowning blunder."

In the Index, with Gradus dead, Kinbote continues to taunt those he can, arranging the wild-goose chase for the Crown Jewels, mocking the Russian spies with Russian terms for "hiding place," and in the process leaving *us* as readers tantalized with not just one problem (where *are* the Crown Jewels?) but three: where are the Crown Jewels; who, if anybody, in the real world are Niagarin and Andronnikov; and what, if anything, in the real world are the Crown Jewels to make Kinbote gloat so over his pursuers' failure to find them?

In the longest entry in the Index, on Kinbote himself, we notice "his contempt for Prof. H. (not in Index) . . . his final rupture with E. (not in the Index) . . . he and *S* shaking with mirth over tidbits in a college textbook by Prof C. (not in the Index)." The final two items under "Kinbote," and the next entry, read thus:

> his unsuccessful attempt to save S's life, and his success in salvaging the MS, *1000*; his arranging to have it published without the help of two "experts," *Foreword*.
>
> *Kobaltana*, a once fashionable mountain resort near the ruins of some old barracks now a cold and desolate spot of difficult access and no importance but still remembered in military families and forest castles, not in the text.

A page later, we meet again "*Niagarin and Andronnikov*, two Soviet 'experts' still in quest of a buried treasure, *130, 681, 741*; see Crown Jewels." The conjunction of the contempt for two sets of "two 'experts'" and of "not in the Index" and "not in the text" should give us our answer to all three riddles.

In the Foreword, Kinbote complains of Sybil Shade: "Instead of answering a month-old letter from my cave in Cedarn, listing some of my most desperate queries, such as the real name of 'Jim Coates' etc., she suddenly shot me a wire, requesting me to accept Prof. H. (!) and Prof. C. (!!) as co-editors of her husband's poem. How deeply this surprised and pained me! Naturally, it precluded collaboration with my friend's misguided widow" (18). Kinbote transmutes the "experts" Prof. H. (Professor Paul Hurley, Jr., "fine administrator and inept scholar" [C.376–377]) and Prof. C. (a fatuous Freudian, C.929), whom he knows cannot have his regal insight into Shade, into Niagarin and Andronnikov, and their frustrated quest for the manuscript into the search for the elusive Crown Jewels by the bumbling Soviet spies.[24] The once fashionable mountain resort of "Kobal*tana*," the only place in Zembla with an entry in the Index but absent from the text, is the hiding place of the Crown Jewels,[25] and it corresponds in the real world of the novel to Cedarn, U*tana*, a small resort, now "again a ghost town" (C.609–614) in "these grim autumnal mountains" (C.71, 100), where Kinbote sits at his typewriter to annotate Shade's manuscript.[26] Even the fatal letter from Kinbote that Niagarin and Andronnikov find in the bureau of Charles II's wife, the letter that sends Gradus on his way and thus, in Kinbote's version of events, leads to Shade's death, corresponds to the contract from Shade's wife that would have enabled "Prof. H. (!) and Prof. C. (!!)" to become Kinbote's co-editors, something that to Kinbote seems tantamount to killing Shade all over again.

Kinbote's End

There are few things Kinbote finds more satisfying than self-glorification and the humiliation of his enemies. The two combine in an unexpected entry in the Index. Kinbote is a devotee of English poetry, but he lists only two poets in his Index: John Shade and, not Shakespeare—although even Kinbote sees that Shakespeare provided Shade with the phrase "pale fire"—but *Flatman, Thomas, 1637–88, English poet, scholar and miniaturist, not known to old fraud, 894.* If we turn to the note to line 894, we find a group of Wordsmith professors discussing how to pronounce the name of their colleague Professor Pnin:

> Professor Hurley: "Think of the French word for 'tire': punoo."
> Shade: "Why, sir, I am afraid you have only punctured the difficulty" [laughing uproariously].
> "Flatman," quipped I. (C.894, 268)

Hurley, who presumably does not recognize the name, must be the "old fraud."[27] Why, especially in this context, even an English professor's failure to recognize a pun on the name of a poet as obscure as Thomas Flatman would stamp one a fraud remains quite unclear, until we seek to find out just why Kinbote thinks him so significant. On the restoration of Charles II in 1660, Flatman wrote "A Panegyric To His Renowed Majestie, Charles the Second, King of Great *Britaine*, &c.";[28] twenty-five years later he responded to Charles II's death by writing a Pindaric ode "On the much lamented Death of Our Late Sovereign Lord King Charles II. Of Blessed Memory."[29] The panegyric begins:

> Return, return, strange Prodigie of Fate!
> Gird on thy Beams, and re-assume thy State.
> Miraculous Prince, beyond the reach of Verse,
> The Fame and Wonder of the Universe!
>
> . . . .
>
> Come, Royal Exile! We submit, we fall,
> We bend before thy Throne, and give thee all.
> Accept Eternal Honour, and that Crown. . . . (11. 1–15)[30]

That is the kind of tone Kinbote seems to wish Shade might have found for *his* Charles II.

But Shade never wrote the poem he *should* have written. Now Shade himself, the focus of Kinbote's pride and hope for the last few months, is dead. Now Kinbote himself has immortalized Zembla, the refuge of his imagination, in the only way left him, by attaching it to the immortality he expects of Shade's poem. Now the moment he publishes his Commentary he will disclose his incognito, despite his fears that "whatever happens, wherever the scene is laid, somebody, somewhere, will quietly set out . . . and presently he will ring at my door—a bigger, more respectable, more competent Gradus" (C.1000, 301). Now he is left in a "desolate log cabin" in these "grim autumnal mountains." What will he do?

The answer seems inescapable. Throughout the Commentary, and even more throughout the Index, he appears strongly tempted by suicide. "Dear Jesus, do something," he cries out. "At times I thought that only by self-destruction could I hope to cheat the relentlessly advancing assassins who were in me" (C.62, 97), he declares, and now concludes that indeed a "more competent Gradus" is already on his way. He writes a whole note on suicide, in which he extols the poetry of self-slaughter, "the perfect safety of wooed death ... the vastness of the Divine Embrace enfolding one's liberated spirit," and hopes that those tempted like him "may be forgiven perhaps the one sin that ends all sins" (C.493).

If he were to take his life, what method would he choose? "Of the not very many ways known of shedding one's body," he writes, "falling, falling, falling is the supreme method, but you have to select your sill or ledge very carefully so as not to hurt yourself or others":

> If you rent a cell in the luminous waffle, room 1915 or 1959, in a tall business center hotel browing the star dust, and pull up the window, and gently—not fall, not jump— but roll out as you should for air comfort, there is always the chance of knocking clean through into your own hell a pacific noctambulator walking his dog; in this respect a back room might be safer, especially if giving on the roof of an old tenacious normal house far below where a cat may be trusted to flash out of the way. Another popular take-off is a mountaintop with a sheer drop of say 500 meters. . . . The ideal drop is from an aircraft, your muscles relaxed, your pilot puzzled, your packed parachute shuffled off. . . . (C.493, 220–21)

Since the year of his birth is 1915, and it is now October 1959, and he is living in mountains that become lonelier and more desolate by the week, his end seems not far off at all.[31] "What can prevent us from yielding to the burning desire for merging in God?" (C.493, 222).

"God will help me, I trust," he tries to encourage himself, at the start of the last paragraph in the Commentary, "to rid myself of any desire to follow the example of two other characters in this work": Hazel Shade and Jakob Gradus. But in the Index the second entry records

> *Acht, Iris,* celebrated actress, d. 1888, a passionate and powerful woman, favorite of Thurgus the Third (*q.v.*), *130.* She died officially by her own hand; unofficially, strangled in her dressing room by a fellow actor, a jealous young Gothlander, now, at ninety, the oldest, and least important, member of the Shadows (*q.v.*) group.

Once as a child Charles Xavier had not dared enter Iris Acht's dressing room, and had beat a hasty retreat through the tunnel. Then as an adult and a king he found a solution to his *solus rex* problem, an escape from the prison his Zemblan castle had become, when he passed through Iris Acht's door into freedom, only to find himself still surrounded by his fears. Now he might find a still better solution, a more permanent escape, from "a personality consisting mainly of the shadows of its own prison bars" (C.549, 227), if he can step again, as it were, into the door of the room where Iris Acht took her own life. Officially, perhaps, Kinbote might seem to die by his own hand, but unofficially, he wants us to know, he, like Iris, will turn out to have been the victim of another Gradus, another Shadow.

The next page in the Index features *"Botkin, V.,"* whose name prompts Kinbote, an expert on surnames, to trace various possible meanings, ending with "botkin or bodkin, a Danish stiletto," in pointed allusion to Hamlet's "To be or not to be" soliloquy and his own earlier note on suicide: "There are purists who maintain that a gentleman should use a brace of pistols, one for each temple, or a bare botkin (note the correct spelling)" (C.493, 220).* On the occasion when Kinbote is identified as "the author of a remarkable book on surnames," he has denied that his name is "a kind of anagram of Botkin or Botkine," but concedes that *"kinbote* means regicide" in Zemblan (C.894, 267). Since he expects a "more competent Gradus" to come for him, since he admits that only by self-destruction could he hope to "cheat the relentlessly advancing assassins who were in me," it seems that he will indeed play the part of his own regicide, that he will take his life but hope his death can be "unofficially" attributed, like Iris Acht's, to regicidal Shadows outside him.

Later still in the Index comes the entry for Hazel Shade. Kinbote has previously rather resented her occupying space at his expense in her father's poem, but this man who has never before been generous to any woman now bestows on her his blessing: "deserves great respect, having preferred the beauty of death to the ugliness of life." It seems so far from the case that Kinbote has rid himself of any desire to follow her example, as he hopes at the end of the Commentary, that we can surely read his suicide as imminent. He has lost the one person whose friendship he valued, and he has exhausted his dream—he even breaks off his Index at *"Zembla,* a distant northern land" without

---

* There are two other references to suicide in *Hamlet* in this note: "ladies should either swallow a lethal dose or drown with clumsy Ophelia"; and "The ideal drop is from an aircraft, . . . your packed parachute shuffled off." Cf. Hamlet's "To be or not to be" soliloquy: "when we have shuffled off this moral coil" (III.i.66), an echo noted in Ackerley, "*Pale Fire*: Three Notes," 101–2.

listing occurrences in the text, as if he is too drained and desolate to continue. "Solitude is the playfield of Satan. I cannot describe the depths of my loneliness and distress" (C.62, 95), he says, thinking of the past spring, but he has never been as alone as now. Surely he will succumb to his despair.

Indeed, when an interviewer asked Nabokov a question about October 19, the date on which Kinbote signs his Foreword, he identified it as "the day on which Kinbote committed suicide (and he certainly did after putting the last touches to his edition of the poem)."[32] Michael Wood regards this as "authorial trespassing," and comments: "We don't have to pay attention to it."[33] But many different strands of evidence converge to place Kinbote on the brink of suicide: evidence within the world of the story, his emotional state, his temptation to suicide, his current situation, his readiness to publicize his incognito despite his dread of the next Gradus, his viewing suicide as an escape from the assassins stalking him, and especially the evidence of particular Nabokovian pointers in the text—like the suicide of Iris Acht, "botkin" defined as a Danish stiletto, "kinbote" as regicide, and the dates "1915 or 1959." Nabokov's interview merely corroborates what *Pale Fire* already establishes.

Even if Kinbote had said within the novel that he would commit suicide on such and such a day in such and such a way, there would be room for doubt: a change of mind, a bungled attempt, an unwelcome rescue. The only way Nabokov could have made Kinbote's suicide as unequivocal as Wood requires would be to provide a declaration within *Pale Fire* external to Kinbote's text, such as the testimony of an editor like the John Ray, Jr., of *Lolita* or the Ronald Oranger of *Ada*, who serve precisely to indicate the deaths of Humbert and Lolita and of Van and Ada. But such an editor would have to identify Kinbote or Botkin, to pronounce on his identity, his sanity, his claim to be king of Zembla, and on the status of Zembla itself: to destroy the book, in other words, to dispel its mystery, to retract its challenge of discovery. Although Nabokov cannot make Kinbote's suicide absolute without destroying the novel, he has done all in his power to make the evidence point to Kinbote's committing suicide as soon as he forever secures his Zembla by sending off the page proofs (he has already returned the galleys [F, 18]), and before publication alerts the Shadows, those "relentlessly advancing assassins," or the "professed Shadeans" whom he knows will swoop on the presumptions of his Commentary.[34]

8.

Problems: Shade and Kinbote

PROBLEMS AND SOLUTIONS

As we reread *Pale Fire*, as we see how part and part correlate, or as we detect a problem that prompts us to look elsewhere, we make discoveries of all kinds, perhaps about Shade and the sources and end of his world, or about Kinbote and the sources and end of his. We encounter problems one of the two writers poses, or problems they try to solve, but in the very act of resolving some, we often become aware of others that had escaped us before or had remained below the threshold of recognition *as* problems.

Some problems are local. After Shade's death one of his short poems is published in the New York magazine *The Beau and the Butterfly*. Why this invented title? Most North American readers will sooner or later recognize the magazine as *The New Yorker*, with its top-hatted beau, Eustace Tilley, peering through a lorgnette at a butterfly every year in a February anniversary cover. Other problems pervade the whole novel. A pattern of green-and-red at times surges to the fore, at times ebbs from sight, and again advances to problematic prominence. It becomes even more provoking when we notice that at one point, talking of his students' papers, Shade says that "I am generally very benevolent. . . . But there are certain trifles I do not forgive. . . . Not having read the required book. Having read it like an idiot. Looking in it for symbols; example: 'The author uses the striking image *green leaves* because green is the symbol of happiness and frustration'" (C.172, 156), while at another, Kinbote produces for Shade's amusement "certain tidbits from a book I had filched from a classroom: a learned work on psychoanalysis, used in American colleges, repeat, used in American colleges . . . : 'The little cap of red velvet in the German version of Little Red Riding Hood is a symbol of menstruation.' (Quoted by Prof. C.

from Erich Fromm, *The Forgotten Language*, 1951, N.Y., p. 240.) Do
those clowns really *believe* what they teach?" (C.929). Even as he wrily
extends the green-red pattern, Nabokov warns us not to read either
color as a symbol.

Shade deliberately poses one problem for us on our first
reading. He evokes Hazel's unhappy student days:

> She was my darling: difficult, morose—
> But still my darling. You remember those
> Almost unruffled evenings when we played
> 360 Mah-jongg, or she tried on your furs, which made
> Her almost fetching; and the mirrors smiled,
> The lights were merciful, the shadows mild.
> Sometimes I'd help her with a Latin text,
> Or she'd be reading in her bedroom, next
> To my fluorescent lair, and you would be
> In your own study, twice removed from me,
> And I would hear both voices now and then:
> "Mother, what's *grimpen*?" "What is what?"
> "Grim Pen."
> Pause, and your guarded scholium. Then again:
> 370 "Mother, what's *chtonic*?"[1] That, too, you'd explain,
> Appending: "Would you like a tangerine?"
> "No. Yes. And what does *sempiternal* mean?"
> You'd hesitate. And lustily I'd roar
> The answer from my desk through the closed door.
>
> It does not matter what it was she read
> (some phony modern poem that was said
> In English Lit to be a document
> "Engazhay and compelling"—what this meant
> Nobody cared); the point is that the three
> 380 Chambers, *then* bound by you and her and me,
> *Now* form a triptych[2] or a three-act play
> In which portrayed events forever stay.

Just what is that "phony modern poem" that Shade says "does not
matter"?

Many keen readers of modern poetry will know at once (and still
more would have been likely to know in 1962). Kinbote suspects, but

will not say, yet his very reserve ups the ante: "I believe I can guess (in my bookless mountain cave) what poem is meant; but without looking it up I would not wish to name its author. Anyway, I deplore my friend's vicious thrusts at the most distinguished poets of his day" (C.376). Both Shade and Nabokov are debunking some major figure.

As so often when Nabokov poses problems, he has already placed pointers to the solution, although he requires we use our memory and imagination to see them *as* pointers. Two notes before Kinbote's refusal to identify the poet, he glosses Shade's "She twisted words": "One of the examples her father gives is odd. I am quite sure it was I who one day, when we were discussing 'mirror words,' observed (and I recall the poet's expression of stupefaction) that 'spider' in reverse is 'redips,' and 'T. S. Eliot,' 'toilest.' But then it is also true that Hazel Shade resembled me in certain respects." (C.347–348) In the next note, Kinbote comments on the rhymes, in the couplets with the first two words from the "phony modern poem," on "then—pen, again—explain": "In speech John Shade, as a good American, rhymed 'again' with 'pen' and not with 'explain.' The adjacent position of these rhymes is curious" (C.367–370). But not if it is a sly comment on the American-born T. S. Eliot's enthusiastic acquired Britishness.[3] Indeed the inquisitive reader can soon find that the three words Hazel asks about all derive from Eliot's "Four Quartets,"[4] which at the time *Pale Fire* was published was widely regarded by Anglophone readers as the greatest poetic achievement of the previous thirty years—a judgment far fewer would make now.

Kinbote highlights some problems deliberately, like the location of the Crown Jewels, or takes few pains to conceal others, as when his gleeful vindictiveness alerts us to the Gerald Emerald behind Izumrudov. Other problems he would never want us to see as problems: the origins of his fantasy of Zembla or the chances of his committing suicide. But there is at least one more problem that is urgent and explicit for him and that *he* cannot solve but we can. Precisely because he is so fixated on suicide, and so anxious about whether it may be a sin, he feels desperate to discern some meaning in the message that the "pale light" in the Haunted Barn spells out to Hazel, presumably some kind of comment on *her* imminent suicide. We cannot decipher the message on a first reading, but on a rereading we can, provided we discard Kinbote's assumption.

Kinbote taxes his mind to construe in "pada ata lane pad not ogo old wart alan ther tale feur far rant lant tal told" some allusion to Hazel's suicide. But as we reread we can now see instead a message to Hazel to tell her "father (*pada*: pa, da, padre) he is not to go across the lane to old Goldsworth's, as an *atalanta* butterfly dances by, after he finishes 'Pale Fire' (*tale feur*), at the invitation of someone from a foreign land who has told and even ranted his tall tale to him."[5] We can decipher the message warning of Shade's death, of course, only *after* his death. Kinbote observes that "The barn ghost seems to have expressed himself with the empasted difficulty of apoplexy" (C.347, 189), but he does not realize that it is the spirit of Shade's Aunt Maud,[6] always so fond of "images of doom" (P.89, 36), who shortly before she dies has a stroke that seriously interferes with her speech (P.196–208, 40).

The clarity of this message, once decoded, and of its hidden speech directions, correlates oddly with the obsession with the afterlife in Shade's poem, where he writes

> why join in the vulgar laughter? Why
> Scorn a hereafter none can verify:
> The Turk's delight, the future lyres, the talks
> With Socrates and Proust in cypress walks,
> The seraph with his six flamingo wings,
> And Flemish hells with porcupines and things?
> It isn't that we dream too wild a dream:
> The trouble is we do not make it seem
> Sufficiently unlikely; for the most
> 230   We can think up is a domestic ghost

yet resolutely keeps out of his poem anything like mere "domestic ghosts," including the poltergeist phenomena around Hazel, and the details of her preoccupation with the Haunted Barn (all Shade says about this is: "She had strange fears, strange fantasies, strange force / Of character—as when she spent three nights / Investigating certain sounds and lights / In an old barn"). The decoded message suggests that the spirit of Aunt Maud, who died in 1950, somehow still survives, or at least did in 1956, and beyond death retains aspects of her personality, her preoccupation with images of doom, and even, in the way she spells out the message, a strange mutation of the paralysis and speech difficulty of her last year.

In a work where of five main characters three (Hazel, Shade and Gradus) are already dead, and a fourth (Kinbote) appears close to suicide, and where there is such a preoccupation with the possibility of an afterlife, the fact that this string of letters can be deciphered, at least by us, outside the novel's world, seems deeply curious. But how does it relate to other aspects of the novel? To the eerie moment in Charles II's Zemblan tunnel, when, as he switches on a flashlight, "The dim light he discharged at last was now his dearest companion, Oleg's ghost, the phantom of freedom" (C.130, 132)? Or to Shade's poem "The Nature of Electricity" that wryly proposes

> The dead, the gentle dead—who knows?—
> In tungsten filaments abide,
> And on my bedside table glows
> Another man's departed bride.
>
> And maybe Shakespeare floods a whole
> Town with innumerable lights . . . (C.347, 192)?

How, above all, does it relate to our sense of devastation when we feel the full force of Shade's death? As in everyday life, we cannot see how to connect something like the light in the barn, so troubling and so potentially meaningful for those involved, with the rest of the world in which it appears. As so often, a new solution only opens up a deeper problem.

On the Brink

From the very beginning, *Pale Fire* sets up a rhythm of successive discoveries, about Kinbote's sexual behavior, about the comic shortcomings of his Commentary, about his secret status as king, about Gradus's real identity as Grey, about Kinbote's sanity, about his true identity as Botkin, about his actual past and likely future, and about many other features, large and small, of the novel's world. But as we reread, we find the most alluring and elusive discoveries are the echoes we can now detect and do not expect between part and part. We have enjoyed the outrageous humor as well as the sheer outrage of the disparity between Kinbote's *apparatus criticus* and his ostensible subject, Shade's "Pale Fire," and we naturally find it mysterious and surely significant when we detect a sustained harmony between part and ostensibly discordant part. Among these covert concords are:

(1) The "pale fire" in the title of a long poem preoccupied with death, the "pale light" in the Haunted Barn, and the "dim light . . . Oleg's ghost" in the tunnel through which Charles II makes his escape.

(2) The recurrences of either the phrase or echoes of the source of Shade's "pale fire" in the Commentary, some clearly deliberate on Kinbote's part (Shade burning discarded drafts "in the pale fire of the incinerator" [F, 15]), some uncertain (the poem's "pale and diaphanous final phase" [C.42, 81], or "their earrings catching and loosing the fire of the sun" [C.71, 105]), some impossible for Kinbote to have fully intended since they echo the source passage he has failed to identify ("have caught myself borrowing a kind of opalescent light from my poet's fiery orb" [C.42, 81]).

(3) The weird presence of Shakespeare: in the *Timon of Athens* source for Shade's title; in the tiny copy of the Zemblan *Timon Afinsken* that Charles II takes with him on his escape through the tunnel and that Kinbote still has with him as a talisman; in the Coriolanus Lane and Timon Alley near the Royal Theatre at Onhava where Charles II emerges from his tunnel; in the avenue of the trees mentioned by Shakespeare planted at Wordsmith University; and in the image of Shakespeare's ghost lighting up a whole town in Shade's "The Nature of Electricity."

(4) The crystalline imagery of reflection and mirroring in the opening of "Pale Fire" and the stress on Zemblan as "the tongue of the mirror" (C.678, 242) and Zembla as "a land of reflections" (C.894, 265), the memorable "azure" of the sky into which the waxwing crashes and Zembla's "blue inenubilable" skies, and the waxwing-like bird in the Zemblan royal crest.

(5) The "shadow of the waxwing slain" and the Shadows of the Commentary, especially odd, if Kinbote is right that "I was the shadow of the waxwing slain" was meant to become, in a ricorso, line 1000 of the poem, since Shade after writing line 999 is immediately slain by the Shadow Gradus.

(6) The mirror-imagery of genius at the start of the poem, and Gradus's occupation as a glass-maker and the fact that his name, "Jakob Gradus," if spelled backward, as a kind of mirror word, becomes "*Sudarg of Bokay*, a mirror maker of genius" in the Index.

(7) The odd links between the end of Canto One, which describes

Shade's childhood fits, when he was "tugged at by playful death" as he played with a "tin wheelbarrow pushed by a tin boy" (whom we discover to be black) and the end of Canto Four and Kinbote's note to line 1000, which contain Shade's anything but playful death, the wheelbarrow of "Some neighbor's gardener" in the penultimate line, and Kinbote's "Negro gardener" who disarms Gradus after Shade has been shot.[7]

(8) The strange moment in the poem where Shade lets his imagination roam across the world as he shaves and composes:

> and now I plough
> Old Zembla's fields where my gray stubble grows,
> And slaves make hay between my mouth and nose.
>
> *Man's life as commentary to abstruse*
> 940 *Unfinished poem.* Note for further use.

(9) And apparently inexplicable echoes like that between Kinbote's background information on Charles II's Scottish tutor, Mr. Campbell, who had "immolated his life, so to speak, at the portable altars of a vast number of hobbies, from the study of book mites to bear hunting" (C.71, 104), and Shade's ironic summary of the kinds of advice given by I.P.H.:

> 560 Precautions to be taken in the case
> Of freak reincarnation: what to do
> On suddenly discovering that you
> Are now a young and venerable toad
> Plump in the middle of a busy road,
> Or a bear cub beneath a burning pine,
> Or a book mite in a revived divine.

(10) Or the fact that a careful reader should find, that Shade, Kinbote, and Gradus all share the same birthday (July 5), although Shade is sixteen years older than the other two.[8]

As we discover these relationships, they interact with both our prior experience of successively deepening discoveries about Kinbote and the sense of a great revelation waiting somewhere ahead that animates Shade to make us feel on the brink of some solution that will suddenly explain all. It can be no accident that Nabokov had first thought of calling Shade's poem "The Brink."[9]

PROPOSED SOLUTIONS

How can we explain the stealthy signals between part and
part, when the central irony of the novel appears to depend precisely
on the *lack* of communication between part and part? Because this
question seems to acquire more urgency the more we reread, the attempt to answer it has led to the longest-running and the fiercest debate in the interpretation of any of Nabokov's works. Participants in
the debate have adopted one of four main positions.

Some have suggested that Shade has written the whole of *Pale Fire*,
not just the poem; others have argued instead that Kinbote must have
written the entire volume, poem included; still others maintain that
Nabokov undermines the apparent dual authorship but deliberately
leaves the attribution question unresolved, so that while there is evidence that *either* Shade *or* Kinbote could have written the whole, the
reader, like someone looking at the perceptual psychologists' pet
image, now sees duck, now rabbit, but cannot settle on a single stable
response. Most Nabokov readers, however, reject with disgust and exasperation the claim that a single internal author may be responsible
for all of *Pale Fire*. For even most advanced readers of the novel, its
integrity and its consummate formal harmony come solely from Nabokov, while the comedy and pathos of its *dis*integratedness, so essential to its effect, derive from the absurd breach between Shade's contribution and Kinbote's.

An often intense debate about who wrote what in *Pale Fire* recently
broke out (December 1997–February 1998) in the Nabokov discussion
group on the Internet (Nabokv-L), drawing on and adding to the published critiques.[10] Of those who opt for a single-author explanation,
Shadeans dominate. The case for Shade as sole author was first made
by Andrew Field in 1967;[11] more arguments were added by Julia Bader
in 1972;[12] I added more in *Vladimir Nabokov: The American Years* in
1991[13] and still more in a long contribution to the Internet discussion;[14]
but others like Gennady Barabtarlo, Chris Ackerley, and Sergey Il'yn
have also taken up some form of the Shadean cause in print or on
screen.[15] The first Kinbotean was Page Stegner (1966),[16] but he offered
no arguments beyond the colorfulness of Kinbote's fancy (if Kinbote
could invent flamboyant Zembla, he could surely invent pallid Appalachia). He has had more support among readers new to *Pale Fire*
than old hands, although there are critics like Pekka Tammi and

Charles Nicol who argue that the equivocal overlaps between poem and commentary can be accounted for by Kinbote's more-or-less consciously reflecting "Pale Fire" in the mirror-world of his Zembla, while D. Barton Johnson stresses the primacy of Botkin.[17] Among those who opt for the fundamental undecidability of the authorship are Alvin B. Kernan (1982)[18] and Brian McHale (1987).[19] The majority who oppose single authorship include Robert Alter (1975),[20] Ellen Pifer (1980),[21] and David Lodge (1996).[22] Dmitri Nabokov, the novelist's son and translator, joined the Internet discussion with his recollection that his father thought the idea that *either* Shade *or* Kinbote could have invented the other barely less absurd than the idea that *each* could have invented the other,[23] but since in one of his own manuscripts Nabokov ascribes the Index to Shade (who would therefore have to be still alive after his reported death),[24] even that does not settle the matter.

In the 1998 Nabokv-L discussion, Ellen Pifer cited her 1980 citation of Robert Alter's "eminently sensible" 1975 comment: "This novel is not a Jamesian experiment in reliability of narrative point-of-view, and there is no reason to doubt the existence of the basic fictional data—the Poem and its author, on the one hand, and the mad Commentary and *its* perpetrator, on the other, inverted left hand."[25] Alter's remark is indeed sensible, but like so many of those made against the Shade-as-author position, it also runs the risk of stopping discussion and inquiry short. The closer we attend to *Pale Fire*, the more it provokes us into explaining the strange resonances between two minds and worlds that seem as remote from one another as Shade's and Kinbote's. The novel is indeed no Jamesian experiment in narrative reliability, but it *is* an eminently Nabokovian exercise in readerly discovery and in the surprises that can leak out from other realms.

Those who have argued against Shade as sole author have rarely paid sufficient heed to the astonishing pressure of significance that wells up as echoes between part and part accumulate, to the way, in Alvin Kernan's words, that "everything in the 'plexed artistry' of the novel seems to lead on to everything else and to tease us with the possibility of a completely articulated structure which if understood will allow us to fly through the barrier of the text into a meaning beyond."[26] (Only Kernan's "tease"—natural enough for someone who believes that the novel sets up an undecidable choice between Shade or Kinbote as sole author—strikes me as wrong.) Those who have argued for Shade, on the other hand, myself included, have been so struck by the need to respond to the tantalizing mystery of the novel's covert coherence and its promise of radical revelation that they have over-looked the objections to the Shadean position that to anti-Shadeans seem so obvious and undeniable as to be positively perverse to dismiss (we will return to those objections, which are indeed decisive, shortly).

KINBOTE

Because *Pale Fire* already offers so much in both poem, com-mentary, and the gap between them—the contrast between Shade's control and Kinbote's chaos, Shade's fulfillment and Kinbote's desper-ation, Shade's readiness to step outside himself in imagination and Kinbote's compulsion to impose himself on his world—and in the fur-ther and deeply poignant gap between Shade's confidence in what is to come and the rude shock of his death, many astute readers like Alter and Pifer feel there is no need to explore further. Yet in doing so they forget the experience and overlook the texture of *Pale Fire*, the sheer number of its pointed interconnections that seem to intimate a revela-tion just ahead, to dangle before us what Kernan calls "the possibility of absolute meanings if only we could follow and assemble the myriad of resemblances which look like clues to an absolute meaning."[27] *Pale Fire*'s echoes and patterns, and especially what Bader calls "all these 'subliminal' connections between the poem and the commentary,"[28] can seem about to converge, to interlock, to fit together into a key that will open a door we still cannot see.

Could Kinbote perhaps have written both parts? According to the first level of the story, he certainly has the imagination to invent the outlandish world of Zembla; why could he not also add the de-murer world of Appalachia? But *Pale Fire* quickly rules out the possi-bility of Kinbote as sole author. The never-modest Kinbote declares himself capable "of imitating any prose in the world (but singularly enough not verse—I am a miserable rhymester)" (C.991, 289), an ad-mission borne out by the woeful meter and rhyme of the variants he tries to fabricate. If he *could* write Shadean verse, he would have no need whatever to implore Shade to commemorate Zembla in a long poem called "Solus Rex"; he could simply do the job himself, and all his desperation, all his ridiculous pride in imagining himself the inti-mate and the inspiration of a poet of Shade's standing, would vanish. Kinbote is far too self-centered and too misogynistic to want to imag-ine the happily married John and Sybil Shade, and he knows too little of America to do so, unless he arranges jokes like "Frankly I too never excelled in soccer and cricket" (C.130, 117) at his own expense—something this conceited and touchy commentator would never do. The scholar who has the impetuosity and minimal self-control to write "There is a very loud amusement park right in front of my present lodgings" (F, 13) has neither the skill at verse, nor the interest in others, nor the discipline, nor the slightest shadow of a motive, to invent a John and Sybil Shade who would only distract from the glory of Charles II.

A subtler and more plausible explanation involving a reduced but still key role for Kinbote has been advanced by Pekka Tammi and Charles Nicol.[29] Perhaps the uncanny coincidences between poem and commentary could be explained by Kinbote's deliberate attempt—after he discovers that the long poem Shade has been at work on is not at all the epic of Charles II he had expected—to fabricate a close relationship between what he can find in the poem and his Zembla. To some extent Kinbote plainly does seek to intensify the connections between poem and commentary. When he writes, "The poor poet had now been turned over and lay with open dead eyes directed up at the sunny evening azure" (C.1000, 295), there can be little doubt he means to recall the memorable "azure" of the poem's second line.[30] When he recollects seeing Shade burn a whole stack of superseded drafts "in the pale fire of the incinerator" (F, 15) he evokes the poem's title, and also his own thesis that despite the poem's undeniably not being about Zembla, it *would* have been much more so had a jealous Sybil not censored these incinerated early drafts: "I realize only too clearly, alas, that the result, in its pale and diaphanous final phase, cannot be regarded as a direct echo of my narrative" (C.42, 81). He even says, "My commentary to this poem, now in the hands of my readers, represents an attempt to sort out those echoes and wavelets of fire, and pale phosphorescent hints, and all the many subliminal debts to me" (C.1000, 297). The added joke here is that in this most elaborately artful echo of the poem's title, he fails to realize he is also echoing the Shakespearean *source* of Shade's title, which he has not bothered to identify. The "wavelets" in his last note contain a ripple from *Timon of Athens*, without his knowing it, just as his admission that he has in many cases "caught myself borrowing a kind of opalescent light from my poet's fiery orb, and unconsciously aping the prose style of his own critical essays" (C.42, 81), which follows the passage referring to the "pale and diaphanous final phase" of the poem, echoes even more closely the source of the poem's title, not directly or consciously, but by way of

the very passage Shade raids—which Kinbote has just quoted in another connection in the previous note (C.39–40, 80), in a Zemblan version which lacks the phrase "pale fire" but obviously continues to
reverberate in his mind.

The subtler of these echoes of the poem's title, then, are jokes at Kinbote's expense, and the more overt ones are undisguised if not inele-
gant allusions, wistful toyings with Shade's title, as if to say: "I offered
you *Solus Rex*, and you gave me *Pale Fire*. Look what I can do with
your title. Why couldn't *you* have made more of my far more mesmer-
izing visions?" But apart from these few reflected gleams of the poem's
title, Kinbote has no reason to maximize the links between Zembla and
Shade's poem. He *had* wanted, had desperately wanted, Shade to write
his story in verse, but Shade did not, and his own professed and dem-
onstrated ineptitude at writing verse means he cannot alter the fact
and rewrite the poem as he wishes. As a result his only option is to
record his urging his Zemblan lore on Shade and his bitterness on
discovering it had not been used. He wants us to *feel* his pain at the
betrayal:

> We know how firmly, how stupidly I believed that Shade was compos-
> ing a poem, a kind of *romaunt*, about the King of Zembla. We have been
> prepared for the horrible disappointment in store for me. Oh, I did not
> expect him to devote himself *completely* to that theme! It might have been
> blended of course with some of his own life stuff and sundry Ameri-
> cana—but I was sure his poem would contain the wonderful incidents I
> had described to him, the characters I had made alive for him and all the
> unique *atmosphere* of my kingdom. I even suggested to him a good title—
> the title of the book in me whose pages he was to cut: *Solus Rex*; instead
> of which I saw *Pale Fire*, which meant to me nothing. I started to read the
> poem. I read faster and faster. I sped through it, snarling, as a furious
> young heir through an old deceiver's testament. Where were the battle-
> ments of my sunset castle? Where was Zembla the Fair? Where her spine
> of mountains? Where her long thrill through the mist? And my lovely
> flower boys, and the spectrum of the stained windows, and the Black
> Rose Paladins, and the whole marvelous tale? Nothing of it was there!
> The complex contribution I had been pressing upon him with a hypno-
> tist's patience and a lover's urge was simply not there. Oh, but I cannot
> express the agony! (C.1000, 296)

Since he cannot fabricate a Zemblan poem himself, his one alternative position is to claim that Shade's poem *would* have had more of

Zembla if he had been free to write as his friendship for Kinbote prompted: "Gradually I regained my usual composure. I reread *Pale Fire* more carefully. I liked it better when expecting less. And what was that? What was that dim distant music, those vestiges of color in the air? Here and there I discovered in it and especially, especially in the invaluable variants, echoes and spangles of my mind, a long ripplewake of my glory" (C.1000, 297). Always jealous of Sybil's closeness to Shade, he concocts the theory that she censors the Zemblan elements out of his poem, and he manufactures the Zemblan variants in proof (C.42, 81). His fabrications are hilariously clumsy and inept, implausible in their alleged place in the poem, clunky in rhythm and sublimely banal in rhyme, and even at this low level sometimes too difficult for him to make the effort to fill out what seems a plausible line (see the variant at C.130, 118). The first forged variant, "Ah, I must not forget to say something / That my friend told me of a certain king" (C.12, 74), which licenses the whole Zembla theme in the Commentary, is later embarrassedly retracted, although Kinbote does not return to excise the lines ("I could strike them out before publication but that would mean reworking the entire note, or at least a considerable part of it, and I have no time for such stupidities" [C.50, 228]), since that would in effect remove his pretext for mentioning Zembla at all. His few other Zemblan variants are half-proudly identified in the Index as "K's contribution," but confirm that he knows and admits, outside of the transparent fiction that the variants are Shade's, that there is no evidence at all that Shade ever planned to write the poem he wanted about Zembla. The most he can claim is that "the sunset glow of the story acted as a catalytic agent upon the very process of the sustained creative effervescence that enabled Shade to produce a 1000-line poem in three weeks" (C.42, 81).

The hypothesis that Kinbote is responsible for the subtle subliminal links between poem and commentary—as opposed to the wonderfully unsubtle variants—would require either that he has adapted the Zemblan material he now recounts in order to fit Shade's poem better, or that he has infiltrated into his Commentary covert verbal associations other than his explicit sad caressing of Shade's title.

The first option makes no sense and contradicts the evidence. If he had adapted the Zemblan story to the poem, he would not now be able to make so much of his disappointment at the disparity between them, and he would not have needed to concoct his variants. Besides, the account of Zembla must be basically in place—its blue atmosphere, the tunnel, the escape over the mountain—for Kinbote's pride in the story's glamour and his persistence in thrusting it before Shade to establish the situation on which everything else in the novel rests. Even Kinbote's relationship with Disa, which it has been suggested might be his creative response to the portrait of Sybil in the poem,[31] must in fact be something he has described in detail to Shade before he sees a word of the poem, since after he sums up this part of his story, he reports: "When in the course of an evening stroll in May or June, 1959, I offered Shade all this marvelous material, he looked at me quizzically and said: 'That's all very well, Charles. But . . . [h]ow can you know that all this intimate stuff about your rather appalling king is true?" (C.433–34, 214). If Kinbote were inventing, he would surely not have Shade say "your rather appalling king": *he* can see nothing but glamour in the King's behavior. The firm outline and the bright tint of what he evokes for Shade as "our blue inenubilable Zembla" (C.991, 288), then, must be securely in place before Kinbote ever sights Shade's azure imagery. Kinbote has *not* refashioned his Zembla to bring it line with Shade's poem.[32]

The other option, that Kinbote has deftly stitched poem and commentary together with gossamer verbal threads, does not in fact account for such key connections as that between Shade's "ready to become a floweret / Or a fat fly" and Sybil's calling Kinbote "a king-sized botfly" (C.247)[33] and seems utterly at odds with all Kinbote's practice. Because of his overblown egotism, he lacks self-control ("and damn that music!", "Dear Jesus, do something" [C.47–48, 93]), and when he does something he considers subtle he wastes no time in drawing it proudly to our attention. He reports with pleasure: "I contented myself on my way out with pulling Gerald Emerald's bowtie loose with a deft jerk of my fingers as I passed by him" (F, 24); he repays the Shades' not inviting him to Shade's birthday party by passing on an "impossibly rude" allusion to Proust, smugly adding, "I am a very sly Zemblan" (C.181, 162). When he tries for an unusual stylistic effect in his Commentary, he cannot refrain from pointing it out and even claiming it as unprecedented: "It is probably the first time that the dull pain of distance is rendered through an effect of style" (C.47–48, 92); "Never before has the inexorable advance of fate"—of Gradus, that is—"received such a sensuous form" (C.131–132, 136).

For the most part, Kinbote is simply so entranced by the picture he has built up of himself as Charles II that he reverts to it shamelessly on the least occasion. Shade mentions "parents," and after half a paragraph on Shade's parents, grudgingly lifted from Prof. Hurley's obituary, Kinbote devotes six pages to Charles II's father and mother (C.71), Shade writes, "one foot upon a mountain," and Kinbote seizes the chance to spend ten pages reliving his own escape over the Bera range (C.149). Kinbote stuffs Zembla into the Commentary without apology or craft, simply because he cannot help it, and not as part of some subtle argument that the poem and commentary are deeply interfused. He admits frankly, plaintively, insistently that there is nothing of his Zembla in the poem, except—to allow *some* suggestion that Shade was deeply moved by his story—in his grossly concocted variants. Kinbote lacks the restraint, the modesty, and the motive to establish the silent signals connecting poem and commentary that trouble and tantalize the good rereader. We need another solution.

SHADE

If the eerie echoes between poem and commentary cannot be explained as the work of Kinbote, might Shade have written both parts? Shade says in "Pale Fire" that he has dedicated his whole life to fighting the "inadmissible abyss" of death (P.179), a fight he conducts through his art, through the incessant exercise of his imagination. At the beginning of the poem he imagines projecting himself beyond the death of a waxwing that has knocked itself out on his window, projecting himself into the azure world beyond: "I was the shadow of the waxwing slain. . . ." At the end of the poem he compares his confidence in the design of things, in a life after death, to his confidence that he will wake up the next morning, but within a few minutes of setting down the last lines of his poem he is killed. According to Kinbote, the killer is a Shadow, a glassmaker, whose birthday, strangely, we can discover to be the same day as Shade's and Kinbote's.[34] Kinbote describes himself as a king whose coat of arms includes a waxwing-like bird (C.1–4, 73); the name of the person who kills Shade, Jakob Gradus, when reversed as if in a mirror, reads Sudarg of Bokay, a "mirror-maker of genius" (I, 314), whose sky-blue mirrors surely reflect the indelible mirror images in the poem's opening lines. Something odd is happening. Has Shade decided to play the part of Gradus, his own killer, and then to project himslf as if beyond death by imagining himself as Kinbote, citizen and celebrant of Zembla's azure world?

During the poem, discussing his time at the I.P.H., Shade says that in death he is "ready to become a floweret / Or a fat fly, but never, to forget" (P.523–34). Now, Sybil Shade calls Kinbote "an elephantine tick; a king-sized botfly; a macaco worm;[35] the monstrous parasite of a genius" (C.247, 171–72), while Botkin in the Index is "American scholar of Russian descent . . . ; king-bot, maggot of extinct fly that once bred in mammoths and is thought to have hastened their phylogenetic end" (I, 306).[36] Kinbote is flamboyantly homosexual, or what his most homophobic foe calls "Quite the fancy pansy" (C.894, 268); of all the flowers and "flowerets" in the English language there are only two that end "-et," "bluet" and the much more common "violet," which happens to be the first rhyme-word of the first couplet in the verse paragraph that includes "floweret" (also placed as the first rhyme-word of *its* couplet). In *Ada*, Nabokov has Van pointedly and vindictively associate the names of violets (pansies) with the homosexual Captain Tapper,[37] and clearly in *Pale Fire* too he has gone to a great deal of trouble to associate Shade's "ready to become a floweret / Or a fat fly, but never, to forget" with the homosexual Kinbote, that "king-sized botfly" so desperate that the world shall never forget his Zemblan past. Are Shade's lines a sly disclosure that in *his* preparation for the hereafter, he is ready to become the "pansy" Kinbote, the botfly "King-bot"?

In her 1980 *Nabokov and the Novel*, Ellen Pifer argued against what seemed to have become a dominant reading of Nabokov in the 1960s and 1970s. She made a powerful case for approaching his novels not as mere literary games but as stories that involve characters and concerns that matter, yet her dislike of treating the novels as puzzles must contend with Nabokov's own comparison of the relationships between author and reader of a novel and between composer and solver of a chess problem. Interconnecting details like those we have just noted have evidently been designed to catch our eye, provoke our curiosity, and invite our explanation of their purpose. Pifer argues eloquently for Nabokovian values, for detail, memory, curiosity, and imagination, but if these things *are* important, why is it not also important that details that we remember relate to other details in curious ways that prompt some imaginative response on our part? Nabokov writes that "The unravelling of a riddle is the purest and most basic act of the human mind."[38] Overlooking the riddling problems Nabokov's works pose will not make them disappear, though it may cause what makes *him* unique start to fade.

The shadow-Shadow, waxwing-silktail, reflection-mirror echoes seem to reflect purpose, not chance, and perhaps Shade's purpose. For Shade begins his poem by showing himself projecting himself imaginatively beyond death: perhaps the waxwing image is a key to the Kinbote story; perhaps Shade has not died but has instead invented Kinbote and killing and commentary. After all, he declares in Canto Three of the poem, after discovering that what he had thought was the corroborating "fountain" in Mrs. Z.'s near-death experience was in fact a "mountain":

> . . . all at once it dawned on me that *this*
> Was the real point, the contrapuntal theme;
> Just this: not text, but texture. . . . (P.806–08)

If Shade were to present the interrelation between his own poem and what *seems* to be someone else's commentary, texture would dominate over text; his projecting himself into the shadow of the waxwing, into the azure, would be a perfect prefiguration of his projecting himself into Zembla, that cloudless "land of reflections" (C.894, 265).

Yet according to the story he is killed. But of course the hypothesis that he had invented the Commentary requires that the killing too would be fictional, requires that if he is to imagine himself dead and inhabiting as it were Kinbote's soul, the life of someone who is a mirror-inversion of himself (exile rather than stay-at-home, lonely homosexual rather than happily married man, vegetarian rather than meat-eater, bearded rather than clean-shaven, left- rather than right-handed, and so on), then he must indeed *seem* dead.

Nevertheless arguments against the Shadean hypothesis rule out this solution. One of the main reasons for the aversion of most anti-Shadeans to the Shadean hypothesis is that Shade has never previously shown himself capable of sustained fictional invention: marvelous images, perhaps, like the waxwing, or Shakespeare's spirit lighting a whole town, but never characters or elaborate plots. If Shade is sixty-one, and as able to construct stories as elaborate as the Shadean hypothesis would require, why has he never written fiction before?

But writers can of course discover their talents late; Sterne was forty-six when he digressed from sermons into *Tristram Shandy*. Perhaps a more potent argument, advanced by David Lodge, is that as a novelist himself he cannot imagine Shade transmuting into poignant autobiographical art the tragedy of his daughter's death only then to offset it against the crazy invention of Kinbote.[39] In *Pale Fire* Nabokov himself transforms his own father's killing into the shambolic farce of Shade's death, and in the margins of his autobiography he turns his father's death into a kind of cosmic chess game; although he does not combine the two strategies in one work, in *The Gift* his narrator Fyodor sets his tender evocation of his own father's life and death beside his scornful, mocking, parodic account of Nikolay Chernyshevsky's life and death. Yet Lodge's argument still has its force.

Still more forceful is D. Barton Johnson's point that whoever writes the Commentary knows Russian, and we have no evidence that Shade knows the language.[40] In the Internet discussion I countered: "This kind of argument could be used to prove Nabokov couldn't have written either *Pale Fire* or *Ada*, since there is no evidence, outside the Zemblan of *Pale Fire* and the Dutch in *Ada*, that he knew any Scandinavian languages or any Dutch: it is very possible for an inventive wordsmith with a particular purpose to do enough poking into another language to play a little with its lexicon." Yet although there is actually little connected Russian in the Commentary (the longest such passage, "Khrushchev's" reported "*Vï nazïvaete sebya zemblerami*, you call yourselves Zemblans, *a ya vas nazïvayu zemlyakami*, and I call you fellow countrymen!" [C.949/2, 274], could be understood by a first-year student of Russian, although such a student would be much less likely to *invent* such a pun), some of the play on isolated words demands a sophisticated knowledge of the language: *taynik* (hiding place), for instance, might be found in an English-Russian dictionary, but the old form *potaynik* would not (I, 314, 312).[41] According to the story, Kinbote does know Russian, even if he is genuinely Zemblan; and Botkin, who seems to stand behind or inside him, is of course a Russian by birth. Kinbote or Botkin seems a much likelier author of the Commentary and Index than Shade.

Where Johnson approaches Nabokov's works as puzzles, Pifer skirts the puzzles to fasten on character and conduct. Her resolute humanism has its power, and in fact provides the decisive grounds for rejecting the Shadean solution. As she argued in support of Lodge's anti-Shadean stance at the 1995 Nabokov conference at the University of Nice, Shade would have to be very immodest, in a way that seems uncharacteristic of him, to construct a Kinbote who writes passages like this: "I experienced a grand sense of wonder whenever I looked at him, especially in the presence of other people, inferior people. This wonder was enhanced by my awareness of their not feeling what I felt, of their not seeing what I saw, of their taking Shade for granted, instead of drenching every nerve, so to speak, in the romance of his presence" (F, 27). The whole contrast between Shade's modesty and kindness and Kinbote's immodesty and blind self-obsession would be undermined by a Shade who covertly presented his modesty as one of the positive poles of the story. Kinbote repeats three times (F, 22; C.47–48, 92; C949/2, 280) that Main Hall on Wordsmith campus has been renamed after Shade's death "Shade Hall," a curious and indeed unimaginable kind of hubris for the normally unboastful Shade to display if he has merely invented his own death.

And if he *had* invented his own death—and this explains the outrage the Shadean idea provokes—how much would the novel lose! I was once so fascinated by the increase in Shade's powers that this reading would imply, by the sense that he all but transcends his situation through the deceptive powers of his art, that, like other Shadeans, I was ready to overlook what it would mean for his world. And to overlook, too, the fact that the Shadean thesis becomes positively incoherent. If we imagine a Shade in New Wye who arranges his own fictive death in order to probe the beyond, as it were, from the other side of the looking glass, what happens on publication day? Does he disappear with Sybil, as Hermann in *Despair* plans to disappear with his wife after staging "his" death (the murder of a supposed look-alike, undertaken for insurance money) to start a new life? Or does he stay in New Wye and face the ribbing, the endless sideways glances at his weirdly vainglorious invention in presenting himself magnified through Kinbote's adulation and his university department diminished through Kinbote's contempt for their folly and fraud? Had he invented Kinbote as a way of passing beyond the "solitary confinement of the self," he would now find himself on publication day, far from transcending the self, subjected to local and national attention, to the gaze of a thousand invasive Kinbotes.

Or do we rescue the Shadean idea by saying that if Shade invents his own death scene, then of course he invents much of his life, too? In *Vladimir Nabokov: The American Years*, I wrote, "Of course the more we accept Shade as the author of both poem and commentary, the less we can be sure that someone who has invented Zembla and his own murder has not already transformed the life he presents in the poem in order to make poem and commentary fit. The more autonomy we see in Shade the artist, the less distinct become the outlines of Shade the man. He begins, in other words, to grade into Nabokov."[42] In *Pale Fire* Nabokov does indeed transform major losses in his own life, actual and imagined—the loss of Russia, the mistaken assassination of his own father, his dread that his only child Dmitri might lose his life in his passion for mountain-climbing and car-racing[43]—so that Shade's coping with his own loss in his treatment of Hazel's death in particular plainly parallels Nabokov's own coping with his loss of his father in the shooting of Shade.

But if Shade invents Kinbote, Zembla, and his own death, he must also be radically reinventing his real life—since Kinbote seems, at least on the surface, a real part of Shade's last few months—to the point where New Wye, Wordsmith, and even Sybil, Hazel, and Hazel's death become dubious. In the Shadean reading, Shade as sole author seems to be trying to cope as inventively as he can with the fact of death, but neither death nor life, neither his own nor Hazel's, is left with enough existence to need to be coped with.

We still need another solution. Let us think.

Part Three

SYNTHESIS: RE-REREADING

Discovery as Story

a synthesis of poignant

artistic delight

9.

Transformation

SOLUTIONS AND PROBLEMS

To solve problems in Nabokov, as in chess or life, it often takes a swerve of thought, a knight move of imagination. Let us for the moment set aside the problem of the echoes reverberating between *Pale Fire*'s poem and commentary and of who might be responsible for them, and focus on one pattern we *can* follow through, and in fact cannot help finding more insistent the more we reread.

Early in Canto Three, after recounting Hazel's suicide in Canto Two, Shade reports on the Institute of Preparation for the Hereafter and the possibility or impossibility of meeting in death those we have loved. Late in Canto Four, he announces himself

> . . . reasonably sure that we survive
> And that my darling somewhere is alive,
> As I am reasonably sure that I
> 980   Shall wake at six tomorrow, on July
> The twenty-second, nineteen fifty-nine. . . .

Of course, he does not wake the next day, and that appears to refute his "my darling somewhere is alive."

The question of whether on not she has survived has been one of uttermost urgency for Shade ever since his daughter died. "I was the shadow of the waxwing slain / By the false azure in the windowpane," he begins his poem, and at dead center he places Hazel's death, triggered when her first blind date recoils:

> After he'd gone the three young people stood
> Before the azure entrance for a while.
> Puddles were neon-barred; and with a smile

She said she'd be *de trop*, she'd much prefer
400   Just going home.

In those neon bars[1] in the azure reflected in the puddles, Shade shows that even in the waxwing image, with its azure reflection and the implied "wax-red streaks" (C.1–4) on the bird's wings, he imagines projecting himself beyond death partly in order to see if Hazel is there.

Throughout the poem, his preoccupation continues. Describing his house and garden in Canto One, he writes:

I had a favorite young shagbark there
50   With ample dark jade leaves and a black, spare,
Vermiculated trunk. The setting sun
Bronzed the black bark, around which, like undone
Garlands, the shadows of the foliage fell.
It is now stout and rough; it has done well.
White butterflies turn lavender as they
Pass through its shade where gently seems to sway
The phantom of my little daughter's swing.

After switching explicitly to the theme of exploring death's abyss in Canto Two, he muses there:

It isn't that we dream too wild a dream:
The trouble is we do not make it seem
Sufficiently unlikely; for the most
230   We can think up is a domestic ghost.

In Canto Three, he looks at Hazel's recent death in the light of his earlier experience at I.P.H.:

That tasteless venture helped me in a way.
I learnt what to ignore in my survey
Of death's abyss. And when we lost our child
I knew there would be nothing: no self-styled
Spirit would touch a keyboard of dry wood
650   To rap out her pet name; no phantom would
Rise gracefully to welcome you and me
In the dark garden, near the shagbark tree.

Shade seems agnostic, even dismissive, about the possibility of Hazel's survival as conventional ghost, phantom, shade, but in Canto Four he ends by affirming his sense of harmony between the order of his verse and his universe, and his confidence that somewhere she is alive. He looks out to see Sybil's shadow near the shagbark, and the "dark Vanessa with the crimson band . . . its ink-blue wingtips flecked with white" that echoes both the red-streaked wing of the waxwing in his opening line and the white butterfly turning lavender in the shadow of Hazel's shagbark. Summoning together these signs, he affirms design even in what seem the random remains of the day.

VANESSA ATALANTA

Shade's stress throughout the poem on the garden, on Hazel's shagbark, on butterflies showing or changing color in the low sun, on shadows and shades and phantoms becomes more urgent the more we reread. And there is one quite spectacular appearance of a butterfly in the garden that plays in the setting sun on the edge of light and shade, just a moment after Shade finishes his poem, a moment before he meets his death.

Even on a first reading of the novel, we enter an aura of mystery in the description of the *Vanessa atalanta* that cavorts exuberantly around Shade just before he is killed. As the time of composition and the time of narration converge at the end of "Pale Fire," Shade gazes around him, searching for his wife ("Where are you? In the garden. I can see / Part of your shadow near the shagbark tree"), and watches as

> A dark Vanessa with a crimson band
> Wheels in the low sun, settles on the sand
> And shows its ink-blue wingtips flecked with white.

Immediately after finishing the poem, he walks over with Kinbote, who has the manuscript tucked under his arm, toward the Goldsworth house. Kinbote tells the story:

Lines 993–995: A dark Vanessa, etc.

One minute before his death, as we were crossing from his demesne to mine and had begun working up between the junipers and ornamental shrubs, a Red Admirable (see note to line 270) came dizzily whirling around us like a colored flame. Once or twice before we had already noticed the same individual, at that same time, on that same spot, where the low sun finding an aperture in the foliage splashed the brown sand with a last radiance while the evening's shade covered the rest of the path. One's eyes could not follow the rapid butterfly in the sunbeams as it flashed and vanished, and flashed again, with an almost frightening imitation of conscious play which now culminated in its settling upon my delighted friend's sleeve. It took off, and we saw it next moment sporting in an ecstasy of frivolous haste around a laurel shrub, every now and then perching on a lacquered leaf and sliding down its grooved middle like a boy down the banisters on his birthday. Then the tide of the shade reached the laurels, and the magnificent, velvet-and-flame creature dissolved in it.

Even when we first encounter this passage it seems charged with promise or foreboding, in its attribution of conscious intelligence to the butterfly, in its extraordinary effects of color and sun and shade, in the suggestion that the butterfly might be either tugging at Shade's sleeve, warning him not to cross into the Goldsworth garden, or acclaiming his newest and finest poem ("sporting in an ecstasy of frivolous haste around a laurel shrub . . . sliding down its grooved middle like a boy down the banisters"). Alvin Kernan comments that "A reader inescapably responds to this butterfly, even as Shade responded to the white fountain, particularly because of its appearance at the moment of death and the verbal associations with 'shade' and the poet's laurels, as a manifestation of some transcendental force in the universe moving in correspondence with human life."[2] That perhaps overstates or overdefines our initial response, but certainly we react with a sense of wonder to something that, given Shade's imminent death, ought to be an omen yet feels anything but ominous.

Nevertheless, where does it lead? Four pages later—and even on a first reading we expect this to happen at any moment—Shade is shot, and the human drama outweighs any incidental butterfly. Yet each time we return to that passage, a little more conscious, too, each time, of the butterfly-shagbark-shade-phantom links within the poem, we feel that same charge renewed. Still it does not lead anywhere. Does this sound a little familiar?

Indeed it does. The "pada ata lane . . ." in the Haunted Barn had also carried a charge of promise from the first, even though the promise had soon seemed neutralized in a bath of skeptical irony. But when we deciphered Aunt Maud's message, it still seemed to lead nowhere. Perhaps we had better return to it.

Though we see little of Hazel, we see she is consistently associated with the paranormal: with the poltergeist that disturbs her just after Maud dies and that seems to reflect Maud's personality, and with the "roundlet of pale light" in the Haunted Barn, which we can also discern spells out for Hazel a message from her great-aunt. But to Hazel both poltergeist and ghostly light seem chilling and disturbing, frustratingly indecisive and meaningless.

Yet unlike her, *we* can not only read a message in the light in the barn, a hint of Shade's still-distant death, but we should also now be able to detect a curious triple flash in "pada *ATA LANe* pad no*T* ogo old w*ArT ALAN* Ther t*A*le feur f*A*r r*AnT LANT* t*A*l told" of the *atalanta* butterfly that greets Shade just the moment before he does in fact "go to Goldsworth's" and his death.[3] This subliminal threefold insistence seems still stronger and stranger when we notice the stress on threefold repetition in the report on the Haunted Barn: "There are always 'three nights' in fairy tales, and in this sad fairy tale there was a third one too" (C.347, 190). On the third night in the barn, there is no sign whatever of the "pale light," nothing to add to the apparently senseless babble of the "talking light." But on a rereading we could decipher its direct message. Can we now, on a re-rereading, also make sense of its *atalanta* undertone?

One of the real difficulties of Nabokov's patterns is that they all interconnect, as things do in this complicated and interesting world of ours. Whatever charge of unresolved import we feel in the description of the *Vanessa atalanta*, a charge boosted immeasurably by the *atalanta*'s flashing through Maud's ghostly message, we cannot dissociate the *Vanessa* from Sybil Shade. After explaining how he first fell in love with his wife, John Shade turns to her directly:

> Come and be worshiped, come and be caressed,
> 270   My dark Vanessa, crimson-barred, my blest
> My Admirable butterfly!

At the end of the poem, again, Shade looks over at his wife just before catching sight of the *Vanessa* that will greet him a few minutes later, and describes it so as to echo the Admirable he described in his appeal to his wife:

> Where are you? In the garden. I can see
> 990   Part of your shadow near the shagbark tree.
> Somewhere horeshoes are being tossed. Click. Clunk.
> (Leaning against its lamppost like a drunk.)
> A dark Vanessa with a crimson band
> Wheels in the low sun, settles on the sand
> And shows its ink-blue wingtips flecked with white.

Although the *Vanessa atalanta* that dances on and around Shade as he walks to his death seems to carry some transcendental charge, Sybil herself is very much alive, and in fact has just driven off to a dinner meeting of her club before Kinbote comes over to invite Shade back for a drink. So how can that mysterious *Vanessa* be as mysterious as *seems* to be suggested by the timing and description of its last appearance in Kinbote's note and by that covert fairy-tale triple invocation in Maud's ghostly message? If the *Vanessa* evokes Sybil, how can it also fit in, as it seems to, to the pattern of references to Hazel, the garden, the shag-bark, shade, butterflies changing color in the shadows, phantoms?

To pose the problem that way is almost to prompt the solution. Shade introduces Hazel abruptly into the poem, just after addressing Sybil as "My dark Vanessa," with the regretful report that, unfortunately for her, Hazel did not take after her mother's beauty[4] but turned out to be the image of his own short, fat, twisted self:

>   . . . And I love you most
> 290   When with a pensive nod you greet her ghost
>   And hold her first toy on your palm, or look
>   At a postcard from her, found in a book.
>
>   She might have been you, me, or some quaint blend:
>   Nature chose me so as to wrench and rend
>   Your heart and mine. . . .
>
>   . . . .
>   . . . . while children of her age
> 310   Were cast as elves and fairies on the stage
>   That *she*'d helped paint for the school pantomime,
>   My gentle girl appeared as Mother Time,
>   A bent charwoman with slop pail and broom,
>   And like a fool I sobbed in the men's room.
>
>   Another winter was scrape-scooped away.
>   The Toothwort White haunted our woods in May.
>   Summer was power-mowed, and autumn, burned.
>   Alas, the dingy cygnet never turned
>   Into a wood duck.

Notice that "with a pensive nod you greet her *ghost*" brings Hazel forward for the first time directly into the poem, and the one fleeting reference to her beforehand had been to "The *phantom* of my little daughter's swing."

But what do we make of the last lines of that passage? Kinbote explains Shade's sly twist on the Hans Christian Andersen story, his wittily reversing the conventional preference for the swan in favor of the multicolored splendor of the duck: "The wood duck, a richly colored bird, emerald, amethyst, carnelian, with black and white markings, is incomparably more beautiful than the much-overrated swan, a serpentine goose with a dirty neck of yellowish plush and a frogman's black rubber flaps" (C.319). Kinbote here is helpful indeed, but he is no naturalist. In the previous note he is powerless to explain Shade's "The Toothwort White haunted our woods in May":

> Frankly, I am not certain what this means. My dictionary defines "toothwort" as "a kind of cress" and the noun "white" as "any pure white breed of farm animal or a certain genus of lepidoptera." Little help is provided by the variant written in the margin:

> In woods Virginia Whites occurred in May

> Folklore characters, perhaps? Fairies? Or cabbage butterflies? (C.316).

The Toothwort White or West Virginia White (*Pieris [Artogeia] virginiensis*)[5] is in fact a woodland butterfly whose numbers are dwindling rapidly through loss of its native habitat. Far from being a "cabbage butterfly," as Kinbote vaguely proposes, it was for a long time not distinguished from *Pieris napi*, the Mustard White, which has suffered population loss through *competition* with the introduced European *Pieris rapae*, the Cabbage White.[6]

After his helpless gloss on the Toothwort White and his helpful one on the dingy cygnet and wood duck, Kinbote has only another short, four-line note before the note on the Haunted Barn, the note where Hazel is continuously present longer than anywhere else in poem or commentary, the note where the *atalanta* recurs three fairy-tale times in Maud's message. But the note begins with Kinbote's description of the owner of the barn, Paul Hentzner, the German farmer with whom Shade had once rambled every other evening, attracted especially by his knowledge of plants and animals: "He esteemed Hentzner for knowing 'the names of things'" (C.347, 185). Coming less than a page after Kinbote's failure to identify the Toothwort White, this ought to strike us as a clear Nabokovian directive: we really should identify that butterfly. Shade certainly knows it: Kinbote has earlier complained about the poet's "coquettish way of pointing out with the tip of his cane various curious natural objects" during their sunset rambles: "He never tired of illustrating by means of these examples the extraordinary blend of Canadian Zone and Austral Zone that 'obtained,' as he put it, in that particular spot of Appalachia where at our altitude of about 1,500 feet northern species of birds, insects and plants commingled with southern representatives" (C.238, 168–69). Had Kinbote paid a little more attention, he might have heard about the Toothwort White, which is indeed mostly a Transitional Zone[7] butterfly, like the *Lycaeides melissa samuelis*, the Karner Blue, that Nabokov himself named in 1943 and first saw on the wing in 1950.[8]

The Toothwort White happens to be "dusky white with smoky gray-brown scaling,"[9] and, like the Mustard White with which it was long confused, "quite shy."[10] The *Vanessa atalanta*, by contrast, is in the words of lepidopterist Robert Michael Pyle, "Unmistakable and unforgettable. . . . [It] will alight on a person's shoulder day after day in a garden. . . . In midsummer it is not unusual to see them chasing each other."[11] As Kinbote correctly notes, the *atalanta* or Red Admirable "is a most frolicsome fly" (C.270). The Toothwort White "haunted" our woods in May, Shade says, in the couplet before he laments of his daughter that "Alas, the dingy cygnet never turned / Into a wood duck." Kinbote explains that correctly in terms of the wood duck's having incomparably richer colors than the dingy cygnet. But the Toothwort White is also a dingy white, with a visible scaling, and shy—like the "difficult, morose" Hazel, who has "psoriasis."[12]

Hazel took after her father, not her mother. In Shade's reversed fairy tale Hazel as dingy cygnet *ought* to have turned into the sumptuous dark colors of the wood duck, but alas, does not. But what if this "alas . . . never" is also reversed? If Hazel as Toothwort White, dingy, scaly, withdrawn, now reappears in death as a *Vanessa atalanta*, now takes after her mother in looks ("My dark Vanessa, . . . / My Admirable"), not her father, and is now transformed in personality from moroseness to exuberance?

If Hazel can inhabit the *atalanta*, that would suddenly explain the singular charge surrounding the butterfly as it greets Shade moments before his death. It would also explain the fairy-tale repetition of the *atalanta* in the message Maud had spelled out for Hazel; add an ironic twist to Kinbote's "Folklore characters, perhaps? Fairies? Or cabbage butterflies?" in the Toothwort White note immediately preceding his gloss on Shade's reversal of the Ugly Duckling fairy-tale; and explain the pattern running through the poem associating the garden, shadows, butterflies, and Hazel's shade. That pattern started with white butterflies changing color as they passed into shade near mementoes of Hazel:

> White butterflies turn lavender as they
> Pass through its shade where gently seems to sway
> The phantom of my little daughter's swing.

Now it seems to end with another butterfly, with a child's slide echoing a child's swing, and with a spectacular deep flush replacing the white:

> It took off, and we saw it next moment sporting in an ecstasy of frivolous haste around a laurel shrub, every now and then perching on a lacquered leaf and sliding down its grooved middle like a boy down the banisters on his birthday. Then the tide of the shade reached the laurels, and the magnificent, velvet-and-flame creature dissolved in it.

When Hazel headed alone to the edge of Dulwich Forest to investigate the Haunted Barn, like the shy Toothwort White that "haunted our woods," she was troubled and sullen. Now she seems transformed from dinginess and depression into the resplendent color and the confident play of the *atalanta* that she animates for the moment. Then she was difficult, morose, inclined to sit and moan in a monotone. Now she seems not only to take after her mother in appearance, but also to offer the same kind of support her mother gives to Shade's work, as she applauds the poem he has just brought to a close.

CORROBORATION

This would certainly offer a solution to the problem of Hazel's survival after death, so insistently posed by Shade's poem, and especially by its unplanned end, by the gap between his confident expectation he will wake the next day and his sudden murder. But such a solution might seem an absurdly bold conjecture—were it not for Shade's, and Nabokov's, lifelong preoccupation with the afterlife (Véra Nabokov even called it her husband's "main theme"),[13] and for pointers within *Pale Fire* and parallels elsewhere in its author's work. Shade briefly mentions Hazel's "strange fears, strange fantasies, strange force / Of character—as when she spent three nights /

Investigating certain sounds and lights / In an old barn" (P.344–47), but says no more. But after several rereadings we can now decode those lights, as neither Shade nor his daughter could, as a message from dead Aunt Maud, a warning about Shade's death, and even a prediction of the *atalanta*'s appearance just as death approaches. If one character in the novel somehow survives death, and the question of another's survival is as forcefully posed as in Hazel's case, it would almost seem strange *not* to provide an answer—even if it takes us still more rereadings to locate it.

The idea that Hazel as the *Vanessa* has caught Shade's eye and even flown into his poem from beyond the grave will still seem a surprise, but part of a pattern, to the reader familiar with other Nabokov works. In the story "The Vane Sisters,"[14] the ghosts of two dead women way-lay the narrator's attention through tricks of light and shade, and without his realizing, guide his actions and words, even as he expresses explicitly the hopelessness of his attempt to discern some glimpse of the sisters beyond death. In the novel *Transparent Things* (1972), the ghost of one of the characters who dies during the course of the book tells the whole story and welcomes the hero over the threshold of death in the last line, as Hazel seems about to greet her father at the moment *he* dies.

Hazel's part in the Red Admirable finds a still more exact counterpart in a matching but more explicit strategy Nabokov used once before, near the start of his storytelling career. A father's negative conclusions after the death of a child—like Shade's "Alas, the dingy cygnet never turned / Into a wood duck," or "no phantom would / Rise gracefully to welcome you and me / In the dark garden, near the shagbark tree"—are reversed into a triumphant positive through the implication, in a description of a magnificent lepidopteron, that the child survives, somehow richly transformed, beyond death.

In the story "Christmas," written in 1924, Sleptsov, who has already lost his wife, must now try to cope with the death of his son, a passionate lepidopterist. On a winter visit to the family summer home in the Russian countryside, the heartbroken father, exploring his son's study, picks up a few mementos to bring back from the unheated main part of the house to the small heated wing in which he is staying on this unseasonal visit. One of the things he gathers is a biscuit tin in which he knew his son had been keeping the cocoon of some exotic moth, as the boy had remembered during his fatal illness, "regretting that he had left it behind, but consoling himself with the thought that the chrysalid inside was probably dead."[15] Reading his son's diary— butterfly catches, an adolescent passion (new to his father!) for a girl vacationing in a nearby dacha, chance doodles—Sleptsov breaks down, unable to bear it any longer, and decides he will take his own life the next day:

> Sleptsov pressed his eyes shut, and had a fleeting sensation that earthly life lay before him, totally bared and comprehensible—and ghastly in its sadness, humiliatingly pointless, sterile, devoid of miracles. . . .
>
> At that instant there was a sudden snap—a thin sound like that of an overstretched rubber band breaking. Sleptsov opened his eyes. The cocoon in the biscuit tin had burst at its tip, and a black, wrinkled creature the size of a mouse was crawling up the wall above the table. It stopped, holding onto the surface with six blurry feet, and started palpitating strangely. It had emerged from the chrysalid because a man overcome with grief had transferred a tin box to his warm room, and the warmth had penetrated its taut leaf-and-silk envelope; it had waited this moment so long, had collected its strength so tensely, and now, having broken out, it was slowly and miraculously expanding. Gradually the wrinkled tissues, the velvety fringes, unfurled; the fan-pleated veins grew firmer as they filled with air. It became a winged thing almost imperceptibly, as a maturing face imperceptibly becomes beautiful. And its wings—still feeble, still moist—kept growing and unfolding, and now they were developed to the limit set for them by God, and there, on the wall, instead of a little lump of life, instead of a dark mouse, was a great *Attacus* moth like those that fly, birdlike, around lamps in the Indian dusk.
>
> And then those thick black wings, with a glazy eyespot on each and a purplish bloom dusting their hooked foretips, took a full breath under the impulse of tender, ravishing, almost human happiness.[16]

In *Pale Fire* Nabokov also draws on naturalistic detail when he suggests the fairy-tale transformation of Toothwort White into Red Admirable: the *atalanta*'s coloration ("like a colored flame," "the magnificent, velvet-and-flame creature"); its time of flight, at dusk; its elusiveness to the eye, the vivid hues of the upper wing and the muted browns of the under wing representing a form of protective coloration known as "flash and dazzle" that "confuses the pursuer"[17] ("One's eyes could not follow the rapid butterfly in the sunbeams as it flashed and vanished, and flashed again, with an almost frightening imitation of conscious play"); and perhaps above all its character, its friendly inquisitiveness and persistence ("Once or twice before we had already noticed the same individual, at that same time, on that same spot").

Nearly forty years earlier Nabokov had chosen the largest of all Lepidoptera, the Atlas moth, with its wingspan of almost a foot, in a similar combination: sharp natural observation, the ascription of all-but-human feelings to the insect, the implication of the supernatural. But the differences between early and late are as striking as the similarities. If he is not as blind as his name in Russian suggests, Sleptsov himself may witness the "miracle," may be changed from his decision to take his own life by seeing the majesty of the unfurling moth, by having his hopes awakened that his son might also, as it were, be growing huge wings himself.[18] Shade sees and admires the *Vanessa*, but so long as he remains alive—even in a near-death experience—he can have no access to any unequivocal sign of the beyond. In "Christmas" we as readers also see at once the irony of the "miracle" that refutes Sleptsov's conclusion that the world is "devoid of miracles." But in *Pale Fire* all we can see at first is Shade's own death, refuting his confidence, mere hours after he expresses it, even in waking the next day, let alone the likelihood that "my darling somewhere is alive." That life gives no direct signs of anything beyond life the mature Nabokov accepts as a condition of his exploration of the hereafter. But that does not rule out that there may be even more astonishing discoveries to be made than any he could imagine when, at twenty-five, he wrote "Christmas."

THE *VANESSA*: PROBLEM AND SOLUTION

In a moment we will find other confirmations within *Pale Fire* that Hazel's haunting the *Vanessa atalanta*, her being transformed from the dingy Toothwort White, her becoming more like her mother, supplies the solution to the problem of her survival after death. But first let us linger for a moment on Nabokov's technique here. As Alvin Kernan articulates so well, even first-time readers sense a special charge in the *Vanessa atalanta* of Kinbote's note. It seems immediately like a promise, a solution, to a problem we cannot yet state. But when we can recognize the extent to which Hazel's death and possible survival constitute a problem that pervades Shade's poem, and even when this problem becomes still more urgent after we see her connection with the Haunted Barn and the *atalanta* in its message, we still cannot easily jump to the *atalanta* as a solution, because Shade has so explicitly identified his wife, not his daughter, with *Vanessa*.

Nabokov is a master problemist on the chessboard as on the page. He compares one of his chess problems to an artistic problem in his early novel *Glory*, but it seems an even closer analogy to what he has designed here in *Pale Fire*:

> The result reminds me of a chess problem I once composed. Its beauty lay in a paradoxical first move: the White Queen had four likely squares at its disposal but on any of these it would be in the way (such a powerful piece—and "in the way"!) of one of White's Knights in four mating variants; in other words, being an absolutely useless spoilsport and burden on the board, with no part whatever in any of the subsequent play, it had to exile itself to a neutral corner behind an inert pawn and remain wedged there in idle obscurity.[19]

Sybil as the *Vanessa* is in a sense the White Queen blocking the solution of Shade's and the reader's problem. We have to realize she is not herself a force in the solution, but that if Hazel is as it were promoted to Queen (a legitimate step in chess, of course, if a pawn reaches the opposing end),[20] she can now take after her mother in death as she could not in life, she now can play the part of the *Vanessa*. There can be *two* White Queens, two *Vanessas* on the board at the same time, and it is the second, not the first, that makes possible the key move that leads to the solution.

CONVERGENCE

If one of our senses identifies something correctly, others will back up the first. Following nature's lead, Nabokov lets us confirm the identification of Hazel with the *atalanta* in several ways within *Pale Fire* itself. The note on the Haunted Barn episode provides a key to identifying Hazel in the *Vanessa*. The "talking light" in the barn whose message Hazel records might be explained away by "an ambushed scamp's toy flashlight," or by Hazel's "own imaginative hysteria," but if such explanations fail, as they appear to, then this message in the barn, even on a first reading, seems to brush closer to the supernatural than anything else in the novel. Yet even Hazel, energized in this scene as nowhere else, can draw only a blank conclusion from the message that cannot begin to be to deciphered until we know of Shade's death. Once we do decode the signal, and once we see the *atalanta* within it, the butterfly that greets Shade walking to his death almost demands deeper explanation.

But the note that records this most supernatural scene in the novel also introduces the novel's most dedicated naturalist, Paul Hentzner, whose "knowing 'the names of things'" stands as an invitation to find out more about the Toothwort White and hence discover the parallel to Shade's reversal of the fairy tale of the Ugly Duckling. And this long note on the Haunted Barn also points us still another way toward Hazel's transformation. It is Hentzner's son who, Shade recalls, once declared, "Here Papa pisses." That "pointless" remark at the edge of Dulwich Forest, as we saw in Chapter 6, suggests that like the modest Pippa of *Pippa Passes*, whom Browning had thought up while walking in a wood near Dulwich, the unassuming Hentzner serves as much more of an inspiration to Shade than the Kinbote who pushes on him his tales of Charles II. But it also points to something else.

In Part II of Browning's poem, the person inspired as Pippa passes by is the sculptor Jules, an admirer and imitator of Antonio Canova. Jules at one point stops reverently before Canova's famous statue of Psyche holding in her hand a butterfly emblematic of her soul.[21] Webster's Second glosses "Psyche" thus: "*Gr. Antiq.* A lovely maiden, the personification of the soul, usually represented with the wings of a butterfly, emblematic of immortality."[22] In *Pippa Passes* a group of jealous artist friends, offended by Jules's high seriousness of purpose, have duped him into falling in love with an unseen woman, supposedly a passionate admirer of his work, through letters, as if from her, that they have in fact penned themselves. He marries the naive young woman whom his fellow artists have intimidated into playing the admirer and whom they have instructed to disclose the hoax just after the marriage ceremony. But even as the young woman dutifully recites the speech Jules's colleagues have drafted for her, Jules senses that his young bride genuinely feels for him. He hears Pippa sing as she passes, and her song at once prompts him to take a fresh look at his bride—

> Look at the woman here with the new soul,
> Like my own Psyche,—fresh upon her lips
> Alit, the visionary butterfly,
> Waiting my word to enter and make bright. . . .[23]

—and to determine on a new life with her and a new course for his art. Browning's poem seems doubly relevant to Hazel: in young Pippa, a woman unseen or overlooked by others but impacting on their lives, and in the statue of Psyche and her butterfly, emblem of the immortality of the soul.

When Hazel explored the Barn, she could not construe that ghostly light's message, and even later Kinbote for all his effort cannot find in it "the least allusion to the poor girl's fate" (C.347, 189). Concluding his note on the Haunted Barn, Kinbote comments, "There are always 'three nights' in fairy tales, and in this sad fairy tale there was a third one too." He dramatizes the imagined scene—rather well, indeed—to show the blank wait of Hazel with her parents that last night. The playlet ends: *"Two minutes pass. Life is hopeless, afterlife heartless. Hazel is heard quietly weeping in the dark. John Shade lights a lantern. Sybil lights a cigarette. Meeting adjourned"* (192). The experiment seems to prove the hopeless gap between even the dim glimmer of hope of an afterlife that the "roundlet of pale light" had suggested and the blank reality of a dark barn. But for us it proves, if we look closely enough, to allude to the "poor girl's fate"—except that we could hardly call Hazel "poor girl" after her astonishing manifestation as the *Vanessa*.

Another line of evidence converges to the same point. In one surprising digression, Kinbote and Shade talk of racial prejudice after overhearing an anti-Semitic intonation at the Faculty Club. Kinbote comments that "a young Negro gardener (see note to line 998) whom I had recently hired—soon after the dismissal of an unforgettable roomer (see Foreword)—invariably used the word 'colored.' As a dealer in old and new words (observed Shade) he strongly objected to that epithet not only because it was artistically misleading, but also because its sense depended too much upon application and applier" (C.470, 217). Feeling he has not quite explained his *artistic* objection to "colored," Shade adds:

> Figures in the first scientific works on flowers, birds, butterflies and so forth were hand-painted by diligent aquarellists. In defective or premature publications the figures on some plates remained blank. The juxtaposition of the phrases "a white" and "a colored man" always reminded my poet, so imperiously as to dispel their accepted sense, of those outlines one longed to fill with their lawful colors—the green and purple of an exotic plant, the solid blue of a plumage, the geranium bar of a scalloped wing. (C.470, 218)

While the "green and purple of an exotic plant" and "the solid blue of a plumage" are unspecific, "the geranium bar of a scalloped wing" can refer *only* to the wing of a *Vanessa atalanta,* as the Index confirms under "*Vanessa.*"[24] Shade, talking of the white image to be filled with the color of an *atalanta,* in a passage provoked by Kinbote's mention of his Negro gardener, anticipates Hazel, a dingy Toothwort White in the "defective or premature" version of her young life, being filled with the vivid "geranium" or "velvet-and-flame" colors of an *atalanta* just before Kinbote's next line and note introduces on stage his "Negro gardener."

The Magic and the Logic of Discovery:

Art, Science, Religion

Nabokov indicates Hazel's transformation beyond death in a variety of ways, and that variety has its own additional point. He recasts the fairy tale of "The Ugly Duckling" into the Toothwort White that becomes a Red Admirable, as if to illustrate his repeated injunction to his students at Cornell and Harvard that "great novels are great fairy tales."[25] But his fairy tales never eschew fact or detail. We must have the curiosity, unlike Kinbote, to find out exactly what a Toothwort White looks like in order to understand how it can represent the Hazel who feels compelled to take her own life. Nabokov suggests that "the Beyond" begins "with the initial of Being,"[26] that we can understand the mystery around life not by evading the complexity and particularity of the real but only by looking more deeply into it.

In *The Real Life of Sebastian Knight* he describes Sebastian Knight's last novel, where "by an incredible feat of suggestive wording, the author makes us believe that he knows the truth about death and he is going to tell it," and when that truth comes, "such shining giants of our brain as science, art or religion fell out of the familiar scheme of their classification, and joining hands, were mixed and joyfully levelled."[27] Nabokov is ready to draw on the Psyche of Greek myth, or the art of Browning, but to them he adds the science of a naturalist. He wants to avoid simply recycling the answers of the past and implies that without a scientific readiness to ask new questions about the endlessly proliferating particulars of our world we are doomed to the repetition of old and steadily decaying answers.

Hentzner supplies Shade with information about natural detail and owns the barn in which Hazel records her supernatural message. Kinbote has no time for Shade's fascination for Transition Zone flora and fauna, but Nabokov sees Shade's enthusiasm for Hentzner's kind of knowledge as an essential component of his art. Nabokov repeatedly proposes that at their highest, science and art share a similar passion, precision, imagination, and inspiration—a similar excitement of discovery, a similar contact with the mystery of things: "During my years of teaching literature at Cornell and elsewhere I demanded of my students the passion of science and the patience of poetry";[28] "in a work of art there is a kind of merging between . . . the precision of poetry and the excitement of pure science";[29] "There is no science without fancy, and no art without facts";[30] "Does there not exist a high ridge where the mountainside of 'scientific' knowledge joins the opposite slope of 'artistic' imagination?"[31]

Here in *Pale Fire*, by means of an exact description of the *atalanta*'s color and character, Nabokov manages to give the butterfly a powerful charge of resonant implication that we can make full sense of once we join it with the myth of Psyche, the art of Browning, Andersen's fairy tale, Shade's own contrapuntal art in the butterfly-and-shade pattern in his poem, his interest in the science of amateur naturalists like Hentzner, and his comments on the "white" and "colored" plates in the artwork of the earliest scientific treatments of "flowers, birds, butterflies and so forth." In allowing us to detect Hazel's spirit somehow transformed into the exuberant *atalanta*, Nabokov himself "mixes and joyfully levels" art, science, and religion.

An Old Friend

Nabokov declares that a synthesis is the thesis of a new series;[32] Popper that a successful new theory opens up new problems[33]— and, he might have added, rapidly solves some of them, as the theory of plate tectonics suddenly made possible new lines of inquiry in evolutionary biogeography and soon suggested solutions to problems of relationship and distribution that had until then been utterly intractable. The discovery of Hazel's survival transforms our view of *Pale Fire* and of the problems it poses, but for the moment it brings us no closer to solving the old problem of the echoes between part and part. Yet it does raise a new problem—and suggests a new solution, that perhaps begins also to move us toward a solution to the traditional *Pale Fire* problem.

"Once or twice before," writes Kinbote, "we had already noticed the same individual, at that same time, on that same spot, where the low sun finding an aperture in the foliage splashed the brown sand with a last radiance while the evening's shade covered the rest of the path." By appearing there on previous occasions, Hazel as *Vanessa* has given Shade the key to completing his poem, by fading into the evening, by covertly echoing in the red bar of the butterfly's wing the red streak on a waxwing,[34] by allowing him to imply an order concealed behind chance. Shade had *meant* his waxwing image to anticipate the "azure" and the "neon-barred" of his daughter's last night alive, but little does he know how richly the *Vanessa* that allows him to close off his poem answers the implicit question about Hazel's own survival that he has raised in his poem's opening.

But her role here provokes another question. If she has already contributed to "Pale Fire," if she is associated with the Pippa of *Pippa Passes*, if Pippa in passing by influences people in numerous different ways, if Hazel by her forays to the barn at the edge of Dulwich Forest is also linked with Browning's moment of inspiration as he walked in a wood near Dulwich, and if Shade lives in Dulwich Road, is it not possible that sometime between *her* death in 1957 and *his* in 1959, Hazel has previously crossed her father's path, has somehow influenced his life, even before she adds such color and splendor to his last lines and his last moments?

Immediately after he concludes his playlet about the "talking light" in the barn with the bleak *"Life is hopeless, afterlife heartless,"* Kinbote notes:

> The light never came back but it gleams again in a short poem "The Nature of Electricity," which John Shade had sent to the New York magazine *The Beau and the Butterfly*, some time in 1958, but which appeared only after his death:
>
> > The dead, the gentle dead—who knows?—
> > In tungsten filaments abide,
> > And on my bedside table glows
> > Another man's departed bride.
> >
> > And maybe Shakespeare floods a whole
> > Town with innumerable lights,

And Shelley's incandescent soul
Lures the pale moths of starless nights.

Streetlamps are numbered, and maybe
Number nine-hundred-ninety-nine
(So brightly beaming through a tree
So green) is an old friend of mine.

And when above the livid plain
Forked lightning plays, therein may dwell
The torments of a Tamerlane,
The roar of tyrants torn in hell.

Kinbote intends his "The light . . . gleams again" as no more than a stylish transition, but the poem's playful image of electricity as the transmutation of the dead does indeed appear to reflect the triple episode of the Haunted Barn, which begins the first night in a loud electric storm and features a light that Kinbote accepts might be no more than "an ambushed scamp's toy flashlight" (C.347, 189) but that we can see has been powered by Aunt Maud.

The New York magazine *The Beau and Butterfly* seems at first merely a playful allusion to *The New Yorker*, in honor of the anniversary cover that features beau Eustace Tilley peering at a butterfly through his monocle.[35] But the transformation of *The New Yorker*'s name looks quite different once we have reason to see Hazel as transformed herself from drab Toothwort White to radiant Red Admirable. In the verse paragraph in "Pale Fire" reporting her sad adolescence, Shade begins with the *butterfly*, the Toothwort White, laments that "the dingy cygnet never turned / Into a wood duck," and realizes that "Out of the lacquered night, a white-scarfed *beau* / Would never come for her" (P.315–34).

Hazel was destroyed after a beau *did* come for her, only to flee at once, but now the sumptuous and ecstatic *atalanta* she animates seems amply to redeem her past misery. Earlier in the note on the Haunted Barn, Maud's "pada ata lane" had tried to announce Shade's death in dark tones, despite that triple flicker of the *atalanta*. Now, Hazel as butterfly more than matches her great-aunt Maud in a much more fertile message from the beyond.

Strolling through a wood near Dulwich, Browning had thought of "someone walking alone through life" and inspiring others unnoticed. Just as the Pippa of *Pippa Passes* inspires those around her, just as

Canova's Psyche inspires Jules, so Hazel as butterfly-soul, in 1958, the year after her death, seems to have sent her father, sitting in his Dulwich Road home, the idea for the poem *he* will send to *The Beau and the Butterfly*. The number 999 in "The Nature of Electricity" cannot help recalling for us the number of the last line of the last poem Shade ever wrote, and the fact that just after writing it, he will pass by the ebullient *atalanta*—an "old friend" indeed—as he walks across the lane to the Goldsworth house and his death. A year before her father dies, and knowing there is nothing she can do to alter the moment of doom her great-aunt had foreseen even earlier, Hazel appears to find a more creative way than Maud's cryptic splutter of weaving her father's impending death into his life.

In place of Maud's negative note that no one can decipher, Hazel also anticipates the moment of her father's death, just after he reaches line 999, but offers him a much more playful, creative, subtle, and celebratory message, the inspiration for a poem, not merely a fleeting code to try to *read* but lasting lines she can help him *write*, a poem that keeps the surprises open, that suggests even if only as a playful possibility that the dead *do* light up the lives of the living, and that, unlike Maud's blurted and illegible message, will keep lighting up readers' lives. After finishing line 999, Shade will indeed cross "an old friend" "So brightly beaming through a tree / So green." She cannot avert his death, but she will be there for him once he dies.

10.

From Appalachia to Zembla:
A Woman Spurned

No Self-Styled Spirit

The experience of the Institute of Preparation for the Hereafter prepared Shade only to expect nothing in the here-and-now:

> when we lost our child
> I knew there would be nothing: no self-styled
> Spirit would touch a keyboard of dry wood
650   To rap out her pet name; no phantom would
> Rise gracefully to welcome you and me
> In the dark garden, near the shagbark tree.

From our position, knowing of Maud's message in the Haunted Barn, knowing of Hazel's manifestation as a *Vanessa atalanta* as her mother stands "near the shagbark tree" at the end of the poem, Shade's confident dismissal seems to call out for ironic reversal, just as the narrator's smug rejection of Cynthia Vane's "theory of intervenient auras" in "The Vane Sisters"[1] is ironically reversed by the aura he has just passed through, and even by the words he sets down at the close of his story, recording his failure to catch the least glimpse of Cynthia in his dream—words that he does not realize are dictated by dead Cynthia and Sybil.[2]

Shade's lines continue with echoes of two other poets, Eliot and Goethe:

> "What is that funny creaking—do you hear?"
> "It is the shutter on the stairs, my dear."

> "If you're not sleeping, let's turn on the light.
> I hate that wind! Let's play some chess." "All right."

"I'm sure it's not the shutter. There—again."
"It is a tendril fingering the pane."

"What glided down the roof and made that thud?"
660   "It is old winter tumbling in the mud."

"And now what shall I do? My knight is pinned."

Who rides so late in the night and the wind?
It is the writer's grief. It is the wild
March wind. It is the father with his child.

Evoking another warm, windy March night exactly a year after Hazel's death, Shade mimics Eliot (Part II of "The Waste Land"), in deliberate tribute to the Eliot lines from "Four Quartets" that gave rise to that treasured three-way conversation the Shades had with their daughter, Canto Two's fondly recollected "triptych or . . . three-act play / In which portrayed events forever stay."[3] The unease in the Eliot lines gives rise in Shade's memory to the deeper unease of Goethe's "Elf King," with its image of a father about to have his child snatched from him into a sinister death. For us, though, the Goethe lines bring just as surely to mind the image of Charles II fleeing in dread and darkness over the mountains of Zembla, muttering these lines to himself. And we will soon understand the depth of the ironic reversal of Shade's sureness that he will hear nothing from Hazel.

If Hazel's spirit has inspired her father sometime in 1958 to write "The Nature of Electricity," and if Kinbote arrives in Dulwich Road early 1959, might Hazel not have influenced Kinbote, too, just as the Pippa whom Browning thought up in his wood near Dulwich influences not just one but a number of different people in Asolo? If, as we discovered in Chapter 7, Kinbote's Zemblan fantasy develops only after he moves into Dulwich Road, has Hazel somehow helped prompt it?

Mirror Words

Immediately after the Haunted Barn note, Kinbote comments on Shade's "She twisted words": "One of the examples her father gives is odd. I am quite sure it was I who one day, when we were discussing 'mirror words,' observed (and I recall the poet's expression of stupefaction) that 'spider' in reverse is 'redips,' and 'T. S. Eliot,' 'toilest.' But then it is also true that Hazel Shade resembled me in certain respects" (C.347–348, 193). The next two notes also refer obliquely to Eliot and point the curious reader toward his "Four Quartets" as the source of the obscure words Hazel queries. Shade finds it oddly disconcerting that Kinbote should echo the Hazel he never met, but the echoes will become much more pervasive and haunting.[4]

The most insistent motif in Eliot's poem is the phrase "In my end is my beginning" and variants upon it, yet that very pattern seems to be replayed in Hazel's penchant for reversing the letters of words, even the letters of "T. S. Eliot," as it is replayed in another way in the *atalanta* at the end of "Pale Fire," whose red flash on its wings recalls the waxwing at the beginning of the poem.

Kinbote claims he has inspired Shade with the "spider"—"redips" reversal, but as so often in *Pale Fire*, the directional sign may itself need to be reversed. By this stage of reading we can not only follow all the novel's patterns, but we will also have reason to believe they are not incidental ornaments but signposts to concealed sense. As a series of patterns of reversed letters, of ends become beginnings, quietly suggests—and other patterns, allusions, and motives will converge on the same conclusion—Hazel has inspired Kinbote, and not only in the "spider"—"redips" inversion. With her liking for "mirror words," she appears a major inspiration behind Kinbote's Zembla, that "land of reflections" whose language is "the tongue of the mirror."

Kinbote's Zembla fantasy develops only after he settles in New Wye, while he lives in the house of the "alphabetic family" of the Goldsworths, whose daughters Alphina, Betty, Candida, and Dee appear to give rise in Kinbote's cracked but crystalline imagination to King Alfin, Queen Blenda, King Charles, and Queen Disa. The quartet of daughters runs from Dee, the eldest, to Alphina, the youngest, as if to echo the "In my end is my beginning" of the "Four Quartets." This pattern seems to be echoed again when the A-to-Z sequences that run through the house (the four sets of children's encyclopedias, Mrs. Goldsworth's novels from Amber to Zen) reverse into Charles II's supposed kingdom of Zembla—whose beginning is the end of the alphabet, whose end is its beginning—or in his supposed journey that begins in Zembla and ends in Arcady.

Soon after arriving in New Wye, Kinbote hides what seem to him the offensive photographs of the four Goldsworth girls under the winter clothes in their closet. After Shade's death he temporarily stows the four cantos of the poem that he still thinks will tell his story "under a heap of girls' galoshes, furred snowboots and white wellingtons heaped at the bottom of a closet, from which I exited as if it had been the end of the secret passage that had taken me all the way out of my enchanted castle and right from Zembla to this Arcady" (C.1000, 295).

Kinbote's story starts with Charles II's father, King Alfin, an evident extrapolation from the Goldsworths' Alphina: again, a double echo of "in my end is my beginning," as the Goldsworths' youngest child reverses in Kinbote's fantasy into the elder of his supposed parents. Hazel drowns in Lake Omega, named after the last letter of the Greek alphabet, and this young woman who loves to reverse letters appears to direct Kinbote toward the *first* letter of the Greek alphabet as the starting point for his imagined life in Zembla,[5] and through that— through the King Alfin who flies into the side of a building in the "land of reflections"—toward the image in line alpha of her father's poem.

LADY OF THE LAKE

As elsewhere, Nabokov allows other routes to his most unexpected discoveries. Hazel drowns herself in a lake, after getting off a bus at a place with the decidedly Scottish name of Lochanhead (*lochan* is Scottish for "little lake")[6] and stepping into the icy swamp at Lochan Neck. Charles II of Zembla has as a tutor a passionate Scot, a Mr. Campbell, who can recite the whole of *Macbeth* and teaches little princesses to enjoy "Lord Ronald's Coronach" from Sir Walter Scott's *Minstrelsy of the Scottish Border* (C.71, 104, in "a clear reference," as Gerard de Vries notes, "to the appreciation Scott's first biographer, John Lockhart, gave of this poem as it awakes 'the childish ear to the power of poetry and the melody of verse'").[7] In Scott's *The Lady of the Lake*, the king of a northern land[8] who remains incognito until near the very end of this six-canto poem, steps forward after clambering through the mountain woods on his own, hears the call of the Lady of the Lake, and speaks—the first human communication in the poem: "'A stranger I,' the Huntsman said, / Advancing from the hazel shade" (I.397–98).[9] Scott, of course, had drawn his title from Arthurian legend, where the Lady of the Lake is a blurrily supernatural figure who in one of Malory's accounts gives Arthur the sword that is the mark of his right to kingship. As the Scott allusion and the Malory behind him appear to imply, Kinbote steps forward to play the covert king of a northern land from under the shadow of Hazel Shade, the lady of the lake. And in inspiring him with Zembla, she will also inspire her father with "Pale Fire," and so arrange for Kinbote to keep the Crown Jewels of his kingdom, the precious manuscript he can hoard as the pretext for telling the story that will *prove* he is a king.

ADVANCING FROM THE HAZEL SHADE

Why would Hazel help Kinbote to develop his wistful wish-fulfillment world of Zembla? Presumably she takes note of him because he has moved next door to her father and admires Shade so. She singles him out for her attention because she recognizes him as suicidal, as she was, and because although Zembla provides him with a radiant if not uninterrupted escape from his despair, it also compels him to tell his story to Shade, offering Hazel a kind of indirect but ultimately very fruitful communication with her father (but let us defer until the next two chapters the evidence that Hazel fashions Zembla into a mirror world that flashes into her father's mind the idea for his autobiographical poem). Her parents did not doubt that her own poltergeist phase was "an outward extension or expulsion of insanity" (C.230, 166); now, as a ghost herself, she seems to extend Kinbote's insanity, offering him in the fantasy life of Zembla an alternative to his solitude and despair.

The story of Charles the Beloved reflects Kinbote's hypertrophied sense of his own importance and reverses the stigma of homosexuality in Appalachia into a sign of nobility, manhood, and style in Zembla. But at the same time, Zembla seems to reflect Hazel Shade's story. On moving into the Goldsworth house, Kinbote dumps into a closet the "pert pictures" of the four daughters, whom he suspects "will soon change from horribly cute little schoolgirls to smart young ladies and superior mothers" (C.47–48, 83). That closet seems to transmute in his imagination into the key to his Zembla story, the entrance into the hidden tunnel through which he can make his escape, while Hazel, anything but a "horribly cute" schoolgirl, destined never to be a smart young lady or a superior mother, appears to inspire him so that each of the four main episodes of the Zembla story includes a woman the King recoils from: his would-be seducer, Fleur de Fyler; the image of Iris Acht; the mountain girl, Garh; and Disa, his queen.

Let me draw attention to a feature of Zembla that I do not think has ever been remarked on, yet should strike us as very curious. Although extremely vain, Kinbote never reports any woman in New Wye as showing sexual interest in him, yet in Zembla, where homosexuality seems almost the enchanted norm, the action focuses for far longer on scenes of the King walking away from women than on his advancing toward other men.[10] That pattern underlies much of the comedy of the Zembla scenes, as well as an unexpected late wave of pathos in his account of his relationship to Queen Disa.

Nor has it been remarked how persistently a breath from the beyond pervades the Zembla scenes, often in the form of echoes from some of the few scenes we witness of Hazel's life: the planchette message for Fleur de Fyler, supposedly from the dead Queen Blenda, which recalls the message for Hazel from her dead great-aunt; the lights on the tunnel walls that the King thinks of as Oleg's ghost and that also recall the Haunted Barn; the image of a red reflection in a bright blue lake that sends "a shiver of *alfear* (uncontrollable fear caused by elves)" through the King, but recalls that azure-and-red reflection in a puddle before the bar that Hazel leaves the night she becomes, as it were, the lady of the lake; and the strong sense of some deeper emotional and moral reality trying to break through the King's tormented dreams of Disa.

If Hazel's shade has helped shape the Zembla fantasy in Kinbote's mind, her role behind the scenes would explain both Zembla's breezes from the beyond and the pattern of the King's turning away from women, in its comedy *and* its pathos. As we shall see, Zembla becomes more clearly than ever an escape, an indulgent dream, yet underneath it all we can now glimpse a new depth of human truth, as we see Hazel acknowledge her past, bravely facing it, playfully transforming it, allowing Kinbote an escape within life that *she* never had, but at the same time reflecting her own past predicament and her present delight in her new freedom from the solitary confinement of her old self.

METHOD AND MADNESS

As in the case of the Red Admirable, Hazel's part in prompting Kinbote's delusions about Zembla also has its own precursor in the Nabokov canon. Early in 1940, Nabokov wrote the story "Ultima Thule," intending it as the first chapter of his last, never-completed Russian novel, *Solus Rex*, which in its name, its preoccupation with death, its revolution in an imaginary northern land, and its radical disjunction between its parts so strikingly anticipates *Pale Fire* itself.

"Ultima Thule" takes the form of a letter Sineusov addresses to his wife, who has died of tuberculosis six months into her first pregnancy. Conscious of the absurdity of trying to communicate like this with someone who has died, Sineusov nevertheless cannot stop himself. He reports to her his meetings with Adam Falter, once his tutor in St. Petersburg, who has recently as it were exploded into knowledge, into an understanding of the ultimate truth of things normally denied to the mortal mind, although in terms of ordinary life he now seems in many ways insane. Despite all Sineusov's probing, Falter refuses to divulge his secret (he did pass it on to one pryer, who died of the shock). Falter—in the light of Hazel's last manifestation in Shade's life, we should note that his name is the German for "butterfly," as if to mark his metamorphosis—nevertheless tells Sineusov that in evading his questions he *has* let slip a clue: "Amid all the piffle and prate I inadvertently gave myself away—only two or three words, but in them flashed a fringe of absolute insight—luckily, though, you paid no attention."[11] If *we* follow that clue we will realize, as Sineusov himself never sees, that Falter's sudden mental metamorphosis "is an eerie transmutation of the child his own dead wife was to have borne, and the sign he had so fervently hoped for from that dead woman."[12]

The situation in *Pale Fire* is in most respects quite different, but in both story and novel a woman somehow surviving beyond death affects the mind of a man still living, inducing in him a degree of madness that offers him a gift—insight in "Ultima Thule," escape in *Pale Fire*—at some cost to his sanity, though not to his intelligence. In Botkin's or Kinbote's case, of course, we have reason to suspect that his extreme egocentrism had already brought him to the brink of insanity long before he began to see himself as the king of Zembla.

FLEUR

Just how do each of the four main episodes of Charles II's story advance from Hazel's shade? After Queen Blenda's death and before Prince Charles is crowned Charles II, Countess de Fyler directs her younger daughter Fleur to lay sexual siege to the heir to the throne. Fleur seems a picture of inexhaustible female beauty, whose image reflected upon itself in a special mirror turns into all nymphs, receding into the mists of time, "an infinite number of nudes . . . , garlands of girls in graceful and sorrowful groups, diminishing in the limpid distance . . ." (C.80, 111). After searching for months "with a porcelain cup and Cinderella's slipper," the society sculptor and poet Arnor finds in her breasts and feet the ideal model for his sculpture. But despite these parodic intimations of timeless fairy-tale beauty, despite the exotic swing and play of her haunches, despite her spending three days of "ridiculous cohabitation" (110) with the young king, Charles remains utterly and comically unaroused by her. The statue for which Arnor needed her is aptly titled *Lilith Calling Back Adam*. Lilith, in Hebrew mythology, the representative of womankind before the creation of Eve, is shunned by Adam and stands as an image of the first female ever rebuffed by a male.[13]

Like Hazel's stakeout of the Haunted Barn, Fleur's assault on Charles's bedroom lasts three nights, nights during which Charles, feeling "a sickly physical fear of [his mother's] phantom" (109), welcomes Fleur's presence at least for her keeping "at bay the strong ghost of Queen Blenda" (111). Before initiating the siege, Fleur's mother had made the Prince "attend table-turning séances with an experienced"— and evidently well-bribed—"American medium," at which Queen Blenda's spirit spells out with the planchette, in English, the insistent but ineffectual message: "Charles take take cherish love flower flower flower" (109). This crude match-making with its threefold "flower" plays out in quite another key the threefold *atalanta* in the ghostly message spelled out in the Haunted Barn. But if the séance, the triple repetition in the medium's message, and the three nights of fruitless vigil create surprising covert connections between Fleur and the Hazel of the Haunted Barn, for all the disparities between the two actresses and the two settings, the connections strengthen still further if we remember the covert but pointed Browning echoes (Dulwich Forest, "Here Papa pisses") of the Hunted Barn episode, for the "American medium" who impersonates Queen Blenda's spirit speaking to Prince Charles in this rigged séance hints at the most famous of mediums, the American Daniel Dunglas Home (1833–86), also no stranger to royalty. (Nabokov evokes him in *Speak, Memory* as "that incredibly agile medium, Daniel Home, . . . said to have been caught stroking with his bare foot (in imitation of a ghost hand) the kind, trustful face of Empress Eugénie.")[14] In 1855 Robert Browning attended a séance directed by Home, whom he had always thought a venal fraud and on whom, as is well known, he based the speaker of his "Mr. Sludge, 'The Medium'" (drafted c. 1859–60, published 1864).

In Canto Two of "Pale Fire," Hazel looks so unprepossessing that she can seem, even to a fond father's eye, only "almost fetching" when she tries on her mother's furs "and the mirrors smiled, / The lights were merciful, the shadows mild." Fleur, by contrast, naked before "a triptych of bottomless light, a really fantastic mirror" evokes immemorial female beauty, "an infinite number of nudes . . . garlands of girls . . . breaking into individual nymphs." In Chapter 12, we will find just how deeply Hazel, lover of mirror words, is implicated, not only in the "triptych" involving her parents and herself in Canto Two, but also in the television picture of a nymph before a mirror that follows. And already in this first image of a woman spurned in Zembla, the beauty who provided the model for *Lilith Calling Back Adam*, Hazel seems to transpose with wry detachment the disaster of her one fatal blind date into the enchanting comedy of Fleur de Fyler's luckless forced tryst with Charles, her failure to stir the least response in him despite her peerless beauty.

IRIS ACHT

An element of the uncanny haunts each of the main episodes of the Zembla story. The tone of comic exoticism in the Fleur de Fyler episode changes to something far eerier in the longest note of all, the escape through the tunnel. As we saw in Chapter 3, chess pervades this whole note, from the "king-in-the-corner waiter of the *solus rex* type" of chess problem to which the King compares the problem of his imprisonment, to the chess game played by Campbell and Beauchamp while the Prince and Oleg explore the tunnel. The solution to the problem is provided by the tunnel to Iris Acht's dressingroom, a solution the King arrives at the very night he is moved to the lumber room:

> The King's wandering gaze stopped at the casement which was half open. One could see part of the dimly lit court where under an enclosed poplar two soldiers on a stone bench were playing lansquenet. The summer night was starless and stirless, with distant spasms of silent lightning. Around the lantern that stood on the bench a batlike moth blindly flapped—until the punter knocked it down with his cap. The King yawned, and the illumined card players shivered and dissolved in the

prism of his tears. His bored glance traveled from wall to wall. The gallery door stood slightly ajar, and one could hear the steps of the guard
coming and going. Above the closet, Iris Acht squared her shoulders and
looked away. A cricket cricked. The bedside light was just strong
enough to put a bright gleam on the gilt key in the lock of the closet
door. And all at once that spark on that key caused a wonderful confla-
gration to spread in the prisoner's mind. (C.130, 122–23)

The light that puts a gleam on the key in the closet door hands him, as
it were, the key he needs to solve the problem of his imprisonment: the
closet under the picture of Iris Acht. The lightning, the electric light,
and the key also recall another famous flash of inspiration, Benjamin
Franklin's experiment with a key on his kite during a lightning storm
to test the nature of electricity. And in fact, the whole ambience here
recalls the note on the Haunted Barn, with its lightning storm and its
light that spells out a message, as well as the poem "The Nature of
Electricity," with its "pale moths of starless nights" and its "lightning"
infiltrating the "night . . . starless . . . lightning . . . moth"[15] of the scene
above, and even, as we shall see, the suggestion that "the gentle dead"
may live on in electric light.

Although the key to the closet under the picture of Iris Acht offers
the King his solution, he does not know *what* door that key will open
at the other end of the tunnel. He relives in his mind the scene from
thirty years ago. When he heads off with his young playmate and recent bedmate, Oleg, he has no idea where the tunnel leads. In the passage underground the scene strikingly reflects the light playing on the
walls of the Haunted Barn: "Oleg walked in front: his shapely buttocks
encased in tight indigo cotton moved alertly, and his own erect radiance, rather than his flambeau, seemed to illume with leaps of light the
low ceiling and crowded walls. Behind him the young Prince's electric
torch played on the ground and gave a coating of flour to the back of
Oleg's bare thighs" (C.130, 126–27).

Like the King three decades later, the boys do not read the signs in
Iris Acht's picture above the closet, or in the green sofa and green car-
pet that anticipate her greenroom. When they reach a locked green
door at the end of the tunnel, they find that the lumber room closet key
fits, and are about to turn it when they hear

> Two terrible voices, a man's and a woman's, now rising to a passionate
> pitch, now sinking to raucous undertones, . . . exchanging insults in Gut-
> nish as spoken by the fisherfolk of Western Zembla. An abominable

threat made the woman shriek out in fright. Sudden silence ensued, presently broken by the man's murmuring some brief phrase of casual approval ("Perfect, my dear," or "Couldn't be better") that was more eerie than anything that had come before.

Without consulting each other, the young Prince and his friend veered in absurd panic and, with the pedometer beating wildly, raced back the way they had come. (C.130, 127)

Just before opening the door to Iris Acht's greenroom, Prince Charles and Oleg recoil at the sound of this mysterious exchange between a man and a woman and race back to their own "manly" pleasures. They neither discover where the tunnel leads nor deduce that it was built because of an affair between Thurgus the Third and Iris Acht, the only passionate relationship between a man and a woman we encounter in all of Zembla. Green rooms stand at both ends of the tunnel—the green of the Emerald-Izumrudov whom Kinbote detests for his "ignoble heterosexual lust"[16]—as if to announce the answer the boys do not arrive at, as if to signal the intensity of Thurgus's and Iris's passionate affair, as if to mark the boys' frightened retreat from the door leading to heterosexual exchange.

Thirty years later, locked in the lumber room that leads to the secret tunnel, the King opens the closet in the dark, removes its shelves, awkwardly pulls over his pajamas some clothes his hands brush against and takes as a talisman what he guesses must be the copy of *Timon Afinsken* he noticed all those years ago. With the closet closed behind him and its shelves replaced from the tunnel side, he can at last safely switch on his flashlight. Again the "dim light . . . ghost . . . phantom" inevitably brings to mind the "roundlet of pale light" in the Haunted Barn that some would explain away as a "scamp's toy flashlight" (C.347, 188, 189) but that by now we see as Aunt Maud's ghost trying to reach Hazel:

> The dim light he discharged at last was now his dearest companion, Oleg's ghost, the phantom of freedom. He experienced a blend of anguish and exultation, a kind of amorous joy, the like of which he had last known on the day of his coronation, when, as he walked to his throne, a few bars of incredibly rich, deep, plenteous music (whose authorship and physical source he was never able to ascertain) struck his ear, and he inhaled the hair oil of the pretty page who had bent to brush a rose petal off the footstool, and by the light of his torch the King now saw that he was hideously garbed in bright red. (C.130, 132–33)

The bright red that the King notices after this wave of amorous joy at the memory of Oleg, or a pretty page boy, confirms as it were his distance from the green of Thurgus and Iris Acht's desire.

Although the Prince recoils from her door, Iris Acht, unlike Fleur, Garh, and Disa, is not in fact a woman spurned by the King. As if to compensate, Nabokov corroborates her relationship to Hazel in several other ways. Not only is Iris "officially" a suicide, and an actress (among the few scenes we witness of Hazel are her roles as Mother Time in a school pantomime, as a participant in "a triptych or a three-act play" on the domestic stage, as "Daughter" in the playlet of "The Haunted Barn"), but her name twice points toward Hazel. The image of Iris stands over the closet that leads into the tunnel and in fact dominates the whole episode. Her name at the beginning of the note hints at the solution to the scene's insistent implicit riddle—where will the tunnel lead?—but also indicates the answer to a much deeper riddle. "Hazel" is rare as a color word in being so preponderantly applied to a single object, the human eye (Nabokov jokes in his introduction to *Speak, Memory* that he shares not only his birthday but even his passport with "Hazel Brown"), or, to be more anatomically precise, the colored part of the eye, the *iris*. And *iris* is also the species name of the butterfly popularly called the Purple Emperor,[17] whose upper fore-and hind-wings are richly covered in a highly conspicuous purple, as Charles II now finds himself a conspicuously red king. Hazel, in her role as butterfly, as Red Admirable (or more commonly, Red Admiral), seems to stand behind the Iris who offers Kinbote his escape as red king or Purple Emperor.[18]

The King emerges backstage in the Royal Theater and has the good fortune to be spotted at once by his staunch supporter, the actor Odon, who is about to whisk him away when the Scenic Director of the theater, an Extremist sympathizer, spots him, "but being afflicted with a bad stammer could not utter the words of indignant recognition which were making his dentures clack." In this blend of comedy and immemorial adventure, Odon and the King just make their escape.

GARH

The next episode follows almost immediately—Kinbote cannot contain his eagerness to tell it—as the King makes his escape over the mountains. Chased by the Extremist police, he has no time to change out of his eye-catching red as he rushes from Odon's car into the bracken and the night. He climbs up into the darkness, and "as a chance accompaniment of drumming fatigue and anxiety" keeps repeating to himself the "haunting lines" of Goethe's poem "about the erlking, hoary enchanter of the elf-haunted alderwood" (C.662, 239).

After two hours of climbing, he follows a pinhead light until he stumbles into a ditch by a farmhouse. The "gnarled farmer and his plump wife ... like personages in an old tedious tale offered the drenched fugitive a welcome shelter" and give him "a fairy-tale meal" (C.149, 140). The next morning the farmer places his "gnarled hand on the gnarled balustrade and directed toward the upper darkness a guttural call: 'Garh! Garh!' Although given to both sexes, the name is, strictly speaking, a masculine one, and the King expected to see emerge from the loft a bare-kneed mountain lad like a tawny angel. Instead there appeared a disheveled young hussy..." (141). She leads him up the mountain and points him on his way. When he sits down "near a patch of matted elfinwood," she settles beside him, strips off the sweater she had put on, "revealing her naked back and *blanc-mangé* breasts, and flooded her embarrassed companion with all the acridity of ungroomed womanhood. She was about to proceed with her stripping but he stopped her with a gesture and got up"(142).

He starts off up the slope, "still chuckling over the wench's discomfiture," when he suddenly finds himself before a small mountain lake:

> In its limpid tintarron he saw his scarlet reflection but, oddly enough, owing to what seemed to be at first blush an optical illusion, this reflection was not at his feet but much further; moreover, it was accompanied by the ripple-warped reflection of a ledge that jutted high above his present position. And finally, the strain on the magic of the image caused it to snap as his red-sweatered, red-capped doubleganger turned and vanished, whereas he, the observer, remained immobile. He now advanced to the very lip of the water and was met there by a genuine reflection, much larger and clearer than the one that had deceived him. He skirted the pool. High up in the deep-blue sky jutted the empty ledge whereon a counterfeit king had just stood. A shiver of *alfear* (uncontrollable fear caused by elves) ran between his shoulderblades. He murmured a familiar prayer, crossed himself, and resolutely proceeded toward the pass. At a high point upon an adjacent ridge a *steinmann* (a heap of stones erected as a memento of an ascent) had donned a cap of red wool in his honor. He trudged on. But his heart was a conical ache poking him from below in the throat.... (C.149, 143)

The comedy of Garh's discomfiture offsets the sudden shiver of dread the King feels as he sees what he first thinks his own reflection start to move. But that dread in turn offsets and intensifies the imminent rush of glorious release awaiting him when he descends to the western coastline and learns the reason for the reflection in the mountains: forty of his followers, rallied by Odon, have dressed themselves in scarlet and led the Extremist police a merry chase around Zembla, and it was the reflection of one of them he had for a moment mistaken for his own. The red outfit that had looked so ominously conspicuous when he first noticed it in the tunnel, and that had seemed so disconcerting in the reflection in the mountain lake, now becomes the source of his greatest pride, as he thinks of the suite of heroic young supporters and admirers imitating him around the country, reflecting his glory, multiplying his image, as if living out a narcissist's dream. No wonder he cannot conceal his delight at this episode, no wonder he ends it: "I trust the reader has enjoyed this note"(147).

But behind the major chord that defines this moment for Kinbote, another key can be heard. When the King looks in the lake and sees the reflection of a man in bright red start to move, he feels an ache of terror as if there is life in his own reflection, as if he is perhaps no more real than the image he casts, as if there is someone unknown in himself. This red king and the pang his reflection causes him bring to a climax a pattern that has been gathering throughout the whole escape. In the chess-problem setting of the tunnel episode, in the chess game played by the doublets Campbell and Beauchamp, in the red king that Charles II becomes as he steps into a half-enchanted tunnel, and now in the red king whose reflection takes on a life of its own, the escape story inevitably calls to mind the tunnel that opens *Alice's Adventures in Wonderland* and especially the long chess game that runs throughout *Through the Looking Glass*, where Alice finds herself confronted by the Campbell-and-Beauchamp–like Tweedledum and Tweedledee and their troubling claim that she is only part of the Red King's dream.[19] Who is dreaming whom, Alice wonders anxiously, but the story ends with her waking fully and all but certain *she* has dreamed the Red King rather than *he* her.

Like Alice, another young woman, Hazel, lover of "mirror words," lady of the lake, seems to have helped Kinbote dream his dream of the Red King, to cross through into the looking-glass world of Zembla, where for this moment in the mountains he suddenly catches sight of someone else in the lake who seems simultaneously to be himself and a stranger.

Suddenly the King's chuckling at the image of Garh's discomfiture as he walks away from her and then stops in his tracks as he sees the red figure in the lake, himself and not himself, takes on a disturbing new resonance. It seems to recall Hazel, the Red Admirable, the dreamer of this mirror world, the lady in the lake who stepped into her lake and her death precisely *because* a man walked away from her. The azure reflected in a puddle barred with neon red the very moment her date walks away flashes behind this image that suddenly troubles the King.

By walking away from Garh, Charles II will of course cause the raunchy mountain girl none of the harm Pete Dean's insensitivity causes the vulnerable Hazel. But there is another pattern that has been accumulating through this episode. Up until the moment the King catches sight of that reflection in the lake and feels "a shiver of *alfear* (uncontrollable fear caused by elves)," echoes of Goethe's "Erlkönig" have been gathering. As he climbs through the mountain, dressed like an elf-king himself, the King repeats Goethe's lines to himself. The next morning, hearing Garh called for, he imagines her as a "mountain lad like a tawny angel," a temptation he would have found hard to resist. The real Garh turns out to be a female and sits down beside the King near some "elfinwood" whose presence signals that had Garh proved to be the mountain boy the King had anticipated, he would indeed have tried to possess him. Again Hazel seems implicated in the pattern, for when Shade thinks of his child in the clutches of death, he too will recall the Elf King who snatches a child away.

For the King and Kinbote the episode of the flight across the mountains ends in a note of high triumph, as the multiplication of red kings not only saves him but shows scores of young heroes paying him tribute as they mirror his image and transform it from something vulnerable and absurd into high romantic adventure. But the deep pang of dread as he confronts his image in the lake and suddenly stops chuckling about Garh, the eeriest moment in the whole Zembla saga, seems to align the damaging self-concern of both the man who walked away from Hazel and of the King or Kinbote as pedophile.

On the one hand, Hazel in dreaming up the episode of the Red King offers Kinbote his image of glory: escape from the prison of his solitude, triumph over the disregard of others. On the other, she allows a shadow of real pain to trouble the indulgent fantasy about to unfold, a shadow of all *her* pain, when she was unable to enjoy the luxury of self-admiration or a shadow of the pain a Kinbote or a Pete Dean can cause because he cannot see others in the mirror of his own self-regard.

DISA

Charles of Zembla ignores Fleur de Fyler and leaves Garh sitting bare-breasted on the ground without an afterthought of regret. But one woman in Zembla whom he rejects troubles him deeply, if only in his dreams. He backs away from Disa as he does from Fleur or Garh, but knows he inflicts on her much more than a passing pang. Helplessly devoted to him, Disa finds her life one long agony because she can neither detach herself from him nor win the least flicker of his love.

Kinbote introduces her in a late note, the last long note of Charles II's story. After his escape, the king visits her in her Villa Disa on the Côte d'Azur. The "tall, sheared and bearded visitor with the bouquet of flowers-of-the-gods who had been watching her from afar advanced through the garlands of shade. She looked up—and of course no dark spectacles and no make-up could for a moment fool her" (C.433–434, 206). The incognito king who "advanced" through "garlands of shade" pointedly echoes that couplet from Scott's *The Lady of the Lake* where the king, concealing his identity, steps forward to the lady of the lake ("'A stranger I,' the Huntsman said, / Advancing from the hazel shade") and at the same time echoes both the first mention of Hazel in *Pale Fire* ("I had a favorite young shagbark there / . . . the black bark, around which, like undone / Garlands, the shadows of the foliage fell./ . . . White butterflies turn lavender as they / Pass through its shade where gently seems to sway / The phantom of my little daugh- ter's swing") and her last manifestation, as the *Vanessa atalanta* all but mimes the image of a laurel garland ("we saw it next moment sporting in an ecstasy of frivolous haste around a laurel shrub. . . . Then the tide of the shade reached the laurels, and the magnificent, velvet-and-flame creature dissolved in it" [C.993–995]).

Hazel seems insistently implied throughout the heartrending de- scription of Charles's queen. Disa's armorial crest contains a *Vanessa atalanta*. "Disa" herself bears the name of a butterfly, *Erebia disa*, the Arctic Ringlet, found in Europe in northern Norway and Sweden and Finland—as closely as we can surmise, in the very location of Zembla itself.[20] Queen Disa's name of course also echoes Dis, the kingdom of the dead. She is Duchess of Great Payn and Mone, in striking echo of live Hazel at her most unbearably wretched:

350   She hardly ever smiled, and when she did,
          It was a sign of *pain*. She'd criticize
          Ferociously our projects, and with eyes
          Expressionless sit on her tumbled bed
          Spreading her swollen feet, scratching her head
          With psoriatic fingernails, *and moan*,
          Murmuring dreadful words in monotone. (Italics added)

In tribute to her name, the King brings Disa flowers-of-the gods, *Disa uniflora*, the spectacularly red flower regarded as perhaps the most showy of all orchids—as if a transposition of the Red Admirable from animal to plant, from one kingdom to another.

All this puts a totally unexpected slant on the most mysteriously urgent tones adopted anywhere in the Commentary. Describing Disa's beauty, Kinbote refers to Shade's description of Sybil in "Pale Fire":

> At the moment of his painting that poetical portrait, the sitter was twice the age of Queen Disa. I do not wish to be vulgar in dealing with these delicate matters but the fact remains that sixty-year-old Shade is lending here a well-conserved coeval the ethereal and eternal aspect she retains, or should retain, in his kind noble heart. Now the curious thing about it is that Disa at thirty, when last seen in September 1958, bore a singular resemblance not, of course, to Mrs. Shade as she was when I met her, but to the idealized and stylized picture painted by the poet in those lines of *Pale Fire*. Actually it was idealized and stylized only in regard to the older woman; in regard to Queen Disa, as she was that afternoon on that blue terrace, it represented a plain unretouched likeness. I trust the reader appreciates the strangeness of this, because if he does not, there is no sense in writing poems, or notes to poems, or anything at all. (C.433–434, 206–7)

If we remember that Hazel as *Vanessa atalanta*, as Red Admirable, seems now, beyond death, to have lost her fateful physical resemblance to her father and somehow to take after her mother, this uncanny resemblance of Disa to Sybil becomes far more uncanny still.

The resemblance of Disa and Sybil offers a key to the whole story of Zembla, "Semblerland, a land of reflections, of 'resemblers'" (C.894, 265). John Shade finds two ways to escape as best he can the finitude of the mortal life that he likens to a cage or a locked hive:

through the transcendence of self he finds in his art, and through the transcendence he finds in his love for Sybil, in sharing his existence with another. The two are intimately linked: "And all the time, and all the time, my love," he begins his last day's verse, "You too are there, beneath the word, above / The syllable" (P.949–50). Every line he has ever written, except, tragically, these lines themselves and the few that follow, he reads to her at the end of the day, as each new batch is complete.

Like Shade, Kinbote, too, feels a powerful need to flee the limits of the self. He, too, does so in two ways: in his megalomaniac self-assertion, which of course only drives others away and accentuates his isolation, and in his rapid turnover of sexual partners. The two combine pathetically in his attempt to avail himself of the transcendence of art, by pressing his story on Shade, and in his finding a thrill in his "glorious friendship" with the neighbor he stalks like "a lean wary lover."

Shade of course can neither return Kinbote's feelings nor respond to his invitation to eternalize his story in verse. But within the Zembla story, Disa herself offers "poor king, poor Kinbote" another way out. Her love places Charles at the center of her existence in a way far more natural and human than Kinbote's craving for the world's recognition seeks to exact. She is the first person to whom he tells the story of his escape, and she would happily listen to much more. But just as Shade cannot respond to Kinbote, so the King can neither feel nor fake desire for Disa, but can only betray her with what strikes her as his endless and more or less disgusting succession of partners.

Filling in the background to the King's encounter with Disa, Kinbote explains how Zembla's need for an heir to the throne obliged him to marry, only for "the anterior characteristics of [Disa's] unfortunate sex" to keep "fatally putting him off." The twenty-one-year-old bride

> found out all about our manly Zemblan customs, and concealed her naïve distress under a great show of sarcastic sophistication. He congratulated her on her attitude, solemnly swearing that he had given up, or at least would give up, the practices of his youth; but everywhere along the road powerful temptations stood at attention. He succumbed to them from time to time, then every other day, then several times daily—especially during the robust regime of Harfar Baron of Shalksbore, a phenomenally endowed young brute (whose family name, "knave's farm," is the most probable derivation of "Shakespeare"). Curdy Buff—as Harfar was nicknamed by his admirers—had a huge escort of acrobats

and bareback riders, and the whole affair rather got out of hand so that Disa, upon unexpectedly returning from a trip to Sweden, found the Palace transformed into a circus. He again promised, again fell, and despite the utmost discretion was again caught. At last she removed to the Riviera leaving him to amuse himself with a band of Eton-collared, sweet-voiced minions imported from England. (C.433–434, 208–9)

"Curdy Buff" comes from *coeur de boeuf*,[21] or "ox heart," suggesting graphically in precisely what respect Harfar is "phenomenally endowed." Here the motif of redness—as the opposite of the greenness of the heterosexual love of Iris Acht and Thurgus the Third, or Gerald Emerald's fondness for "some mammate student's resilient charms" (C.1000, 298), or the Shades on their "square of green"—reaches its most unappealing. Redness and homosexuality had been associated with Shakespeare and *Timon of Athens* when Charles, retracing his childhood exploration with Oleg, took that copy of *Timon Afinsken* with him and unwittingly donned scarlet clothes before emerging through a green door in the Royal Theater and thence into Coriolanus Lane and Timon Alley. Now, redness and Shakespeare deteriorate into a combination repugnant to Disa, "Curdy Buff" of "Shalksbore"; *Timon* recurs in "those with whom he betrayed her [in his dreams]— prickly-chinned Phrynia, pretty Timandra with that boom under her apron" (210),[22] and the "circus" of decadents that disgusts her seems a still more decayed echo of the "elaborate toy circus . . . the brown boy acrobats with spangled nates" (C.130, 124) that young Prince Charles had gone looking for to amuse Oleg when he first found the tunnel. Here redness seems to have become openly pedophiliac, indulgent, and decadent.

For all Disa's sense of his centrality to her life, the King cannot respond to her. Yet Kinbote reports that despite his steadfast indifference to Disa in waking life, he finds himself stirred to anguish when he dreams of her:

> He dreamed of her more often, and with incomparably more poignancy, than his surface-life feelings for her warranted; these dreams occurred when he least thought of her, and worries in no way connected with her assumed her image in the subliminal world as a battle or a reform becomes a bird of wonder in a tale for children. These heart-rending dreams transformed the drab prose of his feelings for her into strong and strange poetry, subsiding undulations of which would flash and disturb him throughout the day, bringing back the pang and the richness—and

then only the pang, and then only its glancing reflection—but not affecting at all his attitude towards the real Disa.

Her image, as she entered and re-entered his sleep, rising apprehen-
sively from a distant sofa or going in search of the messenger who, they
said, had just passed through the draperies, took into account changes of
fashion; but the Disa wearing the dress he had seen on her the summer
of the Glass Works explosion, or last Sunday, or in any other antecham-
ber of time, forever remained exactly as she looked on the day he had
first told her he did not love her. (209)[23]

The dreams that rack him are all agonizing variations on the theme of
his denying that he does not love her. "His dream-love for her ex-
ceeded in emotional tone, in spiritual passion and depth, anything he
had experienced in his surface existence. This love was like an endless
wringing of hands, like a blundering of the soul through an infinite
maze of hopelessness and remorse" (210). In his dreams the King
seems aware of another in a way Kinbote never is in life: aware of the
anguish of *her* loneliness in being shut out from him, *her* grief at his
endless infidelities, *her* high selflessness in rising above her pain to
deal with others in their need.

In developing in Kinbote's mind the image of Zembla, Hazel's spirit
appears to have offered him an escape from the bleakness of his solitude and despair, a consoling fantasy of triumph that reaches its narcissistic zenith in the vision of those heroic young "men of fashion"
imitating the admirable red escapee up and down the land. But at the
same time she also offers first the dream-shadow of his guilt, in the
shiver of *alfear* as he looks in the lake, and then another dream-
shadow, a richer escape from the prison of the self—one that he, being
who he is, simply cannot reach, even within his fantasy world, except
in his dreams—in a Disa who seems a sublimated version of Hazel
herself, hauntingly like Sybil, and with a staunch courage to face her
condition as a woman spurned.

Out of the Dream

Yet the dream that Hazel helps Kinbote dream remains
only that, a dream, a madman's mirage, an evasion of the real. His
vision of Charles II's escape from solitary confinement in the palace
after his dethronement seems a solution to the problem of his solitude

and his sense of displacement from the centrality he so desperately craves, but however exultant the dream, it cannot sustain him forever. Indeed, after recounting his Zembla story to Shade and then preserving it for posterity in his notes to Shade's poem, Kinbote seems to have exhausted Zembla and himself, and when he reaches the end of his Commentary and his Index, he will rediscover himself still alone, still alive, still trapped in the real.

Zembla itself seems to intimate what his next move will be. The central episode of his Zembla story, the key to his escape, is the episode of the tunnel. Insistent overtones of the underworld surround the tunnel scene, both in "the dim light . . . Oleg's ghost, the phantom of freedom," with all its reminiscences of the light in the Haunted Barn, and in such details as the King's encountering, as the passage leads through the foundations of a museum, "a headless statue of Mercury, conductor of souls to the Lower World" (C.130, 132–33)—the world of Dis, in fact.

As we have seen more than once, chess images pervade the escape through the tunnel, which the King even compares to "what a composer of chess problems might term a king-in-the-corner waiter of the *solus rex* type" (C.130, 118–19). The number 1888, saliently recurring through the episode, seems to reflect the numbering of chess ranks from one to eight, and the layout of the chessboard, eight squares by eight. The key to the problem posed for the King is the closet surmounted by the picture of Iris Acht, the closet that leads into the tunnel that once took Thurgus the Third from this corner room in the square palace to Iris Acht's dressing room. Or in chess terminology, the key move is Iris Acht, *Iris Acht* (German "eight"), i8, from the h8 square in the corner of the board to i8, a king's one-step move, but now off the board.[24]

Kinbote's mad belief that he is really Charles the Beloved offers him only a temporary escape. He will be able to break free from the solitary confinement of the self, from the prison bars of personality,[25] he will find permanent relief only when he dies, when he makes that ultimate key move, the move off the board, the move into the greenroom at the end of the tunnel, when like the Iris Acht of the Index he dies officially by his own hand, even if unofficially at the hands of a Shadow, another "bigger, more respectable, more competent Gradus."

Recounting the story of the Haunted Barn that this tunnel episode so often recalls, Kinbote says "There are always 'three nights' in fairy tales, and in this sad fairy tale there was a third one too" (C.347, 190).

The King has twice come up to Iris Acht's door—as a boy who recoils from that door to retreat to his homosexual romps with Oleg, and as a fugitive king about to find the release of a narcissistic fantasy. But the evidence also suggests that he will open that door a third time, that he will commit suicide as Iris Acht "officially" does in her dressing room, and yet hope to have those really in the know recognize his death, like hers, as an assassination by the Shadows.

The Iris Acht from whose door the young Prince recoils, and through whose door he passes in that dream of escape, is an actress and "officially" a suicide. Her very name echoes "act," and passing through the tunnel the King crosses "under the three transverse streets, Academy Boulevard, Coriolanus Lane and Timon Alley" (C.130, 126), as if to spell A,C,T yet again, while the 1,888 steps through the tunnel lead to the actress's greenroom where she took her life in 1888. We see little of Hazel Shade in her short life, but she has acted—onstage ("My gentle girl appeared as Mother Time"), as part of the "triptych or three-act play" that Shade constructs in "Pale Fire," and as one of the three roles in the play of the "The Haunted Barn" that Kinbote reconstructs—and she too commits suicide.

Unlike Iris Acht, Hazel has had no king to love her, has known no greenroom of ardent trysts. Like Kinbote, she has had to face a life of solitude and despair. From the beyond she seems now to have given him the image of fulfillment, "the dim light" of "his dearest companion, Oleg's ghost, the phantom of freedom," freedom from the trap of his solitude, but it is only the mirage of madness. But when he takes the dark passage again to the greenroom where Iris Acht supposedly took *her* life, when he takes his own life, he may find Hazel waiting there as his Iris Acht, his key move, the bright red Disa or Red Admirable to his Red King.

CADENUS AND VANESSA

That may seem an odd prospect for an inveterate misogynist like Kinbote, but then death in *Pale Fire* does offer a series of extraordinary surprises. The first time the *Vanessa atalanta* appears in the Commentary, Kinbote responds:

> It is *so* like the heart of a scholar in search of a fond name to pile a butterfly genus upon an Orphic divinity on top of the inevitable allusion

to *Van*homrigh, *Esther*! In this connection a couple of lines from one of Swift's poems (which in these backwoods I cannot locate) have stuck in my memory:

> When, lo! *Vanessa* in her bloom
> Advanced like *Atalanta*'s star

As to the Vanessa butterfly, it will reappear in lines 993–995 (to which see note). . . .

I notice a whiff of Swift in some of my notes. I too am a desponder in my nature, an uneasy, peevish, and suspicious man, although I have my moments of volatility and *fou rire*. (C.270)

Quite what Orphic divinity Kinbote has in mind I cannot ascertain— although an Orphic divinity would be one who comes back from the Underworld, like Orpheus almost leading his Eurydice with him.

Jonathan Swift seems to have coined the name Vanessa for Esther ("Essy") Vanhomrigh (1688–1723), in the poem "Cadenus and Vanessa" (written perhaps 1713, published 1726), from which the lines Kinbote quotes come.[26] "Cadenus" is simply an anagram of *decanus*, "dean," reflecting Swift's position as Dean of St. Patrick's in Dublin. In the poem, Swift celebrates what he portrays as the unlikeliest of love affairs, one between a young woman and her tutor, a much older man—a stylized portrait of Swift himself, who had had no thought whatever, in view of his age and profession, of being passionately loved by any woman, least of all someone of Vanessa's youth. Yet Vanessa takes an ardent interest in him, and their love becomes reciprocal.

Shade names the person who spurned Hazel on the night of her death "Pete Dean." Now that she is a *Vanessa atalanta*, Hazel seems to find another "Dean," who spurns all women equally, who identifies with Dean Swift, who twists words as both she and Swift do (spider-redips, decanus-Cadenus, Esther Vanhomrigh–Vanessa).[27] Once spurned by all men and made insufferably wretched because of her physical unattractiveness, Hazel Shade now seems somehow transformed, in looks, as it were, whatever that might now mean, and in spirit. Hazel's shade takes an interest in the unhappy life of her father's neighbor and admirer, who cannot be interested in *any* woman, beautiful or not. She provides him in Zembla with an exultant imagined escape from his situation that also reflects, in a vein of comic exoticism, but with the occasional resonant undertone of recollected anguish, her own acceptance of herself now as a woman spurned, while at the same time she feeds him, in the dreams he has of Disa, the image of a relationship of loyalty and trust that could transcend the prison of self.

Hazel's role in Kinbote's life suggests that after he succumbs to his temptation to suicide, after he figuratively takes the tunnel a third time to Iris Acht's room, they may share a singular kind of companionship, the woman who took her life because she felt herself pushed to the margins of her world, and the man she allows a rich fantasy of himself at the center of *his* world, until reality catches up with him again and he too seeks in death an ultimate escape. Kinbote may discover that even though *Shade* could not take the interest in his life that he wanted, his daughter could: someone else who had found life lonely, difficult, unhappy, someone who now from the beyond has allowed him to live a little longer, while he imagines himself central to his world, and who has made him central in hers. And when he discovers that, it might make all the difference.

II.

"Pale Fire": Origins and Ends

THE EVIDENCE Nabokov conceals within *Pale Fire* suggests that Hazel's spirit somehow inspires Kinbote with the idea of Zembla, because she senses an affinity with him, because she wants to offer him an imaginative consolation for his anguish and loneliness, and because she can turn Zembla into a chance both to express and to ironize her own experience as a woman spurned. Her hidden role suddenly explains the peculiar harmony between her humiliations in New Wye and Kinbote's imagined triumphs in Zembla that we may have felt all along but never quite brought into focus. Yet it still does not explain the more audible echoes between poem and commentary that trouble us from early in our encounter with *Pale Fire*.

But we can find the beginnings of an explanation at last in Hazel's deepest motive. By animating Kinbote with the vision of a Zembla in which he plays such a splendid part that he feels his "glorious misfortunes" must be foisted on Shade for him to preserve in imperishable verse, Hazel will be able to communicate obliquely with her father and even to inspire him to the great poem that she can see forms part of destiny's rough draft.

Throughout his work, Nabokov examines not just the possibility of an afterlife but also the possibility of some communication between the dead and the living. Again and again, in works like *The Defense*, *The Gift*, "Ultima Thule," "The Vane Sisters," *Ada*, and *Transparent Things*, he proposes that the dead may indeed communicate with us, influence us, but that from this side of death, no matter how attentively and imaginatively we examine our world, we will not find any unequivocal proof. Indeed, he suggests, our very expression of our inability to detect such signals could be their very sign, or in any case, proof of the inconceivable distance between the conditions of an existence beyond death and ours. The dead Hazel Shade—and she proves to be acting not entirely alone—appears to inspire her father with material for a poem that sums up her death, his life, and his life-long quest to probe the mystery of death. Yet for all his confidence in forces around him "playing a game of worlds," even Shade can detect no sign of her hidden hand or any other in the text and texture of his life.

WHO GAVE YOU YOUR THEME?

Minutes before Shade dies, he confides at last to Kinbote that he has almost finished his long poem: "A few trifles to settle and [suddenly striking the table with his fist] I've swung it, by God." Kinbote responds with an invitation to wine at his house, and another treat: if Shade agrees to show him the finished product,

> "I promise to divulge to you *why* I gave you, or rather *who* gave you, your theme."
> "What theme?" said Shade absently, as he leaned on my arm and gradually recovered the use of his numb limb.
> "Our blue inenubilable Zembla, and the red-capped Steinmann, and the motorboat in the sea cave, and—" (C.991, 288)

Shade evades the question of the Zembla theme but agrees to the wine, while Kinbote relieves him of the manuscript. Recounting this precious moment, Kinbote broods on the miracle of written words: "Solemnly I weighed in my hand what I was carrying under my left armpit, and for a moment I found myself enriched with an indescribable amazement as if informed that fireflies were making decodable signals on behalf of stranded spirits, or that a bat was writing a legible tale of torture in the bruised and branded sky" (289). We know how misplaced is Kinbote's confidence that he has given Shade his theme, but that some "fireflies," some "stranded spirits," have inspired the manuscript he holds, *by means of* Kinbote's telling Shade the Zembla story, though seemingly far more improbable, turns out to be the mysterious truth.

As the image of Zembla forms in Kinbote's mind, he pressures Shade more and more insistently:

By the end of May I could make out the outlines of some of my images in the shape his genius might give them; by mid-June I felt sure at last that he would recreate in a poem the dazzling Zembla burning in my brain. I mesmerized him with it, I saturated him with my vision, I pressed upon him, with a drunkard's wild generosity, all that I was helpless myself to put into verse. . . . My little pocket diary contains such jottings as: "Suggested to him the heroic measure"; "retold the escape"; "offered the use of a quiet room in my house"; "discussed making recordings of my voice for his use"; and finally, under date of July 3: "poem begun!" (C.42, 80–81)

Especially in June 1959 Kinbote urges the story on him:

During our sunset rambles, of which there were so many, at least nine (according to my notes) in June, but dwindling to two in the first three weeks of July (they shall be resumed Elsewhere!), my friend had a rather coquettish way of pointing out with the tip of his cane various curious natural objects. . . . By means of astute excursions into natural history Shade kept [on July 6] evading me, me, who was hysterically, intensely, uncontrollably curious to know what portion exactly of the Zemblan king's adventures he had completed in the course of the last four or five days. My usual shortcoming, pride, prevented me from pressing him with direct questions but I kept reverting to my own earlier themes—the escape from the palace, the adventures in the mountains—in order to force some confession from him. (C.238, 168–69; bracketed date added)

This whole note and Shade's pointing out of natural objects with the help of Aunt Maud's cane stand in close rapport with the introduction to the note on the Haunted Barn, the Paul Hentzner–Dulwich Road–"Here Papa pisses"–"pada ata lane" complex that suggests different levels of inspiration for Shade in the real world and beyond.

Again and again, Kinbote lays particular stress on the escape, especially the escape through the tunnel. He prepares an elaborate plan of the Onhava palace "in June, when narrating to him the events briefly noticed in my comments (see note to line 130, for example)" (C.71, 106). "Retold the escape," he notes in his diary, and on July 3: "poem begun!" Why *does* Nabokov place such a stress on Kinbote's pressure on Shade through late May and June, especially on Kinbote's prompting Shade to imagine the escape through the tunnel, and then have Shade write in such a sustained flow through the three weeks of July until his death?

PALE . . . FIRE

The first long installment of the Zembla story, first chrono-
logically and in the order of reading, comes to us in a note on the word
"parents." In the poem, of course, the word refers to Shade's parents:

> I was an infant when my parents died.
> They both were ornithologists. I've tried
> So often to evoke them that today
> I have a thousand parents. Sadly they
> Dissolve in their own virtues and recede. (P.71–75)

In glossing this, Kinbote divulges a few details about Shade's parents
that he has had to glean from Prof. Hurley's memoir, for although
Shade lives in the same house as his parents had, his neighbor has
never asked anything about them. But as soon as he can, Kinbote the
commentator turns to the parents of Charles II.

Keep in mind Kinbote's sense of wonder as he holds the manuscript
of "Pale Fire"—"an indescribable amazement as if informed that fireflies were making decodable signals on behalf of stranded spirits"—as
we look at the passage where he describes the night Charles hears that
his mother, Queen Blenda, has suddenly and unexpectedly died. But
before citing the relevant passage, may I just focus your attention? I
want to fish out of this passage evidence for something submerged,
but let us not forget Nabokov's mastery of the surface, his capacity to
evoke an imagined experience. This is the first scene set in Zembla, the
first moment of lived Zemblan time, and the vividness, unpredictability, and beauty of its details allow Zembla to leap into life in our
minds, no matter how convinced we are it is Kinbote's fantasy, no
matter how derivative his private myth of escape may be of many
another flight of fancy. Charles has been at an all-night ball, "for the
nonce, a formal heterosexual affair, rather refreshing after some previous sport" (C.71, 105):

> At about four in the morning, with the sun enflaming the tree crests and
> Mt. Falk, a pink cone, the King stopped his powerful car at one of the
> gates of the palace. The air was so delicate, the light so lyrical, that he
> and the three friends he had with him decided to walk through the lin-
> den bosquet the rest of the distance to the Pavonian Pavilion. . . . A
> strange something struck all four of them as they stood under the young

limes in the prim landscape of scarp and counterscarp fortified by
shadow and countershadow. Otar, a pleasant and cultured adeling with
a tremendous nose and sparse hair, had his two mistresses with him,
eighteen-year-old Fifalda (whom he later married) and seventeen-year-
old Fleur (whom we shall meet in two other notes), daughters of Countess de Fyler, the Queen's favorite lady in waiting. One involuntarily
lingers over that picture, as one does when standing at a vantage point
of time and knowing in retrospect that in a moment one's life would
undergo a complete change. So here was Otar, looking with a puzzled
expression at the distant windows of the Queen's quarters, and there
were the two girls, side by side, thin-legged, in shimmering wraps, their
kitten noses pink, their eyes green and sleepy, their earrings catching
and loosing the fire of the sun. There were a few people around. . . . A
peasant woman with a small cake she had baked, doubtlessly the mother
of the sentinel who had not yet come to relieve the unshaven dark young
nattdett (child of night) in his dreary sentry box, sat on a spur stone
watching in feminine fascination the luciola-like tapers that moved from
window to window. . . . Suddenly, down a steep path among the lilac
bushes—a short cut from the Queen's quarters—the Countess came running and . . . spat out the news. (C.71, 105–6)

"Luciola," we need to note, is a variant spelling of the Italian *lucciola*,
"firefly" or "glow-worm."

There is already something haunting in the air—and Kinbote will
tell us two pages later that Charles II had "a sickly physical fear of
[Queen Blenda's] phantom." But notice also the odd, uncertain, echo of
the title of Shade's poem and its Shakespearean source in the earrings
"catching and loosing the fire of the sun." Since soon after *Pale Fire*
was published, its readers have again and again discovered for themselves as they reread *Hamlet*—the play Nabokov has called "probably
the greatest miracle in all literature"[1]—a curious interrupted echo of
Shade's and Nabokov's title, as if *Timon of Athens* were not its only
source.[2] But no one has known whether the echo was by accident or
design. We now have the evidence to declare it very deliberate and
very pointed design. The ghost of King Hamlet, talking to his son,
cries out:

> Fare thee well at once!
> The glow-worm shows the matin to be near,
> And gins to pale his uneffectual fire.
> Adieu, adieu, adieu! remember me. (1.5.88–91)

The eerie atmosphere of this first Zemblan scene, a northern prince's hearing of a parent's death, the hour between night and morning, the "catching and loosing the fire of the sun," the "glow-worm" or "firefly" in the luciola—all point not only to these lines from *Hamlet*, to the ghost of a father talking to a son, but suggest that Kinbote's "as if informed that fireflies were making decodable signals on behalf of stranded spirits" is not just a simile but an unrecognized sign.

King Alfin the Vague dies when Charles is only three, as Shade's father died when his son was three. Alfin has "a passion for mechanical things," especially planes, and a "very special monoplane, Blenda IV" is "his bird of doom" (C.71, 103): he dies flying it smack into the side of a building. Shade's father's "chief passion" is ornithology, as Hurley notes in his memoir, "adding that 'a bird had been named for him: *Bombycilla Shadei*' (this should be '*shadei*,' of course)" (C.71, 100). Notice here Nabokov's expertise in piecemeal disclosure of information. For the vast majority of readers, the genus name will not at this point be recognized as referring to waxwings, and Kinbote's pedantic point about capitalization distracts his attention and ours and diminishes the visual resemblance to the surname "Shade." But ten lines from the end of the Index and the novel, Nabokov offers the attentive reader the necessary clue: "*Waxwings*, birds of the genus *Bombycilla*, 1–4, 131, 1000; *Bombycilla shadei*, 71; interesting association belatedly realized." If we connect this *Bombycilla shadei* with the poem, we will realize that although Shade, like Charles II, could call his father "the Vague," he nevertheless surely thinks of him, and of his own origin, when in the first line of his poem he writes: "I was the shadow of the waxwing slain." He has in mind the void before him as well as the void after.[3]

Alfin the Vague seems to develop in Kinbote's mind from the picture of Alphina in the Goldsworth home, but he in turn seems to develop in Shade's mind (once he hears from Kinbote the story of Alfin flying into the side of a building in a "land of reflections") into that image of the waxwing that Shade finds for the beginning, line alpha, of his poem, as a way of contemplating both his father's death, his own beginning and his own end—and somehow, this passage now suggests, all this seems to come by way of his father's "stranded spirit."

Samuel Shade, remember, is the brother of the Maud Shade who tries to communicate with Hazel in the barn. The parents in the Zemblan saga—Alfin flying into a wall in his Blenda IV—seem to reflect signals from Shade's "firefly" parents that help to trigger the beginning of Shade's poem and Shade's conscious homage, in the waxwing, to the ornithologist parents he barely knew. "Adieu, adieu, remember me," the ghost of one father asks, and in his opening line Shade certainly remembers *his* father as vividly as he can.

PALE LIGHT, DIM LIGHT, PALE FIRE

"I was the shadow of the waxwing slain / By the false azure in the windowpane," Shade writes, and as he imagines projecting himself into death, he also has his daughter in mind, since he will picture her on the night of her death, abandoned by her date, left to cope with her humiliation, standing by the reflection in pavement puddles of an azure entrance crossed by a neon bar. But Hazel, who seems much more deeply responsible than Shade's parents for the whole shape Zembla takes in Kinbote's mind, appears herself to have inspired her father to write the poem he *does* write, through the pressure that Kinbote applies to have him versify his visions of Zembla. She has Kinbote's imagined story of *his* life inspire Shade to recount the true story of his own.

As he strolled through a wood near Dulwich, Browning had an image of someone walking "alone through life" and exercising a profound influence on other lives, and in *Pippa Passes* he shows Pippa affecting others again and again. Shade, too, lives in Dulwich Road, Shade, too, feels the powerful impact of the lonely Hazel, linked both to Pippa and the Psyche-butterfly of Browning's poem in the note on her Haunted Barn.

When Kinbote urges Shade to write about Charles II, he places particular stress on the episode of the tunnel. That episode itself has an almost palpable internal stress as it builds up, for the boy or the man exploring the tunnel, or for us accompanying them, a strong sense of being on the brink of some great discovery: a sense that gathers through the *solus rex* chess problem, through the excitement of imminent escape, but also through the persistent hints of a passage to the underworld, the crackle and gleam of electricity, the "dim light" of Oleg's ghost, "the phantom of freedom," images that recall the electricity and the "roundlet of pale light" in the Haunted Barn. The tunnel episode ends with Charles II emerging into the Royal Theater in the midst of a performance, as the story of the Haunted Barn ends with a miniature play.

The adventure of the tunnel is vivid and urgent in Kinbote's telling, yet Shade cannot write about it. But that story cannot help stirring something in Shade's memory. The story of a childhood exploration through a tunnel that seems like a passage into the underworld—an exploration that begins when a boy looks for his toys—and then an adult escape still further through that tunnel must give a jolt to Shade, must bring back vividly to mind both the image of his own childhood fits, first triggered when he looked at a toy, and experienced as a first tug from "playful death,"and his later adult foray deeper into "the strange world" of death during a heart attack.

In his note to line 130, the tunnel episode, Kinbote writes:

> Line 130 is followed in the draft by four verses which Shade discarded in favor of the Fair Copy continuation (line 131 etc.). This false start goes:
>
> > As children playing in a castle find
> > In some old closet full of toys, behind
> > The animals and masks, a sliding door
> > [four words heavily crossed out] a secret corridor—
>
> The comparison has remained suspended. Presumably our poet intended to attach it to the account of his stumbling upon some mysterious truth in the fainting fits of his boyhood. I cannot say how sorry I am that he rejected these lines. I regret it not only because of their intrinsic beauty, which is great, but also because the image they contain was suggested by something Shade had from me. I have already alluded in the course of these notes to the adventures of Charles Xavier, last King of Zembla, and to the keen interest my friend took in the many stories I told him about that king. (118)

As so often, Kinbote's claims of influence work exactly the other way. He fabricates this variant in order to give himself a pretext to introduce the tunnel episode into his Commentary: these lines were *not* inspired in Shade by Kinbote, but simply penned by Kinbote in a woeful attempt at forgery. But on the other hand, the image of "stumbling upon some mysterious truth in the fainting fits of his boyhood" does indeed seem to have been intensely revived in Shade's mind by Kinbote's pressing on him this particular episode.

Throughout the tunnel story, so central to the romance of Zembla, we feel a strange sensation of someone playing a game of worlds, from the *solus rex* frame Kinbote establishes for the whole episode, to Campbell and Beauchamp playing chess for exactly the length of time the boys spend traversing the tunnel, or the players playing lansquenet outside the King's prison chamber as he redescends. The sensation reaches its eerie climax on the King's second passage through the tunnel, when he passes relics that have wandered down from a museum above, "a headless statue of Mercury, conductor of souls to the Lower World, and a cracked krater with two black figures shown dicing under a black palm" (C.130, 133). And this eerie intimation resonates most peculiarly with the central "Playing a game of worlds" passage after Shade's second excursion into the "strange world" of death.

Recalling his childhood, Shade reports he was too clumsy to have friends, although

> In sleeping dreams I played with other chaps
> But really envied nothing—save perhaps
> The miracle of a lemniscate left
> Upon wet sand by nonchalantly deft
> Bicycle tires.
>
>   A thread of subtle pain,
> Tugged at by playful death, released again,
> But always present, ran through me. One day,
> When I'd just turned eleven, as I lay
> Prone on the floor and watched a clockwork toy—
> A tin wheelbarrow pushed by a tin boy—
> Bypass chair legs and stray beneath the bed,
> There was a sudden sunburst in my head.

140

If Shade plays with other boys only in his dreams and envies "The miracle of a lemniscate left / Upon wet *sand*," the tunnel episode records *Pale Fire*'s one intense scene of boyhood play, revisited by Kinbote with joy, when he sees that a "remembered spread of colored *sand* bore the thirty-year-old patterned imprint of Oleg's shoe." After the definition of "lemniscate" that Kinbote cites and understandably makes little sense of ("a unicursal bicircular quartic"), Webster's Second explains the word by printing in illustration a figure eight on its side. The number eight saturates the tunnel episode, in Iris *Acht*, whose death is recorded as 1888, whose picture hangs over the entrance to the passage and whose dressing room door stood at its exit exactly 1,888 yards way, according to the boys' pedometer.[4] Again, of course, the proliferation of eights here reflects the intense chess ambience of the tunnel episode[5] and anticipates Shade's decision, after his *second* exploration of the passage to death, to find in life "some kind / Of correlated pattern in the game," like those "Playing a game of worlds, promoting pawns / To ivory unicorns and ebon fauns."

Also running through the tunnel episode is the insistent presence of Shakespeare: the "thirty-twomo edition of *Timon of Athens* translated into Zemblan by his uncle Conmal" (125) that Charles finds as a boy; the description of the tunnel as passing under the "transverse streets . . . Coriolanus Lane and Timon Alley" (126); the copy of *Timon Afinsken* he takes as a talisman on his escape through the tunnel as a man; and the search for Odon's car "in a transverse lane . . . in an adjacent alley" (135, evidently Coriolanus Lane and Timon Alley) as they emerge from the Royal Theater. *Timon of Athens* of course supplies the source for Shade's title, again, as if this elaborate episode, so charged in itself, has triggered Shade to write his whole poem.

Not only does Kinbote compare the King's predicament to "what a composer of chess problems might term a king-in-the-corner waiter of the *solus rex* type," but the whole tunnel episode seems from the first a problem insistently and urgently posed for the reader. For the boys who explore the tunnel together, for the King who wants to escape through it, and for the first-time reader, the problem is simple: Where does the tunnel lead? The answer, of course, is that it leads to the dressingroom of King Thurgus the Third's mistress, Iris Acht, in Onhava's Royal Theater, and many clues like the green decor and the 1888 can after the fact be seen to point ahead to this greenroom where Iris Acht died in 1888. For the rereader, though, other problems supervene, as this episode's challenge intensifies to the point where it seems a key to the whole book, even if we do not know why: just why is it so saturated with images of chess, with crackles of electricity, with intimations of the otherworld, with echoes of Shakespeare, with patterns of red and green, with repetitions of the number eight, with such a plethora of design?

Perhaps the deepest answer is linked to the episode's highest comic surprise: when the King switches on the light after he has safely closed the door of the closet behind him, he finds himself clad in bright red. As we have seen, this king of "a land of reflections" has in a sense become the Red King of *Through the Looking Glass*, and as we have also seen, his garb as he makes his way toward Iris Acht's door recalls the butterfly *iris*, the Purple Emperor, with its garish colors fore and aft. And both Red King and Purple Emperor seem to point to the dead girl who loved mirror words, who now can appear as a Red Admirable, and who like Alice has dreamed her Red King.

A year before Kinbote arrived in New Wye, the *Vanessa*-like Hazel inspired her father to write a poem for *The Beau and the Butterfly* that crackled with electricity, with intimations of the afterworld, with the number 999, and with the pervasive glow of Shakespeare. Now she appears to have developed even further since her death and to have transmuted her nights in the Haunted Barn—her own explorations of the abyss—into the tunnel episode in Zembla as Kinbote's image of discovery and escape, and that story in turn into a stimulus to her father to undertake a long poem about his own lifelong exploration of the abyss.

IRONIES OF INSPIRATION

Kinbote has no inkling that he owes to anything but his own past his glorious visions of Zembla, yet, conversely, he has a highly unjustified confidence that *his* Zembla has kindled Shade's imagination. At one point he compares his memory of a man he once saw in Zembla transfigured by a flash of grace to his glimpses of Shade working on "Pale Fire" in a similar glow of inspiration:

> Once, three decades ago, in my tender and terrible boyhood, I had the occasion of seeing a man in the act of making contact with God. I had wandered into the so-called Rose Court at the back of the Ducal Chapel in my native Onhava, during an interval of hymnal practice. As I mooned there, lifting and cooling my bare calves by turns against a smooth column, I could hear the distant sweet voices interblending in subdued boyish merriment which some chance grudge, some jealous annoyance with one particular lad, prevented me from joining. The sound of rapid steps made me raise my morose gaze from the sectile mosaic of the court—realistic rose petals cut out of rodstein and large, almost palpable thorns cut out of green marble. Into these roses and thorns there walked a black shadow: a tall, pale, long-nosed, dark-haired young minister whom I had seen around once or twice strode out of the vestry and without seeing me stopped in the middle of the court. Guilty disgust contorted his thin lips. He wore spectacles. His clenched hands seemed to be gripping invisible prison bars. But there is no bound to the measure of grace which man may be able to receive. All at once his look

changed to one of rapture and reverence. I had never seen such a blaze
of bliss before but was to perceive something of that splendor, of that
spiritual energy and divine vision, now, in another land, reflected upon
the rugged and homely face of old John Shade. How glad I was that the
vigils I had kept all through the spring had prepared me to observe him
at his miraculous midsummer task! I had learned exactly when and
where to find the best points from which to follow the contours of his
inspiration. My binoculars would seek him out. . . . Sometimes when the
poet paced back and forth across his lawn, or sat down for a moment on
the bench at the end of it, or paused under his favorite hickory tree, I
could distinguish the expression of passionate interest, rapture and reverence, with which he followed the images wording themselves in his
mind, and I knew that whatever my agnostic friend might say in denial,
at *that* moment Our Lord was with him. (C.47–48, 88–89)

Once again Kinbote has it all wrong. The red-and-green pattern here,
the first time in *Pale Fire* the two elements occur together, points toward the most emphatic instance of the pattern: the green rooms at
both ends of the tunnel, and the moment the King walking between
them discovers he is in red. The wave of exultation there, the remembered "bars of incredibly rich, deep plenteous music (whose authorship and physical source he was never able to ascertain)," and "the
pretty page who had bent to brush a rose petal off the footstool"
(C.130, 132–33), strikingly echo this scene that Kinbote remembers
as an analogy for Shade's inspiration, as if to confirm the role of the
tunnel scene in dislodging Shade's memories of his own near escapes
from mortality. The hickory under which Shade pauses, and which he
has so strongly associated with his daughter, with butterflies changing hue, and with shadows and phantoms, again points to a different source for his inspiration than the one Kinbote so confidently
attributes.

0 AND 000, 8 AND ∞

But perhaps Kinbote's reference to "Our Lord" invites a
moment of reflection. If Hazel does help shape the Zembla fantasy in
Kinbote's mind, and through that helps her father shape "Pale Fire"
itself, just where does her influence end? Her spirit does not design the
world in which it works. She does not arrange her father's death, of

course, but like Aunt Maud with her "pada ata lane . . . , " she seems to have seen his killing in advance and even to have seen herself at his side at that moment, just as Maud too, nearly three years ahead of time, incorporated the *atalanta* into her warning. If Hazel inspires her father from the beyond to write "The Nature of Electricity" and in the number 999 indicates herself as the "old friend" "So brightly beaming through a tree / So green," and if she also appears as the exuberant butterfly sporting around the laurel after he finishes line 999, she must be able to see ahead in detail, to see even her father's uncompleted poem, and yet she still has her own highly creative and highly personal part to play in destiny's designs.

In the scene in Canto Two where she asks her parents to explain the arcane words in a poem we can now identify as Eliot's "Four Quartets," Shade declares that "It does not matter what it was she read / (some phony modern poem that was said / In English Lit to be a document / 'Engazhay and compelling' . . .)." What does matter for him is

that the three

380   Chambers, *then* bound by you and her and me,
           Now form a triptych or a three-act play
           In which portrayed events forever stay.

That "triptych or . . . three-act play" resounds oddly with the note on the Haunted Barn, which is also a three-act drama, one for each night in the Barn, and which ends in a three-actor play. Both scenes show rare examples of Hazel interacting with her parents, one in a way that Shade treasures and preserves, one in a way he avoids recalling. As if in memory of the first "triptych or . . . three-act play," and in refutation of the second triptych's discordant course and conclusion (*"Life is hopeless, afterlife heartless"*), Hazel seems to offer her father a poem to outdo "Four Quartets," a poem that has its origins in a quartet of daughters much luckier than her in life, whose "end" is in their "beginning" (A comes after B comes after C comes after D), whose photographs in a closet become the basis for Alfin, Blenda, Charles, and Disa and for the tunnel episode that in turn prompts her father to write his "Four Cantos," as his poem is subtitled.

Hazel dies in Lake Omega, but as if to testify that death is not the last letter of life, she seems with the help of her own grandparents to turn Alphina Goldsworth into Alfin the Vague in Kinbote's mind, and Alfin in turn into the opening line of Shade's poem, the image of the waxwing. She does not occasion her father's heart attack, or the apparent coincidence of his death's-door vision and Mrs. Z.'s, or the arrival of a disturbed foreigner for neighbor, but from such events she can begin to make "ornaments / Of accidents and possibilities."

In the immediate but ever-more-complex image that opens "Pale Fire," Shade projects himself as if beyond death as he reflects on his own origin and end, on the ends of the parents who gave him his beginning, on the end of the daughter who he hoped would carry on his line. At the end of the poem, he records the quiet congruence of the evening hour, confident that it testifies to a larger concord.

<blockquote>

                                              I can see
990   Part of your shadow near the shagbark tree.
           Somewhere horseshoes are being tossed. Click. Clunk.
           (Leaning against its lamppost like a drunk.)
           A dark Vanessa with a crimson band
           Wheels in the low sun. . . .
</blockquote>

But even he cannot see the signs that Hazel is still there with him, that even the horseshoes, the shape of a capital omega, testify to her presence and prompting.

From her position beyond, Hazel does not design Shade's world, but she does deepen the design that she detects in the very weave of things. In inventing the tunnel episode to echo her own experience of the Haunted Barn, she acts a part in Kinbote's and her father's life, she plays as it were the role of Iris Acht, whom she has Kinbote imagine dying a suicide in 1888, as she has him imagine the Prince and his "dear companion" measuring out 1,888 paces to her green door. Shade writes in Canto One of his envy of the "lemniscate" another boy might leave in the sand. As we have seen, a "lemniscate" is a curve of the shape of a figure eight, or of the hourglass evoked a few lines earlier, or, if placed on its side, the symbol for infinity, ∞.

<blockquote>

120   A thousand years ago five minutes were
           Equal to forty years of fine sand.
           Outstare the stars. Infinite foretime and
           Infinite aftertime: above your head
           They close like giant wings, and you are dead.
</blockquote>

Hazel as the *Vanessa* seems to refute the finality of "and you are dead," to turn the hourglass of elapsing time into infinity, as if the wings of infinite foretime and infinite aftertime, far from closing in on us, become ours, and bear us up. "Pale Fire" appears to end blankly when Shade dies before he reaches line 1000, as if the last line of death is a blank, a triple zero like Hazel's death in one of three conjoined lakes, Omega, Ozero, Zero. No, she seems to answer, in the repeated 1888 she has Kinbote imagine, death is not a triple zero but a triple eight, a triple lemniscate, infinity upon infinity upon infinity, all we cannot attain in life multiplied unimaginably.

12.

"A Poem in Four Cantos":
Sign and Design

IF HAZEL helps foster Kinbote's fantasy, from the Alfin who flies into a wall to the "Zembla, a distant northern land" that ends the Index, and if she provides the cue for the alpha and the omega, the waxwing and the *Vanessa*, in Shade's poem, does not the very possibility of any such direction from the beyond diminish the freedom of the mortal mind? Nabokov takes good care to suggest this need not be the case. That Kinbote's vainglorious Commentary serves his own inflated sense of himself requires no proof. That Shade's poem bespeaks his own vision in his own distinctive voice we cannot doubt. And even as we discern more of Hazel's hidden part in her father's lines, we discover more signs of Shade's artistic guile as he guides "Pale Fire" toward his own goals.

SHADE: LINK-AND-BOBOLINK

After his hopes have been first raised, by Mrs. Z's reported "fountain" as she dipped near death, and then dashed, by her actual "mountain," Shade feels tempted to "take the hint, / And stop investigating my abyss," but decides—and here comes the climax of his poem—that

> *this*
> Was the real point, the contrapuntal theme;
> Just this: not text, but texture; not the dream
> But topsy-turvical coincidence,

810   Not flimsy nonsense, but a web of sense.
        Yes! It sufficed that I in life could find
        Some kind of link-and-bobolink, some kind
        Of correlated pattern in the game. . . .

The very phrase "link-and-bobolink," with its misleading coupling of a general abstract noun and a particular species of bird, should warn us to expect something deceptive in the patterns Shade will weave, just as he finds something mysteriously playful in a fate that can tantalize him with a coincidence like "fountain" and "mountain."

Shade's parents die when he is an infant, and he is brought up by Aunt Maud. After reporting her death, he muses on the unknowability of a hereafter:

        It isn't that we dream too wild a dream:
        The trouble is we do not make it seem
        Sufficiently unlikely; for the most
230   We can think up is a domestic ghost.

        How ludicrous these efforts to translate
        Into one's private tongue a public fate!
        Instead of poetry divinely terse,
        Disjointed notes, Insomnia's mean verse!

        Life is a message scribbled in the dark.
        Anonymous.

              Espied on a pine's bark,
        As we were walking home the day she died,
        An empty emerald case, squat and frog-eyed,
        Hugging the trunk; and its companion piece,
240   A gum-logged ant.

                    That Englishman in Nice,
        A proud and happy linguist: *je nourris*
        Les pauvres cigales—meaning that he
        Fed the poor sea gulls!

                    Lafontaine was wrong:
        Dead is the mandible, alive the song.

Here Shade boldly reverses La Fontaine's fable: while the ant is life-less, the cicada has flown away from its "empty emerald case." It still lives, it can still sing its song.¹ Since the ant trapped in gum and the empty cicada case that Shade sees on the day his aunt dies resemble the doom-laden objects Maud herself gathers and paints, his robust aphorism implicitly affirms Maud's own survival.

Of course he cannot *know* she survives, but from outside his world we can now see more. Shade's *"Life is a message scribbled in the dark. / Anonymous"* serves his own purpose as an image rich in resonant implication. To us, aware as we are of the message from dead Maud that Hazel jots down in the dark of the Haunted Barn, it also recalls the very evidence, which Shade has no way of seeing, that his aunt does somehow live on.² Shade's later conviction that his near-death vision of a "fountain" provides some kind of clue to death proves an illusion, and leads him to his artistic motto, "not text but texture." The direct message that the "fountain" seems to offer is wrong, and so, he claims here, with his customary structural stealth, is La Fontaine (French, of course, for "fountain"). Yet his reversal of La Fontaine, his implicit affirmation of survival after death, Maud's included, is itself only text, not texture.

But he does more than affirm. Between his initial observation of the cicada case and his aphoristic retort, Shade situates the *"cigales"* (cicadas) that an Englishman in Nice proudly supposes means "seagulls." He lets us assume that a mere association of sense and sound, cicada-*cigales*-seagulls, triggers this recollection, but when he describes the night of Hazel's death and refers again to the man feeding gulls, he discloses that Hazel was in fact conceived during this trip to the Côte d'Azur ("To the . . . sea . . . / Which we had visited in thirty-three, / Nine months before her birth"). Earlier in Canto Two, just after he recalls dedicating himself to exploring death's abyss, Shade announces, as if by the way, "Today I'm sixty-one. Waxwings / Are berry-picking. A cicada sings." But he in fact is very deliberately juxtaposing the waxwing of the poem's opening lines, which he imagines flying on after its death, with the cicada still to come, whose song he will declare remains alive.

He associates waxwings here with his birthday as he has earlier associated them with his own imagined death ("I was the shadow of the waxwing slain"). And just as he covertly links the seagulls-cum-*cigales* with Hazel's birth *and* her death, so he links the initial waxwing itself with Hazel's death—the "azure" of the windowpane in the opening lines anticipates the "azure" outside the Hawaiian bar, as the waxwing (a *cedar* waxwing) prefigures the patrol car whose headlights blaze "Across five *cedar* trunks" (P.485) when the police come to announce Hazel's fate—but also, implicitly, with her survival.

Although Shade cannot know of his aunt's or his daughter's survival after death, he not only affirms in his text his confidence that they have survived but also incorporates into the texture of his poem, from end to end, a pattern of winged creatures—waxwing, pheasant, grouse, mockingbird, seagull, cygnet, wood duck, bobolink, robin, "white butterflies," cicada, Red Admirable, Toothwort White, fat fly, cobra-headed moth, and "dark Vanessa with a crimson band"—that seem to suggest we do not so much fly into death as live on, fly on, like the waxwing, in its reflected sky.

When he feigns to digress as he recalls an apparently incidental *cigale,* Shade in fact pointedly insinuates Hazel into his ruminations on Maud's death and implicates her too in his affirmation that "Lafontaine was wrong: / Dead is the mandible, alive the song." Again, of course, he does not *know* of her survival, but we can see from our unique vantage on his world that on the day of his death, when he makes his last "reasonably sure" affirmation that she is "somewhere ... alive," another insect that has metamorphosed and flown away, the *Vanessa atalanta,* will fully justify his confidence. When he repudiates La Fontaine, he does not know that Hazel, transformed as it were from Toothwort White to *Vanessa,* will after all fulfill his wry revision of that other famous fable, as this "dingy cygnet" indeed turns in a sense "Into a wood duck." Shade's confidence in the detail and design of the natural world, and his ability to reflect them in the "link-and-bobolink" of his art, Nabokov intimates, will be even more richly vindicated than he can possibly know.

SHADE: RHYMES AND REASONS

A pattern of natural imagery, even with a supernatural implication—and the poem contains another such pattern in its trees[3]— still does not amount to the kind of deceptive design that "link-and-bobolink" would seem to promise when it couples an abstraction and a quite particular species of American bird. But like the "aloof and mute" players of the "game of worlds," Shade has other covert moves to make.

Bobo is a French nursery-word meaning "hurt," "sore," "pain" ("lit-tle hurt," Nabokov nicely glosses it in his notes to *Ada*).[4] The opening couplet of Canto One links Shade, an American bird, and a word that rhymes with "pain": "I was the shadow of the waxwing *slain* / By the false azure in the window*pane*." Toward the end of Canto One, an-other verse paragraph opens with a lightly modulated reprise that stresses the recurrence of the rhyme by incorporating its own internal rhyme, "I was the shadow of the waxwing *slain* / By *feigned* remote-ness in the window*pane*." The next verse paragraph begins the last movement of the Canto, the three paragraphs reporting Shade's fits as a child:

> A thread of subtle *pain*,
> 140   Tugged at by playful death, released *again*,
> But always present, ran through me.

The canto ends with a rhyme that echoes its opening couplet and the opening rhyme of its final movement:

> And though old doctor Colt pronounced me cured
> Of what, he said, were mainly growing *pains*,
> The wonder lingers and the shame *remains*.

At the beginning of Canto Two, Shade recalls deciding long ago

> to explore and fight
> The foul, the inadmissible abyss,
> 180   Devoting all my twisted life to this
> One task. Today I'm sixty-one. Waxwings
> Are berry-pecking. . . .

But even before this, the coupling of the "waxwing" and the double *slain/windowpane* and the *pain/again* and *pains/remains* rhymes in Canto One establishes that Shade's image of the waxwing is a con-scious poetic attempt to explore the beyond[5] in a way that responds, in a more deliberate and controlled fashion, to those first advance tugs of "playful death" in his childhood fits.

Shade ends his whole poem with another closing three-paragraph movement. He looks around him, looks back at the end of the day: "Gently the day has passed in a *sustained* / Low hum of harmony. The brain is *drained*. . ." The poem's first rhyme almost returns. It comes closer still to an exact reprise at the beginning of the last paragraph: "But it's not bedtime yet. The sun *attains* / Old Dr. Sutton's last two windowpanes." Then at the end of the paragraph, Shade returns all the way to the original rhyme:

> And through the flowing shade and ebbing light
> A man, unheedful of the butterfly—
> Some neighbor's gardener, I guess—goes by
> Trundling an empty barrow up the *lane*.

But the second line of the expected final couplet never appears. Tragically, he gets no chance to complete the "correlated pattern in [his] game."

But he has been able to extend it even further than we have seen. One particularly odd occurrence of the rhyme that obtrudes its own oddity:

> And I would hear both voices now and then:
> "Mother, what's *grimpen*?" "What is what?"
>   "Grim Pen."
> Pause, and your guarded scholium. Then again:
> 370 "Mother, what's *chtonic*?" That, too, you'd explain. . . .

As he recalls Hazel's query, Shade almost lets us glimpse his smile of appreciation at Eliot's turning the treacherous Grimpen Mire, where the villain of *The Hound of the Baskervilles* keeps his murdering hound, into a common noun. Yet it is a grim smile, for at the end of Conan Doyle's story Holmes's adversary sinks into the mire and drowns, as Shade knows Hazel, too, stepped "Into a crackling, gulping swamp, and sank."[6]

But the allusion, and the rhyme that contains it, disguises something else, for Shade engages with Eliot here in a way that shows that he knows in detail the poet he seems impatiently to dismiss.[7] The two adjacent couplets rhyming *then*/*Grim Pen*, and *again*/*explain*, as Kinbote's puzzled note highlights, draw attention to the strangeness of the American Shade's rhyming *again* with *explain* rather than with *pen*.[8] But the conjunction of *Pen* and *again* as rhyme words, albeit from different couplets, echoes a couplet from "The Waste Land":[9]

> 'That corpse you planted last year in your garden,
> 'Has it begun to sprout? Will it bloom this year?
> 'Or has the sudden frost disturbed its bed?
> 'O keep the Dog far hence, that's friend to *men*,
> 'Or with his nails he'll dig it up *again*.' (71–75)[10]

Eliot's note to these lines points us to Cornelia's dirge in Webster's *The White Devil*.[11] By appropriating Eliot's "grimpen," with its Sherlock Holmes allusion and its echo of what had seemed a supernatural, demonic hound, and then evoking a rhyme involving another gruesome dog and an allusion to Webster's "devilish" drama, Shade elegantly and wittily links Eliot's two most ambitious poems.

Eliot's *men/again* rhyme stands out in its unrhymed context in "The Waste Land," where the poet plays, as he will again in "Four Quartets," on the tension between occasional bursts of rhyme and a bulk of unrhymed lines. Shade seems to reply by showing how he can rejuvenate rhyme even within perfectly regular heroic couplets. In the foreboding, the allusion, and the uneasy rhyme, he seems ready to take on Eliot on Eliot's own terms.

The slight discord in the endings "Grim *Pen*" and an *"again"* rhymed with *"explain"* finds another echo when Shade later rhymes *"again"* with *"pane"*:

> ... And when we lost our child
> I knew there would be nothing: no self-styled
> Spirit would touch a keyboard of dry wood
650   To rap out her pet name; no phantom would
> Rise gracefully to welcome you and me
> In the dark garden, near the shagbark tree.
>
> "What is that funny creaking—do you hear?"
> "It is the shutter on the stairs, my dear."
>
> "If you're not sleeping, let's turn on the light.
> I hate that wind! Let's play some chess." "All right."
>
> "I'm sure it's not the shutter. There—*again*."
> "It is a tendril fingering the *pane*."
>
> "What glided down the roof and made that thud?"
660   "It is old winter tumbling in the mud."
>
> "And now what shall I do? My knight is pinned."
>
> Who rides so late in the night and the wind?
> It is the writer's grief. It is the wild
> March wind. It is the father with his child.

Shade returns to *again* rhymed in the English fashion in another nod to Eliot, since (as we noted glancingly in Chapter 10) these lines, with their game of chess and their edgy conversation about the wind, derive from Part II of "The Waste Land," "A Game of Chess":

> "What is that noise?"
>   The wind under the door.
> "What is that noise now? What is the wind doing?"
>   Nothing again nothing.
>
> . . . .
>
> "What shall I do now? What shall I do?" (117–31)[12]

Hazel's asking for an explanation of words from "Four Quartets" had prompted "Pale Fire"'s first back-and-forth conversation; here, the second conversational exchange again echoes Eliot and again rhymes *again* as "gain," but the "a-gain" marks a loss: with Hazel dead, the conversation can only be two ways now, not the "three-act play" of that night in the past.

Shade pays homage to the poetry of unease and the poetry of obtruded allusion that were perhaps the most emphatically new notes in the early Eliot, but adapts it to work within a coherent narrative context—Sybil's pain and anxiety a year after Hazel's death, on a night whose warm wind recalls the very evening her daughter died.[13] Quietly he argues for rhymes and the unbearably personal reasons of plot and against Eliot's insistence on distancing himself from rhyme and plot and personality.

SHADE: BEAUTY IN THE GLASS

Because of the rich fictive context of Shade's poem, because so much critical energy has been attracted by the relationship between poem and commentary and by the flamboyance of the commentary, too little attention has been devoted to the subtleties of the poem itself. Shade's modulating between the mundane and the magical and the prosaic and the poetic[14] in his "Four Cantos" seems a deliberate response to Eliot's alternating and opposing the rhymed and the unrhymed and the morbidly modern and the transcendentally timeless in his "Four Quartets." Against Eliot's "That was a way of putting it— not very satisfactory: / A periphrastic study in a worn-out poetical fashion,"[15] Shade sets his own "And if my private universe scans right, / So does the verse of galaxies divine, / Which I suspect is an iambic line." In place of Eliot's variations on rhyme and rhymelessness, Shade proffers his own always exact rhymes, sometimes recurring, sometimes misleading, often backed by a barrage of internal rhymes; rhymes that exploit the tension between the photic and the phonic, between calculation (numbers, dates) and incantation, between chat and chant ("The man must be—what? Eighty? Eighty-two? / Was twice my age the year I married you").

And in response to one striking passage in Eliot, Shade advances a counter-example that calls into question Eliot's fragmentariness, his eschewal of plot, his unintegrated allusions. Part II of "The Waste Land," "A Game of Chess," opens with the ornate picture of a woman seated before her mirror and her baroque perfumes:

> The Chair she sat in, like a burnished throne,
> Glowed on the marble, where the glass
> Held up by standards wrought with fruited vines
> From which a golden Cupidon peeped out
> (Another hid his eyes behind his wing)
> Doubled the flames of sevenbranched candelabra
> Reflecting light upon the table as
> The glitter of her jewels rose to meet it,
> From satin cases poured in rich profusion.
> In vials of ivory and colored glass
> Unstoppered, lurked her strange synthetic perfumes,
> Unguent, powdered or liquid—troubled, confused
> And drowned the sense in odours; stirred by the air
> That freshened from the window, these ascended
> In fattening the prolonged candle-flames,
> Flung their smoke into the laquearia,
> Stirring the pattern on the coffered ceiling.
> Huge sea-wood fed with copper
> Burned green and orange, framed by the coloured stone,
> In which sad light a carvèd dolphin swam.
> Above the antique mantel was displayed
> As though a window gave upon the sylvan scene
> The change of Philomel, by the barbarous king
> So rudely forced; yet there the nightingale
> Filled all the desert with inviolable voice

> And still she cried, and still the world pursues,
> 'Jug Jug' to dirty ears.
> And other withered stumps of time
> Were told upon the walls; staring forms
> Leaned out, leaning, hushing the room enclosed. (77–106)[16]

From the opening echo of Enobarbus's praise of Cleopatra in her barge,[17] the passage ironically redeploys centuries of images of poetic splendor,[18] but for all the stylishness of its heady glitter and intentionally disconcerting opulence, it remains a curiously detached bravura set-piece. Of course it serves as a contrast to the demotic language and setting of the pub scene in the second half of "A Game of Chess," in keeping with Eliot's method of fragmentation and juxtaposition, yet in view of its very limited resonance within the rest of the poem, it seems hardly warranted in its length. In editing the manuscript, even Ezra Pound, usually so sympathetic to Eliot's aims, wrote along the margin: "Don't see what you had in mind here."[19]

As if in reply, Shade offers another image of a woman before toilet items, another reworking of a famous set-piece of female beauty seated, another succession of echoes of the poetry of the past:

> A male hand traced from Florida to Maine
> The curving arrows of Aeolian wars.
> 410 You said that later a quartet of bores,
> Two writers and two critics, would debate
> The Cause of Poetry on Channel 8.
> A nymph came pirouetting, under white
> Rotating petals, in a vernal rite
> To kneel before an altar in a wood
> Where various articles of toilet stood.
> I went upstairs and read a galley proof,
> And heard the wind roll marbles on the roof.
> *"See the blind beggar dance, the cripple sing"*
> 420 Has unmistakably the vulgar ring
> Of its preposterous age. Then came your call,
> My tender mockingbird, up from the hall.
> I was in time to overhear brief fame
> And have a cup of tea with you: my name
> Was mentioned twice, as usual just behind
> (one oozy footstep) Frost.

Just thirty-five lines after dismissing "Four Quartets" as "some phony modern poem," Shade surely evokes Eliot here in "a *quartet* of bores" debating "The Cause of Poetry."[20]

Unlike Eliot, Shade integrates his allusions into a consistent narrative context that poignantly augments the ironies.[21] Sybil Shade has switched on the televison while waiting for Hazel to return from her date. But while recounting the start of this fateful evening, Shade also, like Eliot, engages in the dialogue of ancient and modern, of the poetry of the past and the prosaic realities of the present. In fact, by the time the Cause of Poetry program has finished, he has retraced the course of Western poetry from Homer through Pope to Frost.

In the first couplet he deftly appropriates classical myth for modern meteorological science, an ancient weapon for a modern chart, an old metaphor for the new everyday reality of the TV weather forecast. After watching the forecast (the warm winds marked by those "curving Aeolian arrows" have brought the thaw that makes it possible for Hazel to drown herself in the lake), Shade sits through the advertisement for some beauty product until its banality drives him to his study.

In just two quick couplets (as opposed to Eliot's extended description), Shade uses allusion to underscore the irony he sees in this pedestrian modern pantomime of would-be beauty. He draws on the scene and the language of Belinda's toilet in Pope's *The Rape of the Lock*:

> And now, unveiled, the *Toilet* stands display'd,
> Each Silver Vase in mystic Order laid,
> First, rob'd in White, the *Nymph* intent adores,
> With Head uncover'd, the Cosmetic Pow'rs!
> A heav'nly Image in the Glass appears;
> To that she bends, to that her Eyes she rears.
> Th' inferior Priestess, at her *Altar*'s side,
> Trembling, begins the sacred *Rites* of Pride. (1.121–28)[22]

The Eliot passage depends greatly on the mirror ("the glass . . . / Doubled the flames of sevenbranched candelabra"), while in the Pope lines from which Shade's "toilet" and "altar" derive, the mirror is the central fixture ("A heav'nly Image in the Glass appears . . ."). Shade's "altar" is presumably also a vanity, all the more absurd—and all the more typical of the soft-focus pseudo-appeal of television cosmetics advertisements—for being placed in the midst of a wood.

In evoking Pope,[23] Shade makes no simple opposition between past opulence and present decadence. Pope was already mocking the tastes and vanities of his time, and in echoing him Shade highlights the fatuous conventionalism of the commercial that promotes its new product with timeless—or rather timeworn—images. Worshiping the "*Cosmetic* Pow'rs" in private, Belinda had seemed absurd enough a quarter of a millennium ago; now a nation of viewers is supposed to join in the adoration of the cosmetics, an absurdity Shade intensifies by the delicious rhythmic and verbal flatness of "Where various articles of toilet stood" when we eventually arrive at the objects of veneration.

Again this ironic image of the vapidity of the modern world of television advertising, all the more prosaic for its attempt at visual poetry, has an ominous undertone to its triviality, for it is the very insistence on female beauty and grace which the advertisement typifies that will drive the uncomely and ungainly Hazel to her death (in fact by this stage of the poem, we already know that her blind date, on the point of entering the bar with her, has recoiled at the prospect of being seen with such a lousy catch). Shade ascends to his desk to read the proofs of his new book on Pope, checks a line from *An Essay on Man* (2.267) and the comment he has made on it, and redescends to hear himself mentioned "just behind / (one oozy footstep) Frost"—another image that foreshadows Hazel's imminent end.

Shade challenges Eliot with his own ironic adaptation of a famous poetic image of female glamour. Like Eliot, he incorporates in different ways the poetry of the past (the generalized Aeolian arrows, the specific words and scene silently lifted from *The Rape of the Lock*, the explicit quotation from the *Essay on Man*), but just as he motivates each allusion, and the different *kinds* of allusion, so he manages to juxtapose present and past, banality and supposed beauty, in a narrative context that holds in tension the ordinariness of the activity and the gathering oppressiveness of the situation.

He also manages to relate part to part in a way that draws strength from the narrative context. The one at least briefly protracted scene he shows of the Shades, parents and child, in some kind of harmony occurs on the night when Hazel asks about the words from Eliot's "Four Quartets," "a triptych or a three-act play / In which portrayed events forever stay" (P.381–82). In the segment of television viewing framed within the two references to the poetry program, Shade evokes a heartbreakingly ironic image of the timeless, and yet also very modern, adoration of female beauty that deliberately challenges Eliot's "A

Game of Chess," and in so doing stresses the contrast between that
night when Eliot brought all three Shades together and this night
when the parents, despite the attempted distraction of television, are
so anxiously conscious of their daughter's absence elsewhere. Then, a
year to the month after Hazel's death, a tense dialogue between Sybil
and John Shade recalls this fateful night of her death in a passage that
echoes—and pays tribute to—the passage in "A Game of Chess" into
which Eliot's set-piece leads.

A Brighter Shade: Pain and Gain

Shade has his own personal and poetic reasons for his patterns, his allusions, his rhymes. The "link-and-bobolink" that unites
the waxwing with all those echoes of *slain* and *windowpane* allows him
the very kind of texture he feels he needs in order to have his text not
merely describe but embody the mysterious design he detects around
him. In the "playing a game of worlds" passage he resolves to find
"some kind / Of correlated pattern in the game," and he does, in ways
that show that the pattern need not diminish the poignancy. But when
he says "It did not matter who they were. No sound, / No furtive light
came from their involute / Abode," we have reason to believe that it
does matter, and that Hazel herself has played a part in his patterns.
A year after Hazel's death, Shade reports, he expected that "no
phantom would / Rise gracefully to welcome you and me / In the
dark garden, near the shagbark tree," but the lines that immediately
follow tabulate the sounds in the night that disturb her parents' memories. From our vantage point, it seems likely by now that Hazel *is*
indeed already trying to contact her parents amidst the noises of this
unsettled night, and that when, another year later, Shade comes to record the occasion and writes, " 'There—again.' / 'It is a tendril fingering the pane,' " it is Hazel who prompts him to the echo of Eliot's "A
Game of Chess," and to the echo of the *a-gain* rhyme. She is again the
catalyst for her parents' talk, as she was, while still alive, in the passage that circles around "Four Quartets" and first draws attention to
the strangeness of a rhyme with *a-gain*.
It even seems as if Hazel, "no self-styled / Spirit" rapping out her
pet name, but a good deal more resourceful, here adds her signature,
as it were, to the two key episodes in the Zemblan story and their influence on her father. First she evokes the multiple overlay of chess

themes in the Zemblan tunnel episode by overlayering her parents' game of chess and Eliot's "A Game of Chess," after T. S. Eliot has been so closely associated both with her (*grimpen, sempiternal, chtonic*) and with her closeness in thought to Kinbote.[24] Then the equally exact echo of Goethe's "Erlkönig" recalls Charles II's flight over the mountains, during which the royal fugitive recites Goethe's poem,[25] and a cluster of images—Garh spurned by the King, the lake, the red reflection in the blue water, a shiver of ominous *alfear*—all recall Hazel left abandoned on her last night.[26]

These episodes that Kinbote presses on Shade, hoping his neighbor will write a "Solus Rex," instead produce "Pale Fire." By means of the tunnel episode, that childhood foretaste of an adult passage to freedom, with its odd intimations of a passage to the underworld, Hazel prompts her father to link his childhood fits, encased within those *pain/a-gain* and *pains/remains* rhymes, with his adult foray into death and his adult image of the waxwing dying yet flying on in the reflected sky, encased within the double *slain/windowpane* rhyme.

By means of the flight over Zembla's mountains, she seems even to supply her father with the essential ingredients of his poem's remarkable opening image, which he so consciously links with the night of her death, but without quite knowing from where his inspiration derives. Just as Shade imagines himself as the waxwing slain in the false azure, and then against all the odds somehow also living on, flying on in the reflected sky, so Kinbote imagines himself crossing the mountains: at first shuddering with fear, after he quits Garh, as he sees the lake reflecting a "deep-blue sky" and an elusive red streak, but then, as he crosses through the pass, feeling a wave of exhilaration and impending freedom in the bluest of all Zemblan blues. The morning had begun with the "very air . . . tinted and *glazed*"; he approaches the "limpid tintarron" ("a precious glass stained a deep blue," Index) of the mountain lake; at the pass, he looks north to "the final blue" and south to "a tender *haze*" and descends to the gulf and its "arching *blaze*" (C.149, 142–44). The "correlated pattern" of *-aze* sounds, like the emphatic blue in sky and lake, point back to Hazel and forward to the "azure in the windowpane" of the poem.

Kinbote presses the tunnel episode—the *solus rex* scene itself—on Shade with particular insistence. His importunateness that Shade should write a long poem highlighting this episode seems instead to trigger in Shade's mind the idea for a long poem that looks back over his own lifelong exploration, since those first childhood fits, of the

passage to death. Shade introduces those fits with the first oddly angli-
cized *pain/a-gain* rhyme, with no apparent local reason for the diver-
gence from the expected American pronunciation of "again." Those
exact rhyme syllables recur only once more, in the " 'There—*again*. / 'It
is a tendril fingering the *pane*,' " in a passage where the rhyme, the
Eliot subtext, and the chess echo both Hazel and the chess-laden episode of the tunnel, while the reference to the window's "pane" of
course echoes the poem's opening image.

Hazel's "pain" (P.350) led to her early death. Her father's "growing
pains," his childhood fits, were his first exploration of death. By transforming her pain into Kinbote's vision of panic and release as he
crosses the mountains into a blue blaze, she prompts her father to recall his childhood pains and helps him envision the radiant image of
the waxwing in the azure windowpane. And beyond him, as if indeed tapping at that windowpane, Hazel turns her old pain into an
unexpected gain.

In Zembla, land of reflections, Queen Disa not only stands as a
troubling reverse image of Sybil Shade, as spurned by her husband as
Sybil is loved by hers, but reflects at a still deeper level the Hazel who
now, as Red Admirable, in some way mirrors her mother. Disa, Duchess of Payn and Mone, echoes and in fact arises from the Hazel who
"hardly ever smiled, and when she did, / It was a sign of *pain*. She'd
criticize / . . . *and moan*" (P.350–55). Disa's anguish at being spurned by
Charles, though no more than a dream within a fantasy, touches us
deeply, and reflects the agony of Hazel's lifelong rejection. Yet Hazel
can also now inspire Kinbote with such pricelessly comic images as the
equally rejected Fleur de Fyler. Now, beyond death, she seems to smile
far more than she ever could in life, and indeed to radiate an extraordinary imaginative energy as she reworks the intensity of her old suffer-
ing into images of Kinbote's Zembla and thence back into her father's
Appalachia. As she plays with her "pain" from beyond the reflective
pane of death, she transforms it again and again into gain.

A Brighter Shade: Nymphs and Mirrors

As if aware that his death is imminent, Hazel offers her father through Kinbote an urgently sustained stream of inspiration. Yet,
for all that, Shade's poem depends ultimately on his own experience
and imagination, his own intuitions about the relationship of life and

death, his own sense of his need to imply even more through texture than he can state as text. He has his own reasons for his rhymes, and no confusion about his allusions. He knows that he wants to confront and challenge Eliot in a spirit of homage to Hazel and in criticism of what he sees as Eliot's false poetics and flawed metaphysics. But somehow through his aims and even through his very words Hazel finds her own.

Eliot has been associated with Hazel from her first inquiries about "Four Quartets" and from Kinbote's note about her mirror words:

> *Lines 347–348*: She twisted words
>   One of the examples her father gives is odd. I am quite sure it was I who one day, when we were discussing "mirror words," observed (and I recall the poet's expression of stupefaction) that "spider" in reverse is "redips," and "T. S. Eliot," "toilest." But then it is also true that Hazel Shade resembled me in certain respects.

Notice that we cannot be sure from this note that Hazel herself has also directly reversed Eliot's name. But notice also that this note immediately follows the note on the Haunted Barn and the text of Shade's "The Nature of Electricity," and immediately precedes the two notes that hint at Eliot as the target of Shade's "some phony modern poem," partly by way of the "then—pen, again—explain" rhymes. If Hazel while alive never twisted "T. S. Eliot" into "toilets," this woman, who now seems to inspire in Kinbote the image of the "land of reflections" (C.894) where "the tongue of the mirror" (C.678) is spoken, seems here to prime Kinbote to voice these words to her father.

At the point of Shade's Popean passage where he most directly challenges Eliot's allusive image of beauty in the glass, the image of the "altar . . . / Where various articles of toilet stood," we should now also note T. S. Eliot's name in reverse in *"toilet stood"*—and note that these "mirror words" stand right before the mirror, inviting us to read backward. Here, surely, speaks Hazel.[27] Among the words that Shade in his poem explicitly records Hazel reversing is "powder," which she turns into "red wop." A reporter who accompanied Nabokov in pursuit of butterflies in 1959, between his first idea and his final plan for *Pale Fire*, recorded him exuberantly reversing other words and then adding: "T.S. Eliot spelled backwards is toilets. You have to transpose the t and the s. Powder backwards is red wop! Red wop! Isn't that wonderful!"[28] Just as Hazel's "pot"-"top" deftly couples the pot and its lid, and her "spider"-"redips" evokes a spider dipping and redipping on its thread, so her "powder"-"red wop" calls up in a flash an immigrant anarchist planting a bomb. Nabokov's enthusiasm for the find he passes on to Hazel suggests that he intends to reveal behind her sullen taciturnity in life an intense, intricate inventiveness that then explodes into color after her death. And that is just what we see.

Throughout Zembla, mirrors are implicated in the four key images of women whom the King spurns or turns away from. The first and most immemorially beautiful is Fleur de Fyler, whom Charles upon awakening finds

> standing with a comb in her hand before his—or rather, his grand-father's—cheval glass, a triptych of bottomless light, a really fantastic mirror, signed with a diamond by its maker, Sudarg of Bokay. She turned about before it: a secret device of reflection gathered an infinite number of nudes in its depths, garlands of girls in graceful and sorrow-ful groups, diminishing in the limpid distance, or breaking into individ-ual nymphs, some of whom, she murmured, must resemble her an-cestors when they were young—little peasant *garlien* combing their hair in shallow water as far as the eye could reach, and then the wistful mer-maid from an old tale, and then nothing. (C.80, 111–12)

The old-fashioned "glass," the nymph, the image of timeless female beauty and multiplied reflections echoes both the Eliot passage from "A Game of Chess" (and how much more haunting and evocative than Eliot's long verse passage are these few lines of prose, for all their com-edy!) and the reflection of Eliot in the poem's "nymph . . . before an altar in a wood." Note, too, the "triptych" that recalls the "triptych or . . . three-act play" of the night when Hazel first asks about three words from "Four Quartets."

In the tunnel episode, the young Prince turns back from Iris Acht's door to retreat with his friend, just as on Hazel's last night Pete Dean recoils from the entrance to the bar and heads off, so he says, after his "chum." As king, Charles II returns and as it were turns into the Red King of *Through the Looking Glass* when he makes his way now right to Iris Acht's old door. Then, as he heads over the mountains, he encoun-ters Garh and spurns her a moment before being shaken to the core by what he thinks his own reflection in the "tintarron" of a mountain lake. When he escapes Zembla, he meets up with Disa on the Côte d'Azur. Kinbote here recounts the King's heartrending dreams, in which her image "forever remained exactly as she looked on the day he had first told her he did not love her. . . . The shock had fatally starred the mirror, and thenceforth in his dreams her image of him was infected with the memory of that confession as with some disease. . . . The gist, rather than the actual plot of the dream, was a constant refutation of his not loving her" (C.433–34, 209–10).

All these images of mirrors or reflections and women spurned or turned away from in Zembla, then, stand somehow behind the image of the nymph pirouetting before a mirror in a television advertisement that coincides with Pete Dean's recoil from the unlovely Hazel, and also behind that passage's mirror-reversal of Eliot's multiplied reflections of female beauty. Hazel may have died because of her unfortunate looks, but somehow she now seems to be able to make deep beauty out of her loss, in Kinbote's fantasy and in her father's poem.

Shade's Canto One starts with an extraordinary series of virtuoso mirror images far more original and resonant than the coldly glittering reflections with which Eliot opens "A Game of Chess." As we now know, Hazel herself, whom Shade deliberately implicates in the "azure" of the windowpane, lies behind the Alfin whose flying into death seems to inspire the waxwing image of Shade's line alpha. In Canto Two, as he records the night of his daughter's death, Shade stylizes a television advertisement so that, unlike his exordium, it refers to no explicit mirror, yet quietly reflects Eliot's reflections in "A Game of Chess" and Pope's mirror in "The Rape of the Lock." Pope's passage shows the beautiful Belinda adoring herself in her mirror, and Shade evokes it—painful irony, this—at the very hour Hazel is rejected for her drab looks.

But Hazel has herself inspired this image, signing herself into these lines with her characteristic "mirror words" as she reverses Eliot's name. And as the prime source of Zembla, it is presumably she who has previously prompted Kinbote to imagine his royal mother as Queen Blenda, as if to catalyze her father's imagination into recalling Pope's Belinda as a counter to Eliot's allusive image of beauty before a mirror. It is in a plane that he has named after his wife, Blenda IV, that King Alfin flies to his death. The connection between, on the one hand, Blenda and the Belinda behind the implicit mirror of the nymph in the wood, and on the other, the Alfin who inspires the waxwing that flies into a mirrored sky suggests that from the very start of her father's poem Hazel has been helping him answer Eliot.

Eliot's sense of the emptiness of his world leads him to reach desperately for the prop of religious tradition. For Hazel, too, life had also seemed chillingly ugly and empty, but now from the beyond she has found a fullness that she adds to her father's own trust in life's generous design. She helps him reply to Eliot's image of the sterility of glinting beauty in "A Game of Chess" with her own images of reflected beauty, in the dazzling reflections of the initial waxwing image and in the unassertive image of the mirror before the nymph in the woods. So tragically unattractive in life, a much happier Hazel, able now to find a richness even in her own earlier pain, gratefully offers to Kinbote the mirror-world of Zembla, and to her father, image after image of beauty multiplied by reflection.

Reversing Eliot's name in that line of her father's, Hazel's spirit signals that throughout "Pale Fire" she prompts her father to reflect, reverse, and outshine the "Four Quartets" that brought them together one rare night while she still lived. She ensures that Shade's poem has its beginning in its end, in the *Vanessa* who inspires him, in the lady of Lake Omega who leads him to Alphina, to Alfin, to the waxwing, in the line 1000 that leads back to line 1. She ensures in ways that even her father cannot imagine that in *his* four cantos the world of timelessness will intersect time, end will lead back to beginning, in a way far more thrilling and inventive, far more skeptical and yet more magical, than in the postured probing of Eliot's "Four Quartets."[29]

13.

From Zembla to Appalachia:
The Contrapuntal Theme

Resolving the Echoes

It is little wonder that *Pale Fire* ripples with echoes if Hazel has reflected and reversed her own experience, as recorded at the tragic center of "Pale Fire," into Kinbote's Zembla, and shaped Zembla in turn so as to inspire her father. Yet there are many echoes within the novel—perhaps the most resonant of all—that remain unaccounted for.

When he prepares multiple problems for his readers, partly intersecting, partly independent, Nabokov cannot know which problem any individual reader will solve first.[1] As it happens, this next solution was the first I arrived at after rejecting the Shade-as-sole-author hypothesis, but I have deferred it until now both because it belongs at the end of the story, and because it now seems to me that, for anyone not as wedded to the Shadean hypothesis as I had been, the discovery of Hazel's presence in the *Vanessa* would be a more likely first solution. Of course by this late, "synthetic" phase of solving *Pale Fire*'s problems, one solution can easily raise another problem that becomes easier itself to solve because of the solutions already reached. Readers who have followed the argument to this point may well have asked themselves: "But if Hazel is alive after death, what of Shade himself?" After all, although he has felt the pain of Hazel's loss for more than two years, Shade has been obsessed his whole life with the thought of death looming ahead and with the urge to explore the abyss beyond it. He even starts "Pale Fire" by metaphorically projecting himself beyond death, flying on in the azure of the windowpane. *Does* he get to live on, fly on, within *Pale Fire*'s reflected sky?

To pose the question this way seems almost to expect a positive answer by return. Yet Shade dies at the very end of the Commentary. How could we possibly *know* if he had somehow passed beyond death? I propose we step back from the answer we already have to the question of Hazel's survival, and the further question and answer about Shade's survival that it invites, and return to the key problem that besets us from an early stage of reading *Pale Fire*: why do poem and commentary echo each other in so many ways, when they are so preposterously disjunct? At first I and others advocated seeing Shade as the author of the whole text, but while that interpretation respects the intensity of the poet's urge to probe the beyond, it also lapses into incoherence. Others suggested instead that after reading "Pale Fire" Kinbote adjusts his Zembla story to fit the poem more closely, yet he himself laments the lack of connection between Appalachian poem and Zemblan *romaunt*. And indeed, given that he has thrust Charles II's story on Shade as the ideal subject for his next poem, the Zemblan story in the Commentary cannot merely be Kinbote's response to his reading what that poem turns out to be: "Pale Fire," not the "Solus Rex" he expects. Alfin the Vague's vagueness, Fleur de Fyler's languid sexual siege, the King's escape through the tunnel and over the mountains, and his Côte d'Azur meeting with Disa are central to the saga Kinbote offers Shade before he ever reads "Pale Fire."[2] Without his compulsion to saturate Shade with his story, and his disappointment at finding it absent from the poem, most of the dynamics of the Kinbote-Shade relationship, the dominant human relationship in the novel, would vanish.

But almost half—40 percent—of the Matter of Zembla concerns not the King's escape but the assassination attempt against him. All that, all the Gradus material, all the Shadows, the Niagarin and Andronnikov and Izumrudov scenes—must be new, must have been added to the escape story since Shade's death. And that makes all the difference, just as it turned out to make all the difference that Kinbote's Zemblan fantasy itself did not begin until after his arrival in Dulwich Road, New Wye. In Nabokov, attention to the world of time is the key to the world of timelessness.

The man who kills Shade appears to be Jack Grey, escapee from an Institute for the Criminal Insane, who wants to kill the judge who sent him there. Kinbote claims to have heard from Grey that he is really Jakob Gradus, Shadow and would-be-regicide, but his virtually self-refuting evidence ("I did manage to obtain, soon after his detention, an interview, perhaps even two interviews, with the prisoner" [C.1000, 299]) carries no conviction whatever in the face of the official Jack Grey version of events. But the Gradus story swells in Kinbote's mind until it expands the Zembla theme to fill almost half the Commentary. Despite Kinbote's integrating the Gradus story into the Commentary from the first, it must all be a recent invention. Before Kinbote's interview or interviews with Grey, if it or they ever took place, there is no indication in either the Zemblan escape story or even in his account of his night terrors in New Wye that he had any notion that there existed such a group as the Shadows. Although we can see Kinbote as paranoid, although we witness his night terrors of persecution in the solitude of his New Wye home, there is never any hint of an assassination threat, never a modulation from the key of triumph, in all the Zemblan story that he thrusts upon his neighbor.

Yet it is precisely the story of Gradus's pursuit, not the escape story, that is most uncannily resonant with the poem: what Kinbote has added to the Matter of Zembla since Shade's death, not what he had tried to have Shade immortalize in verse: Gradus as a "Shadow" who kills Shade in the note to line 1000, "I was the shadow of the waxwing slain," and Gradus as glass-maker and his reflection as Sudarg of Bokay, "mirror-maker of genius."

What is particularly striking about the Gradus material is that it is so elaborately and insistently counterpointed with Shade's composition of the poem: "We shall accompany Gradus in constant thought, as he makes his way from distant dim Zembla to green Appalachia, through the entire length of the poem, . . . steadily marching nearer in iambic motion . . . moving up with his valise on the escalator of the pentameter . . . while Shade blots out a word" (C.17 and 29, 78); "the force propelling him is the magic action of Shade's poem itself, the very mechanism and sweep of the verse, the powerful iambic motor" (C.131–32, 136). This seems even more surprisingly strange when we note that "Gradus," according to Nabokov's well-thumbed Webster's Second, is short for *Gradus ad Parnassum*, "title of a dictionary of prosody, poetical phrases, etc., once used in English schools as an aid in Latin versification; hence [*not cap.*], any similar dictionary designed to aid in writing Greek or other poetry."

And stranger still if we note that *Gradus ad Parnassum* is also the title of Johann Fux's celebrated 1725 treatise on counterpoint, which laid the basis for musical counterpoint over the next two centuries. For Shade's poem offers itself and is seen by Kinbote as a signal example of literary counterpoint, in several ways: on the verbal level, in the counterpointing of sound and sense; on a narrative level, in the synchronization of Hazel's last night out and her parents' night at home; and on the level of idea and intention, when after the "fountain"/ "mountain" disappointment Shade writes:

> But all at once it dawned on me that *this*
> Was the real point, the contrapuntal theme;
> Just this: not text, but texture; not the dream
> But topsy-turvical coincidence,
> 810   Not flimsy nonsense, but a web of sense.
> Yes! It sufficed that I in life could find
> Some kind of link-and-bobolink, some kind
> Of correlated pattern in the game,
> Plexed artistry, and something of the same
> Pleasure in it as they who played it found.

Kinbote particularly admires and singles out for praise Shade's verbal counterpoint, what he calls Shade's "combinational turn of mind" (F, 15), his "special brand of combinational magic" (C.727–728, 253), "a third burst of contrapuntal pyrotechnics" (C.734–735, 254), or "an apotheosis crowning the entire canto and synthesizing the contrapuntal aspects of its 'accidents and possibilities'" (C.830, 262).

Unlike the rest of the Zemblan story in the Commentary, which is characterized by Kinbote's opportunistic seizing on chance words ("I could make out": "By the end of May I could make out the outlines of some of my images in the shape his genius might give them" [C.42, 80]), the Gradus theme is carefully orchestrated throughout. Gradus's pursuit of the King is synchronized with Shade's composition of the poem; his image becomes less and less distant, and Kinbote's narrative access to him more and more complete, as he approaches the scene of the killing, so that by the time he is flying to New Wye from New York, Kinbote can take us into Gradus's "magenta and mulberry insides" (C.949/2, 278). Why can someone whose self-control is so often vulnerable shape his Commentary with such care in this one respect? And why is the shaping so insistently associated with Shade's composition of the poem? Why is it so emphatically in the counterpoint singled out as the hallmark of Shadean style?

Why too, for that matter, is Shade so pointedly gray? In the time covered by the novel, he is sixty, then sixty-one, and it is hardly surprising that he has gray hair, but there is something less than casual about the "abundant gray hair" (F, 20) of "my gray-haired friend"

(F, 28), whom Kinbote addresses as "you bad gray poet, you!" (C.12, 74), and whom he describes, at the very moment he is shot at by Grey or de Grey, as "gray-locked" (C.1000, 294). Why does Shade not only have the same birthday as Gradus or de Grey, but also a name that can mean the same as Gradus's other alias, Degree?[3] Why all this on top of the identification of the man who kills Shade as a Shadow, when Shade has written "I was the shadow of the waxwing slain," or on top of Jakob Gradus's trade as a glass-maker, and his mirror-reversed image as a "mirror-maker of genius," maker of mirrors of a special sky-blue tint that seem to reflect directly the azure reflections of the opening of Shade's poem?

Jakob Gradus seems a fantasy Kinbote constructs, after Shade dies, out of the name and deed of Shade's killer, Jack Grey. Kinbote of course wants to make this murderer part of his Zemblan world, and has no interest whatever in linking him with Shade: the whole point of the forty-plus pages he devotes to Gradus is that Gradus was out to get *him*, not Shade or Goldsworth. In view of the fact that the correlations cannot reflect Kinbote's intentions, and in view of the fact that only the Gradus elements of the Zembla story unmistakably form in Kinbote's mind after Shade's death—in view of the extraordinary association of Shade and someone as unlike him as Gradus, and in view of the fact that only the Gradus parts of the Commentary exhibit a conscious control and craftsmanship that is alien to Kinbote's usual practice but exactly reminiscent of Shade's, I suggest—I suggested, even before seeing Hazel's role after death—that we are invited to see here that Shade's shade, his ghost, influences Kinbote's paranoia in such a way that his developing fantasy about Jack Grey takes shape as the Gradus story, which is then through Shade's unrecognized guidance shaped into a complex narrative counterpoint to the composition of the poem.

CORROBORATION

Such a solution to the problems posed by the intricate interplay of poem and commentary appears less astonishing, even if still quite unforeseen, to someone who has followed the case for Hazel's large part in the story after her death: Shade joins forces with Hazel, adding to all she has helped Kinbote invent, weaving his counterpoints around her mirror-reversals, working with her in a way they never could manage in life. But for the reader who arrives *first* at this solution, as I did, and has not yet registered the signs of Hazel's survival, Nabokov needs to supply more corroboration than Shade's—and his own—persistent preoccupation with the beyond.

More evidence of Shade's hand in Gradus will emerge, but Maud's message in the Haunted Barn of course offers an internal parallel that anyone in a position to reach this solution will surely have found. A painter fascinated by images of doom, she delivers, in ominous daubs of light, a note of dire warning about Shade's death. After his own death, Shade's much more blithe spirit, by contrast, appears to turn the approach of his death into another occasion for the exercise of *his* art. Just as Maud's predilection for portents of woe and her corrupted speech are reflected in her attempted admonition, so Shade's characteristic fondness for combinational magic and counterpoint, especially in his last poem, seems to find its unrecognized outlet in the Gradus parts of the Commentary.

If Maud offers one immediate internal parallel, Nabokov supplies an even closer parallel through a one-word allusion. Kinbote at least has at hand the text of the "pada ata lane" message in the barn, though he can make nothing of it. But he cannot locate accurately enough an allusion that nevertheless points *us* to another case of communication between the dead and the living. In glossing Shade's "Stilettos of a frozen stillicide," he recalls having encountered "stillicide" (which means, according to Webster's Second, "a continual falling or succession of drops; now esp., the dripping of rain water from the eaves; eavesdrop") "for the first time in a poem by Thomas Hardy" (C.34–35, 79). The Hardy poem, we discover, is "Friends Beyond," in which the speaker tells of those resting in the local cemetery:

> They've a way of whispering to me—fellow-wight who
> yet abide—
> > In the muted, measured note
> Of a ripple under archways, or a lone cave's stillicide:
>
> "We have triumphed: this achievement turns the bane to antidote,
> Unsuccesses to success. . . ."[4]

Since Kinbote is unable, as usual, to remember exactly *where* in this particular poet's work the word occurred, Nabokov can refer us here, behind Kinbote's back, to another work in which a mortal speaker communicates with the beyond. Behind Kinbote's back, because unlike Hardy's speaker, Kinbote remains unaware of the communication, unaware that his Gradus fantasy is as it were "*S*'s contribution" to the

Commentary, as his own fabricated variants are "*K*'s contribution" to Shade's poem. Kinbote then closes his note, with his habitual compulsiveness, and—perhaps with the wry help of his own "friend beyond"—with a suspicion of Gradus: "We should also note the cloak-and-dagger hint-glint in the 'svelte stilettos' and the shadow of regicide in the rhyme" (C.34–35, 79).[5]

But *we* should also note something else in the "svelte / Stilettos of a frozen stillicide." In his Commentary, Kinbote exclaims: "How persistently our poet evokes images of winter in the beginning of a poem which he started composing on a balmy summer night! . . . My dictionary defines [*stillicide*] as 'a succession of drops falling from the eaves, eavesdrop, cavesdrop.'. . . The bright frost has eternalized the bright eavesdrop." As Kinbote sees, Shade's image evokes icicles on eaves, and the insistent "drop . . . drop . . . drop . . . drop" in his Commentary also helps to evoke the opening scene of "The Vane Sisters," in which the narrator, a professor of French, out walking on a bright day after snow, stops "to watch a family of brilliant icicles drip-dripping from the eaves of a frame house. So clear-cut were their pointed shadows on the white boards behind them that I was sure the shadows of the falling drops should be visible too. But they were not. The roof jutted too far out, perhaps, or the angle of vision was faulty, or, again, I did not chance to be watching the right icicle when the right drop fell."[6] The professor's curiosity about the bright eavesdrops leads him past the house where Sybil Vane's lover, D., used to live; at dinnertime, realizing he has wandered far from his usual way, he eats at a chance restaurant, and as he leaves, he lingers a moment on the street to notice the unusual effect of neon lighting on the shadow of a parking meter. At that moment D.'s car stops outside the restaurant, and D. emerges. Recognizing the narrator "with an exclamation of feigned pleasure," he chats and soon casually divulges the fact of Cynthia Vane's recent death. In bed that night, the professor feels uneasy, disturbed by his memories of Cynthia Vane's belief, after Sybil has committed suicide because of D., that her sister's spirit was somehow present as an aura around her. Though he dismissed Cynthia's theory, the professor cannot sleep until dawn, when he finally slips into a dream from which he wakes

> trying hard to unravel something Cynthia-like in it, something strange and suggestive that must be there.
>
> I could isolate, consciously, little. Everything seemed blurred, yellow-clouded, yielding nothing tangible. Her inept acrostics, maudlin

evasions, theopathies—every recollection formed ripples of mysterious meaning. Everything seemed yellowly blurred, illusive, lost.[7]

This final paragraph in the story, read as an acrostic, discloses, unbeknownst to the narrator: "ICICLES BY CYNTHIA. METER FROM ME, SYBIL." In other words the dead women have guided his footsteps to where he would hear of Cynthia's death, so that he would brood on her and Sybil and on Cynthia's hunch about Sybil's aura. Even his very statement of his conviction that he can find nothing of Cynthia in his dream proves to be a message from the dead women.

In *Pale Fire*'s "svelte / Stilettos of a frozen stillicide," then, Nabokov evokes not only Hardy's "Friends Beyond" but also his own "The Vane Sisters."[8] When *The New Yorker* rejected "The Vane Sisters," Nabokov had to explain the acrostic and the point of the story to his editor, Katharine White, and added: "Most of the stories I am contemplating ... will be composed on these lines, according to this system wherein a second (main) story is woven into, or placed behind, the superficial semitransparent one."[9] When "The Vane Sisters" was at last published in *Encounter*, just the year before Nabokov began *Pale Fire*, he had the magazine alert readers to some sort of puzzle in the story, and in the next issue explained its solution and point. When he has *Pale Fire* allude simultaneously to Hardy's poem and his own story, he plants a crucial clue.[10]

Hardy's speaker knows the "friends beyond" are talking to him; in "The Vane Sisters," the professor does not know that the dead sisters are talking not only to him but through him. Cynthia was an artist whose work was much appreciated by her sister's professor, and the icicles she arranges to lead him on reflect both her taste for visual minutiae and his. Shade was a poet whose work Kinbote has long admired, and the counterpoint Shade appears to develop further through Gradus was the feature that Kinbote especially lauded in his poetry. Cynthia in life was curious about the beyond, as Shade was in his much more sophisticated way, and from the beyond both as it were now extend the special features of their art through the thoughts and words of an individual in some way attuned to their work while they lived.

Just as Kinbote reports the "pada ata lane ..." that Hazel scribbled down in the Haunted Barn but fails, despite all his efforts, to construe what it is or what it spells, so the narrator of "The Vane Sisters" fails despite all *his* efforts to construe the message of the sisters. The French professor prides himself on his unusual visual discernment, but cannot see who has been signaling to him through the shadow-and-shine play he records. Kinbote prides himself on his responsiveness to poetry, and to Shade's verbal counterpoint in particular, but cannot detect what lies behind the counterpoint he now introduces into the Commentary. His "stillicide" note occurs just a few lines after the note that begins "By an extraordinary coincidence (inherent perhaps in the contrapuntal nature of Shade's art) our poet seems to name here (gradual, gray) a man, whom he was to see for one fatal moment three weeks later" and that boasts of the counterpoint Kinbote will arrange between Gradus's approach and Shade's composing his poem; the "stillicide" note ends with Kinbote's self-satisfaction in spotting a "cloak-and-dagger hint-glint in the 'svelte stilettos' and the shadow of regicide in the rhyme," without his realizing *why* he feels so pleased to detect in the poem signs of a Gradus that he knows Shade could not have known.

In the other cases of influence from the beyond in Nabokov's fiction, in "The Vane Sisters," in *Ada*, in *Transparent Things*, the mortals who receive the attentions of the dead remain unable to detect them, no matter how hard they seek them, no matter even if they are looking in the right place, like Hazel and Kinbote both attempting to decode a message in the light in the Haunted Barn. Within his fictional worlds, Nabokov "never disregards the limits of the knowable,"[11] but from outside these worlds, in our position as rereaders, in the increasingly timeless relation to the novel's time we gain as we reread, he allows us eventually to see what the characters within the novel—or we ourselves when we first enter their time—could not possibly glimpse.

Nabokov does all he can in *Pale Fire* to keep the dead Shade's intrusion on the mortal world, so much subtler and more complex than Maud's, and with so much less time to develop than Hazel's, hidden and yet ultimately discernible. He arranges after all for "Pale Fire" to be *posthumously* published, to focus repeatedly on the idea of survival after death, and to be written by someone called Shade, a perfectly English word (one of whose meanings is of course "the soul after its separation from the body"), but not otherwise an English surname. He had made Shade seem the unsurprising one, but the New Wye poet who says "Life is a great surprise. I do not see why death should not be an even greater one" (C.549, 225) turns out to offer a much greater surprise than Zembla's king.

ON TO LINE 1000, BACK TO LINE 1

Let us focus on the hours around Shade's death to see just how great a surprise it must be for him. He breaks off his poem, saying to Kinbote: "I have here [indicating a huge pregnant envelope near him on the oilcloth] practically the entire product. A few trifles to settle and [suddenly striking the table with his fist] I've swung it, by God" (C.991, 288). To judge by the symmetry of the cantos, he has been planning a thousand-line poem, and in the course of this last day's work, he has found both a title and an ending. Noting, as he glances back over his career, that he has passed beyond titles lifted from other writers' lines, he now pretends to lapse back into old ways from sheer haste when he steals the phrase "pale fire" from Shakespeare. But as we saw in Chapter 2, his title toys with the very idea of the purloined title by stealing from Timon's denunciation of universal thievery, and at the same time, through the imagery of reflection in Timon's speech, reflects again the bright optical after-image of the reflections in his own initial lines. At the end of his poem, Shade wants to answer its highly wrought beginning with a slow dissolve into the subdued harmonies around him. At the same time, by virtue of the *Vanessa*, with its crimson-barred wings, he can close the poem with a visual echo of the opening—the red streak on a waxwing's wings. The harmonies gently gather, as "the flowing shade and ebbing light" (P.996) again draws on the tide-and-shine imagery from the *Timon* passage, while not interrupting the "sustained / Low hum of harmony" (P.963–64) of his close. No wonder Shade is pleased with the way the end of his poem is working out.

And yet it doesn't seem quite to have ended. The poem is in heroic couplets throughout, and the 999th line has no matching rhyme. Shade declares in the penultimate verse paragraph:

> I feel I understand
> Existence, or at least a minute part
> Of my existence, only through my art,
> In terms of combinational delight;
> And if my private universe scans right,
> So does the verse of galaxies divine
> Which I suspect is an iambic line.
> I'm reasonably sure that we survive

> And that my darling somewhere is alive,
> As I am reasonably sure that I
> 980   Shall wake at six tomorrow, on July
> The twenty-second, nineteen fifty-nine.

After equating the design of his verse and his universe like this, Shade would utterly undermine his serene confidence in the deep concord in things—which he plainly seeks as his poem's final note—were he to leave the last rhyme unfinished. He must surely plan one more line to round the poem off.

But as he accepts Kinbote's invitation for a drink and walks across the lane to the Goldsworth house, he is shot and killed by an intruder. He has asserted that if his private universe scans right, so does the verse of galaxies divine, but suddenly the rhyme is broken off forever, his confidence cruelly mocked, and the meaningless rift of a grotesque death substituted for the promise of continuity and harmony.

His poem seems doomed to remain forever unfinished, yet *if* his imagination survives and prompts Kinbote to declare line 1000 a return to line 1, and then to incorporate the poet's death in a note to that line, if he prompts Kinbote to imagine his killer as Gradus, and to synchronize the approach of unexpected death with the composition of the poem, Shade will now see that his poem spirals round from the couplet broken off at line 999 to a richer significance than he could ever have planned. "I was the shadow of the waxwing slain / In the false azure of the windowpane" can now mean more than he ever intended, when Shade brings the Shadow Gradus to life in Kinbote's mind, Gradus the glazier, whose very element seems to be glass, and who flies his way steadily closer throughout the Commentary. Shade's imagination now lives on in this blue world of the beyond more vividly than even he could have foreseen. Or to put it another way, the very completion of his life and work comes only in their incompleteness as seen from the here and now: the death that breaks off his masterpiece ensures its unimaginable completion. The catastrophic interruption of death turns out to be the perfect ending and the perfect new beginning.

Shade closes the antepenultimate paragraph of his poem:

> Maybe my sensual love for the *consonne*
> *D'appui*, Echo's fey child, is based upon
> A feeling of fantastically planned,
> 970   Richly rhymed life.

Presumably he would have liked to end the whole poem with a *consonne d'appui*;[12] if the next line after line 999 reads "I was the shadow of the waxwing slain" it will indeed have that *consonne d'appui* (the *l* of "lane" and "slain"), and it will indeed disclose a "fantastically planned, / Richly rhymed life."

If we were alert, we should have detected a joke in the opening line of the novel even on a first reading, in "a poem in heroic couplets, of nine-hundred ninety-nine lines." The joke became much more acrid when on rereading we remembered *why* Shade can never complete that last couplet. But now it turns into a much more redemptive surprise as we see how the last line, which only his death can write, stands as proof of a design far beyond any even Shade could have suspected.

Instead of the cold blast of skeptical irony that Shade's murder at first seems to release, a flood of radiant positives now courses through the poem. He had written of his hunch that he could find the answer to his lifelong quest in "the contrapuntal theme; / Just this: not text, but texture," and in "Playing a game of worlds" (P.807–19). Although he had built his own counterpoint of sound and sense into the poem, and played a game of worlds in the counterpoint he devised for Hazel's last night, he can now see that his own life and work have been shaped as moves in some much more sublime game of worlds. And he can now approach still closer to the design behind life by adding the Gradus theme to Zembla: he can create a far thicker texture, in the interplay of commentary and poem, around his original mortal text, devise a far more poignant counterpointing of creation and apparent annihilation, play a far ampler "game of worlds," as he moves Gradus step by step closer through "spacetime" (C.209).[13]

The Point of the Counterpoint

We can see the new meaning in Shade's old work if, by adding Gradus to Kinbote's Zembla, he can in death write line 1000 by rewriting line 1 in an almost infinitely expanded way. But why else would Shade after death *want* to prompt Kinbote's imagination to add the Gradus theme?

At one level his intervention reflects his kindness in mortal life. Kinbote has believed in his special relationship with Shade for no more reason than that Shade has tolerated his eccentric, intrusive, megalomaniac neighbor, has listened to him, has even broken off the intense work on his composition of the poem to take a walk with his distressed companion, and has recognized both the desperation and the creativity in Kinbote's Zemblan fancies (C.629, 238). All the same, this kindness could not extend to composing a major poem at Kinbote's imploring; inspiration cannnot simply be summoned at the bidding of others. Shade had to compose the poem he did for his own human reasons, although from his new vantage point he can see now that it has also been shaped by powers beyond him. Now, as he in turn helps Kinbote from the beyond with the Gradus story, the much closer access he has to his old neighbor's mind allows him to appreciate the extent of his desperation, and to offer him a consolation for the fact that the long poem he worked on through July was *not* the "Solus Rex" Kinbote expected. Satisfying Kinbote's endless and urgent need for importance, suggesting new "evidence" that he can advance to confirm his supposed centrality, Shade keeps him from suicide a little longer by offering him a way of tightly relating Zembla to the poem he wrote that *then* could *not* reflect Zembla, and specifically of integrating the Zemblan elements retrospectively with the very composition of "Pale Fire."

In prompting Kinbote's imagination, Shade, like his daughter, forces nothing in Kinbote's soul—or to put it another way, he can work only with the materials available: Kinbote's obsessive desire for attention and admiration that deep down he knows he does not deserve, his persistent sense of persecution, and his flair for prose despite his incompetence as a poet. Shade can develop the Gradus theme, can turn his killer Grey into a surreptitious Zemblan assassin, through Kinbote's tendency to see the world as focused on himself. Like Hazel, he does not drive Kinbote into madness—Kinbote is already there—but provides him with some sense of control, at least so long as he writes, over the forces he thinks are pursuing him. Only when he ends the last note of the Commentary, when he records Gradus's death, does Kinbote again feel the acute alarm he seems for months to have held at bay.

By developing Kinbote's Zembla in his own unique way, by setting up the elaborate counterpoint of Gradus and the composition of the poem, Shade also helps Kinbote—always in awe of him as an artist—to become as much of an artist as he can, to impose a much tighter form than he can manage elsewhere on the obsessions filling his mind. In this sense Shade says thank you to Kinbote for appreciating the contrapuntal aspects of his art, just as in "The Vane Sisters" the narrator's admiration for visual minutiae in Cynthia's paintings determines the way she and Sybil guide him to the point where he will meet the man who can tell him of Cynthia's death. Now, accompanying Kinbote as he writes the Commentary, he can also provide his old neighbor with something of the close companionship Kinbote had craved from him but that had been impossible between them in life.

In helping Kinbote formulate and integrate the Gradus story into the Commentary, Shade can also perfect his own art and take it to a new plane. He can retrieve from the chaos under which the Commentary threatens to submerge the poem an order, a shape, a mounting tension, despite all Kinbote's manic impulsiveness. He can confirm the "contrapuntal theme," the interplay of life and death, that he had sensed in mortal life and himself now join the "game of worlds" by promoting Gradus's advance. And he can acknowledge his much deeper awareness, from the other side of the mirror, of the "combinational delight" behind things, his recognition that his life and art have been patterned by forces beyond him, and in just such a way that they could reach their perfect completion only in his death.

Shading in the Detail

Shade's "contrapuntal art" was what first suggested that the extraordinary links between Shade and Gradus could be explained by his having shaped the Gradus theme. But there are other aspects of his art, his search for "Some kind of link-and-bobolink, some kind / Of correlated pattern in the game," that we can also find in the Gradus notes. In the previous chapter, we noted the patterns that he quietly weaves through his poem: the images of winged creatures, the rhymes linking *pane* and *pain*. Now he playfully extends these personal signs into his contribution to the Commentary.

Take *pane/pain* first. Shade makes Gradus, as if to fit the opening images of the poem and the initial "window*pane*" rhyme, a glazier, who is assigned his mission to kill the ex-King Charles at a meeting of the Shadows in Onhava's Glass Works. Gradus adores glass animals (C.697), makes a glass eye for his mistress (C.949[2], 276), and claims "to have improved the glitter and rattle of the so-called *feuilles-d'alarme* used by grape growers and orchardmen to scare the birds" (C.171, 152). We learn of his "re-paning a broken window and checking for the new government the rare Rippleson panes in one of the ex-royal hothouses" (C.697). But the "panes" become associated with "pain" in the repeated references to the Glass Works explosion, and the "frightful disfigurement" of an apparent victim (C.149, 145; cf. C.80, 112; C.433–434, 209), or in Gradus's attempt to "castrate himself" after his wife leaves him, with the result that he is "laid up at the Glassman Hospital with a severe infection" (C.697, 253).

Shade's resourcefulness in incorporating the Gradus theme according to the patterns of his own art, yet without in the least impinging on Kinbote's character, can be seen in the initial reference to Gradus, in the first note in the Commentary, in the way he simultaneously introduces both the contrapuntal rhythm and imagery of wings or flying. He places Kinbote's chaotic impulses at the service of his concealed control, when Kinbote reports his "temptation to synchronize a certain fateful fact, the departure from Zembla of the would-be regicide Gradus," with the date Shade began the poem, but concedes that Gradus "actually . . . left Onhava on the Copenhagen plane on July 5" (C.1–4, 74). Later Shade improves on Kinbote's crass attempt to establish synchrony by having him record that Gradus is assigned his orders to kill the King "at 0:05, July 2, 1959—which happens to be also the date upon which"—and even the very minute that—"an innocent poet penned the first lines of his last poem" (C.171, 151). But by having the note to line 1 end with Gradus on the Copenhagen plane, he has also introduced immediately, in parallel with the image of the waxwing aloft, the first of a flock of images associating Gradus and flight.

Kinbote declares that "Although Gradus availed himself of all varieties of locomotion—rented cars, local trains, escalators, airplanes—somehow the eye of the mind sees him, and the muscles of the mind feel him, as always streaking across the sky with black traveling bag in one hand and loosely folded umbrella in the other, in a sustained glide high over sea and land" (C.131–132); ironically, he then continues, unconscious that he is disclosing more than he thinks: "The force propelling him is the magic action of Shade's poem itself, the very mechanism and sweep of verse, the powerful iambic motor." Again and again we catch glimpses of Gradus walking "towards a Russian commercial plane" (C.181, 157), "flying west" (C.209), having "flown from Copenhagen to Paris" (C.286, 174) or "landed at the Côte d'Azur airport" (C.697, 250), ordered to "take the earliest available jet to New York" (C.741, 255), or "walking aboard a jetliner" at Orly airport, "fastening his seat belt, reading a newspaper, rising, soaring, desecrating the sky" (C.873). In parallel to the last day of Shade's composing the poem, which will end with the image of the *Vanessa*, Kinbote describes Gradus as he flies toward New Wye: "We can at last describe his tie, an Easter gift from a dressy butcher, his brother-in-law in Onhava:

imitation silk, color chocolate brown, barred with red. . . . We can even make out (as, head-on but quite safely, phantom-like, we pass through him, through the shimmering propeller of his flying machine, through the delegates waving and grinning at us) his magenta and mulberry insides" (C.949^2, 277–78). The Index identifies the tie under "*Vanessa, the Red Admirable . . . caricatured, 949*," and its colors are indeed those of the crimson-barred butterfly that Shade uses to answer the waxwing at the start of his poem, as he uses it to end this series of images of Gradus flying that began in note 1 with the Zemblan ally of the waxwing and Gradus on the Copenhagen plane.

SHADES OF SELF

The *Vanessa*, of course, brings someone else to mind. After his death Shade presumably detects not simply the astonishing depth of unsuspected design woven into his life and art but also the identity and achievement of one particular designer: his daughter. Not only does he find her "somewhere . . . alive," but he discovers how much she has flourished, and how much she has furnished him, since she died.

As a poet he had played a game of worlds in the counterpoint he devised for Hazel's last night, but now beyond death he can see that she has been playing an equally tender and far more astonishing game of worlds with him. If, even beyond her, some ultimate designer has set the limits of the board on which Shade's life and death would be played out, and provided in Kinbote and Grey the necessary "ivory unicorns and ebon fauns," Shade can now see how Hazel has made the most of the possible moves available. She has inspired Kinbote with his visions of Zembla, and through him has offered her father the impetus for his last and greatest poem, adding her own shadings to his most individual marks, his "link-and-bobolink," his paned rhymes and winged images, and fluttered before him in the form of a *Vanessa* to offer him the end he needed for his poem.

In life she had been morose and remote. Although her bedroom had stood beside her father's study, anything like the scene where she called out for help with "Four Quartets" was a precious rarity. Shade could sense the force of her imagination ("She had strange fears, strange fantasies, strange force / Of character," P.344–345) but rarely had any inkling of her thoughts. Now beyond death she explodes with the creative energy she could find no outlet for in life, and sends a shock wave of belated love toward her father, filling him with a poetic fire that only his death can quell. And now, beyond death himself, Shade adds his Gradus to her Zembla, in admiration for the beauty of her achievement and in gratitude for the generosity of her inspiration.

Nabokov has too much sense to permit us any direct glimpse of Hazel's or her father's consciousness once they pass through death: we cannot see past Zembla's "land of reflections," even if we detect the Shades somehow living on behind the azure. But by allowing us to register the dead Hazel's influence on her father and his neighbor and the dead Shade's additional influence on Kinbote, Nabokov suggests how the transformation and even reversal of the conditions of human consciousness in death might underlie life in extraordinary and unfathomable ways.

He also has the sense not to show Shade reunited with his daughter in the hereafter. He manages to imply the transcendence of personality, without the *loss* of personality, in the transition through death, by revealing nothing of the impenetrable beyond but only its effects this side of death. In mortal terms Kinbote exists in desperate if self-inflicted isolation, yet after their deaths Hazel and her father seem able to feel for him and see with him as they transform his sorrows into a brief blaze of recollected triumph. In life Hazel herself had been difficult and unresponsive, yet now in death she works in instinctive harmony with her father as they intercalate Gradus's approach and Charles II's escape.[14] Somehow Hazel and her father seem to permeate the barriers that once separated them from each other and from Kinbote, and yet to retain their own predilections (her fondness for mirror-reversals, her sensitivity to women spurned; his penchant for counterpoint and control, his patterns of pane and wing), while at the same time allowing Kinbote's personality its amplest possible expression.

Freedom and Design

At first it might seem an affront to human autonomy and dignity to find that our lives enacted moves made by forces above us, however "aloof and mute." Yet although few prize their personal independence as much as Nabokov, his instinct at a moment of rare ecstasy was to feel "a thrill of gratitude to whom it may concern—to the contrapuntal genius of human fate or to tender ghosts humoring a lucky mortal."[15] Like his maker, Shade too feels it not demeaning but liberating to imagine his life as a game played from above. As a poet, he tries to find "something of the same / Pleasure in it as they who played it found," by treating his own life, even the tragedy of Hazel's death, as moves in the game of his art. Once he passes through death, he can detect how Hazel's "tender ghost" humored him while he remained a "lucky mortal," and can then combine with her to humor Kinbote in turn.

In one sense, Shade's shaping Gradus within Kinbote's mind marks a new stage in his own creative expression, as well as the perfect resolution of the masterpiece he could not finish in life. But even this free move of his newly metamorphosed mind has itself been designed by some "contrapuntal genius of human fate" far beyond the plane on which he and Hazel now exist. Just as the dead Aunt Maud foresaw years earlier the danger to Shade if he crossed into Goldsworth's with a man from a foreign land, as an *atalanta* fluttered by, so the dead Hazel seems to have foreseen a year before his father's death that she would be there as an "old friend" at "Number nine-hundred-ninety-nine," at the moment he took his all-but-completed poem next door and met his doom. Now, as Shade exercises his new freedom to infiltrate and animate Kinbote's imagination, he cannot help seeing that even this has all been foreseen and in fact inscribed in detail within "Pale Fire." He had imagined himself in the "reflected sky" of the poem's opening lines, and now he finds himself playing the "shadow of the waxwing" in the azure skies of a "land of reflection." He had declared that he was ready to become in death "a floweret / Or a fat fly, but never, to forget"; now in death he enters into the mind of the "pansy" (violet) or the "botfly" Kinbote.[16] He had innocently written of himself shaving as he composed in his head:

> and up the steep
> Incline big trucks around my jawbone creep,
> And now a silent liner docks, and now
> Sunglassers tour Beirut, and now I plough
> Old Zembla's fields where my gray stubble grows,
> And slaves make hay between my mouth and nose.
>
> *Man's life as commentary to abstruse*
> *Unfinished poem.* Note for further use.

940

As Shade's mind roams freely here while he shaves, the white layer of lather on his face turns him from the Beirut sun to suggest the snowy wastes of the remote north, an image he gives a local habitation and a name by way of his beloved Pope ("At Greenland, Zembla, or the Lord knows where," *An Essay on Man*, 2.224). In his "Zembla," in other words, Shade makes no allusion to Kinbote, since he has far too much tact to refer to the fancies of his troubled neighbor—but now after death he finds himself bringing Jack Grey to life in Zembla, and in the commentary to his own unfinished poem. Yet far from being appalled at the way even his most creative acts and freest fancies disclose a deeper design somehow working through him, he seems to sense an infinite tenderness behind it all, prompting his imagination to the utmost, taking care of his present with an eye to what will come, in a way that not only permits but promotes his freedom.

Just as the Shades find their scope beyond death vastly enlarged, not diminished, by the part they play in some still ampler purpose, so their influence in Kinbote's life only augments *his* freedom. Hazel's images of women spurned kindle Kinbote's imagination to blaze with his own lurid comic light. Shade, always a disciplined craftsman, imparts to the Commentary a control, a rhythm and a direction it would otherwise have lacked, yet nothing curbs Kinbote's rich independence. Indeed, vainglorious as ever, Kinbote cannot help drawing attention proudly to the artistry of *his* counterpoint ("We shall accompany Gradus in constant thought, as he makes his way from distant dim Zembla to green Appalachia, through the entire length of the poem, following the road of its rhythm, riding past in a rhyme" [C.17 and 29, 78]; "Never before has the inexorable advance of fate received such a sensuous form" [C.131–132, 136]; "I have staggered the notes referring to him in such a fashion that the first . . . is the vaguest while those that follow become gradually clearer as gradual Gradus approaches in space and time" [C.171, 152]) in a way that owes nothing to Shade's modesty and restraint. Commenting on Shade's intercutting events on the night of Hazel's death, Kinbote, ironically, writes with condescension: "The whole thing strikes me as too labored and long, especially since the synchronization device has been already worked to death by Flaubert and Joyce. Otherwise the pattern is exquisite" (C.403–404, 196). Yet his next note begins immediately with an absurdly highlighted and clearly unwarrantable synchronization of Gradus's and Shade's combined approaches to line 1000: "On July 10, the day Shade wrote this, and perhaps at the very minute he started to use his thirty-third index card for lines 406–16, Gradus was driving in a hired car from Geneva to Lex" (C.408, 197). The note ends almost six pages later with Kinbote again spotlighting the synchrony: "From far below mounted the clink and tinkle of distant masonry work" above Lex " . . . and John Shade took a fresh card" (202). Even inspired by the Shades, Kinbote remains his uniquely self-satisfied self.[17]

In having Kinbote picture Gradus crossing from Zembla to America, Shade offers him for the first time the chance to play his own small game of worlds, and to imagine from another point of view than his own. But in a sense Kinbote fails this challenge, for in handling Gradus he simply continues to glorify his own image at the expense of someone else. Indeed his crassly—and comically—ungenerous orchestration of Gradus serves to define by contrast the creativity and discreetness, the solicitude and sympathy, and the tender respect for free individuality that Hazel shows toward her father, Hazel and Shade toward Kinbote, and the designer beyond toward them all.

Depicting Hazel on the night of her death, in the tragic counterpoint at the center of his poem, Shade records only fragments of conversation recalled from the horrified discussions that followed her suicide, or details generic to any winter scene. He may choose to relay the evening as a miniature game of worlds, but since Hazel, after all, is a human being like him, he respects her independence and her mystery, and refuses to presume that he knows her mind. But when Kinbote depicts Gradus, as far as he knows also his fellow creature—after all, he seems not to recognize that the Gradus he only imagines is anything but the true identity of the Grey he encounters—he acts like a petty god to a wretch infinitely below him. Instead of the sensitivity and stimulus Hazel and her father offer those they influence, Kinbote gleefully minimizes Gradus's humanity, freedom, and dignity: "Mere springs and coils produced the inward movements of this clockwork man" (C.171, 152); "the chimpanzee slouch of his broad body"; "Morally he was a dummy pursuing another dummy"; "our 'automatic man' . . . this argument necessitates, I know, a temporary granting to Gradus of the status of man . . . our half-man was also half mad" (C.949[2], 277–79). In recounting Gradus's approach, he exults in his narrative control, drawing attention to his artistic ingenuity in having Gradus's image come gradually into focus the closer he brings him to his goal, until by the time the assassin wings his way toward New Wye we are allowed to see right into the turmoil in his insides (C.171, 152;

C.949^2, 277). Kinbote gloats over his power to describe circumstances that he insists Gradus barely notices ("He had never visited New York before; but as many near-cretins, he was above novelty" C.949^2, 274), and even when he deigns to concede he can register a few details, he cannot avoid gleeful condescension: "Gradus . . . could make out, with some help from his betters . . . " (C.408, 202). He rejoices in Gradus's humiliation, unhappiness, and pain throughout life, savoring with particular relish and unsparing detail his stomach troubles on the day of the killing and his explosive visit to a toilet in Wordsmith's Campus Hotel.

Shade's characteristic images and structures determine Gradus's outline—the contrapuntal rhythm, the *pane-pain* patterns that fix his profession, the flight imagery that establishes his trajectory—but nothing impinges on Kinbote's freedom to fill it in as he wishes. Shade offers him a chance to extend himself, to step outside himself as he plays a game of worlds with Gradus, but Kinbote fails to carry on the chain of generosity. Unlike Shade, always searching for ways to transcend himself, Kinbote remains comically, insufferably, pricelessly his selfish self—and we would not want a world where he could not remain so, no matter how little we might wish him for a neighbor—as he uses his freedom only to gloat at Gradus's limits and to glory in his own power to surpass them.

CHANGE OF KEY

Ghost stories are nothing new in fiction, but nobody makes them as central, as serious, or as funny, as Nabokov. And nobody before him has written ghost stories that show the dead saying so much to the living, or saying so much *through* the living, or remaining so unheard. Certainly, no one else has written—and surely no one else has ever imagined—ghost stories where the ghosts remain unseen by every reader, and even by most rereaders. Nabokov heightens the irony and the implications still further when he insinuates an unnoticed message from the beyond into the very words in which a character denies the presence or possibility of such a message. That irony structures the whole of "The Vane Sisters," but as we saw in the previous chapter, it recurs too in "Pale Fire," in the passage that runs from Shade's "when we lost our child / I knew there would be nothing: no self-styled / Spirit would touch a keyboard of dry wood / To rap out

her pet name," through the Eliotesque sounds of the haunting wind, to
"'Let's play some chess.' . . . 'And now what shall I do? My knight is
pinned.'" But Nabokov also repeats the irony in Kinbote's Commentary, and in a very different key.

We began this chapter with echoes that we more or less consciously
detect at an early stage of *Pale Fire* but that haunt us because we cannot
resolve them; let us end it with echoes no one seems to have noticed or
lingered over, in an apparently inconsequential scene that plays lightly
over the themes of the last few chapters: the sources of inspiration for
"Pale Fire," communication between the dead and the living, the game
of worlds.

However artistically and philosophically complex and rigorous the
metaphysics Nabokov develops within *Pale Fire*, it is never far removed from his sense of the deep playfulness of things. A misprint
promises Shade corroboration for the vision that itself promised so
much in his deathlike trance, yet when his hopes prove misleading,
when it seems the fates have merely led him some merry chase, that
very recognition leads him to his "point," his "contrapuntal theme."
When, after his death, he threads the Gradus theme into the fabric of
Kinbote's fancy, Kinbote's taunting treatment of Gradus proves far
less benign—and far funnier—than the *fountain-mountain* fiasco. But
even as Kinbote in turn leads Gradus a merry chase, we can see Shade
playing a game of worlds with *him*, signaling to him in the very lines
of the Commentary where Kinbote reports that he has wished in vain
for some sign from his friend.

Nabokov loved and imitated magicians from his childhood,[18] and
knew how to divert our attention or to lull us into discounting clues.
When Kinbote writes in the note to line 286, "If two secret agents belonging to rival factions meet in a battle of wits, and if one has none,
the effect may be droll; it is dull if both are dolts. I defy anybody to
find in the annals of plot and counterplot anything more inept and
boring than the scene that occupies the rest of this conscientious note"
(177), it should be a sign to the experienced reader of Nabokov to
watch closely what his hands are doing.

While Kinbote echoes "pale fire" several times within his Commentary, Shade echoes it only once in his poem: line 286, "A jet's pink trail
above the sunset fire." Ever eager to be acknowledged as Shade's inspiration, Kinbote overlooks the echo of the title but comments immediately that like Sybil, whose responsiveness to her world Shade is cel-
ebrating here, "I, too, was wont to draw my poet's attention to the

idyllic beauty of airplanes in the evening sky." Then comes the swift transition: "Who could have guessed that on the very day (July 7) Shade penned this lambent line (the last line on his twenty-third card) Gradus, alias Degré, had flown from Copenhagen to Paris, thus completing the second lap of his sinister journey!" (174).

The scene that follows describes the meeting between Gradus and Oswin Bretwit, a Karlist (a staunch Karl the Beloved loyalist) to whom Gradus has been instructed to offer a cache of old Bretwit family letters in return for the chance of being put in contact with the fugitive King. This is the first scene in which Gradus speaks, and since Oswin Bretwit dies in an operation the day after this scene, Kinbote's "evidence" for what happened would have to be entirely Gradus's. In recounting the scene, Kinbote drips with sarcasm at the "Shadows' neat plan" (175). The scene has insistent overtones of a chess problem, but a bungled one. Bretwit is an avid solver of chess problems; his very name means "Chess Intelligence" (180: German *Schachbrett*, "chessboard" and English *wit*), and the two members of his family whose letters he is offered by Gradus have first names Zule and Ferz, meaning, according to the Index, "chessrook" (311) and "chessqueen" (305: Russian *ferz*).

Once he has set out the positions of the trap, Kinbote breaks off with a tribute to Oswin Bretwit:

> From beyond the shining corrugations of the ocean I salute here brave Bretwit! Let there appear for a moment his hand and mine firmly clasping each other across the water over the golden wake of an emblematic sun. Let no insurance firm or airline use this insigne on the glossy page of a magazine as an ad badge under the picture of a retired businessman stupefied and honored by the sight of the technicolored snack that the air hostess offers him with everything else she can give; rather, let this lofty handshake be regarded in our cynical age of frenzied heterosexualism as a last, but lasting, symbol of valor and self-abnegation. How fervently one had dreamed that a similar symbol but in verbal form might have imbued the poem of another dead friend; but this was not to be . . . Vainly does one look in *Pale Fire* (oh, pale, indeed!) for the warmth of my hand gripping yours, poor Shade! (176–77; ellipsis in original).

"Pale, indeed!": Kinbote here pointedly echoes the title of Shade's poem, in a note to a line that, although he does not realize it, shows Shade himself echoing "pale fire." His tribute to Bretwit "from beyond the shining corrugations of the ocean" offers a symbol of male friendship "over the golden wake of an emblematic sun" that also echoes (and again without his awareness, since he does not know Shade's source) the image of broken reflections off the sea that completes the circle of theft in Timon's speech. Kinbote then calls up in contrast to his own image of lofty male friendship an image of "frenzied heterosexualism" in an airline ad that reminds us yet again of the "jet's pink trail above the sunset fire" that he has not registered as an echo of "pale fire"; and, addressing the dead Shade, he laments that such a symbol of male friendship across a vast gulf is not echoed in "Pale Fire."

Yet we have good reason to think that in a sense it is, that all the echoes he does not catch show Shade extending, as it were, a hand from the beyond to Kinbote, allowing his commentator to steal "Pale Fire" and to get as much light from the poem as he can in the course of his Commentary. Shade writes in his poem of wanting to play "a game of worlds, promoting pawns / To ivory unicorns and ebon fauns" (P.807, 819–20), and in this chess-filled note more pointedly and playfully than anywhere else, he now takes his turn. For although Baron A., the Shadow whose father-in-law has the family letters that Baron A. hopes will provide the key to the problem of contacting the King, proves to be dismally wrong—the letters are insufferably dull, already published, and not the originals but a scribal copy—his name provides Shade, that master of contrapuntal structure, with a key move. For the "A., Baron, Oswin Affenpin, last Baron of Aff,[19] a puny traitor, 286" introduced here opens the Index—how could he not, with that name?—so that a Zemblan Shadow in the first line of the Index matches the position of Shade's "I was the shadow of the waxwing slain" in the first line of the poem, just as the unfinishedness of the last entry to the Index matches the unfinishedness of the last couplet of the poem.[20]

Although the letters prove useless, Gradus asks obliquely how he can reach the King; Bretwit thinks, "How obtuse of me! He is one of us!" Since any Karlist agent revealing himself to a superior "was expected to make a sign corresponding to the X (for Xavier) in the one-hand alphabet of deaf mutes" (179), Bretwit's own left hand involuntarily starts prompting Gradus. "On the several occasions Bretwit had been given it, the manifestation had been preceded for him, during a moment of suspense—rather a gap in the texture of time than an actual delay—by something similar to what physicians call the aura, a strange sensation both tense and vaporous, a hot-cold ineffable exasperation pervading the entire nervous system before a seizure. And on this occasion too Bretwit felt the magic wine rise to his head." The "gap in the texture of time" and the "aura" recall both Shade's childhood fainting fits and his adult near-death-experience, those moments that had seemed so packed with inconclusive promise, but nothing comes clear here either:

> "All right, I am ready. Give me the sign," he avidly said.
>
> Gradus, deciding to risk it, glanced at the hand in Bretwit's lap: unperceived by its owner, it seemed to be prompting Gradus in a manual whisper. He tried to copy what it was doing its best to convey—mere rudiments of the required sign.
>
> "No, no," said Bretwit with an indulgent smile for the awkward novice. "The other hand, my friend. His Majesty is left-handed, you know."
>
> Gradus tried again—but, like an expelled puppet, the wild little prompter had disappeared. Sheepishly contemplating his five stubby strangers, Gradus went through the motions of an incompetent and half-paralyzed shadowgrapher and finally made an uncertain V-for-Victory sign. Bretwit's smile began to fade. (179–80)

Kinbote had wished for a symbol of his friendship with Shade, and thinks he has none; Bretwit wishes for a sign from Gradus, and, despite prompting, receives none. But the "shadowgrapher" and the "V-for-Victory sign" suggest that Gradus's failure might be read another way, as Shade's shadow writing himself in, and asserting victory from beyond the grave: even if Kinbote cannot decipher the message, even if Shade knows he will fail, Shade sends him a signal by way of the very moves he puts Gradus through.

Aunt Maud's manifestations as poltergeist and as a portent in the Haunted Barn only disturb and frustrate. Hazel also finds that to try to signal her presence to her father too directly—as when she has Kinbote repeat some of her "mirror words"—only startles and disconcerts. By being far more oblique, by way of Kinbote's "land of reflections," she can offer her father much more, even though he cannot know *who* is the real source of his unprecedented inspiration. Beyond death, Shade, with his still greater imaginative resourcefulness, seems to have found in Gradus a way to set up a haunting fugue of echoes to signal *his* presence, to send out the kind of message from behind death that he himself would so much have liked to detect in life. Sublime egoist that he is, Kinbote comically overlooks the signs, ignores the echoes, even at their most playfully reflexive, but *through* him, we can detect these haunting intimations from an early stage in our reading of *Pale Fire*. For a long time they do little but haunt us, inviting us to look closer. And if we do—and because we remain outside this world—we can eventually decode the signals Shade sends through the Commentary's most pointed counterpoint or through its seemingly most pointless asides.

I4.

"Pale Fire," Pale Fire, pale fire:
The Spiral Unwinds

SPIRALS, SYNTHESES, AND SOLUTIONS

In *Pale Fire* the process of discovery awaiting the Shades and the reader retraces the spiral that Nabokov describes in *Speak, Memory*.[1] John Shade's positives form the first, thetic arc, the serene confidence at the end of his poem in his waking up tomorrow, in his surviving beyond death, in the harmony of galaxies divine. The second arc, the antithesis, the negative counter-curve, corresponds to his murder and its consequences, his uncompleted poem, his travestied life and work and death. In his discussion of the chess problem in *Speak, Memory*, Nabokov describes how in this antithetical stage he entices the would-be-expert solver toward a "fashionable avant-garde theme." The same stratagem recurs here in *Pale Fire*, in the savage irony, the metaphysical debunking, as Gradus's and Kinbote's mayhem undercuts Shade's sense of order.[2] In the third arc the poem continues from line 999 to line 1000 by spiraling back to the beginning, in a sustained explosion of positive ironies that suggests an afterlife might transform even what looks like maximum meaninglessness into a synthesis of radiant sense. Within Shade's life, his confidence in the beyond could never be justified. But from the outside, it is perhaps that very frailty and unfinishedness of mortality that allows for the munificence of the pattern that he can see from beyond.

The confidence that through one's art one can understand the design hidden behind life and death might be completely misplaced, or true in a richer way than one could possibly imagine. Nabokov admits that his own confidence, even more robust than Shade's, could be as misplaced as Shade's appears to be at the moment he is killed. Yet the very possibility of design as concealed, as complex and as confounding as all that he packs into the small compass of *Pale Fire* suggests it might well be possible that there is deliberate design behind our world that we cannot yet see.

Some readers still read Nabokov only as far as his negative irony, his trenchant ability to deflate, to register disappointments, humiliations and horrors, the kind of thing that they think demonstrates his scorn and *Schadenfreude*. As his Hermanns and his Humberts and his Paduks and his Graduses indicate, Nabokov is anything but blind to the darkness in life. But readers who stop there, and think that *he* stops there, in modernist irony or in a postmodernist *abîme*, miss altogether his positive irony, his attempt to encompass all the negatives, as he suspects life itself does, and reverse their direction in the mirror of death. The search for that possibility is what makes Nabokov different, and what makes him write.

Creator and Creature

Shade, too, has an intimation of "the verse of galaxies divine," of something deeply artful—something that ensures every detail has its place and point—concealed behind the apparent accidents of his world. Knowing that he needs to test that intuition against the least tractable parts of his own experience, he makes "Pale Fire" an examination of his thwarted search for something beyond life, and of the greatest sorrow in his life, the event he would have been *least* likely to plan, the suicide of his daughter. He plays a kind of game of worlds with his own quest and his daughter's fate, in the structural symmetries of the poem, in the counterpoint of Hazel's last night, in the camouflaged patterns of image and rhyme. Despite the frustration of his quest and the irreparability of his daughter's loss, he does succeed in demonstrating an order and harmony in his life—until death's brutal breach suddenly shatters his symmetries. Yet Shade discovers beyond death that this very interruption allows him both to see himself as part of a design more perfect than he could have hoped for, and to play a game of worlds more gratifying than he ever could in life.

Shade finds in death that even his most powerful and personal poetry already bears the signature of presences beyond him. In the opening couplet of "Pale Fire," he creates an image with immediate impact for us all; at the same time, however, he covertly alludes not only to his parents and daughter but also to himself as craftsman, as Daedalus, the fabulous "old artificer" (as Joyce calls him) who flew to freedom on wax wings of his own making; and simultaneously, he also initiates the personal patterns, the winged images and paned rhymes, that will surreptitiously shape his poem. Yet he discovers after death not only the influence of his dead parents and daughter, in these lines that had seemed so decidedly his, but also the design of some artificer infinitely beyond him, who has determined that he would die with his poem unfinished, only to spiral back and complete it, along death's ampler arc, through the image of Gradus and the note to line 1000.

Of course from outside the world of the novel we know the identity of this ultimate artificer, the designer of this labyrinthine "Daedalian plan" (C.810). Shade may choose the Latin "Gradus" for Jack Grey, a small step from De Grey or Degree, but behind him it is Nabokov who also knows that the word means "degree" in Russian. Perhaps it is Hazel who, in fostering Botkin's fantasy of himself as Zemblan Kinbote, has reversed the syllables of his name, but it is the Russian author behind her who knew Botkin as a distinguished Russian name, and saw in the English "botkin" and "kinbote" extraordinary opportunities for concealed authorial design.[3] And of course it was not Shade, but the author who invented him, who chose *his* singular name and his singular fate.

After writing his most luminous lines, Shade dies and discovers in these very lines the signs that he has himself been directed by forces beyond him, yet discovers also that this allows him to control things in a richer way than before, and to do so by allowing Kinbote to shape things in turn in a way richer than *he* ever has. If this pattern in any way reflects how things really are—and this is the implication of Shade's discovery of a deeper truth behind life and death—would this not suggest that Nabokov in his turn, in shaping Shade, finds his own moves made by forces beyond him? Or is the possibility that our world forms part of a cascade of worlds within worlds more metafiction than metaphysics, reflecting not so much life, or what lies behind it, as the mere inclinations of ingenious art?

Just as Shade tests his intuition of an art behind life against the one event in his own life least amenable to any notion of generous design, so too, surely, should Nabokov. Indeed, Nabokov himself had already suggested as much in his earlier work. In *The Gift*, Fyodor expresses his own intuition about an artful design behind life by playing a rather bumptious fate in his biography of the real nineteenth-century novelist Nikolay Chernyshevsky—and then realizes that that is not enough. Only when he tests his idea against his own experience, only when he can trace a consistent pattern of solicitous fate through a life that seems to swarm with frustrations, only when he can show that the very frustrations and losses and clutter of his existence may themselves constitute the evidence of a generous design, can he hope to make his case. And by the time he realizes this, at the very end of the novel, *we* suddenly recognize that, from the very first, he has indeed woven into the chaos and constriction of his life the evidence of an unexpectedly fulfilling design that we had been utterly unable to see. But Nabokov would need to take the experiment one step further, surely, to look in this way at his *own* life, not a fictional one? And indeed that is just what he does in his autobiography. As he explains himself, he planned *Speak, Memory* according to the way his life "had been planned by unknown players of games."[4] What may appear a rather loose series of reminiscent essays incorporates and conceals a plethora of submerged patterns—including patterns of poignant loss—that to the attentive eye unexpectedly surface and converge at the very end, in such a way as to suggest an infinitely tender plan behind time and a promise beyond it.[5]

In *Pale Fire*, too, Nabokov, like Shade, tests *his* intuition against the things in his life he would have been least likely to choose, had he been able to design his fate. Just as Shade shapes his account of his life around the worst loss he had to suffer, so Nabokov constructs *Pale Fire* around his own losses and fears: as a father and son, he transmutes his fears for his son's life into Shade's grief for his daughter's death, and recasts the bungled assassination in which his father was shot as the killing of Shade himself; as an exile, he mourns with Kinbote his enforced escape from the distant northern land whose language and landscape were indeed once his to command. Somehow, he manages to turn a father murdered and a homeland lost into the keys to a radiantly munificent design.

And just as Shade finds that at the very point where he signs himself most assuredly into his work, other signatures are already there, so Nabokov, too, both inserts his signature under Shade's and lets us glimpse his sense of wonder at the signs already written into *his* life in ways he never planned. When he has Shade evoke a bird flying into the azure in a window and yet flying beyond as if into eternity, he also makes Shade commemorate his dead parents and daughter, and express an oblique hope for their survival; but at the same time he conjures up his *own* father. Nabokov is rightly renowned as a master sentence-maker, and many concur that perhaps the finest sentence he ever wrote is the one ending the first chapter of *Speak, Memory*. According to the timeless Russian ritual of tossing someone in the air to express gratitude, peasants who have asked and been granted a favor by Nabokov's father hurl him skyward:

> From my place at table I would suddenly see through one of the west windows a marvelous case of levitation. There, for an instant, the figure of my father in his wind-rippled white summer suit would be displayed, gloriously sprawling in midair, his limbs in a curiously casual attitude, his handsome, imperturbable features turned to the sky. Thrice, to the mighty heave-ho of his invisible tossers, he would fly up in this fashion, and the second time he would go higher than the first and then there he would be, on his last and loftiest flight, reclining, as if for good, against the cobalt blue of the summer noon, like one of those paradisiac personages who comfortably soar, with such a wealth of folds in their garments, on the vaulted ceiling of a church while below, one by one, the wax tapers in mortal hands light up to make a swarm of minute flames in the mist of incense, and the priest chants of eternal repose, and funeral lilies conceal the face of whoever lies there, among the swimming lights, in the open coffin.[6]

As I point out elsewhere, "despite the generalized nature of the church scene that materializes beneath the sky's blue vault, Nabokov in fact anticipates here . . . the day he looks down at his father lying in an open coffin. . . . [E]ven as Nabokov envisages the funeral, he also half-affirms his father's immortality: 'like one of those paradisiac personages who comfortably soar. . . .' But style cannot charm the facts away: the body still lies there motionless in the church, the candle flames swim because of the tears in young Nabokov's eyes."[7] Here Nabokov depicts his father flying against an intense blue sky, as seen through a window, in an image that then shifts to intimations of immortality, of perpetual flight, before dropping down to the pain of mortal loss, by way of the wax tapers, as he anticipates the day he will look down at the body of his murdered father. A decade later, when he has Shade evoke *his* parents through a waxwing that dies hurtling against the azure, but that he can imagine flying on in the reflected sky, he also evokes his own autobiography's way of coping with the loss of the father he loved. And if behind John Shade's tribute to his parents and to Hazel in his opening lines we can see the influence of the dead Shades, perhaps, Nabokov implies (as he had in *The Gift*),[8] these lines also inscribe the influence of his own dead father on himself.

If the opening lines of "Pale Fire" dazzle from the first, yet prove more imbued in otherworldly inspiration and implication than even Shade could see, another passage of the poem, apparently quiet and quotidian, shows Shade asserting his art to the fullest just where he seems to be reporting most passively. Yet within this personal poetic signature we again find other signatures already inscribed. At the very beginning of the counterpointed countdown to Hazel's death, Sybil switches on the television:

> You scrutinized your wrist: "It's eight fifteen.
> [And here time forked.] I'll turn it on." The screen
> In its blank broth evolved a lifelike blur,
> And music welled.
> > *He took one look at her,*
> *And shot a death ray at well-meaning Jane.*
>
> A male hand traced from Florida to Maine
> The curving arrows of Aeolian wars.
> 410   You said that later a quartet of bores,
> Two writers and two critics, would debate
> The Cause of Poetry on Channel 8.
> A nymph came pirouetting, under white
> Rotating petals, in a vernal rite
> To kneel before an altar in a wood
> Where various articles of toilet stood.

Under the guise of recording a humdrum evening's entertainment—a contrast, of course, with the momentousness of Hazel's imminent end—Shade demonstrates the deceptive intricacy of his art. He draws on his own scholarly specialty, Pope, to defamiliarize the advertising cliché of the nymph before the "altar in a wood," and to offer a challenge to Eliot's image in "The Waste Land," of a seated beauty amid multiple reflections, and the way it responds to Shakespeare with a kind of deliberately brittle vacuity.[9] Implicitly Shade contrasts Eliot's with his own images of expansive reflection at the start of "Pale Fire," and with his own sense of the vitalizing force of Shakespeare, not least in the image of multiple reflections in *Timon of Athens*, which the very title of "Pale Fire" reflects in its turn. Yet underneath this virtuosic palimpsest of allusion, as we saw in Chapter 12, Hazel already seems present, prompting Shade, by way of Kinbote, through the scene of Fleur de Fyler as a nymph before a mirror, and even signing herself in through the mirror-reversal of Eliot's name. And before she does so, someone else signals *his* presence, and some mysterious presence before him.

Counterpoint is one of Shade's personal signs. Another is the *-ane/-aine* rhyme. Here, however, in lines 407–8, at the very onset of the climactic counterpoint in the poem, Shade's signature rhyme bears someone else's sign. Just whose hand wrote the *"well-meaning Jane"* / *"from Florida to Maine"* rhyme becomes clear to us when "from Florida to Maine" again features in another windy *-ane/-ain* rhyme, as Shade characterizes the year 1958:

> It was a year of Tempests: Hurricane
> 680   Lolita swept from Florida to Maine.

This, of course, is the year that Nabokov's *Lolita*, at last published in the United States, swept to the top of bestseller lists around the country.

Since Nabokov never repeats a phrase so distinctive without inviting us to investigate the repetition, since the *-ane/-aine* rhyme has become such a secret signature yet here serves no purpose for Shade or Hazel, since Shade seems not to know "Lolita" except as the name of a hurricane, Nabokov appears to be sending us a strong if cryptic signal behind his poet's back. The "hurricane/Lolita . . . *Maine*" allusion, surely Nabokov's, winks over Shade's shoulder, suggesting that he may also stand in some way behind the "nymph in a wood" passage that begins with the matching *"Jane/Maine"* rhyme, the "from Florida to Maine" phrasing, and those turbulent winds. And indeed, in glossing the lines that echo *The Rape of the Lock*, Kinbote notes that in place of "A nymph came pirouetting" Shade had first had "the lighter and more musical: 'A nymphet pirouetted'" (C. 413). As Nabokov often amusedly insisted, the word "nymphet," in *that* sense, was practically his own.

What does Nabokov mean by asserting his authorial rights here? Why does he set his stamp down so firmly? Because the "nymph . . . in a wood" that might have been a "nymphet" hints—despite the skill with which it blends into its environment, despite the distracting multiple overlay of meanings and sources, from Pope to Eliot to television to Zemblan mirrors and Hazel's mirror words—at the butterfly known as "Nabokov's Wood Nymph."

Shade is stupefied when he hears Kinbote say that "'spider' in reverse is 'redips,' and 'T. S. Eliot,' 'toilest'" (C.347–48). Nabokov must have been equally flabbergasted when he first heard of "Nabokov's Wood Nymph." It had been his dream since childhood to discover a new species of butterfly; in 1941, just a year after arriving in the United States, he spotted and captured a hitherto unrecorded species on the rim of the Grand Canyon, dubbing it *Neonympha dorothea dorothea*. In honor of his discovery and the classificatory work in the paper where he named it, lepidopterist F. Martin Brown in his 1956 *Colorado Butterflies* bestowed on this butterfly the popular name "Nabokov's Wood Nymph."[10] What is curious about this name is that at that time Brown did not yet know of the existence of Nabokov's "nymphet," of the novel Nabokov had written during—and in one famous sequence partly *about*—the extensive motel trips he had made about the American West in pursuit of butterflies.[11]

When he fled the Russian Revolution, Nabokov had to leave behind the woods of a beloved homeland, and a fortune, and his precious collection of butterflies. Now in America he had not only felt immediately at home, especially in montane forests, but had promptly fulfilled his dream of scientific discovery, and had even, in the unexpected aftermath of *Lolita*, regained his fortune—and all this seemed to be summed up in the surprise of the name "Nabokov's Wood Nymph."[12] No wonder he might have felt that an uncannily generous game of worlds was being played around *him*.

Shade has his own reasons for his "link-and-bobolink," for his patter of *pane/pain* rhymes or his pattern of winged creatures from waxwing to wood duck or Red Admirabe to Toothwort White. Hazel in turn seems to sign herself into his poem via a reversed "T.S. Eliot," an *again/pane* rhyme, or the *Vanessa atalanta* of the closing lines. By the time they are *both* dead, Shade and his daughter seem to join forces in enriching Kinbote's fancies. By adding on the Gradus story, they incorporate Shade's own murder into the Zemblan visions Hazel had first offered Kinbote; they even sign the mirror that reflects Fleur de

Fyler's beauty "diminishing in the limpid distance" with the name of "Sudarg of Bokay," a reversed Jakob Gradus, a reflection of the reversed "T. S. Eliot" in the mirror before the nymph in the wood in Shade's poem—as if in gratitude to the "mirror maker of genius" who has created their life and the ultimate beneficence of their deaths.[13]

Behind the mortal Shade, the dead Hazel, and even the dead Shade, Nabokov in turn places *his* signature on the *Jane/Maine* and *Hurricane/Maine* rhymes that link his nymphet and his Wood Nymph. He incorporates his lifelong personal mark, a butterfly, as if to add another winged image to this endless recession of Shades and reflections. And indeed Nabokov's celebrated personal sign recurs—natural or artificial, exposed or concealed—throughout Shade's verse and Kinbote's Commentary: in the renamed *New Yorker*, *The Beau and the Butterfly*, where Shade publishes "The Nature of Electricity"; in *Disa* and *Embla*, two successive entries in the Index, a queen and a town in Zembla but also two adjacent butterfly species,[14] or Nitra and Indra, twin islands in Zembla, but also the species *Papilio nitra* and *Papilio indra*;[15] and indeed in the novel's whole radiant pattern of blues and azures (the French lepidopterological term for "Blues"),[16] from the "false azure" in Shade's windowpane or his "gradual and dual blue" to "the entire blue bulk" (C.433–434, 212) of Kinbote's 'blue inenubilable Zembla' (C.991, 288), as if to commemorate the subfamily of the Blues (*Polyommatini*) in which Nabokov became in the 1940s *the* leading authority.[17]

Shade can allude to his parents in the opening lines of his poem by way of the fact that his father in particular was an ornithologist and had a Mexican waxwing named after him, *Bombycilla shadei*. Nabokov, too, can sign himself in by way of taxonomic terms he first proposed. After analyzing the forms of the North American members of the Blues genus *Lycaeides* in two major papers published in 1944 and 1945, Nabokov decided to investigate the Central and South American Blues for comparative purposes before writing his definitive 1949 monograph on North American *Lycaeides*.[18] In the course of these 1944 and 1945 papers, he erected a number of new genera of Blues, all still valid today. One was *Icaricia*, named after Icarus, the son of Daedalus, who when his waxwings melt plunges into his death in the blue ocean beneath while his father lives on, flies on, in the reflected sky above. Another is *Pseudolucia*, a name which may indicate that its members resemble the Spring Azure, which Kirby in 1837 named *Polyommatus lucia* (now *Celastrina ladon*): in other words, each is a "false (Spring) Azure."[19] A third is *Cyclargus*, named after Argus, Hera's hundred-eyed watchman, a common suffix especially for genera of Blues. Since the Shadow Gradus has as one of his aliases "d'Argus," and is assigned the assassination which leads to Shade's death at the very moment these lines are written, Nabokov as the ultimate namer of not only Shade and Gradus, but also of *Icaricia*, *Pseudolucia*, and *Cyclargus*, seems to be inserting his own signature again and again into Shade's unforgettable opening couplet, with its "shadow," its "waxwing," its "false azure" that sets the keynote for all the novel's celestial blues. The creator of the novel's entire fictional world, Nabokov strategically places the butterflies within it as maker's marks—some eye-catching, some awaiting discovery behind their complex mimetic disguise[20]— in homage to all that *he* has been allowed to discover in the designs of the real.

ULTIMATE SOURCES

Shade composes his poem, dies, and then helps Kinbote orchestrate his Commentary. Behind her father's life, and before his death, his dead daughter, with help from his dead parents, inspires both Kinbote's Zembla and through it the controlled convolutions of her father's poem. Beyond them all, Nabokov determines the patterns of their world, precisely because he in turn suspects that something beyond him shapes his world and ours.

Like Shade, Nabokov had felt from an early age an urgent need to see life in the context of the impenetrability of death. Like Shade, he had a deep trust in the solicitude of life's underlying design, and, like Shade, he found this confidence put to the severest test in the senseless sudden death of someone he dearly loved. And just as Shade does not shy from the pain of his daughter's suicide, yet can end his poem with a serene confidence in the deep harmony of the ordinary, so Nabokov faces resolutely the "farce of fate" (C.1000, 294) in his father's assassination, when he has Shade, on July 21, his father's birthday, walk out of his poem and his confidence in "the verse of galaxies divine" and, like his father, into the path of a bullet meant for another. Yet from that horror Nabokov wrests an affirmation even richer than Shade's, a grateful participation in the "correlated pattern" fashioned by those "aloof and mute" forces "playing a game of worlds." Like Shade, only at a far deeper level, he makes sublime ornaments "of accidents and possibilities."

"It did not matter who they were," Shade declares. Another of Nabokov's most gifted proxies, Fyodor Godunov-Cherdyntsev, wants in a similar context to offer thanks for his life "but there is no one to thank. The list of donations already made: 10,000 days—from Person Unknown."[21] And in his own words, as he depicts himself standing among rare butterflies, Nabokov records that "thrill of gratitude to whom it may concern—to the contrapuntal genius of human fate or to tender ghosts humoring a lucky mortal."[22] In the fictive world of *Pale Fire* Nabokov can allow us to discover the identities of the "tender ghosts" who shape the lives of the mortal Shade and Kinbote and to catch glimpses of himself as creator and contrapuntal controller of this fictional world. But just as the design the dead Shades sign into poem and commentary is not just *their* design—Alphina Goldsworth existed before a trio of Shades helped to transform her and her closet in Botkin's mind, and someone provided Botkin with a Russian *Timon of Athens* before Hazel could turn it into Kinbote's Zemblan *Timon Afinsken* as she deepened the tunnel behind that closet—so even his own design, Nabokov himself implies, forms a mere part of a much larger world.

He could experience "Nabokov's Wood Nymph" as such an eerily complete surprise precisely because the name someone else innocently bestowed upon it so perfectly fused his art and his science—the nymphet he invented and the *Neonympha* he discovered. Art and science, he always insisted, meet at their highest level,[23] because art and nature merge at their deepest. Art and nature certainly fuse throughout the worlds within worlds of *Pale Fire*. Shade from birth lives in a quiet academic town where "a landscaper of genius" (C.49) has planted an avenue of all the trees mentioned by Shakespeare. In his last weeks of life, Shade himself pays tribute to both art and nature throughout his poem: to Shakespeare's supreme art, in his title, and in the image of reflections and interactions between parts of this world (and, as he implies by extension, between this world and another) in the *Timon of Athens* passage from which the title comes; and to nature, from the waxwing of his opening line to the *Vanessa* at his close, by way of other insects and birds suggestive of transformation and transcendence and by way of trees casting numinous shades.

Hazel's spirit appears to inspire her father to pay an additional tribute, in his poem "The Nature of Electricity," where

> The dead, the gentle dead—who knows?—
> In tungsten filaments abide. . . .

> And maybe Shakespeare floods a whole
> Town with innumerable lights. . . .

> Streetlamps are numbered, and maybe
> Number nine-hundred-ninety-nine
> (So brightly beaming through a tree
> So green) is an old friend of mine.

The evocation of Shakespeare flooding a whole town with light and of
lamps spaced along a town street oddly echoes the trees along Shakespeare Avenue in New Wye, and the sense of something peculiarly
pervasive and haunting about Shakespeare's creative energy is hardly
diminished when Kinbote comments after the poem: "Science tells us,
by the way, that the Earth would not merely fall apart, but vanish like
a ghost, if Electricity were suddenly removed from the world" (C.347,
193).

When Kinbote arrives in New Wye, Hazel extends the pattern still
further as she turns a dark closet into the blaze of Zembla in his incandescent imagination. She names Onhava's streets after Shakespearean
plays, and has the King take a copy of *Timon Afinsken* through the tunnel. She connects an eerie insect with Shakespeare when at Queen
Blenda's death a luciola, a glowworm, recalls the Ghost's "The glow-
worm . . . 'gins to pale his uneffectual fire" in *Hamlet*, and she adds an
Iris and a *Disa* to the women from whom the King turns back in Zembla before she appears herself in Appalachia as a *Vanessa*.

Beyond Hazel and the other Shades, as designer of their world, is
Nabokov himself, and behind him, he implies, as he signs himself in
by the pointed patterning of Shakespearean and other allusions and of
butterflies and other natural kinds, stands the limitless wealth of art
and nature that makes him trust so deeply in the underlying munificence of things.

When Nabokov signs himself into the deepest recesses of "Pale Fire"
by means of his Wood Nymph, it is less to assert himself as the ultimate source of the poem than to pay an almost private tribute to the
unknown source of all that life has granted him. His attitude is the
antithesis of Kinbote's. Kinbote sees himself as center and supplier of

all that matters. He grotesquely declares himself the "only begetter" (F, 17) of Shade's poem—echoing the unidentified "only begetter" of Shakespeare's *Sonnets*—even though he knows that "Pale Fire" bears no traces of the "Solus Rex" he had urged Shade to write, and even though he pays so little heed to it, in his eagerness to recount his own story, that he cannot even make the effort to find out Shade's Shakespearean source for its title. Yet for all the absurdity of Kinbote's vision of himself as source and center, Hazel and Shade generously work through his very selfishness to offer him and us a world that bespeaks a still deeper generosity.

Eliot opens "A Game of Chess" by echoing Shakespeare with a kind of pointed sterility. Just as Shade challenges Eliot in "Pale Fire," so throughout the chess-game of worlds in his own *Pale Fire* Nabokov offers an interplay of the poetic and the prosaic, of chaos and design, of time and timelessness, that stands in marked contrast to the denial of rebirth in "The Waste Land" or the desperate refuge in tradition that Eliot reaches toward in "Four Quartets." Nabokov senses in the intricacy of life's combinations something unimaginably richer than the lifelessness of the disconnected fragments Eliot announces he has shored against his ruins. And he tries to match that intricacy in his own combinations, as he places the Wood Nymph he discovered in nature in front of the mirrors of intricate art, as he backs a banal advertisement's black-and-white screen with the polished sheen of a Popean 'glass,' and then a refraction of Eliot's reflection of Shakespeare, and a muted flash of Shade's waxwing and of Sudarg of Bokay's endlessly receding beauties, and even a final shimmer of moon and sea in Shakespeare's "pale fire." And when *Nabokov* reflects Shakespeare, he does it in a spirit of boundless gratitude to the most concrete instance we have, outside nature itself, of inexhaustible creativity.

Nabokov insists that the cosmic is never far from the comic.[24] In no other novel does he take his title from another writer's work. Here in *Pale Fire* he has Kinbote denounce the very practice (C.671–672) and has Shade wrily toy with it as he steals his "pale fire" from Shakespeare. From start to finish of *Pale Fire* Shakespeare recurs as an image of stupendous fecundity, someone from whom we continually borrow and through whom we can continually pass on our experience of the unending bounty of things, as Shade's parents and his daughter pass on the *Timon* in the tunnel to Kinbote and then to Shade himself.[25] In this novel of worlds within worlds, this "system of cells interlinked

within / Cells interlinked within cells interlinked / Within one stem,"
death borrows endlessly from life and life from death, one level of creative generosity takes from another and endlessly gives. "I'll example
you with thievery," Timon says:

> The sun's a thief, and with his great attraction
> Robs the vast sea; the moon's an arrant thief,
> And her pale fire she snatches from the sun;
> The sea's a thief, whose liquid surge resolves
> The moon into salt tears. . . .

But Nabokov steals from his speech to express not Timon's contempt
for universal thievery but his own vision of an unfathomable creative
generosity behind our origins and ends.

Conclusion

NABOKOV DESIGNED *Pale Fire* so that we make discoveries at every phase of reading, so that the interplay of problems and promise keeps luring us on to still more sweeping surprises. He manages to incorporate an unparalleled succession of readerly vistas into a work accessible and enchanting even on a first encounter. But the generosity of his method is more than a matter of method, for it reflects the generosity of his metaphysics, his hunch that the world itself sets before us the possibility and the pleasures of endless discovery, inexhaustible excitement, which far from stopping even at death might then merely shift into a still higher gear.

He arrived at this trust in the ultimate munificence of things, despite losing a homeland, a language, and a father senselessly murdered, by observing his world with the passion of a scientist and the precision of an artist. He incorporates into his art something of the ever-expanding complexity of the world opened up by modern science, but suggests possibilites far beyond those of scientific materialism. He casts doubt on old creeds yet shows that they may have only underestimated the mysterious powers and potentials that could loom beyond the life we can see.

The discoveries I propose as the "synthetic" solutions to the problems *Pale Fire* poses have not been easy to make, but that is how it should be. They cannot be arrived at without thorough immersion in the novel's world, any more, Nabokov implies, than the idea of cosmic design could mean anything to someone unaware of microcosmic detail. At the start of his course on masterpieces of European fiction he would tell his students: "There is nothing wrong about the moonshine of generalization when it comes *after* the sunny trifles of the book have been lovingly collected."[1]

Nabokov thinks that only by paying attention to the infinitely complex particulars of our world and their inexhaustible combinations is it possible to appreciate the limitless generosity of things. Only by finding these things out *for ourselves*, with all the effort and imagination it requires to master something new and rich and intricate, can we feel in discovery a thrill as close as possible to the rapture of creation. He allows us to find our way steadily further into his fictional world and to attain the new insight into its design that his characters appear to gain access to as they pass through death.

Asked by an interviewer, "Do you believe in God?" he answered: "To be quite candid—and what I am going to say now is something I never said before, and I hope it produces a salutary little chill—I know more than I can express in words, and the little I can express would not have been expressed, had I not known more."[2] What *does* he express through the vistas of surprise he offers us in *Pale Fire*? What *do* we find out?

Among much else, we discover as we reread the succession of ironies in the sources of Shade's inspiration. Kinbote claims to be the "only begetter" (F, 17) of the poem, the begetter of the story of Zembla that Shade *should* have written about, the begetter in any case of the frenzy of inspiration that produced "Pale Fire." We recognize in the course of a first reading how wrong, how deluded, how characteristically egomaniacal is Kinbote's claim. As we reread, we identify both the sources of Kinbote's Zemblan fantasy in his own past life, and the way his compulsive snoopings on the Shades, not the glories of his Zembla, have fed directly into the poem. As we continue to reread we can eventually find that the dead Hazel, with the help of her father's parents, has herself "begot" much of Kinbote's Zembla and, in a way quite unimagined by Kinbote, has shaped it so as to prompt her father to commit to verse the story of his lifelong quest for some escape from the limits of mortality. After death, Shade in turn begets Kinbote's Gradus fantasy and has it impart a shapeliness and suspense to the Commentary, even as he also fashions it into a meditation on the creative power unleashed by what seems the blind force of irresistibly advancing death.

We discover a succession of ironies even in *Pale Fire*'s title. A first reading guides us to the identification that Kinbote is too wrapped up in himself to make, the source in *Timon of Athens* for the title of Shade's poem. Kinbote himself plays with the words "pale fire," but as we reread we detect the ironies of his also unconsciously echoing the very context of the phrase that he dimly knows but has not even bothered to locate. As we reread still further, we rediscover the phrase as a message from the firefly-luciola-glowworm ghosts of Shade's parents to Kinbote and ultimately to Shade, in echo of *Hamlet*'s ghost, or from the dead Shade himself as he inspires the Gradus story, and as part of a pattern of pale lights, dim lights, shadows and Shades that signal un-read messages and underground sources throughout *Pale Fire*.

Nabokov prepares these discoveries for us with extraordinary wit and irony, elegance and economy, but also with real poignancy and pathos, as we learn the part that dead parents and children play in the lives of those who have lost them or even in the life of someone who feels himself utterly alone. He grants full measure to the everyday, to the particulars of the real, whether a Toothwort White central to his design or a tangle of disregarded "willow herb, milkweed and iron-weed." In the vivid, often comic, sometimes painful, contrasts between Kinbote and Shade, he explores the moral imperatives of human be-havior in terms of egotism and its opposites, and the glory and grief of our human need for others. Yet behind all this he also focuses intently on the metaphysical, on the enigma of our origins and ends. While he scrupulously acknowledges the limits of the knowable, he also sug-gests, he makes us *feel*, the ever-deepening mystery of our world.

POPPER: THE LOGIC OF CRITICAL DISCOVERY

Pale Fire is so original in method and meaning that for a long time much of what matters most in the novel has resisted readers, whether fascinated fellow-writers like Mary McCarthy and David Lodge, or Nabokov specialists, monographers and biographers alike. Nevertheless, despite the corrosive relativism of those who think criti-cism can reflect only a particular critic's or school's stance, there has been a real advance in the understanding of *Pale Fire* that bears out Popper's analysis of the process of discovery.

Popper stresses that there is no sure method of discovery, that all our ideas involve conjecture and are subject to refutation. Ideas cannot be built up just from "pure" observation, since observation is already impregnated with tacit theories and particular purposes, and to have explanatory power, new theories must leap beyond the observable, whatever might prompt the leap: imagination, intuition, ambition, tra-dition, or anything else. Where Thomas Kuhn and many in his wake would accept what Popper criticizes as "the myth of the framework," the notion that particular paradigms determine what it is possible to think at a given time, Popper emphasizes the utter unpredictability of new theories, the sheer openness—for those who do not enslave them-selves to intellectual fashion—of the interaction between individual talent, existing traditions of inquiry, and the explicandum itself.[3]

Mary McCarthy's 1962 review of *Pale Fire* set the process of discovering the novel off to an explosive start. Jittery with excitement, McCarthy detected both what Nabokov planned a first-time reader should find and some things much less easy to locate,[4] but added a dizzying confusion of proposed allusions, correspondences, and definitions that showed more enthusiasm than discrimination. In a 1963 article, Carol Williams deftly traced some of the novel's quieter and more haunting internal echoes. In the first book on Nabokov, in 1966, Page Stegner, who found the fancifulness of the Zemblan elements not to his taste, nevertheless casually offered the possibility that Kinbote may have written the poem as well as the commentary, despite the pains Nabokov had taken to exclude such a reading by stressing Kinbote's ineptitude for verse. The next year Andrew Field, in his much more ambitious *Nabokov: His Life in Art*, proposed Shade as the author of poem and commentary.

Why did two writers in two years, working independently of each other, arrive at single-author theories? I suggest three major reasons for the apparent attractiveness of these theories in the 1960s and the difficulty of shucking them ever since. The first is that the novel itself depends on successive surprises of identity. What seem to be two people, Kinbote and Charles II of Zembla, turn out to be one, and then more surprises follow: Gradus is not a Zemblan zealot but Jack Grey, an American madman; Kinbote is after all not Charles II but only a lunatic, perhaps a drab Russian scholar named Botkin, who thinks himself a king. Both the initial surprise that two people can turn out to be one and the succession of further surprises led some to account for the still unresolved echoes in *Pale Fire* by expecting a still greater surprise ahead: the two ostensible authors, poet and commentator, must actually be one.

The second reason for the initial appeal of the single-author theories is that the formal inventiveness of Nabokov's fiction seemed such a liberating shock after most other American fiction of the 1940s and 1950s (things began to change in the early 1960s). Nabokov's probing play with the role of the author as intrusive and elusive controller, even in as quiet a novel as *Pnin*, was breathtakingly new, and *that* seemed to be where readers had to seek the key to a new Nabokov novel.

The third and crucial reason is that what I propose as the real so-lution, the otherworldly one, is not only more complex but was in many ways—despite Shade's preoccupation with the beyond, despite Hazel's poltergeist and her recording the ghostly message in the Haunted Barn—simply unavailable at the time, too much at odds with a writer who seems in so many ways so wrily skeptical. When the first books on Nabokov appeared, he had not yet published *Transparent Things*, his one explicitly ghostly novel; the more elusive but still em-phatic otherworldly patterns had not been detected in his other work; and his metaphysics had barely been noticed, let alone understood.

Besides the immediate surprises of identity in *Pale Fire* and the moiré mask of the author behind all Nabokov's works, Field had three particular reasons for naming Shade the primary author. *Nabokov's Life in Art* sought to demonstrate the strong continuity between Nabokov's English work and his Russian, much of which was at that time still untranslated. Field borrowed from Nabokov's friend, the poet Vladis-lav Khodasevich, the notion of the centrality of the figure of the artist in Nabokov's oeuvre; and he stressed the undoubted similarities be-tween *Pale Fire* and Nabokov's last, uncompleted Russian novel, *Solus Rex*.[5] His third line of argument reflected a critical notion fashionable at the time, unity of theme: that both the Shade and the Kinbote contri-butions were "about" death sufficed for Field to assert that a unity of artistic intent shaped them both.

Field was more confident than careful, but Julia Bader in a much more closely reasoned 1972 study identified and interpreted in terms of Shadean authorship many more of the eerie connections between the two parts of the novel that certainly invite *some* explanation. Two years earlier, as a college freshman who had already become addicted to the surprise of discovery in *Pale Fire* while a student at high school, I had written an essay that found still more connections between the disparate parts and interpreted them, under the influence of Field (I was only seventeen!), in Shadean terms. In 1974, I incorporated the essay, revamped, into a masters thesis that I sent to Nabokov, to re-ceive a gracious general comment in reply and a thundering "No!" in the margin beside one blunder specific enough to correct.

Attributions of sole authorship were very much in the air in the 1970s. They seemed attractive in the wake of Wayne Booth's hugely influential *The Rhetoric of Fiction* (1961), which despite its own judi-ciousness allowed others to turn narrative unreliability into a crude critical rule of thumb, and they seemed even more attractive by the late 1970s as narratology and then deconstruction swept onto the critical stage. By 1977, Peter Rabinowitz, in a study of narrative principles, could present *Pale Fire* as a classic case of undecidably unreliable narration, in which either Kinbote or Shade could have written the whole (and a decade later Brian McHale could even call *Pale Fire* "a text of absolute epistemological uncertainty").[6] In 1982, Alvin Kernan responded with finesse to the promise of hidden revelation in *Pale Fire*, but in the early enthusiasm for deconstructionist ideas he too stressed the undecidability, the "tease" of the novel's narration. In his 1985 dissertation Pekka Tammi, despite his superb command of textual detail, restricted himself to fitting *Pale Fire* into a narratological grid that led him to conclude on purely technical grounds that Kinbote, if anyone, was responsible for the correspondences between poem and commentary.

The prominence of the Shadean or Kinbotean or "undecidable" readings had not gone unchallenged. D. Barton Johnson, attending to verbal and subverbal detail, stood largely outside the Shade-Kinbote opposition when he focused on the Botkin behind Kinbote. Robert Alter, with his subtle sense of the nexus between the technical complexities of literature and the experiential complexities of life, proposed in 1975 that *Pale Fire* probed the relationship between art and life rather than any supposed authorship dilemma. Five years later, Alter's student Ellen Pifer argued, with her own characteristically combative humanism, against reading the novel as an exercise in literary detection and for a reading focused on the tension between Shade's generosity and Kinbote's selfishness.

In 1991, I advanced in *Vladimir Nabokov: The American Years* the most elaborate version yet proffered of the Shadean reading. If I can characterize my work objectively, it reflected not a fascination with narrative unreliability (which has become an appalling cliché of critical thought) but my rather tenacious interest in literary structures as integrated wholes in which, at their most successful, style and sense reflect each other in the profoundest ways. But in my determination to account for the correspondences within the novel—and by 1991 I and others had uncovered still more—I persisted with the Shadean idea, since, as I interpreted it, it reflected in a complex fashion Shade's struggle to probe the mystery of death. I convinced some, but provoked justified resistance from others, in print, at conferences, and on the Internet.

Popper repeatedly stressed that to be scientific (in his later years he would say, simply to be rational)[7] an idea must make itself open to

searching criticism. We propose new theories with the hope of infect-
ing others with their power but at the risk of having them refuted or
ignored. A truly scientific idea is one which can be subjected to a critical test that may falsify it. We should test our own ideas rigorously, so
that by falsifying them ourselves we spare ourselves the embarrass-
ment of having them refuted by others, and may thereby drive ourselves on to new and perhaps less vulnerable ideas. But we are partial
to our own theories, and weaknesses that we may not notice will normally be far more apparent to others.[8] Yet even if our theory appears
to be falsified, we are also justified in some measure in strongly de-
fending the idea against criticism: even an apparent falsification is itself a theoretical proposal, itself uncertain, and an idea abandoned too
quickly because of its apparent falsification may turn out later to have
been worth retaining.[9]

I defended the Shadean reading vigorously in the Internet debate in
late 1997 and seemed to be winning more adherents. But as I prepared
a full version of the Shadean case, I found myself disturbed by details
I had overlooked (especially the Alfin-Alphina connection), by recollections of Ellen Pifer's criticisms (which other examples than hers
made even more problematic), and by Dmitri Nabokov's reporting
that his father's attitude to both Shadean and Kinbotean positions was
far more dismissive than the letter accompanying my masters thesis
had permitted me to believe. I had to rethink.

Since 1979, when Véra Nabokov declared the beyond (*potustoronnost'*)[10] Nabokov's "main theme" and I submitted a doctoral dissertation that focused in part on the theme of the beyond in *Ada* and in
Nabokov's metaphysics in general, keen readers of Nabokov have
come increasingly to recognize his interest in such matters. But although, through disentangling and reconnecting the intricate patterns
of *Ada*, I had discovered Lucette's participation from the beyond in
Van's and Ada's life and work, the experience offered no formula for
Pale Fire. Nabokov's novels all operate through compounded connections and ramified relationships, and they all have a shared foundation
of ideas and attitudes, but none can simply be used as a template for
another.

As I reread and rethought *Pale Fire*, new patterns or extensions of
old ones kept rising to my attention and posing themselves as problems that complicated or perhaps suddenly resolved other problems,
new surprises kept waking me in the night or striking me while I was
"soaping a third time one leg," even when I was so exhausted by new
discoveries that I simply wanted them to stop.

The solutions I propose to the problems Nabokov poses in *Pale Fire* should satisfy Kinboteans, Shadeans, and those hostile to the single-authorship theories. Popper stressed that a successful theory would both refute earlier theories and show them as more distant approximations of the truth, although *what* they approximate to cannot be seen until the new explanation is discovered.[11] The various roles that the Shades play from beyond in Kinbote's Zembla, in Shade's "Pale Fire," and in Kinbote's Commentary explain the tantalizingly suggestive correspondences between seemingly disparate parts in ways much more exact and pointed and less problematic than even the single-author theories, let alone the dual-author descriptions of *Pale Fire* that barely tried to account for the hidden design except by referring to Nabokov or an ironic fate. But of course I may be wrong. There may be flaws in my proposals that I have not looked hard enough for: I had thought I had made a good case for Shade as sole author in the biography, and then again on the Internet, and now wince at what I overlooked because of what seemed to be the superior explanatory power of the theory.

And I have no doubt whatever that there are many more discoveries to be made in *Pale Fire*: perhaps more direct or at least additional ways of reaching the same conclusions, or new consequences of these proposals, or new implications for some of the relationships suggested, or explanations of many parts of the novel I have not accounted for. Both Nabokov and Popper in their different terms rightly insist that no discovery is ever final, that a synthesis becomes the thesis of a new series, that a successful theory will open new problems.

KUHN: PARADIGMS

The tenacity of the sole-author readings of *Pale Fire* appears at first to support Thomas Kuhn's influential notion of the paradigm, but ultimately undermines it. Those who have read *Pale Fire* on the alert for subterranean similarities between poem and commentary have tended to opt for one or another of the sole-author hypotheses, not because Nabokov planted these as false solutions (in fact he rightly thought that the novel excluded them both), but because they were easier to arrive at than the reading I now propose. The Shadean hypothesis in particular provides an explanation that approximates, in its confused way, many of the elements of what I now suggest as the solutions to *Pale Fire*'s central problems. The fact that the explanatory power of the Shadean hypothesis, at least while we focused only on what it sought to explain, was greater than that of any other available proposal, made it difficult for those of us who adhered to it to accept the force of criticisms—which themselves could have been made with more clarity. Had the Shadean hypothesis never been proposed in the first place, the solution of the influence of the dead Shades might have been arrived at some time ago. Or it might still await discovery. As Popper stresses, bold theories are welcome, even if mistaken. Without the critical debate that they engender, knowledge cannot advance.

But even while the Shade-as-sole-author position attracted many enthusiastic readers of *Pale Fire*, and while it seemed to offer the most comprehensive explanation for the constant covert communication between poem and commentary, even as the two parts appear to talk past each other, it was no paradigm, no inescapable frame for critical thought. Other readers favored some kind of explanation involving Kinbote or Botkin as the source of the correlations (and that too approximates, in different ways than the Shadean hypothesis, the interpretation I advance here); a few opted for Nabokov's having deliberately made it necessary but impossible to decide between the Shadean and Kinbotean readings (a notion that had little in its favor except for the vogue for the unresolvable in the late 1970s and 1980s); while a great many read the novel without focusing on the sole-authorship suggestions at all. By concentrating on Kinbote, Shade, and Hazel, on Zembla and "Pale Fire," writers like Alter, Pifer, Rorty, and Wood were able to write superbly about the novel in their own ways. If many of us thought within the terms of a single-author solution, it was not because that was a paradigm, a constraint on thought, but because the truth about *Pale Fire*, the truth about anything very complex, is not easy to discover. But that does not mean that open argument cannot advance us toward the truth.

WOOD: DISCOVERY, DEATH, AND DOUBT

In reading this book in manuscript for Princeton University Press, Michael Wood felt uneasy both that it leads toward a definite interpretation and that it leads toward the *kind* of interpretation I suggest. Since his major misgivings probably anticipate the two deepest doubts others are likely to have, I would like to address them both.

Wood takes issue with what he sees as the resolution, the determinateness, the closure of my argument, of the model of readerly discovery that I propose, and of the Popperian parallel with scientific discovery that I posit. He would prefer doubts and irresolutions: not for nothing was *his* book about Nabokovian magic entitled *The Magician's Doubts*. He assumes that what Popper says about discovery in science cannot really apply to literature. "The notion of 'discovery' in literature," he comments, "has to work quite differently from the way it does in most sciences. What we discover in a persuasive reading of a novel is a range of new understandings, rather than a new settled truth."[12] But Popper's central point is that even the most apparently well-confirmed finding in science (Newton's explanation of motion, say, as it looked the year before Einstein's first relativity paper) can *never* be a settled truth. Wood agrees that "the idea of evidence is important—texts do offer discussable evidence, and the discussion of evidence is not merely the airing of opinions—but the alternative to dogmatic or scattershot doubt is argument rather than any clinching experiment or demonstration." But although Popper stresses a falsifying test can be decisive in science, he also stresses that even registering the results of such a test and construing them as falsifying a theory involve hypotheses, "a web of guesses,"[13] and are therefore open to argument, and in any case can do nothing to settle truth, can at most indicate an apparent falsehood and the need to look further. In employing the Popperian analogy, I imply that although other hypotheses proposed for *Pale Fire* now seem demonstrably wrong, my own new hypothesis, which I suggest explains more of the book than other interpretations directed at the same problem, should also be open to challenge, extension, complication, refutation.[14]

Wood also feels uncomfortable with Nabokov's famous analogy between reading and chess-problem solving, since it too implies resolution. But Nabokov is consistent here—even outside the *Speak, Memory* passage that he presents, albeit obliquely, as his artistic credo, he repeatedly refers to "solutions" to his novels[15]—and with good reason: he thinks that "the unravelling of a riddle is the purest and most basic act of the human mind."[16] Nevertheless, he stressed even in the *Speak, Memory* passage's Hegelian thesis-antithesis-synthesis structure that the synthesis or solution is not a resting-place but a new starting-point.

Novelists by disposition tend to prefer particulars to abstractions, and more even than most other novelists, Nabokov insisted on the ir-

replaceable, unpredictable, refractory detail over the convenient generalization. But he was also interested in the surprising patterns that
could be discovered in particulars and that could perhaps help explain
them at some deeper level. The unusual tension between particulars
and pattern in Nabokov is an intensification of the give-and-take between the clarity of reflection and the clutter of experience in all reading and interpretation, in every interplay between life and thought.
Nabokov's stress (and mine) on the "solution" to some of the problems
his novels can pose no more means that everything is now settled and
unproblematic in *Pale Fire* than cracking the code of DNA meant that
everything was now explained in biology. Like the decipherment of
DNA, one of Nabokov's "solutions" opens up new problems on a new
plane, without shutting off old ones (evolutionary theory and ethology
have developed enormously in the last few decades without much
need for microbiology).

Wood's second major misgiving is the particular solution I propose:
the ghosts. The shades of the Shades offer a startling solution to *Pale
Fire*—and yet the book clearly *is* riddling *and* obsessed with the possibility of a life beyond death. Wood expresses his reluctance to accept
my proposal in this way: "The trouble with it is its cost, what you have
to take with it and give up because of it. . . . Death itself is diminished,
its horror is cancelled, and a desperate sentimentality beckons. It's as
if Nahum Tate had decided to deal with Cordelia's death not by removing it from his version of *King Lear* but by bringing her back as a
helpful spirit." But in fact Shakespeare himself as it were revised his
own recent tragedies when he wrote the late tragicomedies, which
show, precisely, children and parents reunited after what had seemed
gratuitous deaths, and in ways that his stagecraft and versecraft insist
we take as emblems of immortality. Are Shakespeare's late plays
"deeply trivializing," in Wood's phrase, because they don't leave us
with daughters senselessly dead, because they show families reunited
after various kinds of death?

Whether the ghosts that I argue we can eventually detect in *Pale Fire*
suggest a world too sentimental and death-denying is a matter for critics to discuss. But we should recall Fielding's Parson Adams, who insists that in the light of Heaven and Providence we should be able to
resign ourselves to any loss, but then promptly becomes unconsolable
when his own son drowns. Or *Twelfth Night*, where Olivia's fool tries
to cheer her out of her vow of mourning for her brother by insisting he

can prove *her* the fool: "I think his soul is in hell, madonna." "I know his soul is in heaven, fool." "The more fool, madonna, to mourn for your brother's soul, being in heaven. Take away the fool, gentlemen."

I have deliberately structured this book so that the otherworldly solutions are deferred and unannounced until Part 3, until a stage that corresponds with a re-rereading of the novel, because Nabokov, too, has planned *Pale Fire* so that these solutions cannot be reached until the world in which John and Hazel Shade live and die has been given its thorough due. The two main arguments that I develop—about the protracted concatenation of deepening surprises on successive readings, and about Nabokov's treatment of the relationship between this world and a next—would be spoiled by rushing toward the conclusion without taking into account the impossibility of getting there quickly, without dwelling on the life of the book on a first encounter, the death that hangs over a rereading, and the intimations from beyond death that Nabokov eventually allows us to detect on re-rereading. Critics will want to discuss whether or not Nabokov's handling of the theme of an afterlife allows him, as I would claim, to have it both ways, to disclose the possibility of a hitherto-concealed consolation only long after the revealed desolation, to give death its due as well as to suggest the possibility of something beyond it that we cannot ordinarily see.

The Shades in *Pale Fire* who continue to influence the living from the world of the dead can be read in various ways. They are anything but an unequivocal affirmation that "This is how things really are," because Nabokov *always* stresses that any form of consciousness beyond the mortal must be either nonexistent or unimaginable: anything we *can* imagine collapses under the absurdity of trying to transpose the conditions of temporality into eternity.[17] We might, of course, see the otherworldly role of the Shades as a sketch of a hereafter, but we may also read it as a metaphor, a possibility space, a concrete anthropomorphized scenario of the unimaginable, an image of surprise, an intimation of concealed design, the coy expression of an unjustifiable trust, a hint of what might lurk within the intimate texture of things.

To me, what is attractive about Nabokov philosophically is that he knows the particulars of the here and now as well as any writer ever has, and gives them their fullest due, but makes us feel that there could be so much more, that it is absurd we don't know more, and yet that the fact that we don't know more may not necessarily mean that we live in an absurd universe or that there is nothing more to know. Given what science itself has discovered about the "more" on the physical plane, from leptons to light years, it seems odd to presume we know everything about the metaphysical.

In fact, modern physics often approximates metaphysics, as scientists suggest that our universe is only a tiny bubble in a much larger one, or that the universe splits into parallel realities or in effect parallel universes at each quantum instant,[18] or that we may even live in a multiverse in which all logically possible universes exist.[19] Frankly, I find these last suggestions hard to credit, but then Sir Francis Bacon thought it unspeakably absurd to suggest that the earth that felt so solid under his feet was revolving in space, and even at the time when Einstein was already formulating the theory of relativity, no one knew that the Milky Way was only one of scores of billions of galaxies.

Nabokov's worlds within worlds seem almost tame by comparison. But there is one difference. He suggests the presence of conscious design as we move from world to world, and in that he stands at odds with the materialism of modern science. In fact, science has consistently advanced from its mythological origins, from a time when the forces of nature were attributed to a god or gods shaping the lives of the humans at the supposed center of existence, to a view that progressively removes and then dissolves any center and sees not only humans but all earthly creatures, all inhabitants of our galaxy, perhaps now even all denizens of our universe, as part of an unimaginable extension of possibilities in which our own realities loom ever smaller and smaller.

But we do not live our lives on that scale, and each of us stands at the center of a consciousness that extends to the boundaries of all that we see and feel and think. Things matter to us on this individual scale, matter to us indeed almost more than we can bear. As Shade says:

> I'm ready to become a floweret
> Or a fat fly, but never, to forget.
> And I'll turn down eternity unless
> The melancholy and the tenderness
> Of mortal life; the passion and the pain;
> The claret taillight of that dwindling plane
> Off Hesperus; your gesture of dismay
530 > On running out of cigarettes; the way
> You smile at dogs; the trail of silver slime
> Snails leave on flagstones; this good ink, this rhyme,
> This index card, this slender rubber band

> Which always forms, when dropped, an ampersand,
> Are found in Heaven by the newlydead
> Stored in its strongholds through the years.

Yet it is not here, not through the text of Shade's hopes and fears, but by way of the whole texture of *Pale Fire*, that Nabokov suggests that something in the surprising weave of the world itself, in all its endless detail and design, offers hints that our private universes may indeed prove central in ways we cannot fathom, even as we discover how much more there is to reality than we can presently see.

In time Nabokov may be judged the first storyteller since the dawn of modern science and modern literary realism to learn enough from science to invite readers to discover worlds within worlds within the live world of the known—a world that he renders in an immediate and human way far from the technological terrains of science fiction or the abstract infinities of a Borges, and that he suggests may, if we look much more closely, gradually disclose the unknown in ways that even science cannot. Or perhaps he will be seen as staging a last rearguard attempt to resurrect an anthropocentric metaphysics, in which the conscious purposes by which we human beings live are attributed to level upon level beyond us, and in which individual mortal lives remain at the center even of a vastly larger world: an astonishing vision, as he conceives it, yet ultimately only the expression of an all-too-human yearning that the cosmos refuses to accommodate.

Whichever way the debate turns, he has discovered in the extraordinary possibilities of his own art a way of reawakening us to the possibilities of art and nature and beyond.

NABOKOV: DOUBT, DISCOVERY, AND DESIGN

If my proposed reading of *Pale Fire* is correct, it shows Nabokov to be nothing like the fashions of the age. In 1975, at a time when the term itself was not yet the fashion, Robert Alter described him as a postmodern writer; by 1993 he had rightly decided he was *not* postmodern.[20] Nabokov has a biting metaphysical irony and no attachment to old creeds and credulities. Shade's "fountain" becomes a mirage, not a solid proof, when it meets Mrs. Z.'s "mountain." The Haunted Barn, on early readings, suggests *"Life is hopeless, afterlife heartless"*: "That was Dad's tummy, I think—not a spook" (C347, 191). Shade affirms cosmic order and gets shot through the heart by a madman aiming at the wrong person. Nabokov's negative irony matters, his rational skepticism, the intelligence needed to debunk false solutions, indulgent imaginings, impossible certainties. Without it there would be no defense against the naive self-confirmations of the desperate, the foolish, the dogmatic. Nabokov insists that from within the human mind we simply cannot know how the mysteries of our origins and ends might appear to some consciousness not restricted to our time and space and thought.

Shade keeps Hazel's poltergeist phase out of his poem and says no more of the Haunted Barn than "she spent three nights / Investigating certain sounds and lights / In an old barn." The lifelong exploration of the abyss to which he dedicates himself and "Pale Fire," he feels sure, will not be advanced by these crude crashings into our physical space. And yet he ends with a serene confidence in some deeply generous design behind things that Michael Wood aptly calls a "theology for sceptics."[21]

Nabokov then has Shade senselessly shot, as if to rebuke the poet for his confidence, but gradually allows us to discover *Pale Fire*'s endless positive ironies, the generosity, the design, the signs of the beyond that are simply not accessible until we reach a new relation to the novel's time. By hiding worlds within worlds of being even within the compact microcosm of *Pale Fire*, he can make us shiver with a sense of possibilities that we thought we had agreed were ruled out.

He does not "prove" his case, but his very case insists on the unprovability, from within mortality, of modes of being beyond it. He allows for the possibility that anything that we might imagine beyond, even all the worlds of discovery and benevolent design he invents in *Pale Fire*, might merely reflect the depth of our desire, might merely help to define the limits of our imprisonment within a chaotic life that prompt us to dream up a freedom and order beyond. Yet the very fact that he can pack so much into *Pale Fire* that we do not expect and that we can only gradually detect, the fact that he can invent such continually unfolding complexity, suggests possibilities of design that a post-Darwinian world would seem to have disallowed.

Pale Fire shows how wrongly so many read Nabokov. His art dazzles on the surface, but he hides far more below. Many suspect he mocks his audience, but in fact he allows us the chance to discover more for ourselves in the work and in our world than any other author I know. His generosity to his readers matches his sense of the generosity of his world. Who else could write a novel in which four out of five main characters die but which remains so funny and so radiant? Who else could offer a world as fantastic as Zembla yet make its magic pale beside the stay-at-home Shades?

Notes

INTRODUCTION

1. "A Bolt from the Blue" (1991 [1962], v, xxi–xxii).
2. Peter Rabinowitz, for instance, in a study of narrative audiences, sees *Pale Fire* as a "frustrating novel to read, and in some respects an impossible one," because of what he thinks is its planned irresolvability. "As we begin to ask further questions ... the number of possible novels begins to proliferate at a geometric rate." "Truth in Fiction: A Reexamination of Audiences" (1996 [1977]), 224–25. Misled by Rabinowitz's claim, Wayne Booth concludes that Nabokov "was considerably more evasive behind his fictions than anything we have yet seen." *The Company We Keep: An Ethics of Fiction* (1988), 149.
3. Raymond Tallis, a gerontologist, philosopher, and literary theorist, makes this point again and again in his work, especially in *Newton's Sleep: The Two Cultures and The Two Kingdoms* (1995) and *Enemies of Hope: A Critique of Contemporary Pessimism* (1997).
4. Cf. John M. Ellis's perceptive remarks, in the article "Theory" in the *New Princeton Encyclopedia of Poetry and Poetics*, where he singles out Leo Spitzer's *Linguistics and Literary History* (1948) as still "The most sober attempt to develop a careful view of the procedure of literary criticism.... Spitzer suggested that the procedure of criticism, unlike that of science, was circular: we proceed from general impressions of the text to careful inspection of specific features of it, which then leads to amended and improved general ideas, which in turn lead us to look again at other parts of the text.... This view of critical procedure is a sophisticated one, and it shows very well the weakness of a reader-response criticism which makes the reader's response a dead end. What Spitzer did not see was that he had described the typical method of the sciences—hypothesis and experiment—though to be sure in terms which were far superior to the misconceptions about scientific method that have been predominant in theory of criticism" (1288; I have expanded the encyclopedia abbreviations). For an informed and penetrating discussion of the relationship between literary criticism and science, see Paisley Livingston, *Literary Knowledge: Humanistic Inquiry and the Philosophy of Science* (1988).
5. See Brian Boyd, *Vladimir Nabokov: The Russian Years* (1990, hereafter *VNRY*) and *Vladimir Nabokov: The American Years* (1991, hereafter *VNAY*);

Michel Sartori, ed., *Les Papillons de Nabokov* (1993); an ongoing series of nearly thirty papers, many collected in *Neotropical "Blue" Butterflies* (1993–97), by lepidopterists on three continents—Zsolt Bálint, Kurt Johnson, Dubi Benyamini, and Gerardo Lamas—which develops and honors Nabokov's legacy as first reviser of the South American lycaenids; Kurt Johnson, G. Warren Whitaker, and Zsolt Bálint, "Nabokov as Lepidopterist: An Informed Appraisal" (1996); Brian Boyd, "Nabokov's Lepidoptera" (1995); Dieter E. Zimmer, *Guide to Nabokov's Butterflies and Moths* (1996); Kurt Johnson and Stephen Coates, *Nabokov's Blues* (Cambridge, Mass.: Zoland, 1999), which examines Nabokov's legacy for lepidopterists, especially those working in Latin American blues, on which he wrote one key paper in 1945; *Nabokov's Butterflies*, ed. Brian Boyd with Robert Michael Pyle (2000), which collects all Nabokov's butterfly writings, scientific and literary.

6. *Strong Opinions* (1973, hereafter *SO*), 78–79, 100.

7. *Speak, Memory: An Autobiography Revisited* (1989 [1966], hereafter *SM*), 218.

8. See below, Chapter 8, pp. 111–26.

9. *Nabokov's Art of Memory and European Modernism* (1993), 231. Foster considerably overstates Calinescu's contention—Calinescu in fact does not even specifically mention *Pale Fire* in his *Five Faces of Modernity* (1987) (but see n. 11)—but it *is* true that the novel is widely seen as a key early instance of postmodernism.

10. On the list group, Nabokv-L (NABOKV-L@UCSBVM.UCSB.edu), December 1997–February 1998.

11. Matei Calinescu, in his *Rereading* (1993), 123–29, briefly and astutely considers *Pale Fire* in terms of the discoveries possible on a first and subsequent readings.

12. *SO*, 11. Nabokov wrote to Jacob Bronowski (August 16, 1963): "Scientific theories . . . are always the temporary gropings for truth of more or less gifted minds which gleam, fade, and are replaced by others." Vladimir Nabokov Archive, Henry W. and Albert A. Berg Collection, New York Public Library (hereafter VNA).

13. "Zemblances" (1982 [1962]), 144.

14. Popper's main works on the philosophy of science after *Logik der Forschung* (1934, English translation 1959) are *Conjectures and Refutations* (1963), *Objective Knowledge* (1972), and the three volumes of the *Postscript to the Logic of Scientific Discovery* (1982–83). The lecture "The Rationality of Scientific Revolutions" (1973), in *The Myth of the Framework* (1994), provides a useful introduction to his epistemology.

15. *Confessions of a Philosopher* (1997), 189.

16. Ibid., 197–98.

17. *The Open Society and Its Enemies* (1966 [1945]), 2:369.

18. Ibid., 2:378.

19. Richard Rorty in his *Objectivity, Relativism, and Truth* (1991) suggests a

partial overlap between his views of truth and Popper's: "This attitude toward truth, in which the consensus of a community rather than a relation to a nonhuman reality is taken as central, is associated not only with the American pragmatic tradition but with the work of Popper and Habermas" (23n). Joseph Carroll notes in his *Evolution and Literary Theory* (1995): "The suggestion of congruity here is seriously misleading. Rorty holds that some beliefs are more useful than others but are not therefore more accurate 'representations of reality' than others. Popper, like Lorenz, holds that some beliefs are more useful than others precisely *because* they are more accurate representations of reality. . . . The consensus theory of truth with which Rorty seeks to associate Popper is in fact an object of Popper's scorn" (453).

Popper dismisses the possibility of attaining certain knowledge, but, unlike Rorty ("truth is not a goal of inquiry," *Truth and Progress* [1998], 3), not of searching for truth, for a better fit between descriptions or theories and facts. Indeed, without the challenge that the recalcitrance of an independent reality poses to inquiry, it is hard to see why people would make the stupendous efforts needed to make knowledge advance, why merely "carrying on the conversation," in Rorty's terms, would lead to radically new ideas. As Susan Haack argues, Rorty's attitude would "undermine not only epistemology . . . but inquiry generally." *Evidence and Inquiry: Towards Reconstruction in Epistemology* (1993), 182–83. Peter Munz ("Philosophy and the Mirror of Rorty" [1987]) critiques Rorty's *Philosophy and the Mirror of Nature* from a Popperian standpoint.

20. In his political philosophy (especially in *The Open Society*) Popper points out that, since free criticism in an "open society" will allow the weakness of proposals and the dangers of their unexpected consequences to be detected more readily than in a society that does not invite criticism, an open society will in the long run be more efficient, contrary to popular belief, than even the most benevolent of dictatorships, and that democracy is not so much a system of representing the popular will as of allowing the populace to reject without violence governments that seem less attractive than the available alternative.

21. *Confessions*, 200, 204.

22. "Slava" ("Fame") (1942), in *Poems and Problems*, 112, 111.

23. *Lectures on Literature* (1980, hereafter *LL*), 3.

24. *SM*, 290.

25. *SO*, 183.

26. "Truth in Fiction," 213.

27. The context is worth quoting. Krug, who has recently lost his wife, looks on his son: "And what agony, thought Krug the thinker, to love so madly a little creature, formed in some mysterious fashion (even more mysterious to us than it had been to the very first thinkers in their pale olive groves) by the fusion of two mysteries, or rather two sets of a trillion of mysteries each;

formed by a fusion which is, at the same time, a matter of choice and a matter of chance and a matter of pure enchantment; thus formed and then permitted to accumulate trillions of its own mysteries; the whole suffused with consciousness, which is the only real thing in the world and the greatest mystery of all." *Bend Sinister* (1990 [1947]), 187–88.

28. *Selected Letters 1940–1977* (1989, hereafter *SL*), 134.

29. *The Gift* (1991 [1938]), 110.

30. *Bend Sinister*, 106.

31. *SM*, 275.

32. *SM*, 301. For accessible extended discussions of Nabokov's metaphysics in terms of the spiral, see Boyd, *Nabokov's* Ada (1985), 49–88, and *VNAY*, 292–320.

33. Janet K. Gezari, "Roman et problème chez Nabokov" (1974); Chris Ackerley, "*Pale Fire*: Three Notes toward a Thetic Solution" (1995).

34. I suspect Nabokov may even have tried to invent this particular problem *in order to* duplicate the process of discovery he prepared for readers of his fiction.

35. "The Sublime and the Ridiculous: Nabokov's Black Farces" (1979), 73.

36. *SO*, 283. He has also said: "I have the greatest readers any author has ever had." *SO*, 192.

37. *Speak, Memory*'s chess problem has been applied to *Pale Fire* from the time of Carol T. Williams's "'Web of Sense': *Pale Fire* in the Nabokov Canon" (1963) up to Ackerley, "*Pale Fire*: Three Notes" (1995).

38. He told his Wellesley College literature class at the start of the course: "Whichever subject you have chosen, you must realize that knowledge in it is limitless. Every subject brims with mysteries and thrills, and no two students of the same subject discover a like amount of delight, accumulate exactly the same amount of knowledge." From unpublished lecture notes (VNA), cited in Boyd, *VNAY*, 109–10.

CHAPTER 1
FOREWORD

1. All reference are to the Vintage edition (New York, 1989), a corrected version of the first edition (New York: Putnam's, 1962). Where the source is not already explicit, citations will be in the form F, P.xxx, C.xxx, I (for Foreword, Poem, Commentary, and Index), so that readers with any edition can locate a reference; page numbers to the Vintage edition are added, if needed, within the Foreword or long notes in the Commentary: "C.130, 125" means "note to line 130; Vintage (or Putnam's) page 125."

Further textual corrections and brief annotations are available in Vladimir Nabokov, *Novels 1955–1962*, ed. Brian Boyd (1996).

CHAPTER 2
POEM

1. "Reading Zemblan" (1987 [1982]), 106. Shade's image strikingly recalls an even more extended image that the narrator Fyodor Godunov-Cherdyntsev paraphrases from a *Discourse on Shades* by the invented French thinker Pierre Delalande, in Nabokov's last Russian novel, *The Gift*: "I know that death in itself is in no way connected with the topography of the hereafter, for a door is merely the exit from the house and not a part of its surroundings, like a tree or a hill. One has to get out somehow, 'but I refuse to see in a door more than a hole, and a carpenter's job' (Delalande, *Discours sur les ombres*, p. 45). And then again: the unfortunate image of a 'road' to which the human mind has become accustomed (life as a kind of journey) is a stupid illusion: we are not going anywhere, we are sitting at home. The other world surrounds us always and is not at all at the end of some pilgrimage. In our earthly house, windows are replaced by mirrors; the door, until a given time, is closed; but air comes in through the cracks." *Gift*, 321–22.

2. *Partial Magic: The Novel as a Self-Conscious Genre* (1975), 196.

3. *Speak, Memory* (1999), 250.

4. Cf. Elizabeth Dipple, *The Unresolvable Plot* (1988), 69.

5. As Kinbote's note to lines 39–40 shows, without his realizing it, a discarded variant to these lines ("and home would haste my thieves, / The sun with stolen ice, the moon with leaves") indicates that Shade has the *Timon of Athens* passage firmly in mind on the very first day of composing the poem. This suggests he planned to call it "Pale Fire" from the start, and is only feigning, on this last day of composition, to snatch at a title.

CHAPTER 3
COMMENTARY

1. See above, p. 33. Peter Hutchinson, *Games Authors Play* (1983), 38–39, and Matei Calinescu, *Rereading*, 124–25, 128–29, discuss some of Nabokov's strategy in inviting the reader to trace the source, but without considering the trail he leaves throughout the novel.

2. Nabokov explained to one French translator, Raymond Girard, "*to spurt* vieux dire *to squirt* avec un sens obscène" ("*to spurt* means *to squirt* in an obscene sense," [letter of December 27, 1963, VNA]) and to another, Maurice-Edgar Coindreau, "le pauvre et dégoûtant Dr. Kinbote se permet ici le triste luxe d'une métaphore obscène" ("poor disgusting Dr. Kinbote allows himself here the sad luxury of an obscene metaphor," [letter of January 14, 1964, VNA]).

3. Ellen Pifer, *Nabokov and the Novel* (1980), 113, notes "Bera" as an anagram of "bare."

4. He takes particular pleasure in girding the loins of Gordon, a fourteen- or fifteen-year-old lad, Charles II's sexual conquest from the previous year, in coverings that keep metamorphosing before our eyes and behind Gradus's back, from "a leopard-spotted loincloth" into ivy "wreathed about the loins," "black bathing trunks," "white tennis shorts," and a "Tarzan brief . . . cast aside on the turf" (C.408).

5. Such as his misconstruing a note saying, "You have hal . . . . . s real bad, chum" as referring to "hallucinations" rather than "halitosis" (C.62, 98), the "Poor old man Swift" note (C.231), and the "lunatic a king" note (C.417–21).

6. In *VNAY*, 435, I suggest Kinbote's very active homosexuality and extreme paranoia as one of Nabokov's many deliberate counterblasts to Freud, since Freud explains paranoia in terms of *repressed* homosexuality.

7. I have corrected the text's erroneous "principles."

CHAPTER 4
INDEX

1. "Fiction Chronicle" (1962), 421.

2. He does in fact feature on one other occasion, but this reference, the key one (C.172), is omitted from the Index.

3. In the Commentary, Kinbote specifically mentions that Shade "has given the royal fugitive a refuge in the vaults of the variants he has preserved; for in his draft as many as *thirteen* verses, superb singing verses . . . bear the specific imprint of my theme" (C.42; italics added).

CHAPTER 5
PALE FIRE

1. A series of publishing problems delayed its appearance to 1964.

2. *SL*, 201.

3. *SL*, 132.

4. *SO*, 13.

5. Letter to Sylvia Berkman, October 10, 1956, VNA.

6. Letter to Roman Grynberg, January 19, 1957, VNA. Quoted in *VNAY*, 302.

7. And of course out of much else. As has often been noticed, Nabokov touches elsewhere on the theme of the imagined northern land, as a more-or-less warped reflection of Russia, in the Zoorland of *Glory* (1932) and the Ultima Thule of what would have been his last Russian novel, *Solus Rex* (1940–42). For the two chapters of the novel that were completed, see "Ultima Thule" and

"Solus Rex" in *Stories*, 496–541. For other elements of a first version of *Pale Fire*, with the northern land and with footnotes, but without the poem-and-commentary structure or the fugitive king's homosexuality, see *SL*, 212–13 and below, pp. 79–80.

8. *Conclusive Evidence* (1951), 217. Nabokov is writing here about the Russian literary emigration and about the writer there who interested him most, "Sirin," his own pen name in those years.

9. For an astute analysis of *Pale Fire* along these lines, see Ellen Pifer, *Nabokov and the Novel* (1980), 110–18.

10. *A New Mimesis: Shakespeare and the Representation of Reality* (1983), 143.

CHAPTER 6
INTRUSIONS OF THE REAL

1. For an accessible account, see *VNRY*, 189–93.

2. In an interview, Nabokov stated that Wordsmith was "much more to the south than any of the colleges with which I've been connected." Interview with Phyllis Méras, May 13, 1962, for *New York Herald Tribune*, from typescript in VNA. The flora and fauna may indicate somewhere a little further south in Appalachia, but the particular features of the landscape—the lakes, the campus, the academic suburb—remain close to Cornell.

3. *Essay on Man*, 2.224.

4. Jonathan Swift, *A Tale of a Tub* (1958 [1704]), 240.

5. *SL*, 212–13.

6. Slightly adapted from Gennady Barabtarlo and Evgeny Shikhovtsev, "The Republic of Zembla" (1987), 54–56.

7. But not—as D. Barton Johnson was the first to point out in his *Worlds in Regression* (1985), 68—to anything in Zemblan history: despite its synoptic survey of Zembla's past, the Index lists no "Charles I" of Zembla.

8. *The History of the Rebellion and Civil Wars in England Begun in the Year 1641*, 6 vols., ed. W. Dunn Macray, 5:198.

9. For brief line-by-line annotations, see my notes to *Pale Fire* in the Library of America edition. In her extremely erratic *Find What the Sailor Has Hidden: Vladimir Nabokov's* Pale Fire (1988), Priscilla Meyer provides many attempted glosses to the novel in pursuit of a dotty thesis that "*Pale Fire* effects a synthesis of British and American culture, outlining the thousand-year evolution of the Anglo-American tradition from the end of the reign of King Alfred in 899 to the birth of Vladimir Vladimirovich [Nabokov] in 1899" (4), but she repeatedly overlooks relevant information (such as the Clarendon passage above, the Carol II parallel, the Grand Duke Konstantin identification) while introducing endless irrelevancies (she declares for instance that in "Conmal" Nabokov parodies James MacPherson's false derivations of names in the Ossian poems,

such as Caol-mahl, "a woman with slender eyebrows," Cor-mar, "an expert at sea" [58], without suggesting how these might relate to the Conmal, a king's uncle and translator, in *Pale Fire*).

10. Line 596 is dated in C.596, 232; line 698, in C.741, 254.

11. Tenishev school records show that Nabokov studied German at school and examined Goethe's "Erlkönig," which seems to have remained his favorite German poem. See Brian Boyd, "Nabokov's Russian Years Revisited" (1994), 75.

12. *A Handbook to the Works of Robert Browning* (6th ed. N.p.: Bell, [1892], 55), cited in *Robert Browning: The Poems, Volume I*, ed. John Pettigrew and Thomas J. Collins (1981), 1069.

CHAPTER 7
EXCURSIONS FROM THE REAL

1. See Introduction above, pp. 8–11.

2. A point well stressed by Richard Rorty, in his 1992 introduction to the Everyman *Pale Fire*, although he overstates the extent to which we overlook Shade early in a first reading, and underplays the extent to which Kinbote, late in a first reading, distracts us from fully focusing on the death.

3. Estonian, Lettish, Lithuanian, Romanian, Hungarian, and Albanian are all non-Slavic.

4. As if the information comes in reverse order because the syllables of the name are back to front?

5. Although all the surnames he mentions here derive from professions, all but "Botkin" (Rymer, Scrivener, Limner) have something to do with preparing texts. See D. Barton Johnson, *Worlds in Regression*, 70; Johnson was the first to consider Botkin carefully.

6. Meyer, *Find What the Sailor Has Hidden*, 115–17, considers Vasily Botkin but belabors his connection with *Pale Fire*.

7. Another detail links the name Botkin with the other side of Nabokov's family. Kinbote offers the etymology "Botkin (one who makes bottekins, fancy footwear)" (C.71, 100); Nabokov's mother's maiden name was Rukavishnikov, which we could gloss "one who makes *rukavitsy* [gauntlets], fancy handwear." For S. D. Botkin, see *VNRY*, 456; for the etymology of "Rukavishnikov," *VNRY*, 30.

8. As Alexandrov observes in *Nabokov's Otherworld*, 189.

9. Perhaps, after the Russian Revolution, in Riga, a major Russian émigré center in the 1920s while Latvia was independent of Russia. "English and Lettish" forms the first pair after "English and Russian" in Kinbote's hysterical notes on "two languages" (C.615); Gradus is born in Riga on the very day Kin-

bote is born; Zemgale is the name of a Latvian tribe and a former (pre-1939) province.

10. *The Eye* (1990 [1930]), 13.

11. Or perhaps Norway (which was joined to Sweden until 1905), in view of his interest in Icelandic literature, and in view of the fact that his quotation from the *New York Times* of July 21, 1959, p. 12, substitutes Zembla for Norway in the real-life version of the *Times*: "And at a picnic for international children a Zemblan moppet cried to her Japanese friend: *Ufgut, ufgut, velkam ut Semblerland!* [Adieu, adieu, till we meet in Zembla!]" (C.949/2, 275).

12. See also C.347, 185 and C.579, 228. Of course, Kinbote also resents members of the Wordsmith English Department merely because they are institutionally closer to Shade than he is himself.

13. Kinbote may owe a little to two people close to the Nabokovs. Nabokov's wife's sister, Elena Massalsky (née Slonim), converted to Catholicism in the emigration in Berlin, married a Russian prince, and moved to Sweden. Like Kinbote, she became religiose. Nabokov's brother Sergey, a homosexual, also converted to Roman Catholicism in his émigré years.

14. Which has also contributed place names to Zembla, the Swiss resorts of Arosa and Grindelwald becoming "Aros and Grindelwod" (C.149, 138). Voss, "How Not to Read Zemblan" (1990), 45.

15. Nabokov spelled this out for his French translators: "Le petit sac couturé d'un bambin *or better* le scrotum d'un garçonnet (Dr. Kinbote is not a nice man). [A small boy's little seamed pouch *or better* a little boy's scrotum]." *Feu pâle* MS, VNA.

16. Alter, *Partial Magic*, 195, notes the first three but not the fourth.

17. Nabokov noted for his French translator, Maurice-Edgar Coindreau: "Allusion au fameux roman 'For ever Amber' . . . ce bestseller idiot [Allusion to the famous novel . . . this idiotic bestseller]." Letter of January 14, 1964, VNA.

18. "A Perfect Day for Bananafish" (January 31, 1948), "Uncle Wiggily in Connecticut" (March 20, 1948), "Franny" (January 29, 1955), "Raise High the Roof Beam, Carpenters" (November 19, 1955), "Zooey," (May 4, 1957) and (a little late for Mrs. Goldsworth's shelves) "Seymour: An Introduction" (June 6, 1959), all published in *The New Yorker*. Mrs. Goldsworth's bookshelf probably contained Salinger's *Nine Stories* (1953), which included "A Perfect Day for Bananafish" and "Uncle Wiggily in Connecticut," and has as its epigraph, "We know the sound of two hands clapping. But what is the sound of one hand clapping?—From a Zen koan." Nabokov, a regular contributor during these years to *The New Yorker*, regarded Salinger more highly than any other contemporary American writer of fiction and singled out "A Perfect Day for Bananafish" for special praise (*SO*, 313).

19. "Reading Zemblan," 119.

20. The first was first noted in Field, *Nabokov: His Life in Art* (1967), 312; the second in D. Barton Johnson, *Worlds in Regression*, 65 and 76n.27.

21. Mary McCarthy made the identification in her 1962 review ("A Bolt from the Blue," viii).

22. See D. Barton Johnson, *Worlds in Regression*, 65; and Pekka Tammi, *Problems of Nabokov's Poetics: A Narratological Analysis* (1985), 207.

23. Like the names of Hamlet's spying false friends, theirs too are transposed, into "Andron and Niagarushka" (C.741, 255).

24. Although the "two experts" are deliberately a Tweedledum-and-Tweedledee pair, we can work out which is probably which. "Niagarin who had lived in Canada spoke English and French; Andronnikov had some German" (C.681, 245) suggests that Niagarin is Hurley, who offers as a tip for pronouncing the name "Pnin," "Think of the French word for 'tire': *punoo*" (C.894, 268), and that keen Freudian Prof. C., who quotes Dr. Oskar Pfister and Erich Fromm to his classes (C.929, 271), is Andronnikov.

25. As Nabokov pointed out when asked in a 1966 interview (*SO*, 92).

26. Ironically, Kinbote had chosen the spot because the Shades were to have traveled there in August, to stay in the ranch belonging to the Hurleys, who were vacationing elsewhere (C.287, 182—83).

27. As Nabokov indicated in impetuous pencil on the margin of my MA thesis, where I had made a vapidly sloppy identification.

28. Published as a broadside, 1660.

29. In his *Poems and Songs*, 1686.

30. Though she identifies Flatman—but so after all does Kinbote himself—Meyer (*Find What the Sailor Has Hidden*, 158) as usual completely misses the point, discussing other works by Flatman but not noticing his eulogies of Charles II.

31. See also C.802, 258.

32. *SO*, 74.

33. *The Magician's Doubts* (1994), 186.

34. If Kinbote jumps to his doom somewhere above Cedarn, Utana, his death would also link oddly with the waxwing image of the poem, since the waxwing is a cedar waxwing and "cedarn" an adjective derived from *cedar*. The waxwing that flies to its death inevitably calls to mind Icarus, the son of Daedalus, who after aspiring too high on his wax wings plummets to his death. Kinbote, himself aspiring too high when he imagines himself king of Zembla, announces that Charles II's royal coat of arms boasts a bird "closely resembling a waxwing in shape and shade" (C.1–4). The owner of Kinbote's mountain cabin, whose twisted limp reminds him of Shade, passes on to Kinbote the *Letters of Franklin Lane*, U.S. Secretary of the Interior from 1913 to 1915, whose name curiously matches the last word of Shade's poem and whose last written reflection, on the eve of his death, as Kinbote notes, "curiously echoes

Shade's tone at the end of Canto Three. . . . 'And if I had passed into that other land, whom would I have sought? . . . Aristotle!—Ah, there would be a man to talk with! What satisfaction to see him take, like reins from between his fingers, the long ribbon of man's life and trace it through the mystifying maze of all the wonderful adventure. . . . The crooked made straight. The Daedalian plan simplified by a look from above. . .'" (C.810).

CHAPTER 8
PROBLEMS

1. Either a misprint for "chthonic" or, as John Burt Foster, Jr., suggests (*Nabokov's Art of Memory*, 222), Hazel's mispronunciation.

2. Corrected, as in the Library of America edition, from "tryptich." Nabokov spells the word normally at C.80 (111) and elsewhere.

3. Despite the growing strains in their friendship, Nabokov heartily approved Edmund Wilson's essay "T.S. Eliot and the Church of England" when he read it in 1958, and wrote him that "Eliot's image will never be the same." Vladimir Nabokov, *Nabokov-Wilson Letters*, ed. Simon Karlinsky (1979), 323 (the published date of the letter, March 24, should be amended to May 26); Nabokov did not seem to realize that Wilson had first published the essay in 1929. In the essay Wilson quotes Eliot's statement of his position, in the preface to *For Lancelot Andrewes*, as "classicist in literature, royalist in politics, and Anglo-Catholic in religion," and commented wrily: "Eliot has gone to England and evolved for himself an aristocratic myth out of English literature and history." *The Shores of Light* (1952), 437, 439.

4. "Burnt Norton" (1936), "East Coker" (1940), "The Dry Salvages" (1941), and "Little Gidding" (1942), published together as *Four Quartets* (1943). "Grimpen" comes from "East Coker," II (l. 93); "chthonic" from "Dry Salvages," V (l. 225); "semipiternal" from "Little Gidding," I (l. 2) (Eliot, *Collected Poems*, 1963). Peter Lubin identified the sources in his "Kickshaws and Motley" (1970), 205n.7, to which Nabokov responded: "Very beautifully he tracks down to their lairs in Eliot three terms queried by a poor little person in *Pale Fire*" (*SO*, 291). (Nabokov's comment plays on the tracking down of the hound of the Baskervilles—Conan Doyle's novel is the source for Eliot's word—to its lair in Grimpen Mire.) As Foster notes (*Nabokov's Art of Memory*, 223–24), the "grimpen" (swamp) and "semipiternal" (in Eliot's poem: "Midwinter spring is its own season / Sempiternal though sodden towards sundown") anticipate Hazel's death in a swamp, as she steps off the ice on a "night of thaw" when "Black spring / Stood just around the corner" (P.494–96).

5. Nabokov offered a similar decoding to Andrew Field in a letter of September 26, 1966, cited *VNAY*, 454; and Véra Nabokov did the same for

Gennady Barabtarlo (*Aerial View: Essays on Nabokov's Art and Metaphysics* [1993], 207–8) in explaining her Russian translation of the passage in *Blednyy ogon'* (1983). Not knowing what more to say, Field reported only: "Those sounds, by the way,"—a light, in fact, not sound—"are actually a warning to John Shade not to go to the Goldsworth house." *Nabokov: His Life in Art*, 307. Presumably working from this hint, Robert Martin Adams decoded the message thus: "Father Atalantis pleads not to go Goldsworth where tale from foreign lant will be told." *Afterjoyce* (1977), 153.

6. As Véra Nabokov confirms in a letter to Igor Yefimov, July 8, 1980 (VNA).

7. First noted in Williams, "Web of Sense: *Pale Fire* in the Nabokov Canon" (1963), 36.

8. See C.181, 157–61, and C.949/2, 275.

9. From *Pale Fire* manuscript, Box 1, Vladimir Nabokov Collection, Library of Congress.

10. NABOKV-L@UCSBVM.UCSB.EDU; the debate began on 15 December 1997 and lasted until early February 1998, with occasional later aftershocks.

11. *Nabokov: His Life in Art*, 291–322.

12. *Crystal Land: Artifice in Nabokov's English Novels* (1972), 31–56.

13. *VNAY*, 425–56.

14. December 22, 1997.

15. Barabtarlo, *Aerial View*, 242, and NABOKV-L, January 9, 1998; Ackerley, "*Pale Fire*: Three Notes"; Il'yn, NABOKV-L, December 19, 1997.

16. *Escape into Aesthetics: The Art of Vladimir Nabokov*, 116–32.

17. Tammi, *Problems*, 197–221, and "*Pale Fire*" (1995); and Nicol, NABOKV-L, December 16 and 23, 1997. D. Barton Johnson, *Worlds in Regression*, 60–77, is both anti-Shadean and anti-Kinbotean but a semi-Botkinian. Indicating Botkin as the "real" person behind Kinbote, he asks: "Is Botkin perhaps a Wordsmith faculty member who is writing a novel about the entirely fictional characters Kinbote, Shade and Gradus? The idea would be attractive were it not that Botkin and Kinbote are almost certainly the same person. More plausible is that Shade, his poem and his killer are all real as is V. Botkin, a drab Wordsmith faculty member" (70–71); but he adds: "Within the world of *Pale Fire*, V. Botkin is the source from which all else flows" (72).

18. "Reading Zemblan."

19. *Postmodernist Fiction* (1987), 18–19.

20. *Partial Magic*, 184–217.

21. *Nabokov and the Novel*, 110–18.

22. *The Practice of Writing: Essays, Lectures, Reviews and a Diary* (1996), 161–64.

23. NABOKV-L, January 8, 1998.

24. See *VNAY*, 445 and Chapter 13, note 13 below.

25. NABOKV-L, January 8, 1998; Pifer, *Nabokov and the Novel*, 187n.15; Alter, *Partial Magic*, 186.

26. "Reading Zemblan," 122. As an example of the way anti-Shadeans can overlook the covert correspondences between part and part, let me cite Pifer: "The tenuous relationship between Shade's poem and Kinbote's Commentary . . . has disturbed many of the novel's readers." *Nabokov and the Novel*, 117. But it is not the tenuous relationship between the parts that disturbs; that is perfectly understandable as a product of Kinbote's insane egotism, and hilarious, and has troubled no one. What *has* perturbed *some* readers is the intimacy of the relationship between part and part, when at a surface level they indeed appear to be utterly remote.

27. "Reading Zemblan," 114.

28. *Crystal Land*, 37.

29. Tammi, *Problems*, and *"Pale Fire"*; Nicol, NABOKV-L, December 23, 1997. See also Maddox, *Nabokov's Novels in English* (1983), 24–25.

30. As Tammi notes in *"Pale Fire,"* 586n.45, there is no reason to imagine, as Alexandrov supposes (*Nabokov's Otherworld*, 209–10), that Kinbote "does not notice" the echo.

31. Nicol, NABOKV-L, December 23, 1997.

32. Except, of course, in detached incidentals, such as the waxwing-like "*sampel* (silktail)" that Kinbote announces in the first note—before he begins the narrative he has told Shade—forms part of the armorial bearings of Charles the Beloved.

33. See below, pp. 121–22 and nn. 35–36.

34. See above, note 8.

35. The larva of a botfly.

36. D. Barton Johnson notes that "Sybil's '*king*-sized *bot*fly' can anagrammatically refer equally well to either Kinbote or Botkin." *Worlds in Regression*, 69. Chris Ackerley was the first to draw my attention to the echo between poem and index (private communication). Nabokov had *his* attention drawn to botfly maggots at a meeting of the Cambridge Entomological Club in the Harvard Faculty Club on October 10, 1944, where after he spoke on "A Genus of Blue Butterflies," Professor Brues showed "a reel film on Bot fly maggots." Minutes of the Cambridge Entomological Club, in *Nabokov's Butterflies*, ed. Boyd and Pyle (forthcoming, 2000).

37. *Ada or Ardor: A Family Chronicle* (1990 [1969]), pt. 1, chap. 42, pp. 304–6, 600. For more detail on Van's assault on homosexuality in this passage, see J. E. Rivers and William Walker, "Notes to Vivian Darkbloom's Notes to *Ada*" (1982), 286.

38. From chap. 16 of *Conclusive Evidence*, which Nabokov decided not to publish. See Nabokov's *Speak, Memory* (1999), 250.

39. *The Practice of Writing*, 162–64.

40. *Worlds in Regression*, 67–77.

41. In his *Nabokov's Otherworld*, 210–11, Vladimir Alexandrov deals with two other plays on Russian words difficult for a non-expert.

42. *VNAY*, 455.

43. For the convincing suggestion that the Shades' unattractive and ungainly only child, born in 1934 and doomed by her physical awkwardness and withdrawnness, is a mirror-reversal of the Nabokovs' only child, also born in 1934, a daredevil and playboy frequently at risk because of his physical adroitness and adventuresomeness, see Robert Alter, "Autobiography as Alchemy in *Pale Fire*" (1993), 136–37.

CHAPTER 9
TRANSFORMATION

1. Although "neon signs" may now loosely refer to many kinds of display lighting, neon itself burns with a brilliant orangy red.

2. "Reading Zemblan," 121.

3. Barabtarlo was the first to notice the threefold *"atalanta"* here (*Aerial View*, 207).

4. Nabokov stresses the identification of Sybil Shade's beauty with the *Vanessa atalanta*'s by having her portrait painted by a painter named "Lang" (P.682). In *Speak, Memory* Nabokov recalls his admiration in his childhood and youth for the "incomparably beautiful" butterfly drawings of Lang (*SM*, 122).

5. At the time Nabokov was most interested in these butterflies, they were still known by the genus name *Pieris*; that has since been revised to *Artogeia*. "Toothwort White," far from being an accepted common name, seems to have been proposed here for the first time by Shade and Nabokov. Lepidopterist Robert Dirig, who had himself tried to propose a new common name, in view of the fact that the West Virginia White is not confined to West Virginia, thinks Nabokov's proposal far superior to his own proposal, "Woodland White," since its relatives are also named after their food plants: the Cabbage White feeds on cabbages, sometimes; the Mustard White on mustard plants, usually; and the Toothwort White on toothworts, almost always (personal communication).

6. Alexander B. Klots, *A Field Guide to the Butterflies of North America, East of the Great Plains* (1951), 201; and Robert Michael Pyle, *The Audubon Society Field Guide to North American Butterflies* (1981), 359. Shade's lines accurately reflect the timing of the butterfly's appearance: the adult butterfly lives for only two weeks in late April and early May.

7. "The Transition Zone is . . . not well marked in itself, but rather a borderline or tension zone where Canadian and Austral zones meet and mingle. . . . A few butterflies found mostly in the Transition Zone are: *Pieris virginiensis*, . . . *Lycaeides melissa samuelis*. . . ." Klots, *Field Guide*, 25.

8. "The Nearctic Forms of *Lycaeides* Hüb[ner] (Lycaenidae, Lepidoptera)"

(1943). As Robert Dirig notes, Nabokov later came to think this not just a subspecies but a distinct species. "But he did not live to do the taxonomic work necessary to prove this, and the question remains" open. "Nabokov's Blue Snowflakes" (1988), 68–69. The Cornell entomologist John G. Franclemont reports that he collected butterflies with Nabokov in the Ithaca area "on a very few occasions in the spring" in the early 1950s. "He was interested in collecting one of the 'Whites,' *Pieris virginiensis*. One trip that I recall with pleasure was to McLean Bogs in the second week of May; it was an afternoon of delightful weather and discussions, but no white butterflies." "Remembering Nabokov" (1984), 227–28. A few years afterward (May 31, 1959), Nabokov wrote to Franclemont: "In April we stayed for a week in the Great Smokies, Tenn., where we had a delightful time with *Pieris virginiensis*." *Nabokov's Butterflies* (forthcoming). Nabokov caught his first *virginiensis* on April 21, 1959.

9. Pyle, *Audubon Society Field Guide*, 359.

10. Klots, *Field Guide*, 201.

11. Pyle, *Audubon Society Field Guide*, 628.

12. P.357, 355.

13. Véra Nabokov singled out *potustoronnost'* (the beyond) as her husband's "main theme" in her introduction to *Stikhi* (1979), 3. I treated the theme at length in "Nabokov and *Ada*" (1979); in *Nabokov's Ada: The Place of Consciousness* (1985); and in the two volumes of the biography, *VNRY* and *VNAY*. William Woodin Rowe's *Nabokov's Spectral Dimension* (1981) is vulgar and almost always unjustified spook-spotting; D. Barton Johnson's *Worlds in Regression* (1985), although focused on the puzzles individual novels pose, deals with the beyond in terms of the "two-world theme," especially in the introduction and section 6; Julian Conolly examines "The Otherworldly in Nabokov's Poetry" (1991), where it is even more dominant than in the prose; Vladimir Alexandrov's *Nabokov's Otherworld* (1991), introduces the topic well but sometimes pushes associations too far; Gennady Barabtarlo's *Aerial Views* (1993) illuminates some striking details; Maxim Shrayer, *The World of Nabokov's Stories* (1998) traces this theme, among others, in the stories.

14. Published 1958, rpt. in *The Stories of Vladimir Nabokov*, 1995. See pp. 213–15 below for a more detailed discussion.

15. *Stories*, 134.

16. *Stories*, 136. Ellipsis in original; this is the end of the story.

17. Klots, *Field Guide*, 36–37.

18. Maxim Shrayer, *The Worlds of Nabokov's Stories* (1998), 34, rightly stresses the openness of the ending: does Sleptsov see this or not?

19. *Glory* (1991 [1932]), xiii. The problem is unpublished but survives in an undated manuscript, perhaps from the 1940s (VNA). Nabokov notes next to the diagram: "The strongest piece on the board gets in the way of the knights and has to be banished to a remote square!"

20. Shade in the poem writes of "Playing a game of worlds, promoting pawns / To ivory unicorns and ebon fauns." Such pieces, with names and powers different from those in the standard game, belong, aptly enough, to so-called fairy chess.

21. *Pippa Passes*, Part 1, ll. 364–65 (Browning, *Poems*, 1:314). Canova made two versions of the sculpture: the first (1789–92) is now at Blundel Hall, the second (1793–94) at the Kunsthalle, Brema. The second has inscribed on it two lines from Dante: *"non v'accorgete voi che noi siam vermi / nati a formar l'angelica farfalla . . . ?* [are you not aware that we are worms, born to form the angelic butterfly . . . ?]" *Purgatorio*, 10.124–25; Charles S. Singleton translation (1973), 106–7. Canova also made two versions of *Psyche and Cupid* with a butterfly, and two versions of them without.

22. Speaking of his research for his unfinished *Butterflies in Art* project, Nabokov said of the butterfly paintings he was investigating: "That in some cases the butterfly symbolizes something (*e.g.*, Psyche) lies utterly outside my area of interest" (*SO*, 168). This of course was in keeping with the purely taxonomic and evolutionary aims of that project, and did not preclude his himself using the conventional symbolism elsewhere for an entirely different purpose.

23. *Pippa Passes*, Part 2, ll. 288–91 (Browning, *Poems* 1:323–24).

24. Robert Dirig considers Nabokov's unexpected "geranium bar" an "absolutely perfect" image for the red on the Vanessa's wing (private communication). A waxwing's wing could also be said to be "scalloped," but its "wax-red streaks" do not have the velvety red of a geranium petal or the bar on an *atalanta*'s wing.

25. *LL*, 2.

26. *Look at The Harlequins!* (1990 [1974]), 16.

27. *The Real Life of Sebastian Knight* (1992 [1941]), 176, 177.

28. *SO*, 7.

29. *SO*, 10.

30. *SO*, 79.

31. *SO*, 330.

32. *SM*, 275.

33. Popper, *Conjectures and Refutations* (1972 [1963]), 28: "Every solution of a problem raises new unsolved problems; the more so the deeper the original problem and the bolder its solution."

34. The echo becomes even stronger when we note that the *Vanessa atalanta*, as it moves to greet Shade in the note to line 993–995, has "begun working up between the junipers and ornamental shrubs," for in the first note in the Commentary Kinbote observes that he has often seen waxwings "most convivially feeding on the chalk-blue berries of junipers growing at the corner of [Shade's] house." The waxwing of the poem is a cedar waxwing, but as Nabokov noted for his French translator, "Ce qu'on appelle *cedar* en Amérique n'est pas un

cedre mais un genevrier. [What Americans call *cedar* is not a cedar but a juni-per.]" Letter to Maurice-Edgar Coindreau, January 14, 1964, VNA.

35. See above, p. 107.

CHAPTER 10
FROM APPALACHIA TO ZEMBLA

1. *Stories*, 620.

2. See pp. 213–15.

3. For the "Four Quartets" echo, see pp. 108–9; for "The Waste Land," see Chapter 12.

4. See p. 203.

5. D. Barton Johnson discusses Nabokov's pointed play with the first and last letters of the Old Church Slavonic alphabet, again in connection with an opposition between this world and the next, in his "The Alpha and Omega of *Invitation to a Beheading*," in *Worlds in Regression*, 28–46.

6. Cf. the genuine Scottish place names Lochan Fada, Lochearnhead, and Lochinver. The last of course calls to mind the ballad of "Lochinvar" from canto 5 of Scott's *Marmion*.

7. Gerard de Vries, "Nabokov, Pushkin and Scott" (1997), 317; cf. also de Vries, "Fanning the Poet's Fire: Some Remarks on Nabokov's *Pale Fire*" (1991), 254.

8. Scotland, of course, in this case; the king is James V.

9. In her review of *Pale Fire*, Mary McCarthy traced Hazel's name to a famous line at the opening of canto 1 of *The Lady of the Lake*, "In lone Glenart-ney's hazel shade" (xv), but she and others overlooked the line that matters for Nabokov.

10. This, I suspect, happens to reflect Nabokov's attitude to homosexuality. For all his prodigious imagination, he appears not to have been able to imagine in any detail sexual pleasure between men, but he *could* imagine vividly—and only feel as wonderfully absurd—a man's turning away from the beauties of women.

11. *Stories*, 518.

12. Boyd, *Nabokov's Ada*, 73; cf., for instance, Alexandrov, *Nabokov's Other-world*, 210.

13. Nabokov wrote a long poem called "Lilith," a comic erotic nightmare, in 1930 (*Poems and Problems*, 50–55, where he dates it 1928).

14. *SM*, 146.

15. Rowe was the first to note this echo (*Nabokov's Spectral Dimension*, 26).

16. Kinbote uses this phrase in another context (C.579, 228), but it certainly applies to his judgment of Emerald and the imagined Izumrudov.

17. The full scientific name is *Apatura iris* L. *Iris* was also the name of a famous nineteenth-century lepidopterological journal Nabokov cites in the course of his scientific work.

18. In a note in his *Eugene Onegin* commentary, Nabokov comments on the different senses of 'purple' in different European languages: the English violet versus the crimsonish red the word evokes in French and Russian (*Eugene Onegin* 2:520–21).

19. See chapters 4, 8, and 12 of Lewis Carroll's *Through the Looking Glass* (1960), 238, 293, 344.

20. That Nabokov intends to evoke the butterfly *disa* he makes clear in the Index, where the next entry after *"Disa"* is *"Embla*, a small old town with a wooden church surrounded by sphagnum bogs at the saddest, loneliest, northmost point of the misty peninsula, *149, 433.*" *Erebia embla*, the Lapland Ringlet, whose habitat is Finland and the northern part of Sweden, closely resembles its sister species *disa*. See Lionel G. Higgins and Norman D. Riley, *A Field Guide to the Butterflies of Britain and Europe* (1993 [1970]), 283–84, maps 277–78.

21. As Nabokov notes for his French translators, January 11, 1965, p. 24, *Feu pâle* MS, VNA.

22. Phrynia and Timandra are two whores in *Timon of Athens*, IV.iii—the scene from which the phrase "pale fire" derives. In Shakespeare's play, of course, they are unequivocally feminine.

23. This report of the dreams that rack him—and they become more painful the longer he dwells on them—curiously echoes the start of the tunnel episode in the greenroom with the picture of Iris Acht above the closet: the "flash" of signals from the tower that cause the King to be sent down to the lumber room, with its "green silk sofa" and a window that "had once been a glorious dreamway of stained glass, with a firebird and a dazzled huntsman" but was shattered and is now replaced with plain glass (C.130, 121) recur here in the "bird of wonder in a tale for children" the "flash," the "sofa," and the "Glass Works explosion."

24. In continental chess terminology, the files are lettered "a–h" and the ranks numbered "1–8," so that one corner in which the "king-in-the-corner" of the *solus rex* problem could be trapped would be "h8," while "i8" would indicate a move one square beyond that corner, to a non-existent ninth file.

25. Cf. both "the solitary confinement of their souls" (*Conclusive Evidence*, 217), and "a personality consisting mainly of the shadow of its own prison bars" (*Pale Fire*, C.549, 227).

26. Ll. 305–6. Jonathan Swift, *The Complete Poems* (1983), 138.

27. When Alfred Appel, Jr., asked him was it only a coincidence that Kinbote's Foreword to *Pale Fire*, the last part he writes, is dated "Oct. 19," the date of Swift's death, Nabokov replied: "I think it is so nice that the day on which Kinbote committed suicide (and he certainly did after putting the last touches

to his edition of the poem) happens to be both the anniversary of Pushkin's *Lyceum* and that of 'poor old man Swift''s death, which is news to me (but see variant in note to line 231)." *SO*, 74–75.

CHAPTER 11
"PALE FIRE"

1. Unpublished lecture notes, VNA; cited *VNAY*, 100.

2. Williams, "Web of Sense," 35; Stegner, *Escape into Aesthetics*, 125; Peter Lubin, "Kickshaws and Motley," 196; Meyer, *Find What the Sailor Has Hidden*, 113; Herbert Grabes, "Nabokov and Shakespeare: The English Works" (1995), 509; Ackerley, "*Pale Fire*: Three Notes," 99.

3. Cf. the opening of Nabokov's autobiography: "The cradle rocks above an abyss, and common sense tells us that our existence is but a brief crack of light between two eternities of darkness. Although the two are identical twins, man, as a rule, views the prenatal abyss with more calm than the one he is heading for (at some forty-five hundred heartbeats an hour)" (*SM*, 19). The image, ultimately derived from Lucretius, had already featured in *The Gift* ("the receding from primal nonexistence becomes an approach to it when I strain my memory to the very limit so as to taste of that darkness and use its lessons to prepare myself for the darkness to come; but, as I turn my life upside-down so that birth becomes death, I fail to see at the verge of this dying-in-reverse anything that would correspond to the boundless terror that even a centenarian is said to experience when he faces the positive end") (11); and in *Bend Sinister* ("Can we work ourself into a state of abject panic by trying to imagine the infinite number of years . . . which extends on the minus side of the day of our birth? We cannot . . . ") (192–99).

4. Alter, *Partial Magic*, 190, may have been the first to link the lemniscate with Iris Acht.

5. See above, pp. 52–55, 169.

CHAPTER 12
"A POEM IN FOUR CANTOS"

1. Alexandrov glosses the full Nabokovian implications of the riposte to La Fontaine: "'the song,' or art, is linked to transcendence, while utilitarian efforts are not." *Nabokov's Otherworld*, 197.

2. The combination of a statement explicitly affirming the impenetrability of life's relation to death and covertly indicating someone's survival after death recalls the ending of "The Vane Sisters" (see pp. 213–15). Shade does not know

what Hazel recorded, but even if he had, of course, he could not have deciphered it until his own death belatedly clarifies the message.

3. Shade renders the trees he names in "Pale Fire" with a naturalist's sharp eye but has them all cast a supernatural shadow. Hazel's "shagbark" or "hickory" is repeatedly associated with "shade," "shadow," and "phantom" (in such lines as "The phantom of my little daughter's swing"); the "pine's bark" at P.237 bears that empty case of the cicada that has flown away, the day Maud dies, to sing of ongoing life; the "cedar trunks" illuminated by the patrol car link up, like the "azure" of the bar, with the triumphant image of the waxwing; the one other tree specified is a yew, a traditional image of death, again associated here with "shade" and the hereafter, in the name "Yewshade" (P.509), the location of the Institution of Preparation for the Hereafter (I.P.H., "or If, as we / Called it," in further echo of "L'if, lifeless tree," C.501: French for "yew"). "Hazel" of course is a species of tree, and "shade tree" is a loose popular classification.

4. *Ada*, 595.

5. The "azure" of the poem's opening couplet also clearly engages with Stéphane Mallarmé's recurrent image of the "Azur," representing the Ideal, as opposed to the "Ici-bas," the here-below, the here and now, in such poems as "L'Azur," "Retourneur," "Le Soupir," and especially the most important of these early poems, "Les Fenêtres." Nabokov recalled that "ce n'est pas Coppée ou Lamartine, mais Verlaine et Mallarmé qui prirent soin de mon adolescence [it wasn't Coppée or Lamartine, but Verlaine and Mallarmé who took care of my adolescence]." "Mademoiselle O" (1936), 16. He would also use Mallarmé's "L'Après-midi d'un Faune" as a major motif in his 1947 novel, *Bend Sinister*.

6. See above, Chapter 8, note 4.

7. Foster (*Nabokov's Art of Memory*, 219–32) deals with Nabokov's critique of Eliot here, but treats it as part of his positioning himself in relation to European modernism, an abstraction that meant nothing to Nabokov, although he did admire Yeats, Chekhov, Wells, Blok, Bely, Proust, Joyce, and Kafka and disliked Eliot, Pound, Lawrence, Woolf, Faulkner, Mann, and Rilke.

8. See Chapter 8, p. 109 and note 3, for the misleading conjunction of the rhymes as a reflection of Eliot's enthusiastic but uncertain acquired Englishness.

9. I am extremely grateful to Tony Fazio not only for pointing this out to me, but also for alerting me to the repetitions of the *a-gain/pane* rhyme at P.657–58 as a link to "The Waste Land" and to what he rightly sees as the puzzling first *pain/a-gain* rhyme (see below).

10. Italics added. Here an unidentified speaker (American? British?) hails an American-sounding Stetson in a very British context, as he crosses with the dawn crowd streaming over London Bridge to work.

11. "But keep the wolf far hence, / Or with his nails, he'll dig them up again" (5.4.100–101).

12. Foster (*Nabokov's Art of Memory*, 231) notes the echo but sees it as only "a brief, rather episodic parody."

13. Indeed the "tendril fingering a pane" in the wind in March 1958 very closely reenacts the wind they hear "throw / Twigs at the windowpane" (P.479–80) on the night of Hazel's death in March 1957.

14. Alter (*Partial Magic*, 201) shrewdly observes: "the twentieth-century colloquial rhythms of 'Pale Fire'—an eighteenth-century critic would have called them 'nerveless'—constantly work against the formal emphases and tensions of the traditional couplet form, often producing an effect of studied gaucherie."

15. "Four Quartets": "East Coker," 70–71.

16. Eliot, *Collected Poems* (1963), 66–67.

17. "The barge she sat in, like a burnished throne, / Burnt on the water. . . ." *Antony and Cleopatra*, II.ii.190–91.

18. Eliot seems also to draw on Iachimo's descriptions of Imogen's bedchamber, as he stands within it (*Cymbeline* II.ii) and as he reports it to Posthumus in Rome (II.iv); Eliot's notes indicate echoes of *The Aeneid*, *Paradise Lost*, and Ovid's *Metamorphoses*.

19. *The Waste Land: A Facsimile*, ed. Valerie Eliot (1971), 10–11.

20. For further confirmation, see p. 203.

21. Cf. Foster, *Nabokov's Art of Memory*, 224: "*Pale Fire* continues the attack [on Eliot] on another front by showing the expressive power of narrative method, the very approach Eliot had rejected forty years before."

22. Pope, *Poems*, 222 (I have italicized the words Shade borrows; the original italicizes "Toilet" and "Cosmetic"). The "inferior Priestess" is Belinda's maidservant, helping in the exalted task of making her mistress up for the day. Notice that Shade picks one marked Popean word for each line of his two allusive couplets: *nymph, rite, altar, toilet*. For a detailed discussion of Pope in *Pale Fire*, see Lisa Zunshine, " 'Pale Spectres, Gaping Tombs, and Purple Fires': Alexander Pope's *The Rape of the Lock* and Vladimir Nabokov's *Pale Fire*" (forthcoming).

23. Interestingly, Eliot originally intended to begin Part III of "The Waste Land" with a seventy-line parody of Pope (see *The Waste Land: A Facsimile*, 22–23, 26–27): "Pound '. . . induced me to destroy what I thought an excellent set of couplets;' wrote Eliot of his pastiche, 'for, said he, "Pope has done this so well that you cannot do it better; and if you mean this as a burlesque, you had better suppress it, for you cannot parody Pope unless you can write better verse than Pope—and you can't." ' " *Facsimile*, 127.

24. See C.347–48, quoted and further discussed at p. 203 below.

25. See above, pp. 85 and 94.

26. See above, pp. 161–64.

27. And Nabokov, who presumably links the "altar" and the "articles of toilet" to comment also both on Eliot's religiosity and on the veneration of Eliot

that he makes Shade snap at in ll. 378-79, and both of which he derides in a different key in *Ada*'s reference to "solemn Kithar Sween, a banker who at sixty-five had become an *avant-garde* author; in the course of one miraculous year he had produced *The Waistline*, a satire in free verse on Anglo-American feeding habits, and *Cardinal Grishkin*, an overtly subtle yarn extolling the Roman faith. The poem was but the twinkle in an owl's eye; as to the novel it had already been pronounced 'seminal' by celebrated young critics (Norman Girsh, Louis Deer, many others) who lauded it in reverential voices pitched so high that an ordinary human ear could not make much of that treble volubility" (505-6). In 1950, in his mock-review of his own autobiography, Nabokov concludes by saying it will "find a permanent place on the book lover's shelf side-by-side with Leo Tolstoy's 'Childhood' [and] T. S. Elmann's 'Amen Corner.' . . . " *SM* (1999), 261. See also Nabokov's comments on Edmund Wilson's "T. S. Eliot and the Church of England," Chapter 8, note 3 above.

28. Robert H. Boyle, "An Absence of Wood Nymphs," 131.

29. In a pseudo-review of his autobiography, as if by another hand, Nabokov voices, as he pretends to deplore, his own judgment: "Few people will share his contention that Eliot's poetry is essentially platitudinous." *SM* (1999), 261.

CHAPTER 13
FROM ZEMBLA TO APPALACHIA

1. Nabokov was always very conscious of the individuality of good readers. Asked in 1930 whether Proust would have a decisive influence on forthcoming literature, he pointed out in his answer that "One could for instance imagine two writers, A and B, completely different, but both under a certain very subjective Proustian influence; this influence passes reader C by, since each of the three (A, B and C) has taken Proust in his own way." ("Anketa o Pruste," 274: "Mozhno sebe, naprimer, predstavit' dvukh pisateley, A i B, sovershenno raznykh, no nakhodyashchikhsya oba pod nekotorym, ochen' sub'ektivnym, vliyaniem Prusta; eto vliyanie chitatelyu C nezametno, tak kak kazhdyy iz tryokh (A, B i C) vosprinyal Prusta po svoemu.") Cf. also *SO*, 283: "one's audience is the most varied and gifted in the world."

2. Kinbote explicitly records his telling Shade about Alfin, about the escape (which he retells, even providing a plan of palace and district), and about the meeting with Disa (C.71, 102; C.71, 106-7; C.433-34, 214).

3. *Gradus* is Latin, or Russian, for "degree." Julia Bader was the first to note the overlap of Shade's and Gradus's names in this sense (*Crystal Land*, 34).

4. 1898; in Samuel Hynes, ed., *The Complete Poetical Works of Thomas Hardy* (1982), 1:78-79. Michael Long, *Marvell, Nabokov: Childhood and Arcadia* (1984), 241n.11, was the first to note the source.

5. Shade and Nabokov, so sensitive to rhymes, may draw attention to the rhyme-word here in tribute to Hardy's poem, where "stillicide" is also a rhyme-word and where the whole poem is in the difficult *terza rima*, in appropriate homage to the form Dante used in the *Divine Comedy*.

6. *Stories*, 615. Gennady Barabtarlo drew my attention to the echo of "The Vane Sisters" here (private communication).

7. *Stories*, 627.

8. As an additional pointer, Kinbote's "cavesdrop" addition to the Webster's definition of *stillicide* calls up a seemingly irrelevant "stalactite"; the narrator of "The Vane Sisters" refers to the icicles as "transparent stalactites" (*Stories*, 615).

9. *SL*, 117.

10. In *Ada*, too, where a pattern of letters connects dead Lucette with live Van and Ada, Van's "It's one of the Vane sisters" in a dream proves a valuable pointer to another anagrammatic scrambling that seems indicative of Lucette's continuing influence. See Boyd, *Nabokov's Ada*, 227.

11. Boyd, *Nabokov's Ada*, 69.

12. "Supporting consonant": a repeated consonant preceding the vowels normally taken as the beginning of the rhyme. Shade explains his love for this kind of rhyme (generally disapproved of in English verse, but considered in France to impart an extra tang to a rhyme) after ending his previous two lines with "*m*eant" and "*c*ement."

13. Gradus is associated with "space and time" again at C.171, 152; C.741, 255; C.949/2, 277.

14. Hazel's role in shaping Gradus as well as Zembla is hinted at in the note to line 49, "shagbark" (Shade's "favorite young shagbark" under which "White butterflies turn lavender as they / Pass through its shade where gently seems to sway / The phantom of my little daughter's swing"). This note, one of the two most tree-packed passages in *Pale Fire* (hickory, jacaranda, maidenhair, ginkgo, and five generic "trees") ends with Kinbote's "I do not know if it is relevant or not but there is a cat-and-mouse game in the second line" (of Shade's poem "The Sacred Tree": "A muscat grape"), "and 'tree' in Zemblan is *grados*." The "muscat"–"cat-and-mouse" (via Latin *mus*) reversal of syllables is itself characteristic of Hazel, and apart from her strong association with the shagbark and its "shade" and "phantom," her very name is a species of tree. As this same note stresses, trees of course are also another signature of Shade—"Our poet shared with the English masters the noble knack of transplanting trees into verse with their sap and shade"—and are strongly associated with Shakespeare ("an arc of those sacred trees planted by a landscaper of genius . . . at the end of the so-called Shakespeare Avenue, on the campus"). For the succession of signatures, ending as it were with Shakespeare, or a fusion of art and nature, see Chapter 14.

15. *SM*, 139.

16. See above, pp. 121–22.

17. As also, for instance, in his Index entry for "Flatman, Thomas": see above, pp. 102–3.

18. See *VNRY*, 89–90.

19. Chris Ackerley points out that this name derives from the chess term *affidatus*, "immune from capture" (private communication).

20. If Shade's intervention in Kinbote's imagination in this way has helped shape the Index, this perhaps accounts for Nabokov's otherwise astonishing ending to the 1965 draft foreword for his revised *Speak, Memory*:

As John Shade says somewhere:

Nobody will heed my index,
    I suppose,
But through it a gentle wind *ex*
    Ponto blows. (Cited *VNAY*, 445)

—astonishing because it attributes the Index to Shade after his death. Shade's spectral influence may also account for Nabokov's decision to drop the Shade attribution. Naturally I had used this note in *VNAY* in support of the Shade-as-sole-author hypothesis; but if Shade's shade shapes only certain aspects of the Index, Nabokov would have reason both to call it Shade's and then to realize that this might confuse.

CHAPTER 14
"PALE FIRE," *PALE FIRE*, PALE FIRE

1. See pp. 8–13.

2. *SM*, 291. Ackerley, "*Pale Fire*: Three Notes," discusses the chess problem and Nabokov's description of it, and applies it to a Shadean reading of *Pale Fire*. He comments: "*Pale Fire* is not a novel based on any 'fashionable avant-garde theme' of polysemous meaning infinitely deferred" (94). Quite right, although Nabokov in 1961 could have hardly anticipated the deconstructionist dogma that would become so fashionable twenty years later. But he did know the twentieth-century fashion for mordant metaphysical skepticism.

3. As many readers have noticed, "botkin," an obsolete variant of "bodkin," can mean "a person wedged in between two others where there is proper room for two only," as if in echo of this insufferable neighbor's desire to insert himself between John and Sybil Shade; or it can recall the "bodkin" Hamlet evokes in considering suicide, as if in anticipation of Kinbote's end. "Kinbote" means compensation paid after a homicide to the kin of the person slain, as if to signal the peculiar compensation Shade and his daughter derive, after Shade's murder, from their involvement in Kinbote's imagination.

4. *SM* (1999), 250.

5. See *VNAY*, 3–7, 154–65.

6. *SM*, 31–32.

7. *VNRY*, 7–8.

8. *VNRY*, 468–78.

9. See pp. 195–200, 205.

10. After Nabokov named his *Neonympha*, it was subsequently discovered to be a subspecies of a butterfly, *pertepida*, known in Mexico but not hitherto suspected to inhabit the United States; the genus name was therefore reassigned to *Euptychia* and eventually renamed *Cyllopsis*, so that his *dorothea* now bears the name *Cyllopsis pertepida dorothea*.

11. At the end of *Lolita*, in the famous closing epiphany above a mountain valley, Nabokov also commemorated the place where he caught the hitherto unknown female of *Lycaeides idas sublivens* Nabokov. See *Lolita*, 307–8 and 316; and *VNAY*, 202–3.

12. Nabokov seems to have discovered the name "Nabokov's Wood Nymph" in July 1957, when he drew it to the attention of Jason Epstein (to whom, four months earlier, he had offered the synopsis of a first version of *Pale Fire*, *SL*, 212–13): see Brian Boyd and Robert Michael Pyle, eds., *Nabokov's Butterflies* (in press).

13. Alter (*Partial Magic*, 188, 191) considers Sudarg of Bokay as an image of Nabokov, and aptly observes that the "mirror-maker of genius" is "just one remove from the fashioner of *Pale Fire*."

14. See above, p. 164 and n.

15. The Nitra and the Indra Swallowtails, two black butterflies of the American West. (Nabokov once counseled lepidopterist and butterfly artist William H. Howe that "for a real thrill you should go one day to hunt the Grand Canyon subspecies" of *Papilio indra*, *SL*, 369.) Curiously, two real butterflies have recently been named after another pair of Zemblan characters, the brothers Nodo and Odon (*Madeleinea nodo* Bálint & Johnson 1994 and *Madeleinea odon* Bálint & Johnson 1994), before the *disa-embla* and *nitra-indra* pairings in *Pale Fire* had been recognized as butterflies. The game of worlds signaled in Nabokov's Wood Nymph seems to be playing out still.

16. See Boyd and Pyle, *Nabokov's Butterflies* (in press).

17. "He was *the* authority on Blues," Kurt Johnson asserts (cited in Brian Boyd, "Nabokov, Literature and Lepidoptera," *Nabokov's Butterflies*, 24); see also Kurt Johnson and Stephen Coates, *Nabokov's Blues* (1999). To Alfred Appel, Jr., who wanted to bring Nabokov's butterflies into an innocent passage from *Lolita* (Humbert composes a quatrain about the Enchanted Hunters hotel that ends "Query: / What Indian dyes, Diana, did thy dell / endorse to make of Picture Lake a very / blood bath of trees before the blue hotel?" and prompts Rita's "Why blue when it is white, why blue for heaven's sake?" [263]), Nabokov replied: "I protest vehemently against the lycaenization of my

common use of the epithet 'Blue.' . . . What Rita does not understand is that a
white surface, the chalk of that hotel, does look blue in a wash of light and
shade on a vivid fall day, amid red foliage. H.H. is merely playing a tribute to
French impressionist painters. . . . When a lepidopterist uses 'Blues,' a slangy
but handy term, for a certain group of Lycaenids, he does not see that word in
any color connection because he knows that the diagnostic undersides of their
wings are not blue but dun, tan, grayish, etc., and that many Blues, especially
in the female, are brown, not blue" (*SL*, 410–11). But in *Pale Fire* blues and
azures permeate the novel in quite a different way, butterflies from the *Vanessa
atalanta* and the Toothwort White to *disa* and *embla*, *iris*, *indra* and *nitra* play
roles that range from incidental to central, and Nabokov obliquely echoes the
names of butterflies he has himself named.

  18. "The Nearctic Forms of *Lycaeides* Hüb. (Lycaenidae, Lepidoptera)," *Psyche* 50 (1943 [published March 1944]): 87–99; "Notes on the Morphology of
the Genus *Lycaeides* (Lycaenidae, Lepidoptera)," *Psyche* 51 (1944 [published
Feb. 1945]): 104–38; "Notes on Neotropical *Plebejinae* (Lycaenidae, Lepidoptera)" *Psyche* 52 (1945): 1–53; "The Nearctic Members of the genus *Lycaeides*
Hübner (Lycaenidae, Lepidoptera)," *Bulletin of the Museum of Comparative Zoology* 101 (1949): 479–641; see also *Nabokov's Butterflies*. The three *Lycaeides* papers "entirely rearranged the classification of this genus" (Klots, *Field Guide*,
164). The Neotropical paper was a seminal and highly successful first revision
of this group, its impact fully understood only in the 1990s, in the work of
Zsolt Bálint, Kurt Johnson, Dubi Benyamini, Gerardo Lamas and others: see
Boyd and Pyle, eds., *Nabokov's Butterflies*, and Johnson and Coates, *Nabokov's
Blues*.

  19. See Robert Michael Pyle, "Butterflies and Moths Named by and for Vladimir Nabokov," in Boyd and Pyle, *Nabokov's Butterflies*.

  20. Similarly, he places the stamp of his own Russianness overtly on Kinbote and his Botkinian shadow and his "distant northern land," and covertly
on the landscape of New Wye, in the *ozero* (Russian, "lake") of "the three conjoined lakes called Omega, Ozero, and Zero (Indian names garbled by early
settlers in such a way as to accommodate specious derivations and commonplace allusions)" (C.47–48, 92). The Russian and the lepidopteral Blue pattern
reach an exuberant apogee in the note on line 627, on "the great Starover
Blue," the Wordsmith college astronomer, whose grandfather is "a Russian
starover (accented, incidentally, on the ultima), that is, Old Believer (member of
a schismatic sect), named Sinyavin, from *siniy*, Russ. 'blue.' This Sinyavin migrated from Saratov to Seattle and begot a son who eventually changed his
name to Blue and married Stella Lazurchik, an Americanized Kashube"
(C.627). Just as Nabokov specialized in one category of natural objects and associates it in *Pale Fire* with the supernatural, so at the invitation of the Institution of Preparation for the Hereafter the astronomer Starover Blue "reviewed

the role / Planets had played as landfalls of the soul" (P.627–28). Note the mirrored "star blue" in the names of husband and wife, and a hint of the waxwing image in the -*chik* ("chick") of *Lazurchik*: the "mirror maker of genius" who specializes in working with "*Tintarron*, a precious glass stained a deep blue" (Index) is at it again. And once again, the game of worlds plays on: the butterflies *Madeleinea tintarrona* Bálint & Johnson 1994 and *Madeleinea cobaltana* Bálint & Lamas 1994 were named before the "blue" pattern in *Pale Fire* was recognized as a lepidopteral author's mark.

21. *Gift*, 340.

22. *SM*, 139.

23. See above, chap. 9, nn. 29–32, and text.

24. *Nikolay Gogol* (1944), 42.

25. In the same way, in Nabokov's major Russian novel, *The Gift*, the question of the source of the work (and the works-within-the work) that we are reading becomes more and more deeply problematic, until we discover that Fyodor's father's spirit and in a strange way Pushkin's too—the equivalent in the firmament of Russian literature to Shakespeare in English—seem to be inspiring him to write *The Gift*. Cf. *Gift*, 110 ("With Pushkin's voice merged the voice of his father") *VNRY*, 468–78 and Brian Boyd, "Nabokov, Pushkin i Shekspir" (1999).

Conclusion

1. *LL*, 1.

2. *SO*, 45.

3. Kuhn, *The Structure of Scientific Revolutions* (1962); Popper, *The Myth of the Framework* (1994).

4. Especially "In lone Glenartney's hazel shade" in Scott's *The Lady of the Lake*—which others unfortunately accepted, without looking further, as *the* key line in Scott's poem for *Pale Fire*. Cf. pp. 152–53, 164 above.

5. In the "Ultima Thule" part of *Solus Rex*, the distant northern land the artist Sineusov is commissioned to illustrate becomes "the home of [his] least expressible thoughts" after the death of his wife. *Stories*, 507. This served Field (*Nabokov: His Life in Art*, 297) as a springboard for his conclusion that Zembla was Shade's veiled way of expressing *his* least expressible thoughts.

6. *Postmodernist Fiction*, 18.

7. *Unended Quest: An Intellectual Autobiography* (1976), 88–89.

8. *Myth of the Framework*, 7.

9. Ibid., 16; *Conjectures and Refutations*, 312n.

10. Literally, "over-to-that-side-ness": to the other side of mortality or reality. See above, Chapter 9, note 3.

11. *Myth of the Framework*, 12.

12. Reader's report to Princeton University Press, June 28, 1998, quoted by kind permission of Michael Wood.

13. "Even our experimental and observational experience does not consist of 'data.' Rather, it consists of a web of guesses." *Open Society*, 2:388.

14. The decision to accept or reject a theory "is always a tentative decision, and a decision subject to criticism." *Open Society*, 2:380.

15. Of *Lolita*, for instance, he says: "I just like composing riddles with elegant solutions" (*SO*, 16); of *Transparent Things*: "The solution . . . is so simple" (*SO*, 195). The title of one of *Popper's* later books goes so far as to assert that all life is problem-solving (*Alles Leben ist Problemlösung*, 1994).

16. *SM* (1999), 250.

17. See Boyd, *Nabokov's* Ada, 67–83.

18. See David Deutsch, *The Fabric of Reality* (1997).

19. See Max Tegmark, "Is 'The Theory of Everything' Merely the Ultimate Ensemble Theory?" (1998); and Marcus Chown, "Anything Goes" (1998).

20. Alter, *Partial Magic*, 190; "Autobiography as Alchemy," 136.

21. *Magician's Doubts*, 190.

Bibliography

Works by Nabokov

Ada or Ardor: A Family Chronicle (1969). New York: Vintage, 1990.
"Anketa o Pruste." *Chisla* 1 (1930): 274.
Bend Sinister (1947). New York: Vintage, 1990.
Blednyy ogon'. Russian translation of *Pale Fire* by Véra Nabokov. Ann Arbor, Mich.: Ardis: 1983.
Conclusive Evidence. New York: Harper & Brothers, 1951.
The Defense (1930). Translated by Michael Scammell with VN, 1964; New York: Vintage, 1990.
Despair (1936). Translated by VN, 1966; New York: Vintage, 1989.
Eugene Onegin. Translated with commentary by VN. 4 vols. New York: Bollingen, 1964. Rev. ed. Princeton, N.J.: Princeton University Press, 1975.
The Eye (1930). Translated by Dmitri Nabokov with VN, 1965; New York: Vintage, 1990.
The Gift (1938). Translated by Michael Scammell with VN, 1963; New York: Vintage, 1991.
Glory (1932). Translated by Dmitri Nabokov with VN, 1971; New York: Vintage, 1991.
Lectures on Literature. Edited by Fredson Bowers. New York: Harcourt Brace Jovanovich / Bruccoli Clark, 1980.
The Annotated Lolita (1955). Edited by Alfred Appel, Jr., 1970; rev. ed., New York: Vintage, 1991.
Look at the Harlequins! (1974). New York: Vintage, 1990.
"Mademoiselle O." *Mesures* 2 (April 1936): 147–72.
Nabokov-Wilson Letters. Edited by Simon Karlinsky. New York: Harper and Row, 1979.
Nabokov's Butterflies. Edited by Brian Boyd with Robert Michael Pyle. Translations by Dmitri Nabokov. Boston: Beacon, 2000.
"The Nearctic Forms of *Lycaeides* Hüb[ner] (Lycaenidae, Lepidoptera)." *Psyche* 50 (1943): 87–99.
Nikolai Gogol. Norfolk, Conn.: New Directions, 1944.
Novels 1955–1962: Lolita, Pnin, Pale Fire, Lolita: A Screenplay. Corrected eds. Edited by Brian Boyd. New York: Library of America, 1996.
Pale Fire. New York: Putnam's, 1962; corrected ed., New York: Vintage, 1989.
Poems and Problems. New York: McGraw-Hill, 1970.

The Real Life of Sebastian Knight (1941). New York: Vintage, 1992.

Selected Letters 1940–1977. Edited by Dmitri Nabokov and Matthew J. Bruccoli. New York: Harcourt Brace Jovanovich / Bruccoli Clark Layman, 1989.

"Some New or Little Known Nearctic *Neonympha* (Lepidoptera: Satyridae)." *Psyche* 49 (1942): 61–80.

Speak, Memory: An Autobiography Revisited (1967). New York: Vintage, 1989.

Speak, Memory: An Autobiography Revisited. Introduction by Brian Boyd. With previously unpublished chapter. London: Everyman; New York: Knopf, 1999.

Stikhi. Ann Arbor, Mich.: Ardis, 1979.

The Stories of Vladimir Nabokov (1995). New York: Vintage, 1997.

Strong Opinions. New York: McGraw-Hill, 1973.

Transparent Things (1972). New York: Vintage, 1989.

SECONDARY SOURCES

Ackerley, Chris. "*Pale Fire*: Three Notes toward a Thetic Solution." *Nabokov Studies* 2 (1995): 87–103.

Adams, Robert Martin. *Afterjoyce*. New York: Oxford University Press, 1977.

———. "Fiction Chronicle." *Hudson Review* 15 (1962): 420–30.

Alexandrov, Vladimir E. *Nabokov's Otherworld*. Princeton, N.J.: Princeton University Press, 1991.

———, ed. *The Garland Companion to Vladimir Nabokov*. New York: Garland, 1995.

Alter, Robert. "Autobiography as Alchemy in *Pale Fire*." *Cycnos* 10 (1993): 135–41.

———. *Partial Magic: The Novel as a Self-Conscious Genre*. Berkeley and Los Angeles: University of California Press, 1975.

Amis, Martin. "The Sublime and the Ridiculous: Nabokov's Black Farces." In *Vladimir Nabokov: A Tribute*, edited by Peter Quennell, 73–87. London: Weidenfeld and Nicolson, 1979.

Andersen, Hans Christian. *Eighty Fairy Tales*. Translated by R. P. Keigwin. New York: Pantheon, 1976.

Bader, Julia. *Crystal Land: Artifice in Nabokov's English Novels*. Berkeley and Los Angeles: University of California Press, 1972.

Bálint, Zsolt, Kurt Johnson, and Dubi Benyamini. *Neotropical "Blue" Butterflies. Reports of the Museum of Natural History, University of Wisconsin, Stevens Point*, nos. 43–54 (1993–97).

Barabtarlo, Gennady. *Aerial View: Essays on Nabokov's Art and Metaphysics*. New York: Peter Lang, 1993.

Barabtarlo, Gennady, and Evgeny Shikhovtsev. "Zembla in the League of Nations." *The Nabokovian* 19 (Fall 1987): 54–56.

Booth, Wayne C. *The Company We Keep: An Ethics of Fiction.* Berkeley and Los Angeles: University of California Press, 1988.

———. *The Rhetoric of Fiction.* Chicago: University of Chicago Press, 1961; rev. ed. 1983.

Boyd, Brian. *Nabokov and Ada.* PhD. diss., University of Toronto, 1979.

———. "Nabokov, Pushkin i Shekspir." In *A. S. Pushkin and V. V. Nabokov. Sbornik dokladov Mezhdunarodnoy nauchnoy konferentsii.* St. Petersburg: Push-kinskiy Dom, 1999.

———. *Nabokov's Ada: The Place of Consciousness.* Ann Arbor, Mich.: Ardis, 1985.

———. "Nabokov's Lepidoptera: A Review-Article on Dieter E. Zimmer's *Nabokov's Lepidoptera.*" *Nabokov Studies* 2 (1995): 290–99.

———. "Nabokov's Philosophical World." *Southern Review* (Adelaide) 14 (1981): 260–301.

———. "Nabokov's Russian Years Revisited." In *For SK: In Celebration of the Life and Career of Simon Karlinsky,* edited by Michael S. Flier and Robert P. Hughes, 71–79. Oakland: Berkeley Slavic Specialties, 1994.

———. "Shade and Shape in *Pale Fire.*" *Nabokov Studies* 4 (1997): 173–224.

———. *Vladimir Nabokov: The American Years.* Princeton, N.J.: Princeton University Press, 1991.

———. *Vladimir Nabokov: The Russian Years.* Princeton, N.J.: Princeton University Press, 1990.

Boyd, Brian, and Kurt Johnson. "Nabokov, Scientist." *Natural History* (June 1999): 2–11.

Boyle, Robert H. "An Absence of Wood Nymphs." In *At the Top of Their Game.* New York: Nick Lyons Books / Winchester Press, 1983.

Brown, F. Martin, with Donald Eff and Bernard Rotger. *Colorado Butterflies. Proceedings of the Denver Museum of Natural History,* 3–7 (1954–56); repr. Denver: Denver Museum of Natural History, 1957.

Browning, Robert. *The Poems, Volume I.* Edited by John Pettigrew with Thomas J. Collins. Harmondsworth: Penguin, 1981.

Calinescu, Matei. *Five Faces of Modernity: Modernism, Avant-Garde, Decadence, Kitsch, Postmodernism.* Durham, N.C.: Duke University Press, 1987.

———. *Rereading.* New Haven, Conn.: Yale University Press, 1993.

Carroll, Joseph. *Evolution and Literary Theory.* Columbia: University of Missouri Press, 1995.

Carroll, Lewis. *The Annotated Alice: Alice's Adventures in Wonderland* and *Through the Looking Glass.* Edited by Martin Gardner. New York: Bramhall House, 1960.

Chown, Marcus. "Anything Goes." *New Scientist,* June 6, 1988, 26–30.

Clarendon, Edward Hyde, Earl of. *The History of the Rebellion and Civil Wars in England Begun in the Year 1641.* 6 vols. Edited by W. Dunn Macray. Oxford: Clarendon, 1888.

Couturier, Maurice. "'Which Is to Be Master' in *Pale Fire*." Zembla (Nabokov Web Site), http://www.libraries.psu.edu/iasweb/nabokov/coutpf.htm, April 1998.

Dante Alighieri. *The Divine Comedy*. 6 vols. Translated with commentary by Charles S. Singleton. Princeton, N.J.: Princeton University Press, 1973.

Derrida, Jacques. *Of Grammatology* (1967). English translation by Gayatri Spivak. Baltimore: Johns Hopkins University Press, 1976.

Deutsch, David. *The Fabric of Reality*. London: Allen Lane / Penguin Press, 1997.

de Vries, Gerard. "*Bleek vuur* verbeeld: Vladimir Nabokovs *Pale Fire*." *De Tweede Ronde* (Summer 1991): 49–65.

―――. "Fanning the Poet's Fire: Some Remarks on Nabokov's *Pale Fire*." *Russian Literature Triquarterly* 24 (1991): 239–67.

―――. "Nabokov, Pushkin and Scott." *Revue de littérature comparée* 3 (1997): 307–22.

Dipple, Elizabeth. *The Unresolvable Plot: Reading Contemporary Fiction*. London: Routledge, 1988.

Dirig, Robert. "Nabokov's Blue Snowflakes." *Natural History* 97, no. 5 (1988): 68–69.

―――. "Spring Sunbathers on the Forest Floor." *Catskill Center News* (Spring 1993): 9–11.

Doyle, Sir Arthur Conan. *The Annotated Sherlock Holmes*. Edited by William S. Baring-Gould. London: John Murray, 1968.

Edelstein, Marilyn. "*Pale Fire*: The Art of Consciousness." In Rivers and Nicol, pp. 213–23.

Eliot, T. S. *Collected Poems 1909–1962*. London: Faber and Faber, 1963.

―――. *The Waste Land: A Facsimile and Transcript of the Original Drafts including the Annotations of Ezra Pound*. Edited by Valerie Eliot. London: Faber and Faber, 1971.

Ellis, John M. "Theory." In *New Princeton Encyclopedia of Poetry and Poetics*, edited by Alex Preminger and T. V. F. Brogan, 1282–90. Princeton, N.J.: Princeton University Press, 1993.

Field, Andrew. *Nabokov: His Life in Art*. Boston: Little, Brown, 1967.

Flatman, Thomas. *A Panegyrick To his Renowed Majestie, Charles the Second, King of Great Britain, &c*. London: Henry Marsh, 1660.

―――. *Poems and Songs*. London: Benjamin Tooke, 1686.

Foster, John Burt, Jr. *Nabokov's Art of Memory and European Modernism*. Princeton, N.J.: Princeton University Press, 1993.

Franclemont, John. "Remembering Nabokov." In *The Achievements of Vladimir Nabokov*, edited by George Gibian and Stephen Jan Parker, 227–28. Ithaca, N.Y.: Cornell Center for International Studies, 1984.

Gould, Stephen Jay. "No Science without Fancy, No Art without Facts: The Lepidoptery of Vladimir Nobokov." In *Véra's Butterflies*, edited by Sarah Funke. New York: Glenn Horowitz, 1999. In press.

Grabes, Herbert. "Nabokov and Shakespeare: The English Works." In Alexandrov, *The Garland Companion*, 496–512.

Haack, Susan. *Evidence and Inquiry: Towards Reconstruction in Epistemology*. Oxford: Blackwell, 1993.

Hardy, Thomas. *The Complete Poetical Works of Thomas Hardy*. Edited by Samuel Hynes. Vol. 1. Oxford: Clarendon, 1982.

Higgins, Lionel G., and Norman D. Riley. *A Field Guide to the Butterflies of Britain and Europe* (1970). 5th ed. London: Harper Collins, 1993.

Hoyem, Andrew. *On Nabokov's Poem "Pale Fire."* San Francisco: Arion Press, 1997.

Hutchinson, Peter. *Games Authors Play*. London: Methuen, 1983.

Johnson, D. Barton. *Worlds in Regression: Some Novels of Vladimir Nabokov*. Ann Arbor, Mich.: Ardis, 1985.

Johnson, Kurt, and Stephen Coates. *Nabokov's Blues*. Cambridge, Mass.: Zorland, 1999.

Johnson, Kurt, G. Warren Whitaker, and Zsolt Bálint. "Nabokov as Lepidopterist: An Informed Appraisal." *Nabokov Studies* 3 (1996): 123–44.

Kermode, Frank. "Zemblances." *New Statesman*, November 9, 1962, 671–72. Reprinted in Page, 144–48.

Kernan, Alvin B. *The Imaginary Library: An Essay on Literature and Society*. Princeton, N.J.: Princeton University Press, 1982. Chapter 4 reprinted as "Reading Zemblan: The Audience Disappears in Nabokov's *Pale Fire*." In *Vladimir Nabokov: Modern Critical Views*, edited by Harold Bloom, 101–25. New York: Chelsea House, 1987.

Klots, Alexander B. *A Field Guide to the Butterflies of North America, East of the Great Plains*. Boston: Houghton Mifflin, 1951.

Kuhn, Thomas. *The Structure of Scientific Revolutions* (1962). 2d ed. Chicago: University of Chicago Press, 1970.

Lane, Franklin K. *The Letters of Franklin K. Lane, Personal and Political*. Edited by Anne Wintermute Lane and Louise Herrick Wall. Boston: Houghton Mifflin, 1922.

Levin, Harry. "Shakespeare's Misanthrope." *Shakespeare Survey* 26 (1973): 89–94.

Livingston, Paisley. *Literary Knowledge: Humanistic Inquiry and the Philosophy of Science*. Ithaca, N.Y.: Cornell University Press, 1988.

Lodge, David. *The Practice of Writing: Essays, Lectures, Reviews and a Diary*. London: Secker and Warburg, 1996.

Long, Michael. *Marvell, Nabokov: Childhood and Arcadia*. Oxford: Clarendon, 1984.

Lubin, Peter. "Kickshaws and Motley." *Triquarterly* 17 (1970): 187–208. Nabokov special issue of *Triquarterly* reprinted as *Nabokov: Criticism, Reminiscences, Tranlsation and Tributes*, edited by Alfred Appel, Jr. and Charles Newman. New York: Simon and Schuster, 1970.

McCarthy, Mary. "A Bolt from the Blue." *New Republic*, June 1962, 21–27. Reprinted in *Nabokov: The Critical Heritage*, edited by Norman Page. London: Routledge and Kegan Paul, 1982. Enlarged in "Vladimir Nabokov's *Pale Fire*." *Encounter*, April 1962, 71–84. Reprinted in McCarthy, *The Writing on the Wall and Other Literary Essays*. London: Weidenfeld and Nicolson, 1970; and in Introduction to Vladimir Nabokov, *Pale Fire*. Harmondsworth: Penguin, 1991.

McHale, Brian. *Postmodernist Fiction*. London: Routledge, 1987.

Maddox, Lucy. *Nabokov's Novels in English*. London: Croom Helm, 1983.

Magee, Bryan. *Confessions of a Philosopher*. London: Weidenfeld and Nicolson, 1997.

Mallarmé, Stéphane. *Collected Poems*. Translated with commentary by Henry Weinfeld. Berkeley and Los Angeles: University of California Press, 1994.

Malory, Thomas. *Works*. 2d ed. Edited by Eugène Vinaver. London: Oxford University Press, 1971.

Meyer, Priscilla. *Find What the Sailor Has Hidden: Vladimir Nabokov's Pale Fire*. Middletown, Conn.: Wesleyan University Press, 1988.

Meyer, Priscilla, and Jeff Hoffman. "Infinite Reflections in Nabokov's *Pale Fire*: The Danish Connection (Hans Andersen and Isak Dinesen)." *Russian Literature* 41 (1997): 197–222.

Morris, J[ohn]. "Genius and Plausibility: Suspension of Disbelief in *Pale Fire*." http://www.libraries.psu.edu/iasweb/nabokov/morris1.htm, January 1999.

Munz, Peter. "Philosophy and the Mirror of Rorty." In *Evolutionary Epistemology, Rationality, and the Sociology of Knowledge*, edited by Gerard Radnitzky and W. W. Bartley III, 345–98. La Salle, Ill.: Open Court, 1987.

Nabokv-L (NABOKV-L@UCSBVM.UCSB.edu) discussion. December 1997–February 1998.

Page, Norman, ed. *Nabokov: The Critical Heritage*. London: Routledge and Kegan Paul, 1982.

Pavanello, Giuseppe. *L'opera completa del Canova*. Milan: Rizzoli, 1976.

Pifer, Ellen. *Nabokov and the Novel*. Cambridge, Mass.: Harvard University Press, 1980.

Polsky, Svetlana. *Smert' i bessmertie v russkikh rasskazakh Vladimira Nabokova*. Ph.D diss., University of Gothenburg, 1997.

———. "Stikhotvorenie V. Nabokova 'Lilit': uprazhnenie v dvusmyslennosti." *Jews and Slavs* 1 (1993): 188–97.

Pope, Alexander. *The Poems of Alexander Pope*. Edited by John Butt. London: Methuen, 1963.

Popper, Karl R. *Alles Leben ist Problemlösung*. Munich: Piper, 1994.

———. *Conjectures and Refutations: The Growth of Scientific Knowledge* (1963). 4th ed. London: Routledge, 1972.

———. *The Logic of Scientific Discovery* (1934). English ed., 1959. 2d ed. London, Routledge, 1968.

———. *The Myth of the Framework: In Defence of Science and Rationality.* Edited by M. A. Notturno. London: Routledge, 1994.

———. *Objective Knowledge: An Evolutionary Approach* (1972). Rev. ed. Oxford: Clarendon, 1979.

———. *The Open Society and Its Enemies.* 2 vols. (1945). 5th ed. Princeton, N.J.: Princeton University Press, 1966.

———. *Postscript to the Logic of Scientific Discovery.* Edited by William W. Bartley III. 3 vols. London: Hutchinson, 1982–83. (*Realism and the Aim of Science*, 1983; *The Open Universe: An Argument for Indeterminism*, 1982; *Quantum Theory and the Schism in Physics*, 1982.)

———. *Unended Quest: An Intellectual Autobiography* (1974). Glasgow: Fontana / Collins, 1976.

Pyle, Robert Michael. *The Audubon Society Field Guide to the Butterflies of North America.* New York: Knopf, 1981.

Rabinowitz, Peter. "Truth in Fiction: A Reexamination of Audiences." *Critical Inquiry* 4 (1977): 121–41. Reprinted in *Narrative / Theory*, edited by David Richter, 208–26. New York: Longman, 1996.

Rampton, David. *Vladimir Nabokov: A Critical Study of the Novels.* Cambridge: Cambridge University Press, 1984.

Rivers, J. E., and Charles Nicol, eds. *Nabokov's Fifth Arc: Nabokov and Others on His Life and Work.* Austin: University of Texas Press, 1982.

Rivers, J. E., and William Walker. "Notes to Vivian Darkbloom's Notes to *Ada.*" In Rivers and Nicol, pp. 260–95.

Rorty, Richard. *Contingency, Irony, and Solidarity.* Cambridge: Cambridge University Press, 1989.

———. "Introduction." In *Pale Fire.* New York: Everyman / Knopf, 1992.

———. *Objectivity, Relativism and Truth.* Cambridge: Cambridge University Press, 1991.

———. *Truth and Progress: Philosophical Papers, Volume 3.* Cambridge: Cambridge University Press, 1998.

Rowe, William Woodin. *Nabokov's Spectral Dimension.* Ann Arbor, Mich.: Ardis, 1981.

Salinger, J. D. *Franny and Zooey.* Boston: Little, Brown, 1961.

———. *Nine Stories.* Boston: Little, Brown, 1953.

———. *Raise High the Roof Beam, Carpenters* and *Seymour: An Introduction.* Boston: Little, Brown, 1963.

Sartori, Michel, ed. *Les papillons de Nabokov.* Lausanne: Musée cantonal de Zoologie, 1993.

Scott, Sir Walter. *The Lady of the Lake.* Edited by William Keith Leask. London: Blackie & Son, n.d.

Shakespeare, William. *The Riverside Shakespeare*. Edited by G. Blakemore Evans et al. Boston: Houghton Mifflin, 1974.

Shrayer, Maxim. *The World of Nabokov's Stories*. Austin: University of Texas Press, 1998.

Stegner, Page. *Escape into Aesthetics: The Art of Vladimir Nabokov*. New York: Dial, 1966.

Swift, Jonathan. *The Complete Poems*. Edited by Pat Rogers. Harmondsworth: Penguin, 1983.

———. *A Tale of a Tub, To Which is Added The Battle of the Books and the Mechanical Operation of the Spirit*. 1704. Edited by A. C. Guthkelch and D. Nichol Smith. 1920; 2d ed., Oxford: Clarendon, 1958.

Tallis, Raymond. *Enemies of Hope: A Critique of Contemporary Pessimism*. New York: St. Martin's Press, 1997.

———. *Newton's Sleep: The Two Cultures and the Two Kingdoms*. London: Macmillan, 1995.

Tammi, Pekka. "*Pale Fire*." In Alexandrov, *A Garland Companion*, 571–86.

———. *Problems of Nabokov's Poetics: A Narratological Analysis*. Helsinki: Suomalainen Tiedeakatemia, 1985.

Tanner, Tony. *City of Words: American Fiction 1950–1970*. London: Jonathan Cape, 1971.

Tegmark, Max. "Is 'The Theory of Everything' Merely the Ultimate Ensemble Theory?" *Annals of Physics* 270 (1998): 1–51.

Toker, Leona. "Liberal Ironists and the 'Gaudily Painted Savage': On Richard Rorty's Reading of Vladimir Nabokov." *Nabokov Studies* 1 (1994): 195–206.

Voss, Manfred. "How Not to Read Zemblan." *The Nabokovian* 25 (1990): 41–47.

———. "How Not to Read Zemblan—Again." *The Nabokovian* 26 (1991): 51–52.

Webster's New International Dictionary of the English Language. Second edition, unabridged. Springfield, Mass.: G. and C. Mirriam, 1958.

Williams, Carol T. "Web of Sense: *Pale Fire* in the Nabokov Canon." *Critique* 6 (1963): 29–45.

Wilson, Edmund. *The Shores of Light: A Literary Chronicle of the 1920s and 1930s*. New York: Farrar, Straus and Giroux, 1952.

Winsor, Kathleen. *Forever Amber* (1944). London: MacDonald, 1969.

Wood, Michael. *The Magician's Doubts: Nabokov and the Risks of Fiction*. London: Chatto and Windus, 1994.

Zimmer, Dieter E. *A Guide to Nabokov's Butterflies and Moths*. Hamburg: privately printed, 1996; rev. ed., 1998.

Zunshine, Lisa. "'Pale Spectres, Gaping Tombs, and Purple Fires': Alexander Pope's *The Rape of the Lock* and Vladimir Nabokov's *Pale Fire*." Conference paper, Cornell Nabokov Festival, September 11, 1998. In *Nabokov at Cornell: Proceedings of the Cornell Nabokov Centenary Conference*, edited by Gavriel Shapiro. Ithaca, N.Y.: Cornell University Press, 2000. In press.

Index

Nabokov works are integrated in alphabetical sequence; works by others are listed by author's name.